The Kingdom Began in Puerto Rico

THE KINGDOM BEGAN IN PUERTO RICO

Neil Connolly's Priesthood in the South Bronx

Angel Garcia

EMPIRE STATE EDITIONS

AN IMPRINT OF FORDHAM UNIVERSITY PRESS

NEW YORK 2021

Fordham University Press also publishes its books in a variety of electronic formats. Some content that appears in print may not be available in electronic books.

Visit us online at www.fordhampress.com/empire-state-editions.

Library of Congress Control Number: 2020917676

Printed in the United States of America

23 22 21   5 4 3 2 1

First edition

CONTENTS

FOREWORD

George Horton,
Director of Social and Community Development,
Archdiocese of New York

Angel Garcia has given us a wonderful gift in authoring *The Kingdom Began in Puerto Rico: Neil Connolly's Priesthood in the South Bronx.*

Angel has memorialized for us the formative ministry years of Father Neil Connolly, who, along with his compatriot Bronx parish priests, religious sisters, and lay ministers, lived out his ministry in the turbulent South Bronx of the 1960s, 1970s, and 1980s. He has traced Father Neil's developing understanding of his own priesthood as he became immersed in the life of the Puerto Rican community and came to know and be known by the people living there. Angel ably blends the dynamic forces of Church and world that transformed Connolly as he grew into realizing the meaning of his vocation.

Father Neil and his brother priests brought their deep faith, which they had learned in their families and in the seminary, to an encounter with the people of the Great Puerto Rican Migration to whom they opened their hearts and minds. Both anticipating and riding the crest of the wave of Vatican II, they, together with their colleague nuns and laity, heard the radical summons of the opening words of *Gaudium et Spes*, the Pastoral Constitution on the Church in the Modern World:

> The joys and hopes, the griefs and the anxieties
> of the men of this age, especially those who are poor
> or in any way afflicted, these are the joys and hopes,

the griefs and anxieties of the followers of Christ. Indeed nothing genuinely human fails to raise an echo in their hearts.

Father Neil understood the centrality of not only bringing God's Word and the sacraments of the Church into people's lives, but also standing in solidarity with them as they struggled to overcome the debilitating economic, social, and political challenges of poverty and exclusion encountered in their daily lives. He worked with the people to organize communities of love and hope, and to empower them for discipleship, social change, and building God's Kingdom—endeavors often at odds with the institutions of both the government and the Church. Father Neil understood the value of the laity and the critical importance of developing lay leadership for the well-being of the community and for the life of the Church.

Although many of these events took place fifty years ago, in many ways the story recounted here can provide an orientation toward a rejuvenation and enlivening of the Church and ministry for priests and for parish communities. So much of what is told here echoes the call of Pope Francis to go to the peripheries and walk in accompaniment with people living on the margins—in Father Neil's case, burgeoning communities of newly arrived Puerto Rican people who were living in poverty and amidst the destruction of the South Bronx. The 2019 Synod on the Amazon underscored the need to listen to the people, learn from their experience, and create forums of communication across social, economic, and political divides. Father Neil, always intellectually curious, imbibed the language and culture studies in Puerto Rico with Ivan Illich and then applied what he learned to cross boundaries; encounter the people; listen, walk, and dialogue with them; and, yes, learn about God from them.

I came to know Father Neil over the last twenty years of his life, after he had left the South Bronx to be Pastor of St. Mary's Parish on Manhattan's Lower East Side. What I remember most is how engaged he always was in the world around him. He would recount stories with such verve and vividness that it was as if each moment, place, and person remembered were still immediately present to him in a kind of loving embrace. Our conversations usually revolved around his planning of some event for parishioners and priests to deepen their knowledge of Catholic social teaching and to organize for social action, or his attempt to assist some person whom he was concerned about and who was in need of immediate help. Neil's priesthood always operated on both personal and social levels.

I last saw Father Neil when I visited him some two weeks before he died at the retirement home for priests where he had gone when he was faced with his last illness. I attended Mass with him, and afterward we sat together in silent prayer. After a delightful lunch with other resident priests, we retreated to his room where we talked for about three hours. Although he was physically frail, his enthusiasm and intellectual curiosity continued undiminished as he recounted his efforts to organize the resident priests into reading and reflection groups. We sat surrounded by his beloved books. He was slowly making his way through the Bible and he shared with me, as he usually did, his latest spiritual reading.

As always, the Church must be about its mission of spreading and living the Gospel, the work of evangelization. Being in Father Neil's presence, one always felt the pull of conversion through his embodiment of what Pope Francis refers to in his encyclical the Joy of the Gospel. We owe a great debt of gratitude to Angel Garcia, who has captured so well the openness of Father Neil to the urgings of the Spirit and his willingness to respond in joy to the signs of the times. Father Neil loved being a priest, and he both fulfilled and challenged its ideal. He was joyfully engaged in the Lord's work up to the day he died.

The Kingdom Began in Puerto Rico

INTRODUCTION

What Led to This Book?

So, I am not a writer by trade, and some have accused me of not being a good storyteller. But some years ago I read Howard Zinn's *A People's History of the United States* (highly recommended, in order to see that the little people in all corners of the country have not just sat and accepted injustice), and I thought that it would be so good to have a "people's history of the South Bronx." I wanted to share some of the stories of good South Bronx organizing efforts, as told through the leaders involved in them while it was becoming "the South Bronx"—a designation that is only around fifty years old, despite the far longer history of human settlement in the area. My feeling was that these efforts were missing from the history books on the South Bronx and on urban history in general. Since Father Neil Connolly had been involved in founding a social action organization I worked in, I thought, OK, I will start with Neil Connolly. That should be easy, I thought.

Hah.

Neil Connolly, I discovered, was a history of the South Bronx all on his own, given all the initiatives and projects for community and justice he was involved in over the years, so I decided I would focus on him and see what happened. What I found out, as I explored his story over the course of six years, is that a lot of growth happened to this person while he was in his South Bronx era. (A very good story of his Lower East Side era, just as long a period of time, would be well worth telling, too, and may be in the works.)

I got to know Neil Connolly while I was an organizer at South Bronx People for Change. I had the great benefit of becoming part of this organization because my mother told me, just months after I graduated college, to stop whining about things like "Oh, where is community?" and "I want a sense of community" and, instead, join up with the local Social Action Committee at St. Anselm's parish. I was told by my mother to put my money where my mouth is. Since the committee was meeting in the building next door to ours, I had no excuse for not attending.

I fell in love with these concepts of social justice, social action, and organizing that drove this group, and I found my community there—first as a volunteer, then as a staff member, and finally, after a couple of staff and life changes, I became the executive director by default.

Suffice it to say that, as far as organizing or directing, I did not really know my elbow from a hole in the ground. (Ivy League education teaches you only so much, and I wasn't even very good at that.) But I really got into the organizing with the guidance of others, including the chairman of the board, Neil Connolly, who kept coming in, sitting down, and meeting with me and recommending a solution, or, if he didn't have one, talking to someone who could. He brought a great deal of optimism to those meetings.

Then we moved on, as people do. But my contact with Neil Connolly continued, and years later, we reconnected in a more in-depth way. Simply put, it began when he made an offer I couldn't refuse.

At his request, I joined his board of directors for Grand Street Guild, an affordable housing organization sponsored by St. Mary's parish in the mid-1970s, and in the process I found out that he was up to quite a bit in his new community on the Lower East Side. As pastor at St. Mary's, Neil Connolly was automatically chairman of the board, per the Guild's bylaws. He was putting together a panel of new members who were "experts," and he called on me. (Business degree. Don't ask.)

I have to admit, I really, really did not want to join any boards at the time, but again, Neil Connolly was asking, and I couldn't refuse him. He had always been there for me, and I felt I should be there for him. He had helped me years earlier, at a time when I was still growing up, figuring out how to solve problems, and learning how to build an organization. An overwhelming time, sometimes. Okay, often.

I came to appreciate that Neil gave, and asked others to give, so that we could have a community of giving. That's the way things should work in this world, according to Neil Connolly. And the increased interaction gave me an opportunity to find out about his experiences and his evolving views of his priesthood in the South Bronx, one after another. So I have tried to capture some of them here.

The other thing I discovered, in approaching the writing of this book, is that there were always two arenas that Neil Connolly was relating to in his South Bronx era: the Church and the world. It complicated things when I was writing about his growth as a priest, because this took place in a historical context, and there are two histories: one of the Church—mostly the Archdiocese of New York, sometimes driven by events of the Church in the United States, and sometimes by those in the global Church—and another of the world, the secular context in which his priesthood was unfolding. Following his story, and placing him in those two arenas in a historically fair manner, was a big challenge. But it became important to me because his learning to grow in both arenas, I concluded, was important to him.

What is written here are some of the events in Connolly's life, as well as the growth. The stories were told by Connolly in a series of two dozen preliminary interviews, which were recorded and transcribed by me, and edited and converted by me into the original first-person chapters. Then I conducted research related to the stories and included them, with Connolly's approval, in the story. Afterward, I went through a series of revisions, which were reviewed in another two or three dozen review sessions with Connolly. In each round of revisions, I was looking to blend the Connolly story and the history so that they were closely related to each other. If there were events going on or groups carrying out activities that Connolly was not aware of or could not have ever been aware of, with few exceptions, I tried to stay away from them. Eventually, I turned story into a third-person biography within a historical context—the changing of the Church, the migration and poverty of the Puerto Rican community to form what would become the South Bronx, and the powerful institutions which affected both events.

A note about writing style: I try to represent Neil's thoughts as faithfully as possible, using italics to express his thoughts, as conveyed to me over the six years of manuscript sessions with him. Otherwise, if there is dialogue between him and someone else, it is in quotes, as transcribed from quotes in my recorded interviews with him or from quotes I wrote during the sessions. I hope this style works.

Why the South Bronx?

Why not?

First, it has been my home for all of my life in New York City—all except my first five years in Puerto Rico, and a few in New Jersey, when I was in college. I grew up here with my family, having the experience of living in public housing when most tenants were working-class households headed by someone who was working. I also had the benefit of a Catholic education, first at St. Anselm's Elementary School next door, when the nuns still wore habits until 1970, and then at Regis, the Jesuit Catholic high school on the upper east side of Manhattan, where the scene became a little less formal but very positively challenging in the early 1970s. Being in the very stable housing projects, studying downtown, and going to college in New Jersey shielded me from some of the major changes taking place in the South Bronx at that time—what I call in this book the "unholy trinity" of epidemics that swept across the area.

But the South Bronx was still my home. I saw and heard about gangs and drugs and got robbed for change a few times, but I played a lot of handball and some stickball and basketball, and I had some very good friendships with the guys and gals from different floors of the building I lived in. I got to learn to love soul music and a little salsa around the neighborhood, and I heard a lot of salsa at the social club we went to on some Saturday nights, where my college-educated father and his friends from the hometown of Cabo Rojo had a little too much to drink—more times than we liked—and my brothers and I laughed and played. In the meantime, my mother, while being his companion through all this, was steadily working in the local public school, learning to become a teacher in college at night while assistant-teaching during the day at P.S. 25, the first bilingual school in the area. She did that while raising us three boys with all her Catholic, Puerto Rican might to urge us to become good, educated, moral human beings.

Second, South Bronx history has been told less than completely over the years, or it has been told flat-out wrong. This book is far from making it complete, but it makes an attempt at a fuller history, a story that is the result of Puerto Rican migrations, segregation, a people surviving some epidemics and government policies, and their growth as a community within a Catholic setting.

Some people have written books or analyses or have done documentaries about the experiences of a family or a particular community of the South Bronx during its defining period—after the Second World War through to the late 1970s/early 1980s. They have done very good work on how the South Bronx became a large area with several hundred thousand people, with organizations being created by the people working every day to make it a livable area. Thankfully, good works about the South Bronx are often being created to give the right perspective.

The South Bronx is a profoundly American story. Its history reminds us of how a growing number of neighborhoods were hit by poverty and poor housing, then had these issues ignored or addressed in varying ways, mostly poorly, by institutions, like the Church and the federal government, and by landlords.

Also, the South Bronx has been, for me, a largely Puerto Rican story. I have great respect for the experiences of the African American community and the struggles of the African American families who lived in the South Bronx of the 1940s through the 1980s. The Bronx African American History Project, initiated and cultivated at Fordham University under Professor Mark Naison's steadfast leadership, has continued to capture those experiences.

Yet the area has a strong Puerto Rican flavor for me, as someone who grew up in this mostly Catholic setting. So that is my emphasis in this one story of the South Bronx. The Puerto Rican experience also defined the experiences of Neil Connolly during this era, as he learned to serve that community and be part of that community. Does the Puerto Rican experience of that time go beyond the southeastern and southwestern areas of the Bronx? Yes, it does. In the many news articles I read to piece this book together, the city government's inability to react to the unique and ongoing mass migration of Puerto Ricans all over the city gave me the sense of a massive entity playing constant catch-up with this rapidly changing, dynamic people and their situation.

Finally, I wanted to write about organizing in the South Bronx because South Bronx People for Change was a defining experience for me, revealing to me that the South Bronx was a much greater and broader experience than my own upbringing. Everyone should know it as well. When people say "the South Bronx," most are referring to an area south of Yankee Stadium. By the time I got to People for Change in 1980, it had already reached all neighborhoods up to Fordham Road. It was a "city," not a neighborhood. Most proposals we wrote for the organization noted that the South Bronx's population was equivalent to that of the city of Milwaukee,

Detroit, or Boston at the time. By way of comparison, the population and neighborhood size—and the issues related to poverty and segregation—of the South Bronx would be equivalent to six historically poor "slum areas." Think Central Harlem, Washington Heights, East Harlem, the Lower East Side, Bushwick, and Bedford-Stuyvesant all put together.

At People for Change, we addressed some of the issues in this "city" through the network of Roman Catholic parishes, which had stayed in these neighborhoods through all the area's ups and downs. Traveling through all the neighborhoods, going to nighttime meetings in local schools, and visiting leaders' apartments gave me a very good sense of how large and complex this "city" was. Therefore, it is worth many, many stories and analyses.

Why the Church, Why a Priest, and Why This Priest?

These are troubled times for the American Roman Catholic Church. During a long period of immigrant expansion and growing wealth in the nineteenth and early twentieth centuries, Catholics in the United States built thousands of institutions—schools, hospitals, universities, orphanages, and more—along with thousands of parishes organized into nearly two hundred "dioceses" and "archdioceses," each covering a substantial area of land and governed, respectively, by a bishop or an archbishop. Although the Catholic Church began as a despised and feared minority in the United States, by the time Neil Connolly was born and as he entered seminary, it was at the height of its national power and strength. What changed between then and now? Many things, some covered in this book as Connolly experienced them firsthand. But today, many dioceses and religious orders are confronting long-lingering issues of clerical sexual abuse, committed by priests and enabled by their superiors, against young people who trusted them and believed they were agents of God, and whose lives have been damaged or ruined. This has caused great disaffection and disillusionment among those who have been loyal or long-term Catholics, whether they were directly impacted by the abuse (self, family, friend, or a worshipper) or indirectly impacted, hearing about it on the news and ashamed or disgusted by this abuse.

There has also been some bad financial news for several dioceses, and there have been closures of parishes and their schools, despite ever-increasing numbers of Hispanic and Asian Catholics around the country. These negative financial developments have often been related to the abuse issues. But there have also been increasing levels of economic inequality suffered by Latino Catholics, who contributed the greatest growth to the Catholic Church in the last few decades, but who might not have contributed as much financially as they might want, with many having incomes that can barely sustain their families. But, whether they are middle class or working class, I believe the Latinos/as could be wooed to support their Church in every way possible, with a different kind of Church that emphasizes community over institution, that gives them—us—a full stake in every aspect of the Church. With priestless parishes continuing to grow, where can the future leaders of the Church be found? Wherever two or three are gathered . . . those are the leaders.

I am not an expert on priests, or on the life of priests, by any means. But I did get to understand a couple of things in the course of working on this book and in my discussions with Neil. Officially, the priest has been expected to be the leader of the parish, the most basic local unit of the global Catholic Church, carrying an extraordinary, some say impossible, responsibility on his shoulders. Priests have had an ever changing role to play in the American Catholic Church and the lives of Catholics. Their search for understanding what they can and must do has, in my opinion, been influenced and maybe turned upside down by factors in Catholic Church history, including Vatican II (of which more later in this book), and by the postwar era, both of which opened up priests to a fast-changing world full of conflicts and issues.

The fact is that there have been countless priests who have given their lives to help people and done good things, including those who have saved lives; comforted, fed, and housed people; grown communities; and given laypersons and religious full and legitimate roles equal to their own in those communities, and they should be celebrated.

There were others who were very equally worthy ministers—priests, religious, and laypersons—who all worked and lived for what has been called "the Kingdom of God" in the South Bronx. They all built a Church community there. They supported Neil Connolly, and he supported them. Their vision of the Church was that it should be fully committed to realizing the full dignity of every human being, Catholic or not.

But I was captivated by the fact that, at a unique time in history, and in a unique place, this man found his reasons for becoming, being, and staying a priest. Those who knew him often say that he was the best priest they knew. He went on a life journey, defined by his time in history, his place in the nation's poorest and most famous slum, and his drive to reach his highest self.

1

***

Puerto Rico

But at the same time, the Church, sent to all peoples of every time and place, is not bound exclusively and indissolubly to any race or nation, any particular way of life or any customary way of life, recent or ancient. Faithful to her own tradition and at the same time conscious of her universal mission, she can enter into communion with the various civilizations, to their enrichment and the enrichment of the Church itself.

—*Gaudium et Spes* §58, December 7, 1965

Priesthood Accomplished

On May 31, 1958, at St. Patrick's Cathedral on Fifth Avenue, Cornelius A. Connolly, known to others as "Neil," was ordained a Roman Catholic priest of the Archdiocese of New York by Cardinal Francis Spellman.[1] Reaching priesthood had taken twelve years of study—six years at Cathedral Prep on Manhattan's West End Avenue, followed by six more at St. Joseph's Seminary, in the Dunwoodie area of Yonkers, New York. Neil's graduating class, thirty-two strong, was one of the largest in the history of St. Joseph's, an institution with a demanding academic program in both the sacred subjects, such as theology and philosophy, and the profane, such as literature and history.[2]

There were several reasons why Neil Connolly might have wanted to become a priest. Prestige was one: Within the Irish American community, the priesthood was considered elite.[3] In the 1940s and 1950s, many of the

Neil Conolly (*left*) and classmates at St. Joseph's Seminary, January 1954. (Photo courtesy of Fr. Robert Stern.)

best and brightest Irish American men became priests.[4] Popularity was another: Thanks to the widely viewed movie personas of Father O'Malley in *Going My Way* and Father Flanagan in *Boys Town*, the larger American public came to believe that being Irish and being Catholic were one and the same, and that priests were admirable human beings.[5] Power was a third: In Catholic Irish American communities, the Church was the central institution ruling the lives of parishioners, and priests led that institution.

But Connolly had worked toward this moment in his life with a different motivation. Entering the minor seminary at the age of twelve, he had decided to make a lifetime commitment in order to be just like the Our Lady of Good Counsel parish priests, who had been so good to his family in their time of need.

Good Counsel, after all, had paid for his trips as a boy to summer camp in Port Jervis, which his father, the elder Cornelius Connolly, could not afford. It also gave the Connollys money for necessities during the 1941 New York City bus drivers' strike, which his father, a shop steward of the young Transport Workers Union, helped lead against Mayor La Guardia.[6] The elder Cornelius—known as "Con Connolly" to his union brothers, many of whom were his former comrades in the Irish Republican Army[7]—was a

Con Connolly and Frances Connolly, Neil's parents, on their wedding day. (Neil Connolly's personal collection.)

committed Catholic, a committed fighter for labor rights, and a committed father and husband, but he couldn't do it all.

The native of Skibbereen, in County Cork, Ireland, part of the last Irish migration wave in the 1920s,[8] moved to this Yorkville parish from Queens to be closer to work and to the rest of the family because he needed help. Con's beloved wife, Frances, an educated domestic whom he met and married in New York, was a wonderful and supportive partner who raised and taught Denis, Neil, Anne Marie, Patrick, and Billy. But Frances suffered from depression. Sometimes it was so severe that she was institutionalized for months at a time at the massive Pilgrim State Hospital on Long Island.[9] On several occasions when Con made the long trip to visit Frances, the parish priest would accompany him and then invite him over to dinner with his own family members out on Long Island for a little respite. Neil Connolly later reflected on the generosity of those priests; he wanted to be like them, to be there for other families just as they had been there for his.

With the official title of priest obtained and his seminary learning complete, Connolly thought, all he needed was a parish. But as it turned out, the new Father Neil Connolly's education was not complete.

Starting Over

On June 15, 1958, Connolly and some classmates from St. Joseph's boarded a plane and landed in Puerto Rico.

Up to that point in his life, he had only heard of Puerto Rico because of two Puerto Rican students in the entire Good Counsel Elementary School. But on a hot June day, sweating buckets in a black serge suit, Connolly began the next stage of his education by asking the most important question in his young priesthood: "How's your Spanish?"

Waiting with a bunch of others for an oral language exam, Connolly stood outside a classroom in the Catholic University of Puerto Rico, in Ponce, the island's second largest city. He and his classmate Marty Dolan, who loved a good laugh just as much as he did, were standing behind two priests, Father Jim Burke of Brooklyn and Father Dan Sullivan of the Bronx. Both had been working with Puerto Ricans in New York City for over ten years, Connolly learned. Burke was very talkative and confident, with a bit of the Irish "blarney" in him, and he was proud of his rank among those gathered in the hallway as an experienced priest in the Puerto Rican community. Connolly asked him, "Oh. How's your Spanish?"

"Well I can communicate," replied Burke, "You know, uh, pretty good, yeah . . . pretty good."

Burke went in to sit on a chair at the front of the classroom, while Connolly and his friend Dolan were waiting outside. When the oral exam began, things got quiet. Into the room came the examiner, a man known only as Martinez. He took a chair and placed it at the front center of the room, right in front of Burke. To Connolly, it was a scene from one of those World War II–era Fellini movies he had seen in the theater, with a military interrogator seeking a confession. In this case, a priest was confessing to a layperson.

Martinez looked directly and seriously at Burke and asked "*¿Cómo está usted?*"—a simple "How are you?" Burke did not answer. Martinez proceeded to ask again, with no change in the facial expression, but with a little more volume. "*¿Cómo está usted?*"

Burke, clueless, repeated the question in a mumble, searching haplessly through his memory for a moment of understanding. "*Cómo está usted, cómo está usted.*" Exasperated, Martinez asked the question again, this time loudly and sternly: "*¡Cómo está usted!*" Burke was startled. "Hey, hey!" he pleaded. "*Un poco mas despacio, por favor.*" ("A little bit slower, please.")

Connolly and Dolan looked on, and then they looked at each other, incredulous. He couldn't answer that? They found this interaction so

Newly ordained priests *(incl. Connolly, stairway, bottom left)* before boarding plane to Puerto Rico, June 1958. Cardinal Francis Spellman and Fr. Joseph Fitzpatrick *(front)*. (Photo courtesy of Fr. Robert Stern.)

humorous that they began convulsing with laughter. However much they tried, they couldn't stop laughing, while everyone else stood looking every other way. But everything stopped when Sullivan was called in.

Martinez faced Sullivan when he came in, and before a "como esta" could be uttered, Sullivan quickly cut off the exam with Martinez by confessing, "I don't know anything." Brought back to the sober moment of the interrogation, Connolly and Dolan followed suit when they were called in.

"I don't know anything," replied Connolly.

"I don't know anything either," said Dolan.

Word got back to the other members of the university program staff after the exams were completed. "Well then, why did you come here?" they asked Connolly and the others.

Saying, "Well, we didn't know," Connolly realized that this would be a challenging summer.

Connolly—along with fifty-one others sent by the Archdiocese of New York, the Diocese of Brooklyn, and others—was beginning a language and culture educational program.[10] This summer was the program's second at Puerto Rico's Catholic University.[11] Participants included half the Dunwoodie graduating class of 1958. But there were other experienced priests besides Sullivan and Burke—priests whom Connolly would get to know that summer and really come to admire for their wisdom. Father Leo Mahon, from Chicago, was developing a new sister parish program for a community in Panama City, Panama. From New York, there was Father Bob Fox, a trained social worker preparing to establish a Catholic Charities program in Montevideo, Uruguay. There was also Father John Ahern, already an active priest in the Catholic Charities system, who worked in the Bronx. From Youngstown, Ohio, there was Father Jim Young, who was learning how to better serve a large migrant Puerto Rican population brought in by government and business forces to help defeat a steelworkers' union strike. Rounding out the group were other priests, nuns, brothers, and laypersons, creating a large base of future Spanish-speakers and culture experts.

There could not have been too many, nor could they have come too soon, for the Archdiocese of New York.

De-Yankeefication

Beginning in the 1940s, the city of New York saw a continuous influx of thousands of people from Puerto Rico every year. The Great Puerto Rican Migration, or *La Gran Migración*, would result in five hundred thousand new residents by 1958, and the waves continued.[12] With seven million residents of all nationalities, New York knew how to absorb new immigrant waves, but this one was different. This was not an influx of white Europeans, but of Latin Americans with different skin colors and hair textures. Moreover, this one could not be controlled by federal quotas limiting the number of arrivals from a particular nation, as had been the case with Europeans since 1924. The passengers arriving on Marine Tiger ships[13] and Trans Caribbean Airways planes were U.S. citizens, free to travel between Puerto Rico and the mainland. No plan or institution was ready for this unlimited migration—not the schools, property owners, and government agencies, and not even the Catholic Church, already experienced in absorbing prior migrations.

After all, the archdiocese of Connolly's youth was a predominantly Irish institution and community. Street processions were part of the regular public devotions to Jesus, the Virgin Mary, and Saints Patrick and Brigid. These devotions, which sometimes lasted forty hours, were important elements of Catholicism brought over from Ireland, as were beliefs in miracles and the utmost respect for the authority of priests. In the center of each of New York's Irish neighborhoods was the parish infrastructure, usually a full-block combination of church, school, rectory, convent, and parish hall—physical structures which defined the very strong sense of social and spiritual structure in Irish American life. These institutions were established by successive powerful Irish archbishops and maintained by the dutiful contributions of working-class parishioners and their many societies. This network of structures, devotions, contributions, and beliefs helped strengthen Irish Americans' way of life. It also gave them legitimacy and comfort in an initially hostile city.[14]

The Irish-dominated Archdiocese of New York did have experience with non-Irish Catholic migrations. Each new group established "national parishes," dedicated in language and staffing to the nationality of the new group. Thus, Italian, German, Polish, and other national parishes sprang up, and eventually 115 of them dotted the Manhattan landscape. But the intensity and volume of the *Gran Migración*, as well as the lack of Puerto Rican clergy, led Cardinal Spellman to call for a different parish model: an "integrated parish." In such a parish, at least one priest would be trained in the language of the new migrants, and services and sacraments could be provided to them in that language—at least until they could all speak English and would no longer need the dedicated services.[15]

It was not until Spellman's public announcement in 1952, however, that the archdiocese put the integrated parish model into action. That was the year when a whole program of diocesan services would be provided for the new community, all under a new office at headquarters called the Office of Spanish Catholic Action.[16] All of these services were created under the direction of two men, both of whom were highly educated, highly interested in Puerto Ricans, very hands-on, and, most important, highly respected by the cardinal: Father Ivan Illich and Father Joseph Fitzpatrick.

Illich was a Croatian-born priest who, during an encounter in Rome, so impressed Spellman with his intellect that Spellman persuaded him to work in the United States. Then, serving a newly forming Puerto Rican community in Manhattan's Washington Heights, Illich learned Spanish doing pastoral work and spent months in Puerto Rico whenever he could, just to learn how people lived.[17] Fitzpatrick, a Jesuit and trained sociologist, dedicated himself, his studies, his teaching, and his service in Puerto Rico and New York to the Puerto Ricans and their experiences in the United States.[18]

Spellman gave the two priests the freedom to develop a program of full immersion in the culture and the language of the Puerto Rican people. Illich organized the program called the Institute for Intercultural Communication at the Catholic University of Puerto Rico (La Universidad Católica de Puerto Rico), and he became vice rector of the university in order to oversee it. Illich wanted the participants to give up the cultural norms they had grown up with—the Irish American Catholic way of life. As he put it, the goal for all participants in the Institute was simple: "de-Yankeefication."[19]

Like Illich, Fitzpatrick was present with Connolly during that summer of 1958, actively involved in the program he co-created. While he agreed with Illich that "de-Yankeefication" was the way to prepare the clergy and religious for their future ministry, Fitzpatrick, the teacher, had a different role at La Universidad from Illich, the organizer. On many evenings Fitzpatrick taught Connolly and the other participants about the history and values of the Puerto Rican people.

Puerto Rico and Empires

Connolly learned that, located in a globally strategic point in the Caribbean, Puerto Rico had lived under the domination of two empires at different stages in its five-hundred-year history: Spain and the United States. The Spanish conquered the country and its indigenous Taino population at the turn of the fifteenth century and controlled it for the next four centuries. After decimating much of the Taino population, the Spanish instituted African slavery, a system which brought the two peoples together and led to a large mixed-race segment of the population, as well as a mixture of the two cultures.[20] During the nineteenth century, Puerto Rican political organizations, campaigns, and conflicts led to the abolition of slavery in 1873 and to the unsuccessful *Grito de Lares*, an armed rebellion in 1868 against the Spanish empire.[21]

The end of the century brought the country under a new empire, with the United States annexing Puerto Rico in 1898 as the "spoils" of victory in the Spanish-American War. Puerto Ricans were given a limited U.S. citizenship in 1917, a status enabling its men to serve in both World Wars and the Korean War. In 1952, Puerto Rico became a political entity known as a "Free Associated State," neither an independent country nor an American state. Its two best known leaders reflected the political tensions on the island over the role of the U.S. empire in the American era: Pedro Albizu Campos, leader of independence struggles under the Nationalist Party, and Luis Muñoz Marín, who converted from independence advocate to the first elected governor and defender of the Free Associated State. When Albizu Campos and the Nationalists organized a successful national sugar cane workers' strike, counter-actions by the U.S.-controlled government, such as the 1937 Ponce Massacre and the suppression of the 1950 Nationalist uprising, terminated a renewed effort for independence. In the middle of these political conflicts, citizenship status was enhanced several times by the United States, until it eventually gave Puerto Rico's people a right important to their future: the right to travel and work freely.[22]

Under both empires, Puerto Ricans remained largely an agricultural people. Spaniards who settled in Puerto Rico had become self-sufficient farmers, or *jíbaros*, who learned the ways of the land and grew enough to feed their families. Through land grants issued by successive Spanish governments, immigration to Puerto Rico from Spain and other countries was vigorously encouraged, and settlers were called to grow crops beneficial to the Spanish.[23]

Agricultural life persisted after the American takeover: In 1910, 79 percent of the population was described as rural, and in 1940, 70 percent were still considered rural.[24] Underscoring Puerto Rico's agricultural dependence, the hurricane season made its people keenly aware of nature's awesome power over their lives and well-being. In 1899, Hurricane *San Ciriaco* came and destroyed the island's crops, electric power, and telephones; killed more than 3,000; and left 250,000 homeless. It was followed in 1928 by the more devastating *San Felipe Segundo*, which also destroyed crops and utilities and left 500,000 homeless.[25]

After the period of royal Spanish rule, another kind of monarch would radically change independent subsistence farming and agriculture in Puerto Rico and accelerate its poverty: King Sugar. By the late 1800s, several large U.S. corporations had already acquired much of the arable land in Puerto Rico. Replacing other crops with sugar cane, the corporations converted many small farms into vast sugar cane fields and mills.[26] As a result, once-independent farmers became sugar cane cutters and processors on someone else's land. Thousands lived as low-wage workers under the *libreta* (passbook) system, taking work when and where they could find it, earning as little as $0.30 an hour during the 1920s and 1930s. In the *tiempo muerto* (dead season), when there was no harvest, thousands relied on piecemeal work in the needlework industry.[27]

As subsistence farms, crop diversity, and farm jobs disappeared from much of Puerto Rico, one thing grew every decade: its population. The American era saw accelerated growth on the island, from one million residents in 1900 to over two million residents by 1950. With the Depression cutting deeply into the economy and many facing starvation, the Puerto Rico Reconstruction Administration (PRRA) was established to provide basic food and aid to hundreds of thousands.[28] Then, as Puerto Rico grew poorer and more crowded, the government launched a "modernization" program, Operation Bootstrap, in the 1930s and 1940s. The program grew the manufacturing sector, luring U.S. corporations by promising cheap labor and tax benefits.[29] Also, to control the population, it subjected about one-third of the country's women to an involuntary mass sterilization program.[30]

Finally, seeing that the agricultural and manufacturing sectors still left hundreds of thousands of working-age people without a job, Puerto Rico took a major step. The government systematically encouraged its people to move to the United States to find a job, and a new life, setting in motion the *Gran Migración*.

In addition to learning all this about their history, Connolly learned about the values of the Puerto Rican people. They had a general fear and distrust of institutions, since government and corporate actions regularly took away their livelihoods and lands. These institutional actions had also taught them to be self-reliant, to find assistance and resources within their own families and among their neighbors. With everyone's limited chance of surviving to an old age, Puerto Rican families, like those in most agricultural societies, were large enough so that some would extend the family to the next generation. The people Connolly was meeting had a broad definition of "family," incorporating godchildren, children born outside of a marriage (even if this was actually not formalized, but a common-law relationship), and children whose parents had passed away, or whose parents were too poor to raise them.[31]

Facing health crises such as the tuberculosis epidemic, and the natural crises of hurricanes, and the overwhelming economic crisis of the Great Depression, the people had also developed a fatalism, accepting things as they were because *"no hay mas na'"* ("What else is there?"), and a religiosity, feeling that things would work out *"si Dios quiere y la Virgen"* ("if God and the Virgin wish it").[32]

First Immersion: Language

The first Puerto Ricans whom Connolly got to know that summer were his teachers at La Universidad, who were also students there. They implemented the language program directed by Dr. Silva, a Brazilian linguistics professor. Connolly thought they were great teachers, welcoming and responsive to the students. Classes were divided up by initial language capabilities, tested by Martinez's "interrogation." And, despite objections by some in the New York hierarchy, who were getting progress reports on the summer's developments, Connolly and his peers, who had socialized even during their seminary years, accepted the other students' invitations to attend dances and recreational events at their homes or at the school.

Socializing and recreation provided Connolly, who loved taking in

A group of Connolly's summer 1958 classmates taking a stroll on campus of La Universidad Católica.

entertainment at jazz clubs in his seminary days, with lessons beyond the classroom. At a dance in one local hall, one of their teachers, a dark-skinned man, was standing in the corner with Connolly and some class-mates when a good, lively dance number was starting up. Another teacher, a light-skinned woman, was standing at another corner while some of her friends were out on the dance floor. Seeing this, Connolly and the other priests urged him to take a chance and ask her out on the floor to dance.

He begged off.

"Ask her out," Connolly and the others said again. "Go dance. Don't be shy."

After some more friendly lobbying, he finally responded to the priests, with a little hesitation. He explained that he could not ask her out because of the difference between his skin color and hers. It was just an unspoken rule, he said, that different races could not mix together on the dance floor without a negative, and maybe violent, public reaction. The priests and teachers remained a little quiet for a while, and then they continued enjoying themselves. But the moment stayed with Connolly.

Connolly had very limited understanding of racial conflicts and race relations at this point. His Yorkville neighborhood had only known one building with black families in it during his boyhood, before they all moved out of the neighborhood almost overnight. Connolly never knew why they moved, or where.

He learned about the attitude he should personally take toward black people through his family. Connolly's father, Con, drove the Harlem bus route for the Fifth Avenue Bus Company and got along very well with his passengers, some of whom even gave him gifts at holiday time. Con, whom Neil considered a "respecter of all people," insisted on that respect among all his family members. Once, when Neil's brother used the word "nigger" at the dinner table while discussing some black person on the street, Con stopped the dinner, stood up, pointed at the brother, and said, "Get out. Don't you ever use that word here." His brother left the table, and everyone resumed the dinner in quiet. The lesson was learned: *Every Connolly would be a respecter of all people, or else.*

As Connolly grew older, he maintained this attitude during his limited experiences with African Americans. During one of his summers as a camp counselor in Poughkeepsie, he oversaw a mixed-race group of kids and felt they all got along well with each other in camp. Also, his friend Harry Salmon was the only black priest candidate at Dunwoodie he knew, and since Salmon was a kind, soft-spoken man and a basketball player with real talent, Connolly, who was always a sports fan, got along very well with him.

But in Puerto Rico, as he looked at his teacher, he was beginning to realize, race was a real problem.

Back in the classroom, Connolly acquired Spanish through a dynamic method of language learning, focusing on active conversation and repetition. Some other students resisted this approach, calling for more traditional exercises such as learning conjugations and verb tenses, and sentence and grammar structures. Connolly did not resist. He embraced this dynamic approach and, in the process, advanced quickly from the lowest level at the beginning to a couple of levels up by the end of the classroom program.

Dynamic learning just seemed natural to Connolly. When he was socializing and holding conversations with his friends on weekends, visiting jazz clubs on Fifty-Second Street, going bowling and playing cards, he found out how little he knew about matters of the world—current events and social and political issues—compared to his classmates. He barely knew what they were talking about. So he started picking up copies of *Time* magazine and newspapers, reading everything he could get his hands on just to be up on the latest news developments and issues and to hold his own in those conversations. It had him thinking more about the world, especially during the turbulent postwar, Cold War times.

Connolly was quick to learn when the situation called for it. And the veteran priests—Ahern, Fox, Young, Mahon, and Fitzpatrick and Illich—all had much to share about their own encounters with the Puerto Ricans in the United States. They engaged Connolly and his new classmates in discussions about Puerto Rican history and culture. They were very impressive, Connolly thought, and they seemed to have a willingness to immerse themselves in the Puerto Rican communities they were serving.

But all this learning in the dynamic language lessons and conversations at La Universidad, Illich and Fitzpatrick pointed out, would be incomplete without the weekend lessons. While the week was dedicated to lectures and discussions in the classroom, the weekend lessons took place in the countryside, all over the island.

Second Immersion: Campo

The first "weekend school" was in San Lorenzo, a town where he was greeted by Redemptorist Father Dusty O'Malley. O'Malley greeted Connolly that first Saturday in the town church's rectory and prepared him for a full schedule of Masses the following day, beginning at six o'clock in the morning. The Masses were to take place up in an area he called the *campo*.

Connolly took a jeep with O'Malley, all the way up the countryside along paths and dirt roads, and ended up on a hilltop. It was a little cool, and Connolly had an extraordinary view of the countryside there. At six sharp, his worshippers arrived: sugar cane workers, who had already spent part of the morning in the fields. Since it had rained the night before, the ground was muddy, which prompted the workers to all take their mud-soaked shoes off before entering a small chapel. They all walked in barefoot, and Connolly, seeing this, did the same before entering this simple structure. Here on the hilltop, Connolly celebrated his first independent Mass for parishioners as a priest. It was also where he would deliver his first sermon using the Spanish vocabulary he was beginning to build at La Universidad.

Connolly was offering his first Mass at the unlikeliest of places. This was not the seminary chapel. Nor was it the Good Counsel structure built in the early 1900s, much less the grand St. Patrick's Cathedral. Weeks earlier, he had joined thirty-one other men in a full ceremonial Mass, presided over by the cardinal and several bishops, dressed in full vestments, and joined by a choir as well as several hundred family members and friends of the new priests. Here, there were no altar boys. There was no choir. There were no vestments or architecturally complex church interiors. It was just a few dozen workers and Connolly, praying and reciting in Latin.

Afterward, Connolly wondered about this Mass and place. *Was this cel-ebration done well? Did the worshippers come here before? What was this chapel doing here? Where did it come from?*

Through more Fitzpatrick presentations at La Universidad, Connolly learned about the Catholic Church and about Catholicism as lived in Puerto Rico. In the Spanish era, Puerto Rico's churches, hospitals, schools, and orphanages were created and staffed by Spain's Catholic Church, un-der agreements with the monarchy called *concordats*. Community institu-tions relied on the central Church for funds and staffing, and the Puerto Ricans' role was merely to worship and be served. In the American era, Puerto Rico's non-church institutions secularized, and many of the clergy and religious returned to Spain. Eventually, the Redemptorists, a religious order from the United States, took control of the Puerto Rican Catholic Church, with archbishops James Davis and James McManus overseeing the two dioceses of San Juan and Ponce. La Universidad Católica in Ponce was also created by them in 1947. Other religious orders, from both the United States and Europe, were eventually brought in to staff the institu-tions formerly run by the Spanish.[33]

But many local parish communities were still ignored, with only thirty-four of the island's seventy-eight town parishes staffed by a priest. These parishes, with churches, rectories, and convents in the geographic centers of the town, were far removed from the underdeveloped countryside, the *campo*. With few access roads to the *campos*, the clergy and religious were reluctant to visit or celebrate sacraments with the people living in the countryside. Even the American takeover did not change this reluctance, and so the *campesinos* were left on their own. It was usually only for spe-cial occasions, such as a *fiesta patronal*, that the *campesinos* came down to the parish centers.[34]

Just as they were often left to rely on themselves for survival in the world then, Puerto Ricans were also left to rely on themselves for their religion. Once again, Puerto Ricans developed their own solution: a self-sufficient Catholicism, especially in the *campos*. Much of their religious activity was carried out in the homes of the local families. Many homes, even the poor-est, kept a rosary and crucifix, and some even had a *santo* (a carved wooden status of Jesus, Mary, or a saint) or an "altar"—a wooden table with fruits and plants, pictures of family members, candles, and water, organized and positioned in a corner of the house as sacrificial offerings to God. With-out a priest, a community often produced *rezadoras* ("pray-ers"), women who were recognized in the community as leaders of prayer gatherings for families or networks of families in a community. They most often led prayer gatherings for wakes, funerals, and novenas after the funeral, some for seven consecutive years afterward to commemorate the anniversary of a death. On the rare occasion when a priest would arrive, a sacrament was celebrated.[35]

At the beginning of the twentieth century, *campesinos* began to see another kind of religious leader: a lay Catholic preacher. In 1902, José de los Santos Morales of the town of Arecibo spontaneously preached a sermon after a prayer session. A year later, José Rodriguez Medina of Utuado also spontaneously preached, this time after a ceremony on Three Kings Day. Their reception was warm and enthusiastic, and many people and families requested sermons in those communities; then services were organized in hundreds of homes throughout the broader Puerto Rican countryside. When the two Josés learned about each other's preaching and services and then met, they agreed to form a joint effort to reach people more broadly in the *campo*. Demand for the two, known affectionately as the "Hermanos Cheo" ("Cheo" being a nickname for José), was so strong that some communities built chapels and even small residences in the hills to accommodate them on their visits and support regular services. The Hermanos Cheo movement grew to include women preachers who were recognized for their gifts and became known as "Hermanas Chea." This new corps of self-styled preachers encouraged Catholicism in this unique way and was ultimately recognized by the Church hierarchy of Puerto Rico.

The chapel in San Lorenzo was a legacy of that movement. The structure was saved for that Sunday when a priest would make the rare visit to bring the sacrament of the Eucharist. Connolly's was that rare visit.

Confession was the next important sacrament for Connolly to offer, again for the first time in his priesthood. The setting for this was even more unusual. In the *campo* town of Jayuya, on another weekend, Connolly was brought to a general store, known in Puerto Rico as a *colmado*. He was escorted through the store, past the overwhelming smells of *bacalao* (salted codfish), to the back wall where the makeshift "confessional" was waiting: a wooden wine cask, where he would sit, and a crate on either side of the cask. There were dozens waiting inside and outside the store.

When Connolly sat down on the wine cask, the first penitent came over: a pretty girl, about fifteen years old, who quietly took a seat on one of the crates. She looked at the new Irish American priest and without thought, put her head in his lap. Connolly was startled, thinking, *What is going on here? What kind of a confession is this?* He quickly pulled her up and had her sit straight, and she began the confession. Connolly heard and responded to her confession with the best Spanish he could muster and then went to the next penitent, and then the next. It was nonstop, one confession after another, for three straight hours.

By the end, Connolly felt, he must have listened to the confession of all the sins of Jayuya.

This was not what he had expected. There were no dividing walls, no velvet curtains or private booths like those he had knelt in at Good Counsel when he was first confessing his sins to a priest whose face he couldn't see, except through a dark mesh screen. Here, in Jayuya's confession "box," he saw the faces of the penitents as they shared their sins. In some cases, two persons sat down at the same time, and one sat and watched while the other shared her venial and cardinal weaknesses with Connolly. He struggled to maintain protocol and privacy by stopping the confession and asking for some order, and for a softer tone: *"Por favor, hay alguien aquí quien está escuchando tu pecado."* (Please, be careful. There is someone here who is listening to all your sins.)

Connolly was exhausted and confused after the nonstop "confession by fire," which left him with a question: *With no church building or private confession booth present, was this sacrament of confession he was practicing still genuine?* He didn't have a real answer, but he felt certain that those he had heard were sincere and solemn in seeking God's mercy through their American priest, and that he was equally sincere and solemn in listening to them and invoking God's forgiveness. There was no other church available for the moment; this *colmado*, with its *bacalao*, groceries, wine casks, and crates, was accordingly the sacramental site. The people committed to the holy act, and so they made it their holy place, their church, on that day. On a prior weekend, the people of San Lorenzo saw him as their priest, and they were his parish for that day. Now in Jayuya, the penitents had seen him as their pastor, and he was for that day.

On another morning in the *campo*, he completed celebration of a Mass and was expecting to rest before a couple of more Masses. However, a worshipper from the *campo* extended Connolly an invitation.

"Padre, ven conmigo, porque vamos a pasar una hora y media. Yo he invitado a mis vecinos, a mis hermanos y cuñados, van a venir y todo eso. Usted puede comer algo, tomar un cafecito, un poquito de pan, o si usted quiere algo, jamón." (Father, please come with me, because we are going to spend about an hour and a half getting together. I've invited my neighbors, my brothers, my brothers- and sisters-in-law, and they are all coming. You could eat something, have some coffee, have a little bread, or if you want something else, maybe some ham.)

Connolly accepted the invitation and went over to her house. The hostess sat him down in a chair in the middle of a room, and he was surrounded by several dozen people. They heard him say a few words, and detecting a respectable Spanish accent, they jumped right into full conversation with him. He was answering "sí" and "no" to questions he didn't fully understand, and he had little idea what he was telling them. But they were so warm and delighted that he was with them that it took away some of his worries about what he was doing there. Like the cane workers in the San Lorenzo chapel and the confessants of Jayuya, they were very open and welcoming to him.

Why? He wondered.

Were they curious about him?

Were they just grateful that a priest visited them in the campo?

Were they just welcoming him to join their community and live the way they did?

Why bring their whole family to meet him?

Sacred Acts

By mid-September, the program was completed, but the return to the United States left Connolly thinking about how incomplete he felt. He had learned something about administering the sacraments, but not from another priest. The Puerto Ricans, with their own Catholic ways, had been his teachers. They had created their own spaces and their own approaches to each act, and they had shared them with Connolly.

Connolly had realized some important things:

With their presence, strong faith, and seriousness of purpose, they declared:

This act—this Mass in the bare chapel or this confession in the colmado—is sacred.

We share our faith together with you, Father Connolly, and together we make it sacred.

The church is here, in the campo.

In accepting the unorthodox, mundane settings, they did not see limits to holiness, and in so doing, compelled Connolly to not see them either. He wondered again, *Where else could church exist?*

Connolly also wondered, *What was next for his priesthood?* He realized that he was getting prepared to work with Puerto Ricans back in New

York, somewhere. *This could be a good thing*, he thought; he had been welcomed with such openness and warmth by the people of Puerto Rico that he was pleasantly overwhelmed. Going back to New York, he looked forward to seeing these Puerto Rican people again and knowing them better. He again thought about his decision as a twelve-year-old boy to become a priest for people, the way Good Counsel priests had been for him. *Now, he would try to become a priest for people—for these people, in their new world.*

But there was much more to work on in order to become a true priest, including his Spanish. It was incomplete. But it was getting better.

2

###

The New Parish

Although he has obligations toward all men, a priest has the poor and lowly
entrusted to him in a special way. The Lord Himself showed that He was united to
them, and the fact that the Gospel was preached to them is mentioned as a sign
of Messianic activity. With special diligence, priests should look after youth, as
well as married people and parents. It is desirable that each of these groups join
together in friendly associations and thereby help one another act more easily
and adequately as Christians in a condition of life which is often demanding.
　　　　　　　　　　　　—Second Vatican Council, *Decree on the Ministry*
　　　　　　　　　　　　　　　　and Life of Priests §6, December 1965

Unknown Soldier

On September 15, 1958, Neil Connolly set foot in St. Athanasius parish,
arriving at 878 Tiffany Street, a three-story rectory next to a large church in
the Hunts Point–Longwood neighborhood of the Bronx. Just days earlier,
at the assignment meeting in the New York Archdiocesan headquarters on
Madison Avenue, auxiliary bishop John Maguire had told him, "It will be
a challenge, but I think you'll do well there." It was a busy rectory, and he
was immediately given numerous priestly assignments. Within weeks of his
arrival, Connolly was already visiting neighborhood apartment buildings to
give Holy Communion to the sick and the elderly.

　　Among the areas Connolly visited was "Little Korea," a few blocks of
Fox and Simpson Streets between Westchester Avenue and 163rd Street.
It was given the nickname because there were a number of veterans from

the Korean War living there, and because of its "wars"—the constant fights and attacks taking place in its buildings and on its streets. The war-zone atmosphere was heightened by overcrowding. Entire buildings in Little Korea were filled with SROs (single-room-occupancy), with spaces originally built as three bedrooms subdivided and then rented out to three different households. SRO tenants included whole families as well as single men.

One day, Connolly was on an emergency visit to a building at 980 Fox Street. Connolly knew that wearing his cassock—the long black clerical robe over his shirt and pants—gave him instant credibility and recognition from the people on the streets, something he had observed in his days in Puerto Rico. He didn't wear it all the time, but on the street in Little Korea, it was often the right "uniform."

From prior visits, he knew that many of the apartments lacked hallway lights, which made it difficult to reach the right room and the person he wanted to see. Each building had an unfamiliar mix of odors and sounds, and each had a bad reputation, with a lot of drug and alcohol abuse, especially among the single men. After his first couple of visits, he learned, when entering an apartment hall, to call out to get the attention of the person he was visiting: "Is anybody here?" People in adjoining rooms had no relationship to each other, so he couldn't really rely on them to find the person he was visiting.

When he arrived that day at the apartment, Connolly saw a couple of detectives standing in the hallway and a person lying motionless on the floor near them. The middle-aged Puerto Rican man had been stabbed to death. One of the detectives looked at Connolly.

"You been here long, Father? You look like a young guy."

Connolly responded, "I've been here a couple of months, maybe."

The detective looked down and said, "Here, let me pick up the hem of your cassock. You got blood dripping from it."

For Connolly, this was a startling, thought-provoking moment. First, up to this point in his life, he had never seen a dead person outside of a funeral home. Also, this was a death by violence, something he had never seen in Yorkville. He had only once come close to seeing it anywhere—in 1949 in Madison Square Garden, where heavyweight champion Rocky Marciano's punch nearly killed Carmine Vingo during one of the Friday Night Fights his brother Denis took him to.[1]

Extreme unction, or "last rites," were administered to Vingo before his ultimately successful recovery. But there was no fame or recovery here. There was not even anyone to describe the dead man to Connolly; no one with any knowledge of his life history, his dreams, or his struggles. Connolly could only use his own prayers for this man's soul, to give this "unknown solider" of Little Korea some mercy and some meaning. Yet, *even if this battle was over*, Connolly realized as he looked around at the environment and the police, *this was still Little Korea, and warfare would resume soon*.

The detectives were Irish, and they didn't speak Spanish. In fact, they did not speak very much at all, except to communicate one thing: Nobody was going into the room or the apartment. There were no relatives coming around to speak with, so Connolly told the police that he would like to administer last rites to this man. He squatted down, careful to avoid any more blood, and made the sign of the cross on the man's forehead while reciting prayers. Connolly used a Spanish prayer book, which he kept at all times and treasured; with his very limited Spanish, he could not afford to be without it, and so he watched it like a hawk.

Connolly was still taken aback by the detectives' casualness. For his fellow Irishmen, the emergency was over. Both a report and a life were finished. For Connolly, however, there was still a sense of emergency about the lost soul and about the building's other souls.

What kind of place was this, he asked, *which showed no mercy to this unknown solider?*

Why was the building dark and overcrowded, and why was everyone separated?

What kind of owner would let this building reach this miserable point? How many other buildings were there like this, where people were left to fend for themselves?

Also, he thought, *this was likely a recent Puerto Rican migrant. What pueblo did he come from in Puerto Rico? How did he not have family?*

Also, was he a baptized Catholic? What sacraments did he receive during his life? And what about the other apartment dwellers' lives?

He was sure that those living in the rooms surrounding him were also from Puerto Rico. Were they from Jayuya, or San Lorenzo, or Arecibo, or anywhere he had visited just a couple of months ago? There were many stories to hear about the people in this neighborhood and how they got here, he was sure.

Forced Migrations

After arriving in New York City, most Puerto Ricans continued migrating, but now it was done within the city, which is roughly a tenth the size of the island they had just left. They often settled first in densely packed and segregated neighborhoods. Their numbers increased from 244,000 in 1950 to 612,000, or 8 percent of the city's population, in 1960.[2] Often arriving with large families, the Puerto Rican migrants were also a much younger and less educated population than other New Yorkers, with a median age of 21.9 years and an education level of 7.6 years.[3]

In the earlier years of the *Gran Migración*, Puerto Ricans settled in all five boroughs, with a greater presence in Manhattan and the Bronx. They started moving in larger numbers to the Bronx in the late 1950s to early 1960s, and by 1965, the Bronx became the borough with the highest number of Puerto Ricans in the city.[4] In 1960, Hunts Point–Longwood, the neighborhood served by St. Athanasius parish, had one of the heaviest concentrations.[5] As in other Puerto Rican neighborhoods, the settlement was created by several forces—"push" and "pull" migrations produced by laws and institutions.

Among other factors, two major government actions, which the Puerto Ricans were powerless to control, pushed the city's Puerto Rican population northward to neighborhoods like Hunts Point–Longwood. The Federal Housing Act of 1949 authorized and funded "urban renewal," the large-scale governmental seizure, destruction, and replacement of "slum" areas in American cities with new housing.[6] In Manhattan, construction coordinator Robert Moses and the City Planning Department carried out over a dozen urban-renewal projects, also known as "slum clearance," in poor, segregated Manhattan areas where Puerto Ricans and blacks lived.[7] Many of those residents were forced to leave their neighborhoods and find new housing, often in other segregated neighborhoods. In addition, the Act, expanding on the 1934 Housing Act, created more government-subsidized public housing developments for working-class people.[8] Thus, more buildings and neighborhoods were "cleared" to make way for the construction of the new housing complexes, which came to be known as the "projects." Public housing units for 100,000 residents were created as of 1962 in the Bronx alone.[9]

Leaving the clearance areas in the Lower East Side, Upper West Side, Hell's Kitchen, East Harlem, Central Harlem, and Morningside Heights, the Puerto Rican migrants took refuge wherever they could, usually near family and friends. Several hundred thousand people were displaced by New York City's clearance actions, setting in motion an almost constant migration for the newly arrived Puerto Ricans.[10] Not one clearance project was created in Hunts Point–Longwood, however, and so the neighborhood attracted many of those being pushed from other neighborhoods in the Bronx and Manhattan.

The apartments in Hunts Point–Longwood and other southeastern Bronx neighborhoods became available to the Puerto Ricans because of another migration, this one a "pull" migration. During the 1950s, an estimated 1.3 million more white New Yorkers left the city than came in, a phenomenon known as "white flight."[11] Those white New York families mostly "fled" to newly created suburbs in areas north and east of the city, such as Westchester, Rockland, and Long Island.[12] Their new homes were created by another federal housing program, the Federal Housing Administration (FHA) mortgage insurance program, which spurred the creation of millions of homes affordable to working and middle class people in the United States.[13] Reflecting the racial regime of the 1940s and 1950s, the program required many suburban developments to ban home sales to non-whites, making them more attractive to whites and enhancing the "pull" from urban neighborhoods.

More than 240,000 of New York's out-migrants left the Bronx, leaving many apartments available, especially in the Southern and Eastern Bronx.[14] But with both "push" and "pull" forces at work, many Puerto Rican migrants struggled to find affordable apartments. Many moved into the next building or the next block and shared apartments with friends, families, and even strangers—a practice known as "doubling up." Single rooms sufficed as living quarters, as long as families and individuals had access to a bathroom and kitchen. Noting the "doubling up" trend, landlords converted hundreds of apartment buildings into SROs, in neighborhoods often close to the sites of the clearance projects.[15] With public housing developments in the Bronx and East Harlem to the south, thousands of displaced migrants sought SRO buildings and found them along Fox Street and Simpson Street, in Little Korea, and elsewhere in Hunts Point–Longwood.

Hunts Point–Longwood

What the Puerto Rican migrants found was a large and busy neighborhood. There were six subway stations: Prospect Avenue, Intervale Avenue, and Simpson Street on the #2 and #5 express lines, and 149th Street, Longwood Avenue, and Hunts Point Avenue on the #6 local line. One major street, Southern Boulevard, was the second largest commercial corridor in the Bronx, and another, 163rd Street, was a major commercial and traffic road leading to Hunts Point Peninsula in one direction and Yankee Stadium in the other. The Hunts Point Peninsula, with a smaller residential community and a much larger industrial park, was separated from the main Hunts Point area by the eight-lane Bruckner Boulevard and Expressway.

There were blocks and blocks of large five- and six-story multifamily buildings. But as any new arrival could see, there were no open-space recreation areas, just the playgrounds belonging to several public schools in the area and a small Police Athletic League (PAL) indoor recreation center on 156th Street. Hunts Point–Longwood had nearly 89,000 residents officially living in the area as of 1960, 46,000 of whom were Puerto Ricans. It had a median family income of $4,650, which was 25 percent less than New York City overall.[16] Housing conditions and prices in Hunts Point–Longwood posed a challenge for its residents living on these lower incomes, which were earned mostly through factory and service jobs in Manhattan.

Monthly rent increased continuously, from an average of $38 to $60 during the 1950s, but the quality of these more expensive apartments worsened. By 1960, about 28 percent of the neighborhood's housing units were already officially considered "deteriorating" or "dilapidated," compared with 15 percent in New York City as a whole.[17] Also, nearly a quarter were officially considered overcrowded, with more than one person per room, which was twice the citywide rate. In the middle of this overpopulated and decaying neighborhood, all that anyone with a little money could do was to survive, even if home was a single room in an unlit apartment. Or not survive, as Connolly saw during his first administration of last rites, before getting back to his next parish assignment.

There was little time between assignments, even though the parish staff of five was large: The pastor, Monsignor Joseph Mastaglio, was joined by Fathers Tom McDonald, Tom McGarrett, Al DeLuca, John Steltz, and Neil Connolly. There were two Spanish Masses on Sunday, and they were regularly packed with worshippers. Every single pew, as well as the large standing-room-only area in the back, was completely filled. And despite the great number of people to greet afterward, this was the easiest sacrament for Connolly to celebrate and learn, even as he stumbled over his first sermons in awkward Spanish.

First Sacrament

Just by itself, the sacrament of baptism was taking up much of the priests' time. In the early 1960s there were, on average, thirty baptisms on a

Saturday, followed by five on a Sunday, week after week for the entire year. At the crest of this wave, the priests at Athanasius baptized fifteen hundred new Catholics a year. Every Puerto Rican in New York, it seemed, wanted a baptism in those years.

Requests for baptisms came in all forms and at all times. Once, a military family came to the church on a Saturday at the last minute, as Connolly was assembling those already scheduled. With siblings, aunts, uncles, and cousins accompanying the young soldier, the mother began pleading her case: *"Este muchacho necesita ser bautizado hoy, porque Sabrá Dios lo que le pasará cuando vaya a la Guerra."* (This young man needs to be baptized now, because God only knows what might happen to him in war.)

Connolly replied (in his rapidly-developing Spanish), "But he hasn't made any of his preparations, he hasn't taken a course."

The desperate mother, now also infuriated, looked at Connolly and cried out, *"¡Vámonos a la Milagrosa!"* La Milagrosa was a Spanish national church located in Harlem. It was one of four Spanish national parishes in New York, established under the original national parish model created by the archdiocese to serve immigrant Catholics. Pastor Ernesto Mayoral, who had taught Connolly in his Cathedral Preparatory Seminary days, would allow baptisms to take place at his church, on the spot, without preparation, for any Spanish-speaking family seeking one. Even with all the baptisms performed by Connolly and his colleagues, they could not compare with the volume of activity at La Milagrosa. At one point, La Milagrosa was reported to have baptized five hundred new Catholics on a single Easter Sunday.

As often as possible, Connolly and the other parish priests did their best to teach and prepare families in advance of the ceremony. But with so many children and adults to be baptized, it was impossible to prepare them all adequately. So, often, there were large-scale group baptisms with many family members in attendance. Within an often boisterous setting, Connolly would instruct those who were about to be baptized, along with their godparents, in the steps involved in the ceremony. He wanted to make sure they responded appropriately, at the right moment and with the right words, to the ritual questions which tested their understanding of the Catholic faith and the meaning of the sacrament.

One day, a baptismal ceremony began with a particularly large group, with different levels of faith understanding and readiness among the participants. Connolly found himself working at length in the pre-ceremony instructions with one particular man, who was having a hard time remembering the response. But Connolly persisted, still attempting to master his own command of Spanish-in-action: "*Entonces, cuando yo pregunto '¿Qué pide la iglesia de Dios?' tu respondes 'la fe,' entiendes?*" ("So, when I ask you 'What does the Church of God ask of you?' you say 'Faith,' understand?")

The man nervously answered, "OK, OK, *yo entiendo, Padre. La fe, la fe.*" ("OK, OK, I get it Father. Faith. Faith.")

Connolly proceeded with the baptism ceremony and he asked each person present individually "*¿Qué pide la iglesia de Dios?*" and they each answered "*La fe.*" Several minutes later, he came to the man who was given the extra preparation, and asked, "*¿Qué pide la iglesia de Dios?*"

The man looked at him, stopped, and nervously uttered, "*Ca-fe.*" The entire church audience erupted with laughter. And the comical request for coffee instead of faith reminded Connolly how hard it was to teach the faith under these circumstances: so many people to serve, with such crucial concepts to get across, and with his lingering language struggles.

It wasn't always rushed. Connolly also offered a one-on-one baptismal course to individual adults. He appreciated that type of education much more than the large gatherings, because it gave him a chance to communicate his understanding of the Catholic faith and the significance of the sacrament. Yet even that approach was challenging, on occasion.

One student, a Cuban woman, would correct Connolly's Spanish during the session, when she wasn't discussing how her husband was reportedly down in Florida planning a secret invasion of Cuba. She was looking to make her first Communion, to fulfill some personal obligation she felt to become a Catholic. At the end of one long session of explaining concepts, Connolly paused for a reaction from her to see if she understood a particularly important concept. He was surprised when she stared at him and stated flatly, "*Padre, yo no he entendido ninguna cosa que usted me ha dicho esta mañana.*" ("Father I have not understood a single thing you have told me this morning.") But she came back, and she and Connolly persevered until she understood him and completed her coursework.

Another Cuban student also caught Connolly's attention, but for a different reason. Rafael Collado, a former engineer, had enrolled his four sons in St. Athanasius Elementary School, and Connolly told him that, in order to raise his sons correctly, Rafael needed to have a genuine understanding of what it meant to be a Catholic. "*Padre, yo soy una persona de mi palabra. Yo voy a completarlo*" ("Father, I am a man of my word. I will complete the course"), he said. So in the evenings, Rafael and Connolly would go through Catholic teachings in the rectory. Sometimes, the sessions would take place at ten o'clock at night, after Connolly finished seeing other visitors seeking counseling or assistance at the last minute. Connolly was impressed with Rafael—he was always prepared, with materials read, and with an appetite for more knowledge. Rafael began getting more involved in the parish after completing the course. In seeing that involvement grow through the following months, Connolly knew he had taught someone special.

Along with the volume of baptismal courses, ceremonies, and other sacraments, Connolly was still racing to learn Spanish, immersing himself further, absorbing all the language capacity and vocabulary he could handle. In fact, a fellow staff priest showed some displeasure with his industry, but for a reason surprising to Connolly. "Hey listen," he said one day. "Some of the English people, the American people, are telling me that you are here to serve both congregations. They resent the fact that you're working with the Spanish people."

Connolly instinctively defended himself. "Well, I am working with both. It just happens that most of the people here are from the Spanish community." But he learned over the next few months that there had been "wars" in the parish between the English and Spanish-speaking communities, most of them in the early and mid-1950s prior to his arrival, over what languages and cultural groups and activities should be permitted in the church. In fact, except for the one priest imported from Spain every year to help with Spanish-speaking parishioners, the staff of that time was either Irish or Italian, and they were expected by the parishioners to be there for "their" people. As Connolly became more involved with the Puerto Rican and Cuban people, he thus not only created a following but sparked the occasional tension. But Connolly knew from the moment he arrived home from his Puerto Rican summer program that the Athanasius community was "going Spanish," and so was he.

As a priest, his first concern was always trying to catch up with all of the people and their religious and personal needs. Even with a staff of five, the Athanasius priests could not keep up with even the sacramental needs of the parish. Unlike Rafael and the Cuban woman and a few other individual students, so many people were just coming in for the ceremony of Baptism, with a sense of urgency about becoming a Catholic, but without much understanding of what it meant. But some time during those years, Connolly came to realize something about all the new baptism seekers: Maybe they were looking for salvation, just in case. Like the soldier and his family headed in frustration for La Milagrosa, they did not know how long their lives would last, nor how they would end. After all, it had ended too soon and too miserably for the stranger on Fox Street, for whose soul Connolly had prayed in their only encounter.

In Puerto Rico, as he learned from Fitzpatrick and Illich, many had known lives shortened by tuberculosis, poverty, and hurricanes. They were not necessarily concerned about something he was emphasizing—that their baptism would bring them into a church community, a community of other believers who would follow the teaching of Christ to love one another. He wondered: Of the fifteen hundred being baptized each year, who would join their community? Also, if he could not get them to understand and fully join, then what was he doing as a priest?

These existential questions about priesthood and the Church were brushed aside at the rectory one day by a counseling need. When he heard the German-born parish cook, Marianne Muller, sobbing in the kitchen, Connolly asked what was wrong.

"Oh, how do you get a license? Those men are so cruel!"

Marianne, a Manhattan resident, was married to a brilliant German theologian who was unable to work because of a midlife crippling disease. Marianne had to take charge, and she cooked for the Athanasius staff to provide for her family. But as the burdens of looking after five children and her husband increased, she wanted to drive to be able to make and keep appointments for everyone in the family. So, getting that license was as important for her as it was difficult: She had already failed a couple of times.

Connolly asked, "Well, what happened?"

"Well," she stammered in her heavily-accented English, "I took the test, and I don't know why he failed me."

Connolly asked, "Well what did you do wrong?"

She tried to gather her composure and said, "Well, I was driving and then, to park the car, I drove up on the sidewalk and I knocked three garbage cans down. I don't know why he failed me."

Amused, Connolly answered, "Well, you can't hit garbage cans," but he also consoled and encouraged her.

But Marianne did not give up, Connolly learned later. She went back one last time and passed the test. Afterward, Connolly thought, *This ordinary woman has extraordinary determination.* Marianne had struggled again and again with something which he had taken for granted, and which seemed impossible to her. But her choice was between staying in poverty or working every day and learning the seemingly impossible. And after all, he remembered, his own father had five children and a spouse crippled by disease, but he also had worked, and with the help of family, the church, and the union, he gave his family a life with some hope. Marianne's struggle to succeed was rooted in her commitment, just like Rafael's struggle to become a Catholic through many late-night sessions with Connolly.

Connolly understood that this deep commitment was essential for himself as well. Without it, he could not handle the overwhelming needs of his parishioners and his constant struggle to provide for them. *This was what he and the Church had to be*, Connolly thought: *committed to its people*.

New Priests

But while Connolly kept his commitment, the commitment of others in the rectory fluctuated, as the staff underwent changes. Beginning in 1962, the priests who were there when Connolly arrived were starting to find other places to work. Tom McDonald, Al DeLuca, and Tom McGarrett, who had already been serving as parish priests for nearly a decade, were ready to move on. In addition, the pastor, Monsignor Mastaglio, a saintly old man who had been at Athanasius for decades, had become more reclusive and passive. He now only went out to take the parish dog for a walk or to step out in the back garden, where some local drug addicts would regularly ask him for some spare change, knowing that he was a "soft touch." He passed away around the same time, and the grateful parish gave him a full funeral Mass complete with music and flowers.

Connolly was joined in 1962 by his good friend from Dunwoodie, Father Louis Gigante, who loved sports as much as he did, especially basketball. Gigante, another graduate of the Puerto Rico summer program and a graduate of Georgetown University, where he was basketball team captain, came from St. James parish on the Lower East Side. Connolly and Gigante had gotten along very well in their seminary days, and they were both "city kids" used to playing and spending time on the streets. Sports would be a way for Gigante and Connolly to bond with the city kids of their new parish. And as the parish became larger and more Spanish, it was time for new energy. For Connolly, Gigante, and another priest—Father Richard Adams, who came on around 1965—were the sources of new energy and welcome changes.

The most important change, however, may have been the pastor. Monsignor Thomas O'Brien came in from a Spanish-speaking parish, St. Paul's in East Harlem, and he had already worked in a parish up in the East Bronx that was gaining more Spanish-speaking people. O'Brien's Spanish was very limited, but he welcomed new ideas and people, and so he was ready for the dynamics of Athanasius, with a large staff that tried to carry the load of assignments. Connolly, Gigante, and Adams saw O'Brien's interest as a signal to initiate things, rather than hold back and wait for the pastor's permission. They would need both the energy and the freedom to act, especially to engage the many children and teenagers who came over from Puerto Rico. Young people were getting lost in the crowded apartment buildings, in the neighborhoods, and in the often-inhospitable schools with few Spanish-speaking teachers. And the parish priests saw where the lost were being "found" with each passing day.

Saving Youth

After World War II, gangs began operating in neighborhoods across poor and working-class areas all around New York City.[18] By the late 1950s, it was reported, there were eight thousand boys and young men in a couple of hundred gangs in the city, along with three thousand young women in female gangs, often accompanying the male gangs. With names like Egyptian Dragons and the Kingsmen, the gangs served as protectors for their own members and as enemies of the gangs from other blocks. Gangs would chase and beat enemy members who walked on their block, which was seen as an invasion of their "turf" or territory.[19] They also had major confrontations with enemy gangs, called "rumbles," at predetermined locations, which involved every gang member with every weapon imaginable.[20] In the late 1950s, when the numbers of gangs and their memberships rapidly increased, there were reported to be as many as fifty rumbles a year in New York City.[21]

The Bronx was the site of many rumbles in the 1960s as well, primarily in the Pelham Bay Park and Orchard Beach areas, removed from the rest of the borough and the police. But many of the rumblers lived in the South and Southeast Bronx, where young people were used to carrying knives, brass knuckles, and other weapons to defend themselves in case of a schoolyard or neighborhood fight. Hunts Point was the site of some battles as well. One night, at 726 Fox Street, near Little Korea, a battle erupted on a rooftop between Egyptian Dragons, Egyptian Crowns, and Kingsmen, ending in a shooting. The incident led to a trial, which, like other sensational gang stories at the time, caught the attention of the *New York Times* and *El Diario* (the leading newspaper of the Puerto Rican community). Threats to the trial court were sent through *El Diario* offices, warning of death if the defendants were not released.[22]

Many organizations serving the Puerto Rican community were scrambling to save their youth from violent gang life, even as they fought against discrimination and the neglect of their communities throughout the city. In September 1959, almost one year after Connolly entered the parish, these organizations even took out a full-page ad in the *New York Times*, with more than one hundred signatory associations and institutions, including St. Athanasius. The ad denounced juvenile delinquency and pledged programs to confront it, while calling on city residents not to blame the Puerto Rican community for the larger problems of juvenile delinquency.[23]

As he looked at the list of signers on the *New York Times* ad, he was amazed and pleased at the number of groups and organizations active in the Puerto Rican community, including some of the Catholic parishes. One hundred and sixty-two in total.

They included labor organizations such as the Puerto Rican Civil Service Employees Association, the Puerto Rican Workers Association, the Association of Puerto Rican Teachers, and the Puerto Rican Postal Workers Association. They also included unions welcoming Puerto Ricans into their ranks, such as District 65, American Federation of Labor and Congress of Industrial Organizations (AFL-CIO), and several locals of the International Ladies' Garment Workers' Union (ILGWU).

There were also business and professional groups such as the Spanish Grocers Association, the Pan American Benevolent Merchants Association, the Spanish Medical Association, the Hispanic Society of Social Workers, and the Puerto Rican newspaper men and women. They also included newly forming groups such as the Hispanic Young Adult Association, an organization including emerging activists such as Dr. Antonia Pantoja.

The full-page ad message in the *Times*, as well as the organizing effort behind it, was pulled together by two organizations already active in Puerto Rican social, civic, and economic issues: the Spanish American Youth Bureau and the Council of Puerto Rican and Spanish American Organizations. Moreover, the hometown clubs—which had been taking shape since the *Gran Migración*—were on board. In fact, an umbrella group, the Federation of Hometown Clubs, with representation from each *club social* in the city of New York, was brought into the effort, led by a dynamic community worker named Gilberto Gerena Valentín. Even the Spanish language media—with four AM radio stations, like Radio WADO and WHOM, and two major Spanish language newspapers, *El Diario* and *La Prensa*—threw their weight behind the anti-delinquency campaign.[24]

Connolly saw that Puerto Ricans, like immigrant communities before them, came together for social, family, labor, education, and other issues. When they left their island country to find a place in New York to live and work, some of them took responsibility for others' well-being. Sometimes they were educating each other, and sometimes they were supporting one another, and sometimes they were fighting to be heard. With their forces coming together, he thought maybe the gang problems could be stopped. But he wondered if they could reach enough youth.

In the meantime, Connolly's fellow priest at Athanasius, John Steltz, was doing everything he possibly could with youth. When he wasn't teaching at Cardinal Hayes High School, Steltz was serving as the chaplain for Spofford House, the large juvenile detention center in the Hunts Point Peninsula erected during the gang era. And, of course, he was also a parish priest, with the related responsibilities. While his command of Spanish was poor, Steltz developed a special connection with Puerto Rican mothers and teenagers, because he found a way to stop some of the young people who were being menaced into joining a gang or were being threatened with violence for leaving one. For every mother or father who asked, Steltz wrote a letter to the police, warning them that "if anything should happen to this young man, you should investigate such-and-such person, leader of this particular gang." Knowing on what street corner the leader could be found, Steltz made sure he saw the letter. Steltz's counter-threats worked on several occasions, and word spread to other families, who then came to Steltz for this letter.

After Steltz had already been working on the gang problem for several years, the city government and the media finally began paying serious attention to delinquency and gangs at the end of the 1950s. In 1959, Connolly's second year, Mayor Robert Wagner officially declared juvenile delinquency "the number one problem facing New York City" and dedicated hundreds of additional police officers to patrol parks and beaches that summer.[25] The New York Police Department created a Juvenile Aid Bureau (JAB) to handle youth under the age of sixteen who were considered "antisocial." Tens of thousands of youth were referred as "juvies" for monitoring and services, and the numbers did not decline.[26] An agency called the Youth Board, created in 1947, also ramped up its activity and staffing, funding youth-related projects operated by local social service agencies and institutions. A Street Club program placed "gang workers" in fourteen targeted areas of the city, including the South Bronx neighborhood, which officials labeled "Morrisania" but which actually included Hunts Point–Longwood.[27]

At one point in the 1960s, seventy "detached workers"—so named because their work was not attached to a specific local organization, giving them flexibility to make decisions and serve at certain hours and locations where the youth could be reached—were working to divert gangs from rumbles and persuade their leaders to enter into recreational, educational, or summer youth employment programs.[28] The workers estimated that five times as many were needed to truly make a dent in the problem.[29]

One such worker in Hunts Point–Longwood was Jack Lyons. A Korean War veteran who played baseball for Manhattan College in the Riverdale neighborhood of the Bronx, Lyons was the sports program director for Athanasius, while also serving as a detached Youth Board worker. With a crushingly hectic schedule, shuttling back and forth between jobs, Lyons gave the parish and neighborhood youth a chance to be safe on the streets. He organized baseball, basketball, and other teams for the Youth Board, and he managed championship level baseball teams for Athanasius at the elementary, high school, and college levels.

Connolly and Gigante worked closely and often with Jack, since they were all sports enthusiasts, and they got to know many of the teenagers that way. They often played pickup basketball games with the youth, on the streets, or in the gym at the small elementary school. But for Connolly, the most important thing was building relationships with the youth and getting them engaged and away from the gangs. Occasionally, their young opponents accused Connolly and Gigante, who were older, heavier, and stronger, of "playing dirty." Connolly didn't disagree; in the game of street-level basketball he was quick and tough, because that was what he knew from his own youth.

Connolly had always been ready for a game since his days growing up in Yorkville. He played basketball for hours on end, whether it was in Central Park with his brother Denis, or for a neighborhood team against other neighborhood teams. It was in some of those games against other neighborhoods that he faced some opponents with a rough edge. In one close game against a team of Italians from a Catholic league school team in East Harlem, while waiting for his teammate to take a free throw, Connolly was standing at the foul line, pushing for position. The opponent, frustrated with the stronger Connolly, turned to him and whispered, "You let me get the rebound, or I'll break your fuckin' kneecaps." Although surprised, Connolly got the rebound himself. As soon as the game was over and his team won, he and his friends ran out of the gym before they could even savor the victory. Connolly learned to survive those days, but that era was different from this one, which he called the "zip guns" era, named after the makeshift guns the gang members made at home and often carried in his neighborhood.

Sports programs and Steltz's letters were working to keep many young men away from trouble, but Connolly and the staff knew they needed to

Fr. Louis Gigante, college basketball team captain, teaches dribbling skills to St. Athanasius boys. (Photo by Chris Sheridan. Courtesy of *Catholic New York*.)

do more. They began to build up the program of religious education in the parish to guide the children and teenagers through their faith formation. Father James Wilson, who was assistant pastor under Mastaglio before leaving to direct the Spanish Apostolate at the archdiocese, had jury-rigged a religious education program using whatever resources he could find. Wilson had worked in the Philippines before coming to St. Athanasius, so he had learned to work within a culture different from his own. He saw the great waves of Puerto Rican migrants coming into Athanasius and knew the younger migrants needed education. Knowing that there was little room at the parish to handle them all, he found a space removed from the church but in the neighborhood: the Hunts Point Palace. The popular dance hall on the top floor of a building on the corner of Southern Boulevard and 163rd Street was large enough to hold the youth.[30]

Hunts Point Palace was known to the Puerto Rican community of New York City as an entertainment attraction. Connolly would sometimes call the busy Palace—which brought in Latin bands, mambo orchestras, and big crowds every weekend—a "bucket of blood." Weekends at the Palace always involved dancing and drinking, which often led to fights ending in police and ambulance calls. During the week, however, it became a site for teaching over a hundred school-age children who could not fit into the church hall.

During Wilson's time, as the class sizes grew and more teachers were needed, the parish reached out for teaching candidates—far out, all the way to Texas. Through a contact, Wilson found four Mexican nuns from Taylor, Texas, who agreed to come each summer and teach religious education. They would travel for days by railcar, sleeping overnight in them, and eventually find their way to Hunts Point–Longwood and the church. When Connolly arrived at the parish and began working with them, he was impressed. They were often dressed like laypersons, rather than religious—often in bomber jackets and dresses—and they carried their own coffee pots with them, a habit acquired from working in camps with migrant Mexican families along the border. He admired how resourceful they were, refusing donations from the parish to pay for airfare and opting instead for the railroad. But Connolly was most impressed with their warmth and openness to the young people. One or the other would often sing religious children's songs while walking the streets to the church, and they drew children along the way, like modern Mexican Pied Pipers.

More youth were coming in each year, and the parish turned to more places for teaching help. A group from the Convent of the Sacred Heart, an exclusive Upper East Side Catholic women's school, agreed to teach classes for Wilson, and they stayed on through Connolly's years. Another group, from the College of New Rochelle, a Catholic women's educational institution in Westchester, north of the Bronx, also came on board during the early 1960s as summer interns. Finally, in 1964, Casita Maria, a Catholic social service organization from East Harlem, began providing recreation opportunities for the Athanasius students.[31] Connolly and Gigante often got together with a couple of Casita's youth workers, John Wright and Milton Robinson, to coordinate programs that would engage neighborhood youth and keep them safe, while supporting the religious education program. In the summer, the parish offered religious education in the morning, then closed up the streets around the church, and Casita Maria organized structured and pickup games. With the help of trained recreation staff from Casita Maria, the parish was also able to organize full-day summer trips to Bear Mountain and other area state parks.

Connolly and Gigante became close enough to the Casita staff that they were regularly invited to attend the organization's annual fundraising gala

Without parks, the streets surrounding the church became the playgrounds. (Fr. Neil Connolly's personal collection.)

at the Waldorf-Astoria. Casita's leadership, higher-echelon Irish Catholics, along with their friends from the Park Avenue area of the Upper East Side of Manhattan, threw lavish events, and Connolly would occasionally attend. The cardinal and the high-ranking leaders of the city would also attend, as Casita was the premier Catholic settlement house in New York. At one of those events, Connolly, who was never completely comfortable at these high-powered affairs, was asked by an animated Casita board member to say a few words on the radio: A live broadcast of the event was being brought to listeners by the Voice of America, an American-owned government station created during World War II to increase American influence with listeners around the world. His high-society board friend was so excited about Connolly speaking that his awkward message did not matter to her: "I'm Father Neil Connolly, and we are live in the Waldorf-Astoria with Casita Maria, and we are from St. Athanasius parish in the Bronx. Thank you." *With that,* Connolly thought whimsically, *I have now communicated to the world. Everyone in the world now knows about our special community in Hunts Point–Longwood.*

This collaboration with Casita Maria was a great boost to the parish's efforts with young people. Prior to that time, parish recreation activities were randomly organized, and trips were challenging to manage. A trip to Bear Mountain was hard to staff, with only a couple of priests who could handle all the Spanish-speaking youth, and so Connolly took help wherever he could find it. They often had priests join them from abroad, especially during the summer, often through some arrangement with a diocesan contact in Spain or elsewhere. One summer, without prior notice or approval, a priest came to Athanasius from Rome, where he was studying. "My name is Chow," he announced as O'Brien opened the rectory door and saw a Chinese priest. "What's he doing here?" O'Brien asked. Connolly realized that the Vatican office where Father Chow was studying had never received the rejection letter from Athanasius, saying they were already full of priests. After learning that Chow spoke Spanish and wanted the experience of pastoral work, though, Connolly appealed to O'Brien.

Father Chow remained through the summer and accompanied Connolly and Gigante on their trips to Bear Mountain. On the first, he unintentionally entertained the rest of the Athanasius delegation at the large swimming pool, a popular attraction for the staff and the youth. Chow climbed up to the ten-foot-high diving board and hurled himself into the water, creating enormous splashes and alarming the lifeguards. Connolly and the others pleaded with him to stop, but he declared, "I will get this right." By the end of the day, Chow had taught himself the fine art of diving, impressing Connolly with his determination and success. Despite all the entertainment value he brought to the day, Chow's biggest contribution was that he spoke Spanish, so he could communicate with the young people. That meant a lot to Connolly, who was always followed by a large crowd of youth at the park.

When he looked at all of the teenagers in the parish and thought about all those still being recruited by the gangs, Connolly decided that the religious education program needed to do more to reach these young people. So he convinced the others on staff and the volunteer teachers that they needed a full program just for the teenagers, and they agreed to use the little elementary school for this program in the evenings. John Steltz, the lead priest in the parish on youth programs and on the threat of gangs, hesitated, saying, "Neil, I don't think you need to do this. I think that what we have with the teens is going well, and we shouldn't mess with that."

Connolly responded, "But John, so many kids are still getting lost, and we are not catching them. We have to try something."

Steltz answered, skeptically, "Well, I hope you get some."

The first night of Connolly's new program, four hundred teenagers showed up at the door of the little school. They came in from every corner

of the neighborhood. Connolly had been so worried about the gangs coming that night, and about fights and shootings near the school, that he called
on "reinforcements." Joe Ryan, a former defensive end with the New York
Titans football team, was a brother of Connolly's seminary classmate and
a Youth Board worker like Jack Lyons. Ryan was recruited as the program's "muscle" to protect the parish school that night. The six-foot-two,
235-pound athlete stood at the entrance alongside Connolly and others as
they hurriedly pulled the teens through the doors of the school, with its
eight classrooms and tiny gymnasium. The experiment was underway and
went beyond everyone's expectations. Not one incident took place.

After a year, the program found space at 830 Southern Boulevard, a new
five-story, forty-room, $10 million structure. On October 17, 1965, several
hundred residents were sitting in a makeshift outdoor "auditorium" with
folding chairs in the middle of the street, and a stage occupied by Cardinal
Spellman, Mayor Wagner, Bronx Borough President Joseph Perricone,
Monsignor O'Brien, and the priests and religious of the parish, to celebrate
the opening of the new St. Athanasius Elementary School.[32] It marked the
beginning of a better religious education program for neighborhood youth,
including the four hundred new teenagers in the program Connolly had
initiated a year earlier. Within a year, there would be six hundred full-time
students and more than two thousand religious education students at the
elementary school.

At the inauguration ceremony, Monsignor James Hart of Blessed Sacrament parish, on Beach Avenue in the East Bronx, gave a speech in English
to a predominantly Spanish-speaking, mostly Puerto Rican crowd, which
created some confusion. The often-bombastic orator puzzled Connolly and
the others with continuing references to the threat of the "red devil" on
First Avenue. After listening for a while, Connolly realized that he was
talking about the United Nations and the threat of Communism.

At first, Connolly could not believe it. However, his father, Con, like
many a Catholic of his time, was also strongly anti-Communist. In their
little apartment on 87th Street, Con had listened to the fiery Sunday afternoon radio speeches of Father Coughlin denouncing the Communist
threat and other threats to Catholicism and America.[33] Connolly also remembered, as a young boy, hearing political speakers like Lou Budenz
denounce Communism at Holy Name Society breakfasts thrown by his
old parish.[34] But the young Connolly was not concerned about Communist
threats, either then or in his current parish.

There was another thing Connolly didn't understand when he attended
those Communion Breakfasts, or this day attending the school dedication
ceremony: why the government officials and political people were there.

This was an event of the Church, he thought—*of St. Athanasius and the archdiocese*. But there was the mayor of New York, seated next to Cardinal Spellman, the two most famous leaders of the city, on the stage above the audience, along with the borough president. Connolly thought, *Well, they were supposed to be the most powerful, so maybe their forces could have joined together and stopped the gang problems*. These leaders were certainly well protected by the police officers he saw standing around the stage and the audience. But to Connolly, these officers seemed just like the detectives he met on that extreme unction visit in the SRO. The parish could not really rely on the officers to have all the answers about solving crime and juvenile delinquency, which kept on growing and terrifying the families sitting on that very street where the officers protected the powerful people. In fact, Connolly heard, the local police had often relied on the parish, like the day when they called in Steltz a few years earlier to talk a young man out of jumping off the roof of a building on Fox Street.

So, was it just a show of united power between government and Church leaders? Connolly thought. *Did they want to use this power for the people? Because, those poor people really needed it.*

Also, thought Connolly, *none of the officials on the stage—Wagner, Spellman, Perricone—could speak the people's language. Along with Hart, with his "Sermon Against the Red Devil," they seemed removed from the hundreds of lives before them. None of these powerful leaders understood the places the faithful audience members had come from in Puerto Rico; or the overcrowded apartments or SROs they were living in; or what they were hoping to find in their new neighborhood, or church, or even the new school. Maybe they needed to get to know these families and their young people*, Connolly thought. *If they didn't understand Spanish, they could listen to Connolly, Gigante, and the Sisters coming to the new school. These staff at Athanasius were working with these families and youth every day, and they knew none of those families were worried about a "Red Devil" on First Avenue.*

Hart seemed to be living in the old Irish Catholic world of Con Connolly, or the world of St. Athanasius parishioners who fought the culture wars. Like the other staff priest who challenged Connolly about serving the "Spanish" people, and not the "American" people of Athanasius, Hart could not accept the new world in front of him, and he was "taking sides" against the Communists. Connolly, meanwhile, was no longer in the old world of Hart, or his father, or the former parishioners. He was not in the world of the powerful people on the stage, or taking their sides, either. Now, he took sides with the people in the audience and in their streets and homes. They needed his help. And much more than his help.

Connolly celebrates with his teenage Catechism graduates. (Fr. Neil Connolly's personal collection.)

What Connolly did understand was that he and the staff and volunteers in the religious education program had heard of "devils" on the rooftops of Fox Street, or on the street corners or basement apartments of buildings on Longwood Avenue, Beck Street, and Simpson Street. The threat of Kingsmen and Dragons taking their young men and women away from their families and into a world of zip guns, knives, and chains; initiation-ceremony beatings; and revenge shootings on rooftops—*that* was the devil their church was protecting them from. For Connolly, this devil came in many colors, those of the jackets each gang member wore as their uniforms for war. Not the Korean War, and not the war in Little Korea, but the war for control of the block and for the souls of the young in Hunts Point–Longwood.

Connolly realized that all the programs for Athanasius youth were created by his predecessors. Wilson had seen that there were needs for religious education, and so he found the Hunts Point Palace and converted a dance hall into a place for building young Catholics. He had recruited the Mexican nuns from Texas and the high-society ladies from the Upper East Side and the women from the College of New Rochelle to fill all the gaps in teaching. He had even found a lawyer and social worker to donate their services to parishioners at the rectory. And there were the sports programs which had been initiated by Mastaglio and elevated to championship status by Jack Lyons, also brought on by Wilson. These programs were the fruits of organizing work done by priests.

Eventually, Connolly came to realize that in a large place like this, a priest could not just serve everyone who came through the rectory door, or just teach each person, one at a time. He had to create programs in the church for religious education, using all the ideas and resources and perseverance he could muster. If he was going to make any kind of a difference to his parishioners, he had to be a program organizer. When he launched the new teen religious education program that drew hundreds of students, Connolly joined the ranks of those organizer-priests.

See-Judge-Act

Religious education was not Connolly's only assignment, since every parish priest had to take on a few. A second staff assignment gave him another chance to bring in people from the neighborhood into the church. The Christian Family Movement, known to the Spanish-speaking Puerto Ricans as El Movimiento Familiar Cristiano, was one of the parish groups Connolly had to staff as a "lead" priest. It met every Sunday night at six thirty, with twenty-four couples in four groups, each group being served by a different priest, all coordinated by Connolly. Connolly was again forced to grow his command of the Spanish language. During these meetings, he discovered some especially thoughtful and effective members, such as Paul Martinez and his wife, Angie. Connolly found out quickly that they and the other participants were part of a worldwide effort involving thousands of Americans.

Movimiento Familiar Cristiano had international and national roots before arriving at Athanasius. In the early twentieth century, it began as a branch of "Catholic Action," a movement developed in part by Belgian Canon Joseph Cardijn, a cleric who supported the idea of Catholic laypersons bringing their faith and values into society.[35] After World War I, the movement caught on rapidly in countries throughout Europe facing global and industrial upheavals. It united Catholics in groups based on their age and occupational status, with many variants across different sectors of European society. All used a small-group reflection-action approach to exploring Christian values and thinking and applying them to needs "in the world," however that world was defined—a neighborhood, a workplace, a college campus, or a larger metropolitan area or nation.

The "Young Christian Workers," known in French as Jeunesse Ou-
vrière Chrétienne (JOC), harnessed this approach into a method called
"Jocism."[36] This was a process known as "see, judge, act." As a first step, a
group of participants had to review some of the current conditions of the
world that merited attention and select one that was a common concern
("see"). Then, using the values of Catholic social teaching, as well as research and diagnosis, the group would analyze the condition to determine
causes and solutions ("judge"). Finally, the group would develop and carry
out a plan of action based on the analysis and the group's capacity ("act").
"See, judge, act" was accessible and effective to many other Catholic Action participants, who numbered several million people in Europe.

In 1949, Jocism made its way into the United States, when a few dozen
married couples coming together to solve community problems, founded
the Christian Family Movement in Indiana. A national coordinating committee was formed to advance and spread the practice of "see, judge, act,"
which would help American Catholic couples to deepen their faith and
marriages by bringing them into the service of the community. Local affiliates were created, along with guide booklets for discussion topics, such as
"economics and family life." Projects initiated by the affiliates included foster parenting, prison ministry, refugee sponsorship, and couples counseling. With a national magazine, *Act*, and a convention which drew up to five
thousand participants, the nationally successful, lay-led Christian Family
Movement gave meaning to Catholics throughout the 1950s and 1960s.[37]
In a recognition of the growing Spanish-speaking Catholic population in
the United States, the movement assumed a role in the integrated Puerto
Rican–serving parishes in the Archdiocese of New York as Movimiento
Familiar Cristiano.

Connolly's Movimiento group met to look at the realities of Hunts
Point–Longwood. One they began to focus on was the difference between
the isolation of their New York neighborhood and the openness of Puerto
Rican communities, where neighbors and families came together and related to each other in the *campo* or the small *pueblos*. Their current neighborhood was block after block of large, crowded buildings with hundreds
of apartments and rooms all locked off from each other, and no public
place to gather, or a way to pass by a neighbor and say "hello." It was
difficult to build bonds. Neighbors were not so much neighbors as they
were strangers, and Movimiento members had a hard time being their
"brother's keeper."

They needed to break the isolation and harshness of city life and find
a way to experience "country life" in Hunts Point–Longwood. So the

Movimiento decided to organize a series of summer day trips to the "country" for neighborhood residents, parishioners, and nonparishioners. With Connolly and the other priests, they organized four such summer trips to state parks such as Bear Mountain and Heckscher State Park. Each trip mobilized a large delegation from Hunts Point–Longwood to the outside world, a motorcade of seventeen buses filled with nearly seven hundred people.

Inevitably, these trips had small adventures.

On one trip, a woman was suddenly jumping up and down in her toreador pants. She needed to go to the bathroom, and she was moving around because she could not contain herself, and she wanted to let others know. Connolly was on the bus, and as the leader of the entire trip, he saw this and acted quickly. They couldn't wait to get to the park, so he told the bus driver to find a place to stop.

"Where do we stop, Father?" the driver asked.

Connolly spotted a place on the road. "That gas station over there. Stop right in front of it."

Not wanting to stop directly at the small station with a large group of buses, Connolly had the driver stop on the other side of the road. The door opened and the woman ran right across the road, with Connolly running right behind her.

He asked the gas station attendant, who was white, "Could she use the bathroom?"

The attendant looked at Connolly and the woman and said, "OK, yeah."

Then, while she was in the bathroom, the attendant looked around and saw the bus lineup across the road, one bus after another. He counted them. Seventeen in all.

Connolly thought that the attendant probably never saw a Puerto Rican in his life.

The attendant gave Connolly a worried look, asking, "Are all those other people going to use the bathroom, too?"

Connolly confidently said, "No, don't worry."

However, in a minute, everyone was getting off the buses, thinking they were going to use the bathroom, too. Connolly and the movement leaders turned around and yelled, "Please get back onto the buses!"

When they got back on the road, already behind schedule, one of their cheap orange rental buses broke down, and they arrived at the park much later than they planned. They discovered that all of the shady spots in the park, where the shadows of large trees provided cool relief, were taken already by their chief "rivals"—the New York African American churchgoers who also organized large trips to the park. It was a long, hot day. But the delegation of parishioners and neighbors ate, played games and music, and had a good time in the country, in their own version of the *campo*.

On another day, the summer heat created yet another challenge. Some of the people were feeling a little sick on the return trip from another large trip to a state park, after eating mayonnaise that had spent too many hours in the sun. When they arrived at Athanasius, someone told Connolly, "Father, there's a lady who's very sick here." Connolly took the woman and her husband to St. Francis Hospital on 143rd Street, which was owned and operated by the Archdiocese of New York and had a better reputation than nearby Lincoln Hospital, run by the city government.[38] Knowing that a Sunday emergency room would be packed, Connolly "ensured" accelerated service. Before entering the hospital, he reached into the trunk of his car, took off his polo shirt, and put on his clerical black shirt and white collar. He entered the hospital with the woman and her husband and went to the emergency room. An emergency room nurse saw him and said, "Father come here, we've got a doctor right here."

Into the examination room, where they were waiting, a doctor came in, speaking in a German accent. "Father, for what is she here?"

Connolly explained, "I don't know the whole story, but she ate something. She is sick to her stomach and she has diarrhea, and she was running around wanting to go to the bathroom."

"Oh. What kind of event did you have?"

"A picnic."

"A picnic, you say?"

"Yeah, we had a picnic, about seven hundred people, and then she ran off the bus. We had to get her here quickly."

"I see. Are the other seven hundred coming in too?"

Connolly laughed and said, "No they're all right."

While the German doctor was afraid of caring for a massive group, Connolly was taking every step he could for them. He realized, even with such large numbers of participants and occasional emergencies, what these trips meant. *To the people who were just from the neighborhood and didn't know the parish, this was a fun chance to get outside of the neighborhood, of the overcrowded apartments with doors and windows and radiators that often didn't work. The park represented the beauty of nature, which they had known in their home towns and campos in Puerto Rico. This trip gave them a chance to bring their own foods and drink and music and to share them, and to rekindle the spirit of the home country. It also allowed them to get to know others and, as the Movimiento Familiar Cristiano group*

had wanted, to break the barriers and isolation that were enveloping the
neighborhood, beneath all the noise and busy activity.

Connolly and the staff regularly looked for ways to bring the Catholic
faith into the cultural context of the Puerto Rican community in Hunts
Point–Longwood. They supported another group, Juventud Acción
Católica (Young Catholic Action), which brought together teens and young
adults to examine their own issues. Each year the parish was involved in
the Fiesta San Juan Bautista, sponsored by the Office of Spanish Catholic Action of the archdiocese, which occurred at Randall's Island Stadium
near the Bronx.[39] Also, they celebrated the feast of Nuestra Señora de la
Providencia, the Virgin Mary, patroness of Puerto Rico.[40] Spanish-speaking
societies for both men and women were also supported by the parish staff,
including the Santo Nombre, Sagrado Corazón, Legión de María, Cursillo,
and Carismático groups.

These activities were all encouraged by the Office of Spanish Catholic Action, which had been created in 1953 to guide the archdiocesan
response to the *Gran Migración*.[41] This office was an important source of
support for Connolly and the Athanasius staff, as well as every other parish
serving the Puerto Rican migration and establishing "integrated" parishes
in the archdiocese. Other programs took shape besides the Institute for Intercultural Communication, the summer immersion program at the Catholic University of Puerto Rico. The office initiated a language-and-culture
program at Cardinal Hayes High School in the Bronx, which prepared
several hundred priests and religious and laypersons staffing the integrated
parishes. It established a table at the airport in San Juan to direct migrants to parishes in New York City neighborhoods so that they could find
a connection with a Catholic community already active with Puerto Ricans.
In upstate New York, a farmworker support program reached out to the
Puerto Ricans who came to work in those farms but lacked any kind of
community connections.

The Family Services Office at the archdiocese, meanwhile, was providing vital social services to the needy families of the archdiocese, whether it
was maternity support, housekeeping, home visitations, family counseling,
or youth services. Bronx native Monsignor John Ahern, one of Connolly's
summer 1958 immersion program classmates, was running the borough's
branch of that office, so he often came into contact with Connolly and
his colleagues at Athanasius and the other Bronx parishes serving Puerto
Ricans.[42] All of these programs at the archdiocese, and the building of the
new school and the operations of the Catholic Youth Organization's sports
programs, gave Connolly and the others vital support.

The Movimiento experience, meanwhile, gave Connolly something else to think about, especially as he struggled to serve a parish with so many needs. Laypersons, he realized, could do some special things in the parish and the neighborhood. After all, they were the ones who had implemented the "see, judge, act" method used throughout the world, right there in Athanasius. It was laypersons who had organized seven-hundred-person trips to help them enjoy the parks and to build relationships upstate with strangers. They identified concerns of the world for Connolly, enabling the people inside the church to engage the people of the world outside the church.

As the priest assigned to Movimiento Familiar Cristiano, Connolly found himself in an unexpected role: He was an "authority-priest," the one who had to make sure nothing got out of hand and everything was in keeping with Church doctrine, but he was also a "supporter-priest," the one who helped the laypersons take their process wherever it would lead them. Even if it was just an emergency visit to a gas station bathroom in the suburbs, he could be there to support their initiative. *What they thought was a priority was what mattered; that was central to the way "see-judge-act" worked.*

Scotch, Tab, and Mission

In setting their own priorities, Connolly and the Athanasius priests had their own work cut out for them, from religious education; parish societies; baptisms, last rites, and Communions to all the counseling and family assistance that people seemed to need. They knew from their early encounters with neighbors, like the visits to Little Korea, and from the sessions with the volunteer lawyer and social worker, that living conditions were getting worse in the buildings, in the schools, and in the streets. They had to start deciding how to respond to these worsening conditions.

Connolly, Gigante, Adams, Steltz, McDonald, and O'Brien discussed ideas during their own priestly "ritual" in the rectory living room. Every night, after a long day, they would pour themselves a glass of scotch—or, in O'Brien's case, a glass of Tab—and watch the ten o'clock news show. Someone would ask how the day went, or someone would begin to recount some incident they were part of that day. Others would chime in, and sometimes the stories would connect. "Can you believe it" or "I just don't understand" would enter the conversation as well.

Occasionally, someone would say, "You know what I think we should be doing?" Many ideas were floated on those television-scotch-and-Tab nights, but only a select few actually made it to an action or a plan. But the discussions and the suggestion that the group of priests should act together on some ideas were not just an intellectual exercise, but a social one—a reminder that they were forming some bonds and perhaps even a team. Connolly realized, *It was because O'Brien gave them the freedom to create and take action that they took some steps. O'Brien created the climate for those discussions and the resulting projects, and he was proud of it, often boasting about all the amazing work done by "my boys."* The boyish element of their personalities was sometimes manifest in the priests, especially in Connolly and Gigante. They were friends with many of the teachers and staff in the elementary school, including Maria, who was also a stewardess for a major airline. Maria had occasionally mentioned to the priests that she could get seats very cheaply anytime she wanted, for herself or her friends. If Connolly and Gigante ever wanted, she said, they should just let her know, and she could easily get them a pair of tickets.

One Easter period, when their fellow priests McDonald and Steltz were still on the parish staff and had gone down to Puerto Rico for vacation, Connolly said to Gigante, "Hey, let's go down there and surprise them. We can take Maria's offer, get the tickets, and we'll come back in a couple of days before it gets busy." Within twenty-four hours, they were on a plane to San Juan. Thinking they knew the likely places to eat in the area where other priests had gone, they went to find a place in the Old San Juan district, known for its pastel-colored, Old World buildings, cobblestone streets, and nice restaurants. They strolled along the street at lunchtime and walked up to the windows of a familiar restaurant, guessing they would find their priest friends. Seeing McDonald and Steltz at a table eating, they stopped, smiled, and waved at them.

McDonald and Steltz looked up, stunned, and looked twice to make sure they were not fooled. When Connolly and Gigante came in, McDonald asked, "What are you guys doing here? Who's back at the rectory?" Gigante and Connolly explained that it was the beginning of the not-so-busy Easter week and that they would only be in Puerto Rico for a couple of days before heading back. They all enjoyed the surprise and, over the next couple of days, a camaraderie that had been developing over the last few years.

Soon, McDonald and Steltz moved on to other assignments. In the meantime, Connolly, Gigante, and Adams were developing a seriousness of purpose as well. They found themselves in a series of staff meetings, creating a mission statement and then using that statement for every meeting after that. The statement affirmed their priorities as a parish team, of committing to the neighborhood and to building parishioners into leaders. At each subsequent meeting the statement, a laminated poster card, was brought to the middle of the room and set up before everyone. As a visual reminder, the mission statement card would occasionally be picked up by one of the priests to make a point challenging someone else's idea. "What does it say on the card?" Connolly would say to the others. "Does this idea fit with any of our priorities? No. We have to work with our priorities." Connolly saw that this tool gave him some clarity and some comfort when they were discussing all the possibilities in an increasingly busy agenda.

By 1965, the rectory looked and felt a lot different than the one Connolly saw when he first set foot in 878 Tiffany seven years earlier. So many more initiatives were being carried out than before, and they still weren't enough, because there were so many more parishioners and neighborhood people than before. Also, people were starting to face harder times, as more people were losing their jobs at the factories that were starting to move away from New York. Connolly and this team of priests needed to do something about these social conditions, but they weren't quite sure what further steps to take. *Whatever they did,* he thought, *they had to do it together, and it had to be done the same way as Wilson did it when he was running things at Athanasius. They had to be organized about things, and they had to build things the way they were building up the church groups, education programs, societies, and movements.*

The "de-Yankeefication" process, which Ivan Illich had hoped would occur within his Puerto Rico program student-priests, had been completed with these Athanasius priests. They were now fully immersed in the lives, language, culture, and fates of their Puerto Rican parishioners. After surviving the thousands of baptisms, the large Sunday Masses, and the ever-expanding religious education and sports programs for the young people, Connolly and his team felt stronger. Connolly felt that he was not just a member, but a builder of a true community in the parish and in the rectory. He was a priest of St. Athanasius, a very busy church, but one that he could finally understand and serve—like the priests of Our Lady of Good Counsel had done for him and his family. Connolly thought, *Maguire was right. He was doing well there.*

Then one morning Connolly looked up from his mission statement, his busy schedule, his groups and movements, his round of last and first sacraments, and his fellow priests' scotch-and-Tab television talks, and found that the Church, which he had known all his life, and which he had trained for as a priest, was about to change.

So was he.

3

A Changed Church, a Changed Role

... But she (the Church) is already present in this world, and is composed of men, that is, of members of the earthly city who have a call to form the family of God's children during the present history of the human race, and to keep increasing it until the Lord returns.... Thus the Church, at once a "visible association and a spiritual association and a spiritual community," goes forward together with humanity and experiences the same earthly lot which the world does.... Through her individual members and her whole community, the Church believes she can contribute greatly toward making the family of men and its history more human.
—Second Vatican Council, Pastoral Constitution on the Church in the Modern World (*Gaudium et Spes*) §40, December 1965

A World of Priests

It was a lively Friday night in December 1965, in the living room of St. Athanasius rectory. With a few days to go until Christmas, things were busy at the parish, but there was always a little time to socialize. Neil Connolly was getting a drink for a fellow priest, while Al DeLuca played piano for the umpteenth time in the last few years. The chatter was lively, as everyone was getting updates about what this guy from the seminary class was doing and what parish so-and-so was working in now. Vacations and holiday visits with families were also on their minds, as DeLuca's renditions of show tunes sparked memories of growing up in the 1940s and 1950s. The socials that St. Athanasius priests threw every few months were a good tradition.

Connolly was well aware of how lucky he was. Not everyone he'd known in seminary had fellow priests like Gigante, Adams, Steltz, and DeLuca, who enjoyed each other's company and spent time together. Also, few had an open-minded, supportive pastor like Tom O'Brien. On a night like this, those who enjoyed their parish assignments less than Connolly could appreciate the conversation and company of their friends from seminary who were now spread around parishes in the Bronx, Manhattan, and various upstate counties. Some had become regulars at these socials, which also occasionally included guests like the people from the Puerto Rico program. Even Ivan Illich was expected to drop in this evening, which Connolly was looking forward to.

As he looked around from his post at the refreshments table, Connolly savored the scene, but beyond the chatter and the laughs, he also heard about some struggles. As on other social nights at Athanasius, some shared the personal difficulties of being without familiar faces to turn to. Some were stationed with pastors who were too rigid in their ways, or who were too "old-school" Irish to welcome the new Puerto Rican parishioners with open arms. Being a priest, like becoming a priest, was a sometimes overwhelming and solitary responsibility. The setbacks and demands were many, and they could fill you with doubt, Connolly thought.

Connolly needed this fellowship with his fellow priests personally, especially during periods of self-questioning. There was one in particular that he was remembering that night. During the summer before his final year in seminary, as he was relaxing on the beach, Connolly had thought about what he would become in just one year: a real live, ordained priest. Connolly had taken his seminary studies seriously because he had to—everyone from his parents to his teachers to the Church at large expected a good academic performance from him. But he had sometimes struggled to focus, as he rarely did when he was working with other people, whether on sports teams or in the seminary's other social activities. A recent church history class had portrayed the priest as playing a central role, in the local towns, across Europe, and elsewhere, as the "keeper of names"—the scribe. The name *clericus* (Latin for "scribe"), which would soon become *clergy*, identified a person with an unusual level of education and, therefore, higher authority and power.

But this kind of role was not what Connolly wanted. He had wondered, sitting on that beach, if he was going to turn out to be just an administrator, a record-keeper in some "hallowed hall," an institutional figure. *No*, he answered himself, *I thought I was going to be preaching in the streets, "thumping the Bible" and saving souls and helping people.* He vowed, in that moment, that while he would complete the seminary studies he had sometimes found challenging, his priesthood would not end in records. His priesthood would be meaningful. It would not be institutional, it would not be clerical, and it would not be administrative. It would give meaning to the people, like the Good Counsel priests had given to him.

Years later, in the rectory of St. Athanasius, in December 1965, the path of priesthood indeed seemed to have been meaningful. Despite the hurried world of hundreds of baptisms (including "scribing" all those names!), running from one sacrament to another, and shuttling from society meetings to school activities, his life as a priest was giving meaning to others and to himself. And the teamwork at Athanasius made it even more meaningful. On this December night, after years of struggles, trial, and error, he understood priesthood well, just like his Spanish.

At that moment of reflection, he was interrupted. Ivan Illich came into the rectory. He walked up to Connolly and began a spirited conversation. Connolly remembered how Illich had challenged him in that Puerto Rico program in 1958. Besides sending him to say Masses and hear confessions in the furthest reaches of the *campo*, in his still-developing Spanish, Illich also sent Connolly other places. Once, he was sent to speak to a group of lawyers, who were thankfully better at speaking English than he was at speaking Spanish. Why he had singled out Connolly for these challenging experiences was not clear, except that Illich probably saw something in Connolly that summer: the quest for something more dynamic and engaging, and the desire to learn. Also, Illich was always emphasizing the need to break away from old institutional practices and meet people where they were.

"Neil, how are you?" said Illich.

"I'm doing great, Ivan. How about yourself?"

Connolly explained the things going on at St. Athanasius—the baptisms, the religious education programs, the Movimiento Familiar Cristiano, and the team ministry. But Illich interrupted.

"Yes, Neil, that's all very good. But let me ask you—are you getting ready?"

"Getting ready for what, Ivan?" Connolly asked, suddenly feeling uncertain.

"The council, Neil. Did you follow it?"

"Oh, the council! Yes," Connolly, relieved, said. "It's great isn't it? All the debates. History in the making."

Illich paused and looked at him. "You don't understand, do you, Neil?"

Connolly paused in kind and looked at him quizzically. "Understand what?"

Illich said softly, but emphatically, "Neil this whole Church is going to change. Your life as a priest is going to change."

Connolly was puzzled. "How?"

Illich said, "Neil, you will have to give up these ways of priesthood." He refused to say any more that night.

A World of Bishops

For Connolly, this earthshaking challenge to the "ways of priesthood" began in 1962, when he and other readers of the *New Yorker* opened the magazine's latest issue to find an article entitled "Letter from Vatican City." Written by a priest with the nom de plume "Xavier Rynne," it detailed the circumstances behind the beginning of an event called the Second Vatican Council, which was underway in Rome.[1] This article would be the first of twelve which covered the council, and his regular news updates became a familiar topic to Connolly and his priest friends. At the Athanasius socials, an inevitable question now was, "Hey, did you read the latest from Xavier Rynne?" While other periodicals covered the goings-on of Vatican II, no report compared with Rynne's level of detail, his insight, and his "color commentary" style of describing the council's figures and developments. For Connolly, the "Letters from Vatican City" was both a series of entertaining stories and a chance to observe, from afar, history in the making.

On October 1962, more than two thousand bishops from around the world had gathered at the Catholic Church's global headquarters in Rome. The twenty-first such "ecumenical," or universal, gathering in Church history, it was only the second to be held at the Vatican, and so it was called the Second Vatican Council, or "Vatican II."[2] It had taken three years to prepare. Voting in the Church, a hierarchical institution not known for democratic practices, was a rare phenomenon, an act taken only in the election of a Pope or in an ecumenical council. The council was an opportunity for bishops to frankly discuss the state of the modern Roman Catholic Church, in the wake of the devastation of World War II and at the height of the Cold War, and to vote on recommendations for change.

Connolly knew that he and his friends were following a once-in-a-lifetime event; the First Vatican Council, this council's predecessor, had occurred nearly a century ago.[3] The Archdiocese of New York's own longtime leader, Francis Cardinal Spellman, flew to Rome in October 1962, bringing along a Jesuit theologian named John Courtney Murray, an international expert on the subjects of Church-state relations and religious freedom.[4] Like the many other theologians who accompanied bishops, Murray was expected to contribute by offering his opinions on the topics as a *peritus*, or expert, though he could not vote on the council's resolutions.

This particular gathering was organized to accomplish four broad and lofty goals: "To define more fully the nature of the Church, especially with respect to the position of Bishops. To promote the restoration of unity among Christians. To renew the Church. To initiate a dialogue with the contemporary world."[5] The chief convener of this complex and comprehensive event, which was expected to be completed in two months, was a man of eighty-one years who came from a humble background. Angelo Roncalli had been raised in a large family of sharecroppers in the small Italian town of Bergamo, and he received an education that cultivated his strong interest in social issues, even as he entered the priesthood. After serving in the military and ministry through two world wars, Roncalli eventually became the patriarch (archbishop) of Venice. There, he expanded the Church in structure and outlook, building a seminary while welcoming the Venice Film Festival and the Socialist Party as good developments for the Archdiocese of Venice.

Once elected Pope John XXIII in 1958 by the College of Cardinals, by his peers who had few expectations from an older, quiet cleric, he surprised them all. Over the strenuous and persistent objections of his own entrenched bureaucracy, the cardinals who worked for him at the Vatican government, Pope John XXIII called for the council.[6] The Pope said it was time for an *aggiornamento*, a renewal or "updating," of the entire Church. "It's time to open the windows and let the fresh air in," he declared, making the global Church a truly global Church.[7]

Connolly read about the beginning of the council and the life history of Pope John XXIII with enthusiasm and thought, what an amazing man, and what a priest. To have survived such a financially deprived upbringing and reached the position of priest was in itself a major accomplishment. But to have made it through two world wars—that must have given him such a broad and unique perspective on the world and on the Church, and it must have given him a wisdom far beyond what any priest like Connolly could know. And then, for him to announce a major new venture at over eighty years old and fight his own bureaucracy over it seemed courageous. Although he had been chosen in a traditional process, this man was very nontraditional, and he seemed determined to see change through to the end.

Although the Vatican bureaucracy gave in and began planning for the gathering as ordered, resistance to Pope John's agenda did not cease. Like a political convention, the council was to debate thirteen core issue areas, all about the Church, including: theology; the roles of various kinds of Church members; and the Church's relationships with other Christians, non-Christian religions, and the secular world. Commissions created "schemas," or draft platforms, for discussion and vote, to address all these areas.[8] The issues had been the subject of intense struggles in the Church, some for decades and even centuries, and Connolly had studied some of their history at seminary: How is the Mass to be celebrated? How is the Bible to be read and interpreted? What does the Church say about other Christian groups and possible unity with them? Can the truth be discovered only in Catholic doctrine?

The original schemas, however, were written not to generate open dialogue but to promote conservative viewpoints on most of these issues. The idea was that the gathered bishops would mostly rubber-stamp them. However, when the council actually met, a series of unexpected speeches and votes forced all of them back to the drawing board, this time to be rewritten by a more balanced group of theologians and bishops before returning to the full council for a real debate.[9]

Thus, when the first and only planned council session came to a close in the fall of 1962, it had not approved a single document. It would have to be extended to another fall session in 1963. But before the beginning of that second session, Pope John XXIII passed away, and the future of the proceedings was in doubt. However, in June the College of Cardinals elected as his successor a man who was committed to the continuation of the council and the fulfillment of its goals of renewal. In another "Letter from Vatican City," Connolly read about Giovanni Battista Montini and found him, too, worthy of great admiration. He was just as experienced about matters of the world as Pope John XXIII. The son of an intellectual mother, who was active in the Catholic Action movement, and a father, who was a lawyer, newspaper editor, and elected official, Montini was exposed to social concerns early on. Then, as a priest, he obtained a uniquely global perspective when he was assigned to serve the Vatican Secretariat of State, which he did for thirty years. His missions included an especially difficult one: the critical post–World War II operation to find and care for political prisoners, Jews, the displaced, prisoners of war, and refugees. Then, upon his appointment as archbishop of Milan, he worked so actively with the city's factories and neighborhoods that he earned the title of "the Workers' Archbishop." Finally, as Pope Paul VI, he immediately called for the resumption of the council, which had so much unfinished business to be addressed.[10]

As he read with enthusiasm about the new Pope, Connolly also paid attention to some of the leading persons at the council.[11] There was Anibale Bugnini, who became a leading advocate for the Liturgical Movement, an international effort to get more lay involvement in liturgy and the sacraments. Another bishop, Augustin Bea, was recognized for his expertise on relations with other Christian denominations. Cardinal Josef Suenens of Belgium was an advocate of the council's "renewal" goals. So he was given a leadership position as one of four moderators of this assembly, which now included well over two thousand bishops; thousands of *periti*, or assistants; observers who were officially invited from a variety of Christian denominations and non-Christian religions; news reporters from around the globe; and interested spectators. A particularly dedicated contingent of cardinals, bishops, and *periti* came from Latin America, including Dom Hélder Câmara from Brazil, and a theologian from Peru named Gustavo Gutiérrez. Both of them were advocates for Church involvement in confronting the "developing" world's living conditions.[12] Connolly always looked to learn from other priests who shared the greater pastoral and theological understanding he had.

To Connolly and other readers of Xavier Rynne, it was clear that a majority of the world's bishops were ready to challenge the institutional status quo at the Vatican. After boldly asking the assembly of bishops if they were planning a revolution, Cardinal Alfredo Ottaviani, the most vigorous and powerful opponent of the council agenda, was cut off for speaking too long, to which the bishops responded with a round of applause.[13] Then, when traditionalist forces (the minority in most debates) secured delay on a key vote, a petition driven by the forces of change generated more than a thousand signatures in a day, and a special meeting with the Pope was suddenly secured to obtain a promise for the vote.[14] Another highly anticipated vote, scheduled before the end of the third session, was postponed by a last-minute maneuver, forcing a delay into the last session, and the very real possibility of new changes not being realized. The move prompted a leader of the vote drive to denounce those behind the maneuver: "the bastards!"[15] The intensity of the debates over the schemas was increasing, as the Second Session of 1963 spilled over into a third in 1964, and a fourth and final one in 1965. But the steady hand of Pope Paul VI and the broad-based commitment among participants to resolve most issues secured overwhelming approval votes for all the rewritten schemas, which became official documents of the "updated" Church.

Connolly enjoyed Rynne's great stories about maneuvering and counter-maneuvering far away in Rome, but mostly they didn't seem like they would have a huge effect on his day-to-day life, and he continued his usual work at the parish. Even after the conversation with Illich, he thought, *The Chancery office—the headquarters of the archdiocese—will tell us what to do, when to show up, and what to learn.* He was a parish priest, and his parishioners needed him; he didn't have much time to figure out for himself what all these changes might mean.

Learning and Teaching

Then, in the winter of 1966, Neil Connolly found himself where he had never expected to be again after the Puerto Rico progam—in the middle of a classroom. And then another, and another, as he became an avid student of the teachings of Vatican II. Lessons were given all over the United States, and Connolly attended whenever and wherever he could go.

One of these events found him watching pictures of wartime explosions and battle scenes projected on a screen. Members of the Catholic Worker Movement were leading a presentation on the Vietnam War and the need for understanding confession and penance in a new light, in terms of forgiveness and reconciliation on an international level. In this dramatic workshop on the campus of the University of Notre Dame in Indiana, Connolly and his classmates heard an argument for a Church that practices peace and encourages nations of the world to do the same.[16] At a time when the Vietnam War was hotly debated in American society, this workshop brought into sharper focus Vatican II's ideas about how the Church should relate to and look at the world.

In another event, this one on the campus of St. Louis University, Connolly heard Eddie Bonhomier, the chief organist at the Church of St. Thomas the Apostle in Harlem. Bonhomier stirred the audience of worshippers, playing keyboards and leading them in a combination of gospel, jazz, and blues hymns. Connolly clapped, swayed, and sang along with this rousing modern style of musical prayer and worship. Bonhomier introduced the workshop to a new form of liturgy, one that demonstrated that listening to the Latin Gregorian chant of the old days was not the only way to celebrate Mass with music. That day, Bonhomier taught Connolly, who grew up loving jazz music, that his favorite music of "the world" could become the music of "the Church."

This jazz Mass, celebrated in English, was brought to life because of the Pastoral Constitution on the Sacred Liturgy, also known, like most Vatican documents, by its first two words in Latin—in this case, *Sacrosanctum Concilium*. This was one of the four council documents (out of a total of sixteen) to be accorded the highest status of "constitution." Approved with near-unanimity, this Pastoral Constitution was the first to be voted on, as the bishops agreed on the need for greater participation by laypersons in the liturgy and in all sacraments. *Sacrosanctum Concilium* allowed the language, the music, and the art of the local diocese's people, in whatever part of the world, to be used in all Church rituals and celebrations. Each bishop was encouraged to respect local values and cultures and allow them to inform the Church's community and life. Bonhomier's jazz liturgy lesson gave Connolly an example of what was possible inside a church.

Sacrosanctum Concilium unleashed a sense of freedom in local dioceses and parishes during this learning period. Now any bishop or priest—whether in Recife, Brazil; Jakarta, Indonesia; or in a Spanish parish in Hunts Point in New York City—could give new expression to the liturgy and potentially reach thousands more in the process. Connolly realized that the Church of Vatican II could truly go to the people. With this new freedom, Connolly did something he had never done before as a priest: He faced the people throughout the Mass. Then, he took responsibility for teaching the parishioners by leading them in speech and prayer and song. *"El Señor este con ustedes,"* he would call out, and he would teach them to respond, *"Y con tu espiritu."* As each Sunday passed, the call-and-response took on more rhythm and more volume. Parishioners took to the new look and sound of a ritual they had treasured as sacred and comforting. Within months of Connolly's initial lessons, the centuries-old tradition of priests celebrating with their backs to their congregation was gone. The language of Latin was gone. The quiet and passivity of the laypersons at Mass were gone.

Connolly also helped parishioners discover their voice in the other sacraments. Baptisms, once celebrated at Athanasius with assembly-line speed or in large, disorganized, crowded events to meet crushing schedule demands, were now going to be celebrated differently. The ceremony was now treated as a deliberate event, in which all families were intentionally brought together to be welcomed into the parish community. Each act of baptism, Connolly learned at workshops and, in turn, taught his parishioners, would now be an act of the whole Church, the living body of Christ, celebrating in the people's language and thus allowing them to fully understand the significance of the act.

The last sacrament of life, like the first sacrament, was given new meaning with the new language as well. "Extreme unction" or "last rites," as the

Post–Vatican II, Connolly performs revolutionary acts of concelebration and facing parishioners. (Fr. Neil Connolly's personal collection.)

sacrament was known, would now be called the "sacrament of healing," signaling a different purpose. The family of a terminally ill person would hear a different message than the hope for a cure from Connolly and other priests: "May God heal you if that is in His will. And if it is not in His will, may he give you the strength to undergo what is entering your life, so that you may reconcile with Him." Connolly found real meaning in this sacrament, much more than he had on the first day he administered it in that darkened SRO hallway years ago.

As Connolly learned in post-council conferences and lectures, this new approach to healing and to all the sacraments was an attempt to return to the origins of the Catholic faith, to the early centuries of the Christian movement. In that time, all activities were conducted in small, still-forming communities. Early Christians shared their food and their homes, and they prayed and read and reflected together. They strove to continuously understand what was asked of them as a Christian community, both in relationship to each other and to the world. Connolly saw this emphasis on the original community as something worth cultivating. Otherwise, he thought, to the lay parishioner the Church could often just seem like a large, imposing, and uninspiring institution, or sometimes a spiritual "filling station" where you stopped in briefly between other important activities to fill up your tank.

With the interest in returning to Scriptural roots and original communities, Connolly created a new event for Easter season at Athanasius. He sought to unite the elements of the Old Testament and the New Testament, but in a different way—on the street and in the Church. He got the support of Gigante and Adams for his idea of a ceremony before the Easter Mass. But he also wanted to introduce this carefully to the parishioners, who were still learning to embrace the changes in the sacraments. So he and the staff chose a few dozen parishioners who had been most receptive to the Vatican II changes already underway in the parish. They would be his participants in this new "Ceremony of the New Fire."

On Holy Saturday, the evening of the scheduled event, it was raining lightly, but a few dozen invited faithful appeared anyway. They stood out on Southern Boulevard a couple of blocks from the church, and each person was given a candle. Someone was called to read scripture, telling the story of Moses and the people of Israel traveling to the promised land, led by a tower of fire provided by God. Connolly and the other priests led the group in prayer and song; then, after a round of lighting candles, they processed, still singing, toward Tiffany Street and finally to the church. Symbolizing the journey out of darkness for Moses and his people, the procession gathered more people and grew as the moving field of flickering lights cut through the darkness of the streets and reached the church. The Ceremony of the New Fire was complete, yielding to the ceremony of the resurrection that was the Easter Mass.

After Mass, many of those who had participated in carrying the new fire gathered for coffee and snacks to enjoy some music and some conversation. The parishioners spoke about the original ritual with great satisfaction and gratitude that they were given a chance to participate. They were moved by the song, the prayer, and the symbolic fire; they said they felt the presence of the Holy Spirit out on the street. Connolly thought, *We created something. We created the presence of the people of God, in the place and language and act of the people. This night, we brought the Vatican II Church—and the original Church—to life and into the street. As in Puerto Rico, wherever the people were, that's where the Church was.*

Was this what the bishops in Rome wanted or expected? It was not what he himself had expected during his years of reading about the council and then returning to his busy round of parish activities. But it was a little of what he had wanted to see when he vowed to be a meaningful priest. Something was inspiring him now.

New Roles

Even while he was busy traveling around the country and learning from the emerging American experts on Vatican II, Connolly found some time at Athanasius for quiet reading of all sixteen major documents. In the process, he discovered the work which had captured the imagination and passions of the bishops over those four years in Rome. Taken together, the documents reflected all of the major debates that had been the Church's focus for decades in some way or another. As he read the documents, Connolly marveled at the thought put into them, and he felt inspired about the future Church and its possibilities. However, some of the writings left him with questions and doubts.

There were documents that opened up the Church to other faiths. The Decree on Ecumenism asserted that the Catholic Church needed to actively explore and find the opportunity to work and celebrate, and even worship, with the clergy and ministers of other Christian faiths.[17] The Decree on Eastern Catholic Churches recognized the Eastern Orthodox Church as a variation of the Catholic Church and called for efforts to find common ground with and, perhaps, officially reunite with that Church and its membership.[18] Finally, the Declaration on the Relationship of the Church to Non-Christian Religions acknowledged the presence of truth and holiness in these other religions and, in a significant move responding to the horrors of the Holocaust, affirmed that Jews were not responsible for Christ's death.[19] In line with the postwar secular consensus on "human rights," the document proclaimed that minorities in the nations of the world, whether religious, racial, ethnic, or other, should be free of discrimination and persecution. This all contradicted the Church's long-held official position that "error" (that is, non-Catholic religions) "has no rights." But for Connolly, this new message of reconciliation and relationship was true to the Christian message of love he had been taught.

Connolly was also intrigued by the documents addressing theology and religious education. The Dogmatic Constitution on Divine Revelation urged continuing and active scholarship to understand the time and the context in which the scriptures were written.[20] This position reaffirmed the Church's progressive trend to find the truth and meaning in scriptures with the help of the arts and sciences, articulated years earlier in the papal letter *Divino Afflante Espiritu*.[21] The Decree on Religious Education praised and affirmed the work of Catholic schools and Catholic religious education, which had been important to Connolly's first seven years as a priest. But it also supported the importance of academic independence in

Catholic colleges, again declaring that openness and truth-seeking was vital to education and scholarship. Connolly heartily agreed.

Other documents proclaimed a new identity for the Church and its members, beginning with the bishops. The Decree on the Bishops' Pastoral Office in the Church, along with *Sacrosanctum Concilium*, gave much greater and clearer power to the Church's bishops around the world, as opposed to the central staff at the Vatican in Rome.[22] From now on, each bishop was to be recognized as the primary power in his diocese. He would be expected to lead the diocese and its parishes in a way that reflected the culture of the people who worshipped there. Bishops' power was also to impact the global Church, reflected in their participation at this council and their votes to approve the sixteen documents. And another of the council's four major documents, the Dogmatic Constitution on the Church, or *Lumen Gentium*, recognized the responsibility for the Church as a whole that each bishop shared with the Pope as their leader.[23] Finally, each bishop was encouraged to join with others in his country to address Church concerns there. Connolly's own bishop, Cardinal Spellman, was already a powerful leader in the Archdiocese of New York, and Connolly thought that his newly shared power with the Pope would make him even stronger.

The council's expanded sense of the identity of the Church itself was more challenging to grasp. *Lumen Gentium* now defined the Church in several ways. It was still an institution, with its sacraments as "signs" to the world, identifying it as God's Church. But the document also renewed an ancient scriptural emphasis on the church as a "mystery," and as a spiritual community.[24] Every one of its members—priests, religious sisters and brothers, and particularly laypersons—was, by right of his or her status as a baptized Catholic, one of the "people of God." This concept made each Catholic equally responsible for the life and direction of the Church, both as community and as institution. This encouraged Connolly, who was striving to create a spiritual community at Athanasius, to continue the work of religious education. But even with the positive news, some things were still not clear to him and left him with questions. How is everyone in a parish responsible for the parish? If the St. Athanasius parishioners were the people of God, what should they do?

Just as intriguing and puzzling to Connolly were two new concepts of priesthood. *Lumen Gentium* determined that laypersons would now be seen as possessing their own category of ministry, in living out and sharing their faith: the "priesthood of the faithful."[25] Each layperson, again by virtue of baptism, had the same responsibility as priests to be messengers of the faith and model the life of a true Catholic. They were to be served in this new "priestly" capacity by ordained priests, bishops, and religious, whose role was now defined as the "ministerial priesthood." In the same spirit of revising the liturgy and sacraments to reflect the language, customs, and values of laypeople, these two concepts of priesthood re-oriented ministry in the direction of laypeople. These newly designated priests would need to be supported in order to carry out their mission.

As Connolly read these sections of the Pastoral Constitution, he thought about his own experiences at Athanasius. What would "priesthood of the faithful" mean, practically speaking? Did the laypersons in the parish need to act differently? Was there a special kind of attention or orientation which Connolly must provide them which he hadn't up to this point? No one provided workshops or manuals, like the Sunday missalettes and catechism books and the conferences about the Pastoral Constitution on the Liturgy, for developing or serving the "priesthood of the faithful." And what did it mean for him to be a "servant priest," as the Pastoral Constitution now defined him? Hadn't he been doing everything he could to prepare his parishioners for all the sacraments, to provide religious education to the children, and to support the societies? With more and more questions shaking his confidence in his own priesthood, he looked to initiatives coming out of the Vatican and the archdiocese to give him answers.

Action and Reaction

Even before the final closing of the council, the leader of the global Church wasted no time in carrying out the messages of the Church in Renewal. In October 1965, Paul VI followed in the footsteps of his namesake, the apostle known for his travels around the world to spread the message of Christ and the new Christian movement. Pushing for a global movement of world peace, he appeared in New York City before the gathering of the world's leaders as the annual United Nations General Assembly, urgently calling on the leaders to end conflicts and achieve lasting peace. He spoke with the weight of decades of experiences as a witness to the horrors of war and the suffering caused: all those who had lost lives, families, communities, and futures. Paul pleaded for peace before representatives of 114 nations, asking also for an end to the threat of nuclear weapons. The leader of the global Church wanted to turn the council's words into meaningful action. But he also called on the bishops of the world to do the same.[26]

In his travels to different parts of the United States to learn the teachings of Vatican II, Connolly also learned about other council-inspired action, this time in his home country. Though the American bishops had occasionally gathered since the mid-nineteenth century and had been more formally organized since World War I, a new body called the United States Conference of Catholic Bishops (USCCB) now took shape. Under its first president, progressive archbishop of Detroit John Dearden, they embarked on a broad-based social justice agenda.[27] American bishops declared their support for striking farmworkers, and they inspired growing national support for the many Mexican and Mexican American Catholics who had called for a boycott of lettuce and grapes.[28] The bishops also advocated for peace negotiations in Vietnam and supported conscientious objection to war. Moreover, they advocated for the creation of the Catholic Campaign for Human Development, a fund to support grassroots civil rights and related activities. The spirit of change was already capturing the attention of the broader American society in the 1960s, and with Vatican II's directive to bishops to take part in their respective national matters, it was compelling the American Catholic Church and its hierarchy to action.

But initiatives for change were also emanating from the grassroots in the U.S. Catholic Church, as laypeople realized they had a role to play as "the people of God." Women religious, or "sisters," as they were commonly known, were asserting their rights to participate in activities beyond elementary school classrooms and hospital nursing.[29] After leading in the nation's Catholic school systems and hospitals, many women religious decided to lead elsewhere. They created and ran community service organizations to help young people, poor people in need of social services, immigrants in need of English language education, and families in need of medicine and nursing care. But, in the socially activist spirit of the time, they also walked picket lines with farmworkers, marched for civil rights, and petitioned for better housing in inner-city and rural America.[30] And they often did these things in ordinary attire, not the distinctive and restrictive "habits" of the past, after the Vatican Council Decree on the Adoption and Renewal of Religious Life gave them a new freedom to do so.[31]

In the world of Catholic laypersons, who were also empowered by their new ministerial status as "the priesthood of the faithful" and "the people of God," new organizing efforts emerged. New laypersons' organizations were founded throughout the country.[32] Particularly in middle-class communities, laymen and laywomen called for a greater say in their parishes and their dioceses. In places like Long Island, Chicago, Los Angeles, and Dallas, local entities developed into chapters of national Catholic organizations. Their concerns ranged from the liturgy in their local parish to the need for Church action against the Vietnam War. Those concerns

Fr. Neil and Sr. Ann Marie in new post-Vatican attire. (Fr. Neil Connolly's personal collection.)

were being brought up elsewhere in the Church, as the bishops' initiatives proved. But the fact that these organizations were created outside parish structures or formal diocesan programs and outside of previously recognized laypersons' movements and societies signaled an independence unfamiliar to Church authorities.

Not all of the bishops who had voted to approve the council documents that had sparked all this change were ready to accept these grassroots movements. When the archbishop of Cincinnati sanctioned the Glenmary Sisters over their efforts to dress as laypersons and directly live with and serve the Appalachian community in Ohio and surrounding states, over ninety members resigned en masse and reorganized themselves into a new order, independent of the authority of the archbishop.[33] In Texas, a bishop banned parishes in his diocese from playing folk music in their liturgy,[34] and Dallas laypersons' organizations staged protests over the decision.[35]

Similar conflicts, which often involved laypersons, erupted throughout the country. Connolly was surprised by them, but it was other conflicts that felt more personal because they involved priests. In one case, a Milwaukee priest was ordered by his bishop to quit his involvement in a civil rights boycott.[36] In another, Vatican officials stepped in against a priest at odds with his bishop in California.[37] Then, in New Jersey, another bishop suspended a priest for holding mass in people's homes.[38] Having heard confessions in the back of a *colmado*, in the Puerto Rican *campo*, Connolly found this bishop's action surprising, especially since the priest was bringing the Gospel message into people's homes. There were many more conflicts arising than there had been in the early days of Connolly's priesthood, reflecting the tensions over new council roles: the bishops, with their newly given authority over their dioceses, and the priests, sisters, and laypersons, with their newly given responsibility for the Church as the "people of God," did not always find it easy to figure out who had the last word.

Stories about these conflicts compelled Connolly to ask even more questions than those that came from reading the documents. Does a priest have a right to defy his bishop? Can a bishop ban a priest, or suspend or punish him if the priest feels that his actions are following the new teachings of Vatican II? Yes, the council gave the bishops plenary power over their dioceses, and all priests were ultimately accountable to the bishops who ordained and led them. But could these priests challenge the bishop if they saw something wrong? And if the priests, sisters, and laypersons are all "the people of God," are *all* the Church, what did they have the power to decide about the Church? There were so many unanswered questions and new difficulties about the way the Church would work after the council, even as the new possibilities were exhilarating.

The Church and the World

Of all the council documents he read, nothing caught Neil Connolly's attention quite like the last one. *Gaudium et Spes*, the Pastoral Constitution on the Church in the Modern World, was issued, or "promulgated," on December 7, 1965, the last day of the council, and just a few weeks before Illich told Connolly that his life was about to change.[39] It was fitting that the last schema introduced into the council was the last one to be resolved by the bishops. Originally known only as "Schema 13,"[40] it was actively promoted by bishops from the poorer countries and continents known as the "Third World," including the bishops of Latin America. From the occasional Latin American priests visiting and staying at Athanasius, and from reading articles in New York's the *Catholic News* and the *National Catholic Reporter*,[41] which emerged during the council years in Kansas City, Connolly knew there were serious challenges facing those bishops, including Hélder Câmara of Brazil.

Reading this Constitution was like hearing Father Fitzpatrick's lectures on the Puerto Rican people those summer evenings in Puerto Rico, making it clear to Connolly that he and the Church were a part of history. The Church did not just exist alongside humanity; it was living within it. It shared the fate of the rest of humankind and, as such, owed its long-term well-being to its ability to work and coexist with all humankind, recognizing and realizing shared goals. One of these goals, according to the document, was to help realize the full potential of every human being on earth, Catholic and non-Catholic. In achieving that goal, the Church could realize its other significant joint goal: creating a world of dignity and well-being for all.

While celebrating the accomplishments of civilization that humankind and technology had brought about, *Gaudium et Spes* focused on the central issue of inequality. The bishops noted in this Pastoral Constitution that there were many people living in conditions of misery. These people were not reaping the benefits of economic progress that the developed world had experienced. And their suffering, it was pointed out, was not merely accidental or the result of a failure to move forward as quickly as Western Europe and the United States. Rather, it was the result of structures and institutions creating unequal and exploitative economic relationships across the globe through the colonization of the last few centuries. Inequalities, in turn, meant hunger, illness, and substandard housing. And importantly for the Church, situations that were harmful to the well-being of families were contrary to the goal of realizing the full potential of every human being.[42]

The Pastoral Constitution did not leave the discussion at the point of stating that the inequality existed between poorer and richer nations of the world, or poorer and richer regions within developed nations.[43] The bishops said it was the Church's responsibility to address not only the inequalities but also the conditions caused by those inequalities. And declaring those conditions was not enough. It was incumbent upon the Church to identify particular situations of injustice, such as when a large corporation takes the property of farmers, leaving them dependent and landless. Or it might mean identifying the exclusion of a community of indigenous people from a role in governing their homeland. Or the injustice might be workers not receiving fair wages to raise their family with dignity or workers enduring inhumane working conditions.[44] Whatever the situation, the bishops said, the Church had a responsibility to identify injustice and to call it out.

Moreover, since the Church had been identified as the "people of God," *all* of its members were responsible for finding and challenging injustice. The institutional Church *and* the people of God had to take action as well as play the prophetic role of denouncing injustice. The entire Church was expected to side with those organizations peacefully working to address injustice. Supporting laborers' efforts to form a union, as well as those of human rights organizations, workers' cooperatives, and farmers' associations, was a responsibility.[45] And while remaining independent of partisan political activity, the Church was expected to challenge and pressure governments over policies that would impact the economic and social well-being of people, especially the vulnerable.

Connolly found these mandates resonating with his experiences. Of course, his father's history as a local leader in the Transport Workers Union taught him what decades of Irish labor struggles in America had taught the people in general: that a fair wage and fair working conditions were things to be fought for. The sacrifices endured by Con Connolly's family were a part of Neil's upbringing, and the principles behind the transit workers' strike were reinforced by older Catholic teaching: for example, "On Capital and Labor," an 1891 document by Pope Leo XIII that supported workers' rights, including unionization and a living wage.[46] The teachings on workers' rights, growing significantly after the industrial revolution and through the labor struggles of the twentieth century, anticipated other areas of broader Catholic social teaching that became more widely known and better-developed following Vatican II.

Connolly himself had also taken steps on labor issues during his time in seminary. He had helped organize a seminar on "The Church and Labor" during his last year at St. Joseph's, involving some guest speakers. Most prominent among them was Father John "Pete" Corridan, a Jesuit priest who worked in the shipyards of the New York waterfront and became a friend of the longshoremen working there. His visits to the docks endeared him to the workers, even as he faced the wrath of some union "leaders" corrupted by the influence of New York's organized crime rackets. Corridan's efforts to give the workers honest wages and better conditions led him to denounce corruption before Congressional Waterfront Commission hearings. His work was featured in Pulitzer Prize–winning articles and the Academy Award–winning movie *On the Waterfront* (1954). Corridan's crusade inspired Connolly, and he was thrilled to invite him for a talk before the future priests at St. Joseph's on his role and experiences as a "workers' priest."[47]

But Connolly's confidence about labor issues were not enough to help him understand another council concept. The bishops emphasized that their call to work for justice was in the service of cultivating the "kingdom of God on earth." This kingdom, the bishops wrote, drawing on scripture, already existed, like a seed or a young plant ready to be brought to fruition. Every member of the Church was on the journey toward that kingdom, to be realized as an era of peace, dignity, and justice for all humankind. It was up to Church members to take action now, in order for the kingdom to "be brought into full flower. . . ."[48] Instead of preparing exclusively for heaven, the bishops wrote, "the expectation of a new earth must not weaken but rather stimulate our concern for cultivating this one. For here grows the body of a new human family." Connolly realized that these lofty words, proclaimed to humankind as part of the last message emanating from the council, signaled a brand-new level of interaction with the world. They were also words he would need some time to make sense of. What was the "Kingdom of God on earth"?

From Doubts to New Responsibilities

As he thought about the council documents, the conferences, and the conflicts he was hearing about from around the country, Connolly was feeling doubts about his priesthood again. Despite two council documents about priests, there was no real new place in the Church for priests, nor was there a new job description like there seemed to be for bishops and laypeople. Connolly was still called on to take care of a parish and its people, to preach the Gospel message and perform the sacraments, though in a more dynamic way that engaged the people. And even with the introduction of new entities called "Presbyteral Councils" to allow priests to advise their bishop, priests still answered to their bishops.

But he was reassured by a recurring theme he heard from the council documents and his various trainings: shared responsibility. First, *he* had to take responsibility for building a different kind of Church, a "people of God." The thousands of *parroquianos* (parishoners) at St. Athanasius whom he had baptized over the years were now the people of God, responsible for the parish. As their priests, Connolly and the others were responsible for serving them, rather than leading them. In turn, he had to teach them to be responsible for their parish, and not just for their Sacred Corazón, or Santo Nombre, or Movimiento part of the parish. For the *whole* parish, a responsibility new to their Catholic identity.

Connolly also saw another responsibility for himself: the Church. Not just St. Athanasius but St. Anselm, St. Anthony of Padua, St. John Chrysostom, and all the other parishes around him in the Bronx. And the ones in Manhattan and Yonkers, and Newburgh, and those in the *capilla* in Jayuya and the other *campos* in Puerto Rico. And the parishes of those priests, sisters, and laypersons he met out in the conferences in Missouri and Indiana and elsewhere in the United States. *Somehow*, he thought,

I am responsible for the current and future life of the Church, and for its fulfillment of the new council teachings.

Moreover, he knew that if he were to carry out those teachings, then he could not continue doing things as he had for the last seven years. He couldn't just react to every situation or solve every problem that came along. Instead, he would have to be intentional in his actions within and outside the parish. Also, it could not be an "automatic" Catholicism anymore in the parish, where you're baptized, you receive Communion, so you're automatically Catholic, you're a "member of the tribe," and there is nothing more to think about or understand. He would have to challenge parishioners and others to be intentional about their Catholicism, to understand the message of responsibility for the whole Church.

There was another responsibility Connolly decided was his: to bring the Church into the world. As a priest, he would need to teach his parishioners to bring their parish into the world, a little like he had done with the Movimiento Familiar Cristiano. But while he engaged some parishioners in the Movimiento to "see, judge, and act" on matters of the world, *Gaudium et Spes* was calling for something more from Connolly, more than the labor seminars and more than community trips to Bear Mountain Park. He would need to speak about unjust conditions in the world and somehow teach his Church—the whole Church—to do the same. It seemed overwhelming, like those hard days in the seminary he was remembering that December night in the rectory when he saw Illich.

He wondered what he might be capable of accomplishing with these new council teachings. It would take a while to find out and to do it right, just like it had taken a while to learn Spanish, to "de-Yankeefy" and understand his parish. *But how to accomplish these teachings in the world? As a priest? What was he capable of? What was any priest capable of in this new Vatican II Church?*

He started to remember one of those Saturday nights when he and fellow seminarians would regularly go out to unwind from the difficult days. They played cards at someone's home, or went out bowling. But the jazz clubs were their favorite place to go and have some drinks, and talk about life for a while, while listening to the popular acts of the time—Illinois Jacquet, Charlie Parker, and others—in Manhattan, either on "Swing Street" (52nd Street) or in the Village. On this night, it was Eddie Condon's, a place in the Village, featuring Teddy Wilson, a well-known cornet player of the time. One of the seminarians, a Spanish man named Rafael Verdejo, started bragging about how he knew the club owner.[49]

"You know, that Condon is my family."

Connolly and others laughed and rolled their eyes at Verdejo's remarks. "Ah, you're full of shit," one of the men barked, as the others chuckled.

Not ready to let the subject go, Verdejo said, "I'm telling you, Condon's my uncle. He even lets me play here sometimes."

More laughter erupted as someone yelled, "Cut the malarkey."

Then he stopped the comments by raising his hand. "I'll tell you what," he said with a sly smile.

"What?" said another man, laughing.

"I'm gonna go up there and play."

"You?" asked Connolly, and the laughter resumed. "C'mon," said Connolly, "Give me a break. What makes you think you can—" But before Connolly could finish his question, Verdejo bounced up and started walking over to the stage where Wilson had just finished playing a set.

Verdejo looked at Wilson, pointing to the piano, and they both nodded. In seconds, Verdejo sat down at the piano bench and asked Wilson about something which Connolly couldn't hear. Then his fellow seminarian counted "one, two, one, two three four" and began to play. Wilson joined in, and the two went back and forth, punto a punto, one song after another, in an impromptu jam session.

Connolly and the other seminarians stared, stunned, and muttered, "Holy shit."

As he sat in awe watching the two perform, Connolly thought about how Verdejo really surprised everyone. He realized that you can never tell what a person is capable of. That night he wondered what he himself might be capable of. It was a question that was coming up regularly in the year leading up to his ordination and in the beginning of priesthood.

Verdejo showed Connolly something that night, in addition to demonstrating his own talents. He just got up, went into the center of it all, and, without worrying about the larger audience, he let go and immersed himself in the performance. That was what Connolly had to do—let go and immerse himself. Connolly kept that moment and that lesson in his memory, and he applied it later when major challenges presented themselves in his life. That was what Illich called on him to do in Puerto Rico, and it was what he again called on him to do that December night in the Athanasius rectory after the council closed. Let go of the old Church and the old priesthood. Walk into the unknown and improvise, in partnership with any other musician who would play with you.

Connolly was ready to learn more about building the Church into the people of God. He was ready to take responsibility for the whole Church. He was also ready to bring the Church into the world and create "the

Kingdom of God on earth." And yet, while he had some ideas about the people of God and taking responsibility for the Church, he had little idea of what creating the Kingdom would involve, or where to start. Fortunately for him, there was someone who would give him a first answer. It was not Illich, but rather another extraordinary member from the 1958 summer class in Puerto Rico.

4

⠿

Summer in the City

... Rather than being some strange, isolated kind of problem, a problem out there, the poor are our mirror. And if the society of the United States ... wants to see their problems revealed to them in a graphic way, well, let them look on the streets we are going to be working this summer.
—Speech given by Monsignor Robert Fox, Summer in the City Conference, College of Mount St. Vincent, Bronx, New York, June 1966

A War on Poverty

Vatican II's call for the Church to serve and collaborate with the world was exciting, but at first it was also confusing. How was he to do this? What did it mean for his daily life as a priest? But even as the council was moving swiftly toward its conclusion, the domestic events that would help to change Connolly's priesthood were already ramping up. On March 16, 1964, the president of the United States launched the campaign that would eventually help Neil Connolly become a priest of the world.

Connolly watched on live television as President Lyndon B. Johnson asked the U.S. Congress to pass the Economic Opportunity Act (EOA) and create a set of programs that became known as the War on Poverty, which he had first mentioned in the State of the Union address a few months before.[1] Johnson declared that the U.S. economy was strong enough to create a "Great Society," one which could support economically vulnerable populations including the elderly, military veterans, the disabled, racial minorities, and the rural and urban poor. He argued that it was possible, for the first time in the country's history, to eliminate poverty—a situation affecting 35 million people, or one out of every five Americans. Johnson promoted new programs such as Medicare, unemployment insurance expansion, and housing and community development.[2] Moreover, concerned about a lack of opportunities for youth, he also initiated school programs like Head Start and college work-study, and youth employment schemes such as the Neighborhood Youth Corps and Job Corps.[3]

Poor communities such as Hunts Point–Longwood got special attention from Johnson as key battlegrounds in his newly declared war. The Community Action Program (CAP) was to "strike at poverty at its source—in the streets of our cities and on the farms of our countryside, among the very young and the impoverished old."[4] A new Office of Economic Opportunity (OEO), created to oversee the War on Poverty, would be led by Sargent Shriver, one-time chair of the National Catholic Council for Interracial Justice and brother-in-law of John F. Kennedy and Robert F. Kennedy.[5] Shriver's OEO wanted to get the people of poor communities directly involved in initiatives to solve their problems. The persistent poverty in these areas of the country, Shriver and Johnson theorized, could be broken by requiring "maximum feasible participation" from local people in the use of anti-poverty funds and creation of anti-poverty strategies.[6] CAP became the most visible battle in the War on Poverty, because it was expected to be played out "on the streets." As a result, it captured the attention of political and community actors in the inner cities of the United States.

The New York City government answered Johnson's call to join the War on Poverty. Under Mayor Robert Wagner and then under his successor, John Lindsay, city hall created both the Economic Opportunity Corporation and a New York City Council on Poverty, a broad-based entity that included representatives from the Archdiocese of New York and the Diocese of Brooklyn.[7] Because Johnson called for community participation, the city called on 852 community groups to elect community committees to decide where CAP funds would go.[8] Political conflicts erupted as soon as elections were called for, and they would continue for a long time, in every arena—at the neighborhood level, between political clubs, and even at the Council on Poverty.[9]

The Council on Poverty selected thirteen government-identified "slum areas"—high-poverty areas in need of services and neighborhood improvement—to receive what would be known as "anti-poverty funds," which totaled $52 million in 1965.[10] Five were in the Bronx, which attracted the greatest number of Puerto Ricans in the city; the planners named Highbridge, Tremont, South Bronx, Morrisania, and Hunts Point, Connolly's own neighborhood.[11]

New York's Catholic Church, with dozens of parishes struggling with poverty, also answered the call to join the War on Poverty. Cardinal Spellman created the Archdiocesan Commission for Community Planning on December 29, 1964, a full year before the release of *Gaudium et Spes*, "enlisting" local parishes, schools, agencies, and Catholic Charities field offices as his "army."[12] The commission's chair was Spellman's vicar general, Bishop John Maguire, who was already responsible for overseeing the integrated parish program to answer the *Gran Migración*, and who assigned the Puerto Rico summer program graduates, including Connolly, to these integrated Spanish parishes.

Monsignor John Ahern was the logical choice to direct the commission.[13] Ahern, a Bronx native and East Harlem parishioner, was a trained social worker who knew firsthand the community's needs and the affected parishes. For eight years, Ahern and his colleagues at Catholic Charities Family Services field offices had been addressing income, employment, housing, and health and mental health needs in many neighborhoods. Ahern, who had good relationships with Connolly and the other parish priests since their days in the Puerto Rico summer program, believed in involving the parish staffs in the War on Poverty. He personally held meetings with clusters of priests from the Lower East Side, East Harlem, Central Harlem, Washington Heights, the South Bronx, and upstate New York. At the Bronx priests' meeting, organized with Connolly's help, Ahern urged them to join the community committees, apply for the CAP funds, attend meetings, and advocate for their needs.

Then, in May 1965, the commission initiated a unique area-wide effort to be funded by the Community Action Program. With a $250,000 grant, Spellman announced "Summer in the City" and appointed Monsignor Robert Fox, coordinator of the Spanish Community Action Office, as its director.[14] This new program would take seriously the mandate of "maximum feasible participation." But it would do so differently than other programs in New York City, or even in the country. Summer in the City enlisted the priests and religious of thirty-nine parishes to "strike at poverty . . . in the streets of our cities." This included Connolly and his colleagues at Athanasius, who would now bring their parish into the world.

Bob Fox and the Three Principles

In June 1966, Connolly, Gigante, and Adams went up to the College of Mount St. Vincent, in the northernmost Bronx neighborhood of Riverdale, to prepare for Summer in the City. Joined by dozens of priests from the other Spanish-speaking parishes of the Archdiocese, Connolly heard Fox, whom he had first met in the Puerto Rico program eight years earlier, explain the essential issue that drove his creation of the new program.[15] As Fox saw it, the lack of relationships within families and communities was the central problem in modern American society. Focusing his special concern on New York's poor neighborhoods, Fox remarked that modern urban life created isolation.[16] This, in turn, led to a deep lack of trust and was detrimental to having healthy, productive relationships and thus to vibrant, peaceful communities in the "urban jungle."

For Fox, however, this problematic isolation was not confined to the "inner city," then a relatively new term. Like Johnson, he recognized the problems and struggles of the American inner city, but he saw them as symptomatic of a wider issue. Isolation was an American problem, not just an inner-city problem. The suburban American lived in isolation as well, both within and outside his community. The inability of the American suburbs and their middle-class inhabitants to understand and relate to the low-income and inner-city areas of America was keeping the isolation entrenched on both sides.[17] Calling for an understanding of the inner city, Fox awakened the consciousness of Connolly and the others, who had grown up in their own isolated worlds and worked somewhat apart from their neighborhoods. "Rather than being some strange, isolated kind of problem, a problem out there," Fox told them, "the poor are our mirror. And if the society of the United States . . . wants to see their problems revealed to them in a graphic way, well, let them look at the streets we're going to be working this summer."[18]

Fox was not ignorant of the increasingly revolutionary climate, of demands for civil and political rights and what would shortly become calls for "power to the people," the slogan of the Black Panther Party, founded later that year. He wanted to create a program to address individual and community powerlessness. In Fox's eyes, the inner-city resident understood the power situation in his life and could take any one of several approaches to that situation: "People either accept powerlessness and move on, or else they turn to illusion. Some people accept the illusion of power, and others turn to destruction—if I can destroy what I feel powerless in front of, then I have power. . . . Another illusion is withdrawal: they won't let me do anything, so I'm pulling out. I'm going to sit and watch it crumble."[19]

Connolly heard these messages about isolation and was reminded of his summer trips with the Movimiento Familiar Cristiano. The Movimiento leaders agreed with Fox: Isolation was the problem facing his parishioners in the Hunts Point–Longwood neighborhood. They wanted to build relationships and community by getting people together outside of the harsh buildings and streets of the neighborhood. Hundreds of people, feeling powerless on their streets, came together and built relationships on those trips. But Connolly heard something different from Fox than what the Movimiento leaders had offered as a solution when they "saw, judged, and acted": *It wasn't necessary to go elsewhere. Isolation could be broken on those very same streets where they lived, and people could reclaim some power in their own life on those streets.*

Fox explained his new approach by describing the groups of people who were in the college auditorium. Connolly and the other priests in attendance were all dressed in their traditional black clothing with white "dog collars." Also, there were a large number of religious—both sisters and brothers—dressed in their traditional garb. But then, as Fox was speaking, Connolly, Gigante, and Adams looked around and saw unfamiliar faces: young men and women dressed in tie-dyed T-shirts, jeans, overalls, or flowery skirts, with some of the men in shaggy beards and long hair. "Who the hell are these people?" they muttered.

Fox noted that he had hired these artists for a central part of his program. To the modern American individual in the inner city, dignity was essential, and it could be achieved if he could express himself within his environment.[20] Fox emphasized the importance of having a poor resident, in approaching his own environment, develop an artist's creativity: "Each and every person," he said, "has to be able to come up with that which an artist has to come up with when he approaches a canvas, the disposition to invest himself and to express himself, even though he knows the poverty of the canvas in front of him. . . . The people here . . . don't have a very pleasant canvas and they have the temptation or tendency to reject that canvas. . . ."[21] As a result, Fox had brought in people who could teach residents to be creative. There were visual artists, sculptors, musicians, dancers, and theater artists, all of whom would join with the parish staffs and religious to carry out the mission of Summer in the City.

Fox emphasized three principles inextricably linked to each other and to the mission of Summer in the City: creativity, relationships, and the public forum. The program brought together artists, religious brothers and sisters from outside communities, parish priests and sisters, and residents to engage each other in "projects" applying the principles. Under the "public forum" principle, everything—every aspect of the project or every activity—had to take place right out on the street, to allow people to come out of their isolation and to see and experience the activity or project. The "relationships" principle—that both strangers and known neighbors had to interact with each other while being on the street—was also expected of everyone involved in Summer in the City. Finally, the "creativity" principle began with the artist, who would initiate a project and instruct and support residents as they came out to the streets and got involved.[22]

Summer in the Peninsula

Fox described these principles as a framework for engaging people who were unknown to the parishes. But Connolly was a little uncertain how well this would work out. *It involved him and the rest of the staff engaging with non-parishioners outside of the parish, and in activities that had nothing to do with being a Catholic or a Christian. He would need to go out and meet strangers and create something with them to build a relationship with them. He just never did anything like this as a priest. What would this program do to make him a better priest?* And how, Connolly wondered, would this answer the problems of poverty?

The Athanasius parish staff accepted the general approach of Summer in the City, but they wanted an approach that fit their team. By 1966 they were already making internal commitments as a staff to divide up responsibilities for the parish, which was so large and had too many people, into three neighborhood areas. Gigante took the area of the church and the immediate neighborhood, and Adams took the neighborhood around the school. Connolly, meanwhile, crossed Bruckner Boulevard into the more distant part of the parish, Hunts Point Peninsula.

They had to start a program on a street, so Connolly had to organize a committee in order to be credible and accepted in the Peninsula, which he didn't know very well, except for some of his Cuban and a few Puerto Rican parishioners who had ended up living on that side. He worked with a couple of parishioners whom he knew to recruit their own contacts in the area. There were Haydee Colón and her brother Ray, who were baptized and then made the rest of their sacraments at Athanasius, and who regularly organized activities in the Peninsula. They introduced Connolly as they reached out to people.

"Hi, I'm Father Neil Connolly," he said over and over, shaking hands. "We want to form a committee of community people to run activities on the street. Do you want to be on this committee? . . . We want to come on this street, but we will not do so unless you want us. But we think we can provide some recreation and fun. Who wants to be just sitting around, suffering from the heat?"

The group decided to focus on recreation activities and selected a playground next to the public school for the Peninsula community, P.S. 48. In the beginning, the playground was dominated by drug addicts and occasional dealers. As the Parks Department worker assigned there told Connolly, they were open to the public, which meant anybody. Undaunted by the presence of the addicts, Connolly went into the playground with Haydee, Ray, and some others from the neighborhood, and they set up a volleyball net and stands. He asked some passersby, "Hey, you want to help? We're going to set up a volleyball game." A couple of them stopped and helped put up the equipment. They began a conversation with Connolly and the Colóns, and they eventually started a game. Summer in the City's first public forum was underway in the junkie playground.

Connolly knew this process of bringing the residents out to the playground and to this new program had to be done carefully. He thought about it after they finished their first games and saw the neighbors watching them with some curiosity and maybe some suspicion. *He and the parish staff who were with him didn't own the street. They were going as guests of the people on the street and the people who used the playground—even of the addicts. If the addicts were in the church and out of control, he could say to them, "Get out of here." But not on the playground.*

However, the addicts started to show up less and less as the program kept coming back every day. During the day, they would play volleyball and basketball with whoever showed up, and at night they would bring out a screen and projector and show movies. Children and their family members came out to play during the day, and mothers came out with their baby carriages to watch movies and hear some music.

The "public forum" theme was being put to the test in positive and negative ways every day. One night, the program started a bonfire in the street. With a man leading a group in song while playing his guitar, some people stood up and danced. At one point, a very attractive African American woman started dancing, after having drunk a little extra. Some man yelled, "Take your clothes off," and she began doing so, until Connolly and another man, a Puerto Rican whom Connolly knew and liked, went over to stop her. He said gently, "Honey, don't. You don't want to make a spectacle of yourself. I'm gonna walk you down the corner and get you home, okay?" Connolly saw how well he handled this, and he was happy that it ended so well, and that everyone had a nice time together, sharing music.

But he also saw difficult things on the street. Some people would throw eggs or water balloons off the roof at an activity that was taking place. People at the activity would be angry and say something to the egg-throwers, but they would also sigh in hopeless acceptance. Another time, two men were in a fight, and one was swinging away at the other with a tire iron. Just across the street, two boys were throwing a ball back and forth to each other. They never stopped, even though they knew what was going on. Connolly chased away the fighters, but he thought about the ball-playing boys. *There was such a harshness on the street. This was what Fox spoke about at Mount St. Vincent. That was the isolation and powerlessness and destruction he was being called on to change.*

After the initial success, the Peninsula team expanded Summer in the City to another block, Barretto Street, that sat on a hill. At one end of the block were some private homes owned by a mix of Italians, Puerto Ricans, and a few blacks. At the bottom of that hill was an apartment building primarily occupied by black families. At the top, Puerto Rican youth were hanging around in front of a home, and at the bottom, black youth were standing outside the building and on the street corner. Everyone kept to themselves, and no one was actively involved on the street.

A white Summer in the City volunteer, a cadet on summer break from West Point Military Academy, decided to change things. Connolly observed the cadet, who didn't speak a word of Spanish, as he went down the block, spoke to the black teens, then went up the block to the Puerto Rican teens, and then back and forth between the two groups over a few days. He managed to create some communication between the groups and finally found agreement on different joint actions.

The first step was for the two groups to go together to play volleyball in the playground at P.S. 48. Then, they agreed to go to St. Mary's Park in the adjoining St. Anselm's parish, which had a large recreation center, including a swimming pool. Finally, they agreed to go out of the city, on a bus trip to Bear Mountain, with the black and Puerto Rican teens finding a little community far from Barretto Street. And in the meantime, of course, they had an artist teaching them arts and crafts on the street, as Summer in the City had called for.

Connolly saw the program expand and draw in more new people, and as he observed, he wondered about its significance for them. He thought, *From the outside looking in, from neighboring streets, people didn't know what was going on. Even a group of older ladies sitting on their folding chairs, who were watching and supporting the games and the players all summer—they didn't know. They were probably thinking, "Oh . . . Father Connolly's just out there playing basketball with other people."* The gentle, talkative old ladies saw everything though, even noticing when Father Gigante tore his pants playing stickball. They also solved problems, in this case sewing up the rip while he continued playing in borrowed pants. But when a group of central staff members from Summer in the City headquarters came to evaluate the program, even those involved older ladies still couldn't explain its special features. They asked one of the elderly women who regularly sat outside, "*¿Qué piensas sobre lo que hace esta iglesia con el Verano en la Ciudad?*" ("What do you think of what the church is doing here with Summer in the City?")

The woman replied, "*¡Bueno, yo no sé exactamente lo que esta tratando de hacer, pero yo sé que a Padre Gigante le gusta jugar el esteekbol!*" ("Well, I don't know exactly what they are trying to do, but Father Gigante does love playing his stickball game!")

Connolly knew that the elderly women could not verbally express the themes of public forum, creativity, and building relationships which Fox had promoted at Mount St. Vincent. But they all did engage in the street activities, even if some were just observers. Others used their creativity in music, arts and crafts projects, and organizing events. He saw, most importantly with participation in the public forum, *that strangers built relationships with each other—priests and religious and volunteers built relationships with people they had never seen in the church.* This was made clear to him by another staff member, who said to him, after the summer was over, "You know, you weren't always comfortable, because you didn't know people."

Connolly, hearing this, understood *Gaudium et Spes* a little better. *"The Church going out into the world" seemed to be a fairly simple concept, but it was an uncomfortable one to live out. They needed to meet the world,* Connolly realized, *not on the Church's "turf" but on the people's "turf."* He had met people in their communities in Puerto Rico, at a *colmado* for confessions and at a makeshift chapel in the hills for Mass, *but those were for Church life, which after all, is what a priest was expected to be a part of. This Summer in the City program pulled him into world life, which a priest had to be a part of, as well.*

In July 1967, as Connolly's second year of Summer in the City was underway, he learned from news reports how fundamentally useful Summer in the City was to its founder, Bob Fox. In Fox's East Harlem neighborhood, a race riot had broken out one night, as happened all around New York's poorer neighborhoods and in many cities of the United States that summer. The day after, Fox mobilized his team of religious and laypersons to the storefront where they were operating Summer in the City. They hurried over to St. Cecilia's rectory and called parishioners and neighbors to the front of the church on 106th Street. Several hundred people gathered, bringing banners, posters, and candles. Prayers were said, the candles were lit, and the group marched in a procession of prayer and song through block after block, while neighbors who had been part of Summer in the City came down from their apartments to join in.

That night, as more than a thousand people reclaimed their neighborhood, the riot did not return to East Harlem. The neighborhood remained calm. And Fox and his storefront team had gone against the recommendations of Mayor Lindsay to get off the streets. As Fox said, "I felt this would be counterproductive. . . . We didn't want the people to surrender the streets to the cops and the rioters—the two groups that believe in force. That's why we marched."[23]

Summer in the City was becoming an inspiring project and gaining a reputation citywide. Even three weeks after the assassination of Dr. Martin Luther King Jr., a special Summer in the City event called "The Thing in the Spring," a neighborhood beautification project, brought volunteers from the suburbs and neighborhood residents together to work side by side in the streets and share a meal. Five thousand people participated, and there were thirty-five parishes involved, including fourteen from the Bronx.[24] Connolly would get to work with or know about many people from these parishes over the years.

Partly in response to the program's success and partly out of its ongoing effort to implement the call of Vatican II, the Archdiocese of New York created an office, the Institute for Human Development, to help the parishes raise funds and form boards and organizational structures that could continue the work of Summer in the City during the school year. The year-round program, called Project Engage, was to help Summer in the City parishes take deeper, more permanent roles in their neighborhoods.[25] Gigante was already underway on his side of the parish, taking the reins to start an organization on Simpson Street. But Connolly wanted to see how far the project would continue in the Peninsula during the year, and who would commit to the project long enough before starting anything new.

The outside volunteers, including some of the laypersons, stayed on through the fall and winter as the Peninsula "chapter" of Summer in the City continued. They included Tom Sexton and his wife, Pat. Tom was a lawyer working for an American corporation with facilities around the world, including Puerto Rico. He and Mike Dunleavy, a corporate employee at Con Edison, were part of a large contingent of suburban Catholic volunteers recruited by Fox and the archdiocese to support Summer in the City, as they sought to break the barriers between the suburbs and the inner city.

Connolly understood how much Summer in the City meant to Tom when he learned about his medical condition: Pat let him know that Tom had multiple sclerosis. While Tom spent much of his time teaching young adults how to pass exams for police, firefighting, and Con Edison positions, he also made occasional visits to Connolly at the rectory. He explained increasing absences related to his condition and to his urgent need to meet work and volunteer commitments: "You know, Father, I'm working my tail off in Puerto Rico for this corporation, because I don't know how much time I have left in my life. Right now, you can't notice, but you'll start to notice it later on, when my foot starts to drag." On the last night Tom visited the rectory, Connolly was watching him walk down the staircase, and he indeed saw the foot drag down each step. *Poor guy*, Connolly thought. *What a noble guy he was, doing all this*.

A Permanent Center

The Summer in the City Committee, which had done everything in the street, also held its meetings there, making decisions about the progress and future of the program. Connolly joined every meeting as one of the committee members, but one night, in the summer of 1968, the neighborhood residents all challenged him with a request. "Please, you guys came here from the church. We now have a foundation, a community here. Please don't leave us. We want you to stay over here. Can we get some place?"

Connolly, intuitively, challenged them right back. "Look, if we do, I'm going to tell you something. I'm not going to run this. I'm willing to work, but I'm not going to run this. And I'm going on vacation next week." He went further: "Now, as a committee, you could hold a meeting on the street, let the people bring their chairs down." Turning to someone who had emerged as one of the Summer in the City leaders, he said, "Godfredo, you can run the meeting. The parish staff will stay, as long as you're willing to share the leadership on this."

When Connolly came back from vacation, they met again on the street, and told him: "Well, we had the meeting. We're willing to do it. We're willing to cooperate."

Connolly was pleasantly surprised; he looked at them and said, "Okay." Something new was going to happen to his involvement in the Peninsula.

The committee did not just want a storefront for community services. They wanted a church as well, so they began a search for a space with a particular set of requirements. They found a series of offices next to each other on Spofford Avenue and Longfellow, which were owned by a steel factory planning to move out of the Hunts Point industrial area. Connolly and the committee members turned the offices into classrooms and offered typing classes, guitar classes, programs for teenagers, and indoor movies. Since it was also the site of the "church," they offered religious instruction programs as well, and even a Mass. In the meantime, Connolly made a Sunday appeal to the parishioners at the main church, asking for their support, since the church people of Hunts Point were also their fellow parishioners, and they could not use government funds for religious services.

From the very beginning, Connolly's vision and message were clear: *If this chapel and community program were going to work, the people were going to have to take full responsibility. Vatican II had defined the renewal Church as the "people of God," in which laypersons took responsibility for the Church alongside priests, bishops, and religious.* Connolly decided, *the people of God would be the builders of this new church.*

In this case, the people of God were the people who had led Summer in the City over the two years at the Peninsula: Haydée Colón; Ray Colón and his wife, Nati; Godfredo Lebrón; Joe and Sylvia Kringden; Rosie and Peter García; Daniel and Felida Figueroa; Julian Collado; Mike Figueroa and his wife, known as "big Tootsie"; Lillian and Orlando Camejo; and Aida Rodriguez.

With the space on Spofford being sold, the new church center soon needed a new location. From a former addict who was streetwise and knew

Full house at Seneca Chapel on Mother's Day. (Photo by Kathleen Osberger.)

all the nightlife in the neighborhood, the committee members learned of a social club on Seneca Avenue that was going out of business, and they took the space. Eventually, they also obtained the two spaces next door—a Pentecostal church and a coffee shop, which were both closing as well. The Pentecostals had been a challenge in the early days of the church when the committee used the social club for a chapel, as their next-door neighbor's services were longer and sometimes loud enough to be heard through the wall. When they took over the two spaces, a new, permanent home was established on Seneca Avenue. It would be both a place of worship and a place to hold meetings for church activity. It would also serve as a community center. In 1968, the Seneca Center was born, with the committee as the board of directors, and Connolly as the executive director.

First One Program, Then Another

Seneca Center wanted to provide social services to the neighborhood, so Connolly and the board built a program. With the help of the Institute for Human Development, Connolly wrote a proposal for senior services and a staff person to provide them. They took the first step forward when they received a grant from Catholic Charities. Lillian Camejo was hired to operate the program three days a week. It served all of the Peninsula's seniors, including a notable Jewish population left over from the early days of the neighborhood in the 1940s and 1950s.

Seeing the strong response from the elderly Jews of the neighborhood, Seneca decided to go further. Connolly wanted to obtain religious program support for them, and reached out to an organization, the New York Board of Rabbis, whom he found in the phone book.

"Hi, listen, we need a rabbi over here, for Saturdays, for worship," said Connolly.

They asked Connolly, "Who are you?"

Connolly replied, "Well, this is Father Neil Connolly. I'm a priest over here in Hunts Point."

"You're a Catholic. Why would you want a—"

Connolly interrupted, "Yeah, but we have this program for seniors, and Jewish people come to it, and we want as many people as possible. But they miss their own cultural and religious activity, because there's no synagogues here anymore. There used to be, but not anymore."

The representative on the other end of the phone, baffled by the request, said, "We'll get back to you. We've got to talk this over."

Connolly never heard back from the board. But during another "ecumenical" encounter—this one with Rabbi Stern from a Scarsdale synagogue, whom he met through a mutual friend—Connolly raised the question of support for Jewish programs. As a result, a delegation of twelve synagogue members came down to the Seneca Center to meet the program participants. Two of these elderly men, Harry Dyer and another man known as "Mister Beshrantsky," were regulars at the main church. They would visit the rectory to chat up the staff, and perhaps more importantly, to ask for money for a pack of cigarettes. When visiting the Seneca Center senior program, Connolly saw Dyer and Beshrantsky there as well, and chatted with them.

The Scarsdale delegation expected a welcome free of controversy, and Rabbi Stern smiled as he was introduced by Connolly to the Hunts Point seniors.

"Hello, so good to see all of you," said Stern.

Before he continued, Dyer interrupted with a shouted question: "Where ya been??"

Stern paused and tried an explanation, "Well, you know—"

"C'mon now!" shouted Dyer, who then pointed at Connolly. "I now believe in Jesus Christ because of him!!"

It was an embarrassing introduction for Stern and the delegation, as well as for Connolly, even while some of the audience chuckled or nodded at Dyer's comments. But the delegation was given a tour of the program and they saw that Seneca was really serving Jewish seniors in the area.

Connolly, Camejo, and the board persevered and grew the Hunts Point Program for the Aged and other programs at the center. But while they avoided many of the ongoing conflicts across the country over federal and local funding for their programs, an occasional controversial question would come up. When the center requested funds from a group called the Greater New York Fund for a teen program, the board received visitors who pointed out the presence of a community storefront from another organization in the area. In fact it was right next door, and the prospective funders challenged Connolly and the other board members. "Wait a minute," said the lead fund representative, "You guys got a poverty program right next door to you."

Connolly came to the center's defense: "Believe me, there's no work being done there. The Youth Corps kids, they just sit around there, with their feet up on the desk all day. Nobody goes to them. They're not competing with us at all. We'll get people." They were granted the funds and then received another grant from the New York City Youth Board, the same one which supported Jack Lyons for his work with street gangs.

With the success of the senior and youth programs, Connolly and the center looked elsewhere to help grow some of their work related to community health issues. They learned of a federal program within the National Institutes of Health of the United States Department of Health Education and Welfare, which would be the biggest grant available for the kind of work they wanted to do—if they were able to obtain it. They submitted the application and were told that there would be a site visit by a team of professional evaluators on behalf of the Institutes. Connolly and the Seneca Center Board knew this visit would be significant. Everyone had to be ready, so they prepared themselves, creating and answering a range of questions suggested by the application materials. On the day of the visit, they found they had guessed well; the leaders answered many of the questions they had practiced while giving the tour and afterward.

However, a couple of unexpected questions were raised—but not about the center. They were about Connolly. One evaluator said, "Father, I understand that your position here is executive director of the whole center."

Connolly responded, "Yeah, I'm really pastor of the church here, but I work in this area. But if you want to say that I am, then, yes, I am. I am not running the program that you have in the proposal. We have somebody doing that already."

Right afterward, a second evaluator came into the dialogue, almost like an interrogator, saying, "Everyone sitting at the table is of color, or Hispanic. You're a white man. How come you're doing this kind of stuff?" This interrogator, who was white, seemed to Connolly to be the leader of the evaluation team.

Connolly was furious. "Why am I doing it? Well, first of all, there's a need to do it," Connolly said, sitting up straight while raising his fingers, one by one, to confront the evaluator. "Second, the people want me to do it. And third, I want to do it." Connolly could barely contain himself as he barked the end of his debate points, "What's the difference if I'm white, black, or whatever??"

No sound was made for a few seconds. Finally, another evaluator broke the awkward silence and moved the discussion quickly to some procedural question. The visit ended shortly afterward. But before the visit team's departure, the "interrogator" took Connolly aside and complimented him. "Father, I'm so glad you answered the way you did." He continued, "Because sometimes people, when you ask them a question like that, they kind of apologize for their presence. You didn't do any of that."

Connolly thanked him, but was not sure whether he meant what he said. He also realized, *this was not going to be the only time people would question his presence in the middle of this Puerto Rican and Cuban community. But he was not going to have his commitment criticized, especially since he had spent ten years going Spanish, and he had made clear to the community that they would have to be leaders of their community, not him. This interrogator had no idea how much they had worked to create an organization led by the people.*

Tough Compassion

Connolly and the board knew who was largely responsible for the success of Seneca Center. This was Lillian Camejo, a Puerto Rican woman who, along with her Cuban husband, Orlando, came up to Hunts Point from Miami as an adult. Camejo was a savvy woman who had learned to work in the community by just becoming involved. She was directed by a friend to the Peninsula when the center was still just an extension of Summer in the City, and she joined the committee and then the board of directors. Taking on new responsibility whenever it was required, Camejo joined the Seneca staff, first as the senior services director, and then eventually as the director of the Family Services Program.

In Camejo, Connolly saw a leader who combined determination and resourcefulness in the face of challenging situations. As the board met to hear about what Camejo's staff was facing, they identified other needs in the neighborhood that they wanted the organization to handle. As a result, Camejo was eventually managing nine people in three programs: the senior services center, the community services office, and then, across the street, a housing program to combat the deteriorating conditions in the Peninsula's apartment buildings. Like Camejo, the staff members were residents of the Hunts Point–Longwood neighborhood, or people who knew the neighborhood well. Connolly and the board thought it was important to have the organization staffed and led by those who understood the people, their history, and their conditions.

The new community services office for the Seneca Center, where Camejo managed several staff persons who all attended to the sometimes desperate situations families were finding themselves in, was at 832 Hunts Point Avenue. Camejo understood how harsh conditions could be for women who were raising children. She and Orlando were raising two boys, Daniel and David, in a neighborhood with working-class families and a small, supportive church community. But some of the life situations that

Lillian Camejo (*rear*) advises a woman at Seneca Center. (Lillian Camejo's personal collection.)

she heard about from the women who walked through the doors of Seneca Center both broke her heart and heightened her resolve.

On one morning, a woman in her thirties, accompanied by children aged five, six, and seven years old, came in. She had just walked all the way over from Tinton Avenue in neighboring St. Anselm's parish, and she intended to continue to walk until she reached the Bronx River at the end of the Peninsula. But she stopped as she walked by the Seneca Center and went in to share her life situation. She explained to Camejo, who was smoking a Salem cigarette while listening, that she was going to take the three children to the river and drown herself and all of them together. She was in a bad relationship with a negligent husband, had reached a breaking point, and could neither handle her life anymore nor leave the care of her children to this husband.

Camejo, who had no training in psychology or counseling, was stunned. But she looked at the three children and the woman, put out her cigarette, and said, "Come with me." She took them out of the office, escorted them to her car, and drove them over the Forty-First Police Precinct on Simpson Street, which was always very busy, and was becoming known as "Fort Apache." She brought them to the desk sergeant and explained the woman's situation.

"This woman needs your help. Do something!!" she demanded.

The police sergeant responded, putting the woman immediately in contact with other agencies while keeping an eye on her and the children, and they eventually found her a new life and a new apartment in Brooklyn. One and a half years later, the same woman appeared at the door of the Seneca Center. She came with a carton of Salem cigarettes, remembering that Camejo had smoked several of them the morning of her first visit. She told Camejo that she was immensely grateful for saving her life that day.

Another time, Camejo had a visit from a woman who walked in barefoot. Camejo gave her coffee, told her to relax, and let her speak about her family situation. Like the other woman, she was desperately trying to leave a bad relationship. Her husband regularly beat her and her four girls, she told Camejo.

Not waiting to be paralyzed by yet another tragic relationship story, Camejo asked, "Did you call the police??!"

No, replied the woman.

Calling on the desperate woman to assert herself, Camejo asked, "Do you want to get rid of him?"

"Yes," she said.

Camejo got her on the phone with the police and helped her report the most recent beating. In two hours, the police came and took the wife-beater away, and he never returned. But months later, a man came to visit Camejo to complain about how his wife had sent the police to throw him out. She realized that this was the same man whom the shoeless woman had spoken about. She listened to him but said and did nothing. The man left frustrated at this hard-edged, unresponsive woman caseworker.

Camejo became known for her tough, no-nonsense approach to community services. But she and the board knew, especially after hearing many of these stories, that harsh conditions required true compassion, sometimes including decisive action.[26]

A Community of Communities

As the Seneca Center was building its ability to serve the needs of the world, the spiritual and religious community was taking its own steps. In the early days, the community center was also the chapel space. But while the services program moved to other spaces and began to be furnished with desks and equipment, the chapel facility was being ignored. Connolly told the new parishioners, "Don't worry about not having a big ornate church. This is us. We have a community here."

But things reached a breaking point with one parishioner one Sunday. An African American woman said to Connolly after Mass, "Father Connolly, I been comin' to this church here for a while now, and there's only one light bulb left that works."

Connolly was reminded of the request a year earlier not to leave the Peninsula community at the end of Summer in the City and of his challenge to them to lead. "Now, you have to bring it to the assembly after Mass," he told the woman. "Maybe we have fifty people here. You know, Ma'am, I'm not an electrician, I don't know how to fix anything." At the assembly, Connolly followed up about the lighting issue. "Does anybody here, any of you guys know anything about fixing things?" he asked the group. "Because I can't fix it. If you cannot fix it, then, next week we'll be in the darkness." Connolly was clear about his approach to the religious community here, as he was with the service center: *He was going to develop leadership and ownership. They could not develop if they were going to rely on him to do everything.* Within a couple of days, some of the chapel men came over and fixed the whole electrical system.

While this was heartening evidence of the people of God taking responsibility for the church, when the weather warmed up again the light bulbs didn't matter so much. Connolly and the board found that the summertime gave them a chance to help the chapel grow in terms of both space and attendance. They started celebrating Masses outside, on the sidewalk. Neighborhood residents walked by and paused to watch. Connolly thought, *They must be wondering, what the hell is going on? People are sitting outside with these chairs, singing and praying, before this man dressed in this costume? Who are these people?* Connolly was joined by several nuns from the Summer in the City program, playing guitar and leading the worshippers in song. Gradually, others joined in the Mass and attendance grew.

During one of those Masses, a short, dark-skinned Cuban man walked by with his guitar. He watched the Mass and then came up to Connolly and introduced himself with a question. "*Yo no sabía que se podía tocar guitarra en la misa,*" he said. "*En Cuba no se podía tocar guitarra en la misa.*" ("I didn't know you could play guitar in Mass. In Cuba you couldn't play guitar in Mass.")

"*Sí, aquí se puede,*" Connolly reassured him. "*Soy Padre Connolly,*" he added as he shook the newcomer's hand.

"*Mucho gusto, padre,*" replied the Cuban guitarist. "*Pío Mendez, un servidor.*"

"Nice to meet you, too, Pío," said Connolly, who was always recruiting. "Why don't you bring your guitar to our Mass next Sunday?"

After the chapel expanded its reach to the street and secured its new place at the old social club and former Pentecostal church, the leadership team worked to reach more of the neighborhood. They decided to build their church in a different kind of space: in the homes of their neighbors. Chapel leaders were going to visit the apartments of every interested resident in the Peninsula. There, they were going to create "Christian Base Communities," or Comunidades Eclesiales de Base, a different kind of church group than any that Connolly or committee members had ever worked with.

They heard about these communities from Father Edgard Beltrán, a priest who, growing up in Latin America in the wake of Vatican II, came from Colombia to the United States to discuss new approaches to Catholicism.[27] After hearing him at a Florida conference, Connolly invited him to lead workshops in St. Jerome's parish, south of Athanasius, on Alexander Avenue. At the workshop, laypersons from several parishes heard a new kind of message: *You have a meaningful role in the life of the Church. As a baptized Christian, you have a direct responsibility to fulfill the mission of the Church.* Beltrán suggested that laypersons could form small groups to fulfill the mission to understand and discuss scripture and their faith.

Inspired by these messages, Connolly and the Athanasius staff committed to forming "Small Christian Communities" in the parish.[28] Each priest was responsible for creating this program in their part of the parish. Connolly recommended it to the Seneca chapel leaders in the Peninsula, also. He explained the thinking behind the proposed program: *A parishioner can be an anonymous Christian, coming in and out of a church and having no life in the community of the church. It was almost commercial,* Connolly explained; *a parishioner entered a church like a "supermarket" that was holy, and he or she acquired Sacraments from it, as well as Holy Water and Devotions, and other products. But Vatican II, which emphasized the "people of God," a community Church as much as an institutional Church, was a call to end the anonymity.* Referring to the Hebrew term *gahal*, the "Assembly of God," Connolly suggested what Beltrán recommended: *Let us form small communities in the parish. They can meet during the week, and then all come together on Sunday in the big church as a "community of communities."*

Accepting Connolly's recommendations, the chapel leadership joined an international movement, as the parish outpost of the Movimiento Familiar

Cristiano had done a few years earlier. Christian Base Communities were groups of Catholic individuals who met together in neighbors' homes to pray, read scripture, and discuss it in concert with the state of society in the world. These groups would meet regularly, according to a format established by a local parish or diocesan or national program supporting them. With a structured agenda and a facilitator trained to guide the sessions, the Communities were able to involve dozens of groups in a parish and thousands of people in a particular region or country.

The Communities had strong roots in Church history, as Connolly knew from his seminary classes, going back to the beginnings of Christianity as a movement.[29] They followed the words of Jesus encouraging community prayer and fellowship, cited in Matthew 18:20: "Where two or three are gathered in my name, there I am in the midst of them." They also followed the practices of some Jewish communities in their time, of coming together in people's homes to live and worship together. Participants of the early Christian movement gathered to share bread and drink, and they prayed and commemorated the Last Supper. They would also reflect on their lives and on the direction of their movement. For the first three hundred years of Christianity, the "Church" did not mean a centralized institution or building; it only existed in people's homes.[30]

In the twentieth century, the practice of meeting, praying and sharing bread, and discussing the state of the world took on new life in the homes of Catholics again. The Catholic Action movement from Europe, the Christian Family Movement in the United States, and other programs using a small-group format had revitalized Church life for many and encouraged Catholic laypersons to get more involved in society even before Vatican II. Some of these groups encouraged ongoing political action. The Catholic Worker Movement, for example, brought small communities together in prayer and reflection but also advocated for peace, nuclear disarmament, civil rights, and economic justice.[31] Christian Base Communities, emerging from Latin America, were the newest type of small group created with an eye toward building up the Church as both a community and a new society.

Connolly, who had seen his predecessor priests building Athanasius with religious education programs, new societies, and even free legal and social services, wanted to build a new kind of Church through the chapel in the Peninsula. The converted social club would offer indoor Masses and street Masses, but it would also offer more: It would be a network of small religious communities in the apartments on Spofford, Seneca, Bryant, Barretto, Lafayette, and Hunts Point Avenue. The Church of the Peninsula in 1968 would be the Church of the early Christians.

Visits and Relationships

The leadership team of the chapel organized visits to apartments in the neighborhood. Each of the visits followed an agenda developed by one of their leaders, Rafael Collado. Collado, who first became an Athanasius parishioner when Connolly taught him personally for many nights in the rectory, had immersed himself in parish life. An educated Cuban refugee with an electrical engineering degree, Collado joined the chapel leadership team in the Peninsula and developed discussion materials for the team leaders to use in their visits, breaking the sessions into forty-five minutes of prayer, reading, study, and reflection. Teams included priests and religious as well as laypersons, who met regularly to prepare for and later evaluate the visits.

In one weekly session, for example, every apartment group would hold a discussion about the death of Jesus Christ. The group used selected passages from the Bible and asked, "What was the purpose of His death?" Participants in the small group would offer their insights on the question. Each participant was asked to connect the readings and the question with other, broader questions: *What relevance does this have in our lives and in the lives of the people in our neighborhood?* Connolly and the chapel leaders saw these visits as a way to form religious communities and to give faith a meaningful and relevant place in the broader neighborhood. In addition to the work of the Seneca Center, the visits were seen as a way for this growing chapel community to know and analyze the conditions of the neighborhood.

One of the buildings regularly visited by a team was 1314 Seneca Avenue, since some of the leadership lived there. The building had a tenant who was not a chapel member, or even a Christian, but became a friend of Connolly. He was a Jewish doctor who had lived there for decades and still had an active medical practice. Connolly admired the man, not just for being a good neighbor but also for continuing to make house calls even as the neighborhood became more dangerous. Because he was carrying drugs and medicine, however, there was a chance of his being robbed, so he required that anyone asking for a visit have a friend or family member meet him at the front of the building and escort him into and out of the apartment. With that assurance, the doctor visited throughout the neighborhood—even the Little Korea area of Fox Street where Connolly had first administered the sacrament of last rites early in his time at Athanasius. Connolly admired this man for making his own meaningful visits.

The building at 1314 Seneca became a central part of another important chapel activity in the neighborhood: the *parrandas* (group caroling visits) at Christmastime.[32] Seven days before Christmas, a group from the chapel, including Connolly, went to buildings in the area to sing *aguinaldos*, traditional Puerto Rican Christmas songs. Since 1314 had a well-designed, ornate lobby, a leftover from its days as an upper-middle-class building for people moving out of cramped immigrant neighborhoods in Manhattan, the chapel group put up a Christmas tree there and sang the *aguinaldos* there as well. Connolly enjoyed the surprised faces of residents and visitors as they walked in and out of the lobby during the *parranda*.

The *parrandas* were also part of Christmas Eve. After celebrating Midnight Mass in the chapel, the *parranda* group would come together, accompanied on guitar by Pío Mendez, who had become both a faithful parishioner and the semi-official church musician after he saw that street Mass in the summer. They went from one apartment building to another, standing at a friendly door of someone they knew, and began singing from a classic *aguinaldo*, "*Abreme la Puerta, abreme la Puerta. . . .*" Tenants would open the door, smiling and singing, and invite the group in for a drink and song. The *parranderos* would then move on to another apartment, and then others, and finally to the firehouse near the chapel.

On a snowy, cold Christmas Eve in 1968, Connolly celebrated Mass in the chapel with about seventy-five parishioners crowding into the space. In addition to Pío Mendez, a piano player and violinist brought their instruments and provided the music. There was great joy and a sense of community that seemed to be even stronger than the prior year. This was the second Midnight Mass at the chapel, and Connolly felt it was one of the most beautiful things he had ever experienced, or could imagine.

But the following year was even more special for Connolly, because he was joined by his mother, Frances, his brother Denis, and one of Denis's friends. Having heard from Connolly all about this new community, they wanted to see it. Connolly introduced them to the congregation, who gave them a warm welcome. After the Mass, Connolly explained the *parranda* tradition to his guests: "You know, we have a custom here. We sing at some of the apartments in the neighborhood and then we end up going to the firehouse and singing to the firemen. You're welcome to join us, but I know it's cold. I'm not sure if you want to go home but—"

"Oh no," said his mother and brother. "We'll go along."

The newly reinforced *parranda* choir made its rounds and found its way to the last stop. This year, the firefighters had waited up for them and had prepared a table with food and refreshments. Pío played as they sang more *aguinaldos*. Then Denis's friend, a professional Broadway singer, stood up and began singing Broadway show tunes. Connolly sang and talked too, and enjoyed the evening with his family, the parishioners, and the firefighters, as they showed appreciation for each other and the spirit of fellowship.

Connolly sat back and looked at his mother and brother. It reminded him that *there was a time when the Connollys enjoyed their time together as a family. Con Connolly could not afford vacations when they were growing up, but he did make sure to spend time with Frances and all the children in Central Park. The Park was their escape from the city life of a crowded Irish and German neighborhood, a different world just five blocks away. With the children going out to play in this vast park and then returning for food before going back again, the couple savored the leisure time, a time when Frances was healthy. The Connolly family's summer outings in Central Park were the closest thing Con and Frances could get to the life of the old country.* Now, in a firehouse in a remote corner of his neighborhood, Father Neil Connolly could celebrate with his old family and his new one at the same time—which was not something he had envisioned when he was preparing himself for priesthood at Dunwoodie.

As Connolly looked at his parishioners, he also thought with joy about Lyndon B. Johnson's War on Poverty. *It started the process for Summer in the City, which in turn led to the Seneca Center, this special community church and community service organization led by the people. The Peninsula did not actually lose much poverty over these four years and might actually have gotten poorer. In fact, there might not have been much change*

Church on the streets—Seneca Chapel procession in Hunts Point. (Photo by Mili Bonilla.)

in material poverty across Bruckner Boulevard, either, where Gigante and Adams were working closely with the larger part of the parish.

But that was not what Bob Fox was working for, was it?

Fox had taught Connolly and the audience at Mount St. Vincent to see the isolation and desperation among individuals in poor communities. He taught them not to fight against poverty but against the isolation by working for creativity, public forums, and relationships.

Connolly looked at his parishioners and the firefighters, singing and eating and talking in the middle of the night, and he remembered the years of work with the people here that had brought him to this special moment of community. He thought, *We have built relationships with the world here.*

And he thought, *This is an extraordinary bringing together of Church and humankind, with everyone being treated with equal and full dignity. Together, we are sharing this earth, this life, and living in true community, even if for just this one evening. We are old Church, new Church, Puerto Rican, Cuban, African American, Irish, and Italian, singing Spanish folk songs and Broadway tunes, celebrating Church, the neighborhood people, and our neighborhood protectors. I think this is what* Gaudium et Spes *thought the flowering of the kingdom of God on earth might be like. This was not the kingdom—not yet. But if it was even a sneak peek at it,* Connolly thought, *it was good to know they speak Spanish in the kingdom. This night, he had come a long way from Puerto Rico to the Kingdom.*

5

:::

World Struggles, Parish Struggles

Now a man can scarcely arrive at the needed sense of responsibility, unless his living conditions allow him to become conscious of his dignity, and to rise to his destiny by spending himself for God and for others. But human freedom is often crippled when a man encounters extreme poverty, just as it withers when he indulges in too many of life's comforts and imprisons himself in a kind of splendid isolation.

—Article 31, The Community of Mankind, *Gaudium et Spes*, Pastoral Constitution on the Church in the Modern World, 32

Good Night

On a warm Saturday night in 1969, in honor of their pastor's birthday, Neil Connolly and Lou Gigante took out Monsignor Tom O'Brien to the *Bon Soir*, a cabaret in Manhattan's West Village. Gigante, who had grown up in the Village, knew the maitre d' and made reservations for a nice table and arranged for special treatment for the birthday guest. He knew the *Bon Soir* always featured great jazz singers and ensembles, and he selected a night when a favorite singer was scheduled to perform. A surprise replacement, a beautiful Brazilian singer, appeared instead, and she sang a few songs before making an announcement to the audience.

"We have a special guest here tonight," she said as she walked over to Connolly, Gigante, and O'Brien, who wore his collar with the red dot to signify his title as monsignor.

"We have a monsignor here from the Catholic Church, and it's such a pleasure to honor him."

The audience went quiet, wondering what was going on. The lights went down, except for the single spotlight focused on their table, and the Brazilian siren sang "Happy Birthday" to O'Brien, who basked in all the attention. Then, the audience chimed in, and Connolly and Gigante sang and smiled. They were proud to have supported O'Brien, who had created such an open and supportive parish for them, especially during a time of such great change.

In O'Brien's era at Athanasius, as the population grew, the parish also grew in programs and services for the Puerto Rican parishioners. Sunday Mass attendance, which had already reached 5,000 by 1957, reached 8,300 by 1965, and ten Masses were required to support all those participants. Baptisms had already reached almost 1,300 in 1965, and religious education, after all of the programs added by Connolly, reached more than 3,000 children by the same year. Athanasius built upon the Spanish societies, first initiated in 1954, with a Spanish choir, the Christian Family Movement, and Juventud Acción Católica. The sports programs, Summer in the City, Summer Day Camp, and Summer Religious Instruction, as well as the new elementary school, were all launched or expanded at the height of parish growth in 1965. After Vatican II, the parish added even more, organizing a liturgical committee, a school board, a parish finance committee, and a credit union. And, of course, two community organizations—Gigante's Simpson Street Development Association (SISDA) and Connolly's Seneca Center—were special creations of "the Church in the world."[1]

So much had been created through that time for so many parishioners, and yet there were more to reach. A community had to be strengthened further, with more time and help. As the migration into Athanasius slowed down, Connolly thought, *He had a chance to solidify a community that was already dynamic and engaged and ready to become stable and committed to the Church and the world*.

But the O'Brien era would not last forever.

The workload was getting to be too much for him, and he did not have the same energy as he had in 1962. After the *Bon Soir* celebration, a serious bout of pneumonia landed O'Brien in the hospital for several weeks and Gigante, Connolly, and Adams took turns visiting him.

Also, O'Brien was making many more trips down to the archdiocesan headquarters to explain why the parish continued to lose money each year. Connolly noticed how this leader, who had been so garrulous, positive, and open to creativity all those years, would come back so dejected from his trips to headquarters and the "finance people," as the Athanasius priests called them. With all this pressure and his weakening condition, O'Brien obtained a transfer to St. Malachy's (known as "the Actor's Church") in Manhattan's theater district. For him, St. Malachy's would be easier to manage.

Then, in June 1969, Father John Byrne came in to replace O'Brien as pastor, bringing a personal history of activism.[2] A former teacher of Connolly at Cathedral Prep, the "minor seminary" in Manhattan's Westside, Byrne was a part of the community of worker-priests in the times of national and local labor struggles of the 1940s and 1950s. He was a supporter of the Labor Schools created to provide education and support to Catholic workers and union members, and he even taught courses himself.

Byrne's commitment was not confined to the classroom either: In 1949, when the cemetery workers went on strike at the archdiocese–owned Calvary Cemetery in Queens, and Cardinal Spellman countered by sending in seminarians to dig the ditches, Byrne spoke out against Spellman's actions. As a result, he was transferred to Corpus Christi parish on the Upper West Side of Manhattan, an assignment far removed from his real interests in education and labor. And when he spoke out to urge the archdiocese to reorganize its priorities and its resources in 1968, Byrne was again transferred, this time to Athanasius.

In Byrne, Connolly found a decent, hardworking man who stood up for his principles, but not a spontaneous, open-minded man like O'Brien. Byrne allowed continuation of the team ministry approach, especially the team meetings that helped Connolly and Gigante focus on priorities while also creating new programs. But he was very focused on order and administration, and he was more comfortable with budgeting and organization, which he knew, than he was with communicating in the language of the Puerto Rican people, which he never had to learn, or with taking action "on the go." Often, when entering the rectory kitchen, he encountered a spread of folders and piles of paperwork—which Connolly and the team had left to "work on later"—covering every inch of the large table. Seeing this seemingly chaotic paper landscape, Byrne would yell, "We gotta clean this place up!"

Rather than engage in much of the day-to-day rectory activity, Byrne often went to the elementary school to work with the principal and discuss their financial needs and to coordinate the sharing of parish collections to meet those needs. Byrne was fighting a quiet fight against an increasingly impossible reality: The parish was losing people and money.

Connolly had started noticing that some changes were taking place, as the usually heavy parish sacrament workload was beginning to ease. For the years after the big school opened, in 1965, so much new activity was being created by Summer in the City and Vatican II that Connolly did not have much time to pay close attention. Although there were still 2,200 children receiving religious instruction in 1968, a good achievement by any standard, it was still a drop from the 3,000 students in 1965. Baptisms, which had been so important for the new migrants from Puerto Rico a decade ago, went from 1,300 a year to 900 in 1968. And in the most noticeable and essential area of parish life, Sunday Mass attendance, which had reached over 8,000 in 1965, dropped to 3,300 in three years, and then to under 2,000 in Byrne's first year.[3]

Connolly knew that some faces which he had often seen were missing, but when Byrne presented reports on these developments to the team of priests, and everyone heard the numbers, Connolly wondered: *What is going on? Where are the people? Is the parish in trouble? What did we miss?*

There were larger forces at play beyond parish actions and control. The world was changing for Puerto Ricans in New York, as they were hit by three social epidemics—what Connolly would later call an "unholy trinity" of forces that would consume Hunts Point–Longwood.

First Epidemic: Poverty

For decades, families and individuals of Hunts Point–Longwood had depended on wage income to support themselves. Its Puerto Rican adult men and women, who had gone from being half of the neighborhood to two-thirds through the 1960s, were heavily dependent on factory work for that income. And it was just this type of work that was disappearing in New York City during that time.

As Connolly was learning from the *New York Times*, by 1967, New York City officials reported that the city lost over 170,000 industrial jobs since 1950, much of it in the 1960s.[4]

A year later, more bad news about the economic state of Puerto Ricans was coming out. Puerto Rican workers were already receiving low pay, with less than half receiving pay of at least $100 a week.[5] One-third of the city's Puerto Rican families were living on annual incomes under $3,000.[6] With such a heavy dependence on factory jobs, the losses of those jobs also meant very limited options for a population still improving its education levels and English-speaking ability. As a result, as American citizens, they qualified for public assistance and sought it out, in big numbers. By the end of the 1960s, Puerto Rican New Yorkers became 35 percent of all public assistance recipients, the largest of any ethnic group in the city.[7]

In heavily Puerto Rican Hunts Point–Longwood, the income issues made day-to-day life difficult, but the housing conditions even more so. Of the more than 20,000 housing units in the neighborhood, one-third were occupied by poor households.[8] Apartments were more overcrowded in 1969 than in 1960 as more migrants came into New York from Puerto Rico and as poorer family members or entire families shared apartments with relatives who could still afford their apartments.[9] Affordability became an issue as well: Just as households were losing wage income, the average rent in that neighborhood had gone from $76 to $98 during the 1960s.[10] Over three-quarters of the poor households in Hunts Point–Longwood were giving over 35 percent of their income to rent.[11] The housing situation was becoming more desperate, and people needed relief.

So they looked for relief, moving outside of Hunts Point–Longwood in droves.

By 1965, as Puerto Ricans reached 242,000 in number in the borough, the Bronx became their population center.[12] Puerto Ricans were learning about family members who had found apartments in other neighborhoods. Many were feeling less hopeful for their future in Hunts Point–Longwood, which was identified by the Census as the second largest poverty area in the Bronx. Yet people were still moving in, as the Census reported that nearly half of the people at least five years old did not live there in the last five years.[13] But the changes in addresses—many came from other neighborhoods displaced by housing clearance projects—forced Athanasius staff to grapple with changes in the pews and in their programs.

Collections from Sunday Mass were declining rapidly over the decade for a few reasons. Puerto Ricans, who came from a centralized island Catholic Church system that supported its parishes, had not been used to supporting their own church, and it took some time to build a donation tradition within that community. Then, with all the migrations in and out of the neighborhood, it was hard for the parish staff to build a relationship with the newcomers, to get their commitment to the parish. And with the loss of jobs in manufacturing that the Puerto Ricans had relied on, their incomes dropped, and so there were fewer dollars and coins filling the collection box. In the meantime, knowing they could find help at the rectory, at the Seneca Center, and at SISDA for their income and housing and social service needs, the newcomers went to those places. As a result, Connolly and the parish staff came to feel the struggles of their parishioners more closely and more often.

Year after year, the archdiocese kept calling O'Brien down to headquarters to explain why he could not come up with the resources to fund the parish, and a frustrated Connolly was asking questions. He knew that the archdiocese was providing support, but he still wondered: *What does the archdiocese expect? We have done our part, providing the sacraments to thousands of people, counseling people and attracting so many into our parish life and organizations, with just five priests, and now a couple of them have left.*

The archdiocese—with its great facilities on Madison Avenue and the Cathedral on Fifth Avenue, and a vast network of schools and organizations—has found a way to build, and they had wealth from collections and rich donors. What about the people here who came from Puerto Rico, who have struggled and remained, and are now poorer? Could they expect the headquarters staff of the archdiocese to be "in the world," as Vatican II called for, to come up to Hunts Point–Longwood and see the conditions of poverty for themselves and solve those conditions? Or was it just going to be Neil and the Athanasius staff, on their own? Why did this Church have to be this way?

Connolly would soon find, in a different way, how the Church would meet the world. The full immersion in the fate of these Puerto Rican people, for Connolly and the parish staff, had begun in the 1950s and grew through the 1960s. So even as things were declining, and the pockets of the parishioners became emptier, there could be no change to their commitment to parishioners. Connolly could not turn back on going Spanish, on the journey he had traveled through ten years. Their history and their fate would have to be his. Like the birth family he had brought to the Christmas Mass in the Peninsula chapel, the parishioners were his family—for richer, for poorer, in sickness and in health . . .

When in Need . . .

So Connolly, Gigante, and Adams made a decision with Byrne, after many team meetings, to make a simple, risky change. They looked at the budget of the rectory and decided to let go of the cook until things got a little better. Instead of expecting someone to volunteer as a regular cook for the priests, they considered the relationships they had built with their parishioners and appealed to them directly for help.

"Our financial position," said *Connolly* from the lectern during the end-of-Mass announcements, "is such that we would appreciate it if you would invite us to your homes to eat."

"But don't take us all," Connolly continued, explaining how no one family would be asked to take on an unfair burden of feeding all the priests, or even of feeding one priest all the time. Connolly, Gigante, and Adams would accept a schedule that involved eating out in different places.

"We'll go each individually to different homes in the parish," he offered, so that the food preparation would not require anything special to serve one extra guest on one evening every few weeks. He wasn't sure how the people would respond to the unusual request, but they had to try something different, and they had to look inside their parish. The archdiocese would not approve any requests for additional funding, and too little was available from the collections to support any more staff.

But the parishioners responded with delight, as phone calls started coming in to the rectory.

"¿Mira, Padre Neil, porque no pase por la casa esta semana? ¿A usted le gusta la comida hispana?

("Listen Father Neil, why don't you pass by the house this week? Do you like Hispanic food?")

"¿Padre Gigante, tu puedes venir este jueves a las seis?"

("Father Gigante, can you come visit this Thursday at six?")

Even Father Byrne, who couldn't speak a word of Spanish and didn't really know or experience the Puerto Rican culture, found occasional opportunities to share a meal with some of the English-speaking families, including the "leftover" Irish and Italians still living in the neighborhood who worshipped at the English Mass.

This made for a hectic evening schedule for Connolly and his fellow priests. They were always running to and from the dinners and finding a different location to visit almost every night. But Connolly saw an advantage to this hectic and major change: It brought him and the other priests very close to the people, because they were now part of their parishioners' homes. Even in the apartments of less familiar households, Connolly experienced a positive and dynamic mix of curiosity, caution, and pleasant engagement.

Once, when visiting the family of an altar boy, Connolly sat at the dining table with just the altar boy—with the boy's family standing and watching from the kitchen, wondering whether Connolly knew how to eat the food, or whether he would appreciate it. Once he cleared the plate, the family realized that Connolly would be all right with them, and they could perhaps eat together with him in the future.

Connolly went to many apartments where he was the not-so-well-known leader of a church to which the host belonged. Usually, by the end of the evening, he became much better known to the host family, and in the process belonged more to them. To him, they were opening up their apartments, which showed their economic situations. They had old kitchen furniture and equipment, but always enough food to serve every member and a guest. Used sofa furniture, sometimes covered with plastic covers for long-term cleanliness and durability, surrounded a small television and a radio or record player. Everything in the apartment, he noted, was clean—immaculately clean.

By the end of such a visit, after back-and-forth conversation, he would have proven to the host that he felt at home in the Puerto Rican culture. He was not just a priest who spoke Spanish; he had been to the *campos* in Puerto Rico, he celebrated in the *Fiesta San Juan Bautista*, he had played volleyball in the summer with the children and neighbors. He had gone Spanish, and with this visit, he showed he was sharing part of their life with them.

Connolly thought, *This is how a priest can live: He can tell the laypeople of his community that he is vulnerable, without as much power as he might seem to have, in their eyes. He can turn to them and say, I am trusting that you will care for me when I am in need, as I care for you when you are in need. The "Church in the world" was not something just theoretical, out there*, he thought. *It was right in this apartment.*

He saw his host family and thought, *I am the priest of "the church," without the power of "the church," at your mercy, in your world, here in this apartment, and the next one, and the next one. The "servant priest," whose role was defined by Vatican II as caring for "the priesthood of the laity," the "people of God," was being cared for by them. A priest can live that way and still be a priest*, he thought. *Maybe even more of a priest than before.*

A Resourceful School

The financial problems with the parish, Connolly knew, came from Athanasius Elementary School, the same one which had been welcomed with joy and anticipation at the grand opening in 1965.[14] In making a commitment to greater education for the low-income children of Hunts Point–Longwood, along with all other schools in Spanish parishes, Spellman and the archdiocese found themselves in a situation comparable to the urban dioceses across the country.

Sunday collections in the inner-city parishes of these dioceses were expected to support the day-to-day operations of the school as well as the church. Schools faced a major loss of women religious, who had been the teaching workforce to the nation's Catholic school system for decades.

Many religious were opting for a more active role in social services and community organizations, especially after Vatican II. In their place, lay-persons who went to teach in the inner-city schools cost more than the religious. In addition to the school costs, school revenues were lower in the 1960s, as many of the lower-income families who moved into the inner-cities could not afford the tuition.

St. Athanasius Elementary School had seen a lot in its fifty years, under the guidance of the Sisters of Charity. Based in the Riverdale community of the Bronx, this religious order had been active in inner-city and poor neighborhoods of New York City, including Hunts Point–Longwood. The Sisters of Charity were led by Sister Margaret Dowling, who had worked with Monsignor Robert Fox to create Summer in the City as a pilot program in St. Brigid's on the Lower East Side before it became the signature War on Poverty program of the archdiocese.[15]

Since 1913, the Sisters of Charity had a teaching presence in St. Athanasius Elementary School, beginning with the little building behind the church on Fox Street. They lived in the neighborhood, in a convent at 955 Bruckner Boulevard, and moved to the top floor of the new elementary school building on Southern Boulevard after its opening. Beginning in the 1960s they were an active presence in Hunts Point–Longwood and became involved in services, in Summer in the City, and in the founding and growing of the SISDA and Seneca Center organizations.

One of those active in the parish, and a founding board member of the Seneca Center, was Sister Ann Marie Lafferty.[16] After taking vows as a novice to join the Sisters of Charity, Lafferty went to Athanasius Parish in the summer of 1967, when she joined Connolly in the Peninsula for Summer in the City.

Lafferty began teaching that year in the new elementary school and, after a few years, became its principal. Living in the convent at the new school was a benefit for Lafferty and her colleagues in the order, since they were closer to the goings-on in the neighborhood as well as the school. With a working-class background, a sensitivity to children's needs, and a determination to get things done, as well as a sense of humor, Lafferty was a natural for the parish.

Parents who registered their children at Athanasius were fearful for their children in the public schools and enticed by Athanasius's strong reputation for quality education. But meeting the monthly tuition was a challenge for many of the families. The school, conscious of the burden tuition could place on families, tried to lessen other household costs. For starters, in addition to nourishing the young minds, the school nourished their bodies as well. At first, the school offered free breakfast and lunch to all students. Then it went further: All of the food and drink not consumed on any given day at school would be donated to school families the following day. Many mothers took full advantage of both food offers.

Most parents at Athanasius Elementary were first-generation, working-class Puerto Ricans, with a smaller group of Irish families. And although most could only show their appreciation to the school with a thank-you or a gift at Christmastime, some found other ways. For example, Sixto Rojas, who worked at a large publishing company with an abundance of unused copying paper, brought reams to the school on a regular basis. Also, Adela Rivera, who worked as a cleaning woman at a major commercial bank, regularly brought boxes of paper clips. Their contributions were often just what the staff needed to make ends meet on supplies.

The students were dedicated and hopeful, even if some were challenging. One favorite of Lafferty was a boy named Hector, whose behavior in class was so bad that he spent nearly every day of his school life in her office. Lafferty knew his family situation, as she did that of every student in Athanasius Elementary. With no father living there to help, and a mother with three boys, Hector was not receiving much attention. Yet Lafferty's regular interaction with Hector helped him get the attention, and he managed to graduate.

In another sign of how challenging some students could be, the first principal, Sister Rita Nawasky, learned to look beyond the smiles of her youth to know them. One time, she was surprised to see three schoolboys walking down the block near the school, smiling and waving at her as they were carrying some groceries. She asked what they had, and they showed her the contents: some ham, some cheese, and some baked goods.

Nawasky, thinking that the boys were gentlemen running an errand to the grocery store for their families, replied, "That's very nice, boys. See you tomorrow." At the school, when she looked at Lafferty and the other sisters there and told them about her encounter, they just grinned.

"What happened?" asked Nawasky.

They explained that the kitchen had just been checked for the following day's supplies. They were missing three items: ham, cheese, and baked goods.

With all the good work her school was doing to instill values in the children, Nawasky realized that even a principal had to learn to be streetwise. In the struggle against "the streets" for the minds of the young, Athanasius Elementary School sometimes lost.

"The streets" were a deceptive, two-sided coin for the parish school staff, playing the role of giver and taker of community and life. These were the same streets where they, along with their colleague, Trudy Collins, known as Sister Thomas, and with Connolly, Gigante, and Adams, had created and carried out the Summer in the City program in the three areas of the parish. With those streets, they met strangers, built relationships, formed organizations, and served even more than the thousands they were already serving in the parish. Often these streets were active with shoppers on Southern Boulevard, Westchester Avenue, and Simpson Street, or people on their way to work or to appointments.

But they were also active with groups of younger and older men. Some looked out on the street, waiting for someone, while others exchanged small bags and cash, and one or two were standing, staring down, nodding their heads and bent at the knees and waist. In building lobbies and stairways, in front of local bodegas, at busy street corners, and even across from the church and school, those groups of men were in the world that the school and parish were fighting to keep their young people from.

The world of heroin.

Second Epidemic: Heroin

Like the Puerto Ricans, heroin migrated significantly into New York City after the Second World War. Unfortunately for them, the heroin trade also arrived in the same neighborhoods where the Puerto Ricans were concentrated and in their neighboring black communities.

As early as 1950, there were warnings about heroin for young people from Hunts Point–Longwood and New York. The New York County Medical Society warned about a rise in narcotics addiction, with the greatest rise among the city's teenagers occurring in the Bronx.[17] Then, testimony by a social worker in 1953 put the number of addicts in New York under 21 at 7,500.[18] In Connolly's first year at Athanasius, in 1958, a local Protestant pastor was providing comfort and support to the addicts of East Harlem, by then one of the fast-growing Puerto Rican settlements in New York.[19] Reverend George Calvert was calling for large-scale public medical action to fight the heroin epidemic, which was claiming an estimated 25,000 New York addicts by then.

In one decade, that number grew four times. The newly appointed Addiction Services Commissioner, Puerto Rican doctor Efrem Ramírez, estimated that by 1967, there were 100,000 heroin addicts in New York City, and another 100,000 nonnarcotic drug users.[20] Addicts were spending about $23 a day on their habit, and committed regular theft to support that spending. The addiction was costing the city $10 million a day in drug-related thefts.[21] Those funds were going to an industry that had reached sophisticated levels of organization and reach. This included the Bronx, where young adults reportedly served as "packagers" in twenty-six heroin "factories," apartments used to collect, prepare, and distribute heroin throughout the borough.[22]

Schools in poor Bronx neighborhoods saw the problem. In Morrisania, for example, uniformed and plainclothes police detectives made many arrests of teenage heroin users and dealers at the Morris High School playground and surrounding schoolyards. Many of the users stole from cars and buildings to maintain their habits; car radiators sold at 48 cents a pound and tenement copper pipes at 38 cents a pound.[23] The school was filling up with younger students who bought "snorting" heroin, which was inhaled, for $21 a bag, and older ones who bought "skin-popping" heroin (injected through the skin) at $3 to $5 a bag.[24] Users often had to become dealers as well as thieves to support habits ranging from $8 a day to $50 a day. But the police in the area knew that the heroin industry was not as serious as it was in neighboring Hunts Point–Longwood.

Those who tried to avoid the problems of heroin by staying off the streets found it in the buildings of Hunts Point–Longwood. Not only did the dealers and users take to the lobbies and stairways of those buildings; apartments were clustering as well with heroin consumers and producers. At 1029 Simpson Street, a building two blocks from the Forty-First Precinct, several apartments in several floors were occupied by teenagers. After a tenant's family vacated an apartment there, some of the teenagers would "settle" and claim the apartment without resistance from the landlord. There, they popped and snorted heroin and sniffed airplane glue, the "drug of choice" for those poorer users living near a hardware store with an unknowing or unscrupulous owner. More apartments were vacated and then reoccupied by another group of teenage users, until much of 1029 was controlled by these groups, who came to collectively identify themselves as the "Glue Angels." The precinct, despite protests and calls from many tenants, did not remove them.[25]

Nobody in authority, it seemed, was stopping the epidemic of heroin addiction, or enforcing laws to stop the epidemic from taking the neighborhoods.

An Innovative Program

In early 1969, Athanasius staff were facing the drug epidemic striking at Hunts Point–Longwood. Without any treatment programs in New York City at the time except for the Ferbstein Clinic at Beth Israel, and the only connection outside being a treatment program in Lexington, Kentucky, Connolly and the others had few options. Drug addicts were coming into the rectory every week, sometimes day after day. Through trial and error, the priests learned to turn away most of those who asked for money, knowing that they likely would turn to robbery and burglary on the streets.

When any mother of an addict came looking for assistance, Connolly and the others recommended a "tough-love" approach, telling her to take away the keys until he went to a rehabilitation or treatment center.

"Straighten him out, or he will rob you again, and again, and keep using heroin."

Very often, the mother would say, "Oh no, I couldn't do that kind of thing. I couldn't abandon my son." Connolly and the other priests did not have any answers, but they knew one thing: They were burying overdose victims as regularly as they were counseling the mothers.

For several years, whenever that tough-love conversation was over, Connolly would wonder: *Where is the archdiocese on this? From the parish statistical reports we are sending down, they might not know a thing. But they must know, from the reports that John Ahern was sending from the Bronx Catholic Charities office, that the parishes are facing an epidemic. Do they not want to help us? Why don't they call us down to headquarters, bring us together on the drug problem, and create some answers? They called all the priests down for conferences and workshops when we were all changing the language and music of Church sacraments after Vatican II, didn't they?*

Connolly thought, *It was as if the parish were invisible to them now. They came up for the dedication of the big new school just a year or two ago, and then . . . no more. They would have to face the drug addiction problem as they had faced the poverty of the parishioners at Athanasius, he realized—on their own.*

Then, in the fall of 1969, Athanasius opened the doors of its former convent, a three-story house at 955 Bruckner Boulevard, to a new drug treatment program.

An organization called Odyssey House, founded by therapist Judy-Anne Densen-Gerber, would run the program at the old convent. Despite not having a New York State license to operate the program, Densen-Gerber and her staff persuaded the parish staff that this program was needed, that it could work, and that it could not wait. Densen-Gerber, a tireless and vocal advocate for treatment programs for addicted teenagers, pointed out that there were about 25,000 such teenagers in Harlem, East Harlem, and the South Bronx combined.[26]

The entire state, meanwhile, had funded the creation of four thousand treatment "beds," fewer than those needed for the 100,000 addicts within its borders.[27] Odyssey House's program for teenagers at the old Athanasius convent was the only one of its kind in the state. Connolly and the staff, desperate for answers, agreed to Gigante's recommendation to establish this program for treating some of the young addicts in their neighborhood.

Connolly, Gigante, and the staff found the Odyssey House program to be helpful in a few ways. It gave Connolly a thorough understanding of what therapy was and what particular approach was being applied in this therapy program. It also gave him more clarity about what was actually going to give a young person another chance at life, at a new life. Besides the comfort of shelter and food, as well as the security of a watchful staff, the therapy itself was disciplined. There were marathon one-on-one sessions with a given resident, with questioning that was intended to "break down defenses," to make the person become vulnerable again and learn to live with their vulnerabilities and seek support from others. The session could continue for several hours—sometimes as long as 24 hours—just so that the staff could achieve the point where the resident was "stripped" of their old ways and ready for a new one. There were up to thirty-five residents at a time, aged fifteen to eighteen, male and female, living in the Odyssey House program.[28]

Odyssey House staff also helped the Athanasius staff better handle the neighborhood addicts who came to the rectory looking for money. Their financial needs appeared reasonable to Connolly at first.

"It's just this once, Father."

"You know, I gotta go to treatment."

"I don't have the carfare for getting to my appointment."

"I have to get away to be with my relatives in New Hampshire."

But Connolly found many of the same people came back, again, still giving those explanations.

Connolly was taught by the Odyssey House managers to call their staff when an addict came looking for money, whatever their explanation.

"Call us, Father," a staff member would say. "We know. We've been through this."

After that offer, Connolly had such a visitor, and he called the Odyssey House person, who told him, "Father, tell the guy to wait. We'll be right over."

In a few minutes, the Odyssey House staff member came in and Connolly brought him to the waiting room to meet the visitor. Connolly then stayed to observe the dialogue and therapy in action. After the visitor answered some questions that got progressively tougher, the Odyssey House staff person stopped the explanation with a confrontation.

"Don't give me any of that bullshit, man!"

Connolly was startled and fascinated, as the staff person continued with the confrontational style: "I've been on the streets like you've been on the streets. I know what the fuck you've been looking for."

The staff member then told the addict that he could take him down to a treatment program right then, or he could call him later and get him to treatment. Or he could leave. In any case, there would be no money.

In a neighborhood with so many young people being lost to addiction, Odyssey House was a welcome presence for Connolly. Yet just as the program was getting through its first year, the rectory got a call from the archdiocese: The consulters were coming uptown to discuss parish properties.

Connolly and the staff knew what that meant: The consulters were priests designated by the archdiocese to conduct team visits to parishes to assess the condition and repair needs of properties owned by the archdiocese—rectories, schools, land, and even convents. In this case, Connolly was told, they wanted to see the convent, and the visit team included Bishop Head, Catholic Charities executive director. Connolly and Gigante, who never told the archdiocese about their leasing the convent to Odyssey House for a dollar, could not refuse or cancel the visit. Yet, they could not let the consulters see the property and risk losing the only teen treatment program around that was actually saving some lives.

So they greeted the consulters—whom they often jokingly referred to in private as the "insulters"—and sat them down in the rectory dining room. There, they offered the guests some coffee and snacks, and Connolly and Gigante began talking . . . and talking . . . and talking even more. Connolly would discuss some subject, and Gigante would follow up and engage the consulters in discussions about the parish, about the properties, and about anything and everything. Gigante even led conversations about sports events—"Did you guys see that game last night?"

Then, with five minutes left on the scheduled visit, a consulter asked, "Hey, shouldn't we go over and see the convent? We're really out of time."

Head responded, "Oh, I think we've gotten an adequate explanation from these guys. We don't need to see anything," and the team left, to the relief of Connolly and Gigante.

After the visit, Connolly was joking around with Gigante about how crazy they were for thinking they could pull off a diversion and marveling at the fact that they did. But at the day's end, all sorts of feelings rushed forward in Connolly's mind.

Here he was, hiding a good program to "live another day," to give those young people a chance to live another day. But these were just a few dozen out of several hundred, maybe a thousand youth, in Hunts Point–Longwood, who were condemned to addiction, to suffering alone, to either a fast or slow death sentence. Their families—the ones who loved them so much they could not confront them with an eviction threat—were condemned to serve out the same sentence. Connolly, who had expected as a seminarian to counsel a number of people during his priesthood, was counseling too, too many.

The one answer was there, in Odyssey House, where people knew what to do. Yet he had to "protect" the program from his own Church, or they would certainly face a shutdown. Why couldn't he trust that his Church, which was funding programs in other properties, would allow this one? Why couldn't they put their resources to serve the people?

He realized, *he and Gigante had challenged the authority of the Church, because they had to: These were desperate times, when the parish was losing many people to other neighborhoods in just a couple of years. In addition to those people, the parish was losing the same generations of young people whom he had worked so hard to recruit through the religious education programs at Hunts Point Palace and the makeshift playgrounds on Tiffany Street and Simpson Streets and the trips to Bear Mountain Park. Now they were being recruited by dealers into a death march. He was a priest for those young people through the years and he had to build a community for them every chance he could. Now, even if it was only a community of thirty-five, even if it was only saving this community rather than building it, and even if he had to defy the Institutional Church to do so, he would do it.*

Meanwhile, the Church of New York tried to catch up. The Archdiocese of New York, after years of the rapidly accelerating epidemic, attempted to do something by funding some treatment programs in other parts of the region. Father Daniel Egan, known as the "Junkie Priest" for working with addicts for years, operated a program on the campus of Graymoor Monastery in Rockland County, north of the Bronx, for female addicts aged fifteen to twenty-one. A program in Mount Kisco, run by ex-addicts, served other current addicts and provided group therapy. The Catholic Youth Organization (CYO), known for its vast sports programs for urban dioceses, operated the American Mobilization to End Narcotics (AMEN), an honor system to commit tens of thousands of youth not to use narcotics. Services Through Organized People (STOP), a new effort based in five East Bronx parishes, provided education to mostly middle-class young people.

Motivational Guidance Associates, in Manhattan, used self-motivation rather than discipline to help in-patient and out-patient addicts recover.

All were experimental and drug-free, but the archdiocese also supported a new form of program—known as "methadone maintenance," using a heroin substitute called methadone, which was considered less lethal—at St. Vincent's and St. Clare's Hospitals in Manhattan, at Misericordia Hospital in the Bronx, and at St. Frances Hospital in Poughkeepsie. There was controversy over the methadone maintenance strategy, with some calling it a substitution of one addiction for another. However, Bishop Edward Head, director of Catholic Charities in the Archdiocese of New York, defended the use of all approaches to the epidemic:

> The scale of narcotics addictions and the associated problem of crime has reached alarming proportions.

Third Epidemic: Crime

While they struggled against the epidemics of poverty and heroin in Hunts Point–Longwood, Connolly and the others were confronted by another epidemic, one that would strike at every aspect of parish life: crime.

In the 1960s, crime came in greater numbers into New York City. In 1965, when the Athanasius population was at its height and the new school opened, there were 26,000 felonies in the Bronx. By 1969, the number of Bronx felonies nearly tripled to 70,000.[29] Much of that growth was in robberies and burglaries, which were in the streets, the buildings, and even the cars of the Bronx.

Where poverty was concentrated, in the city of New York, so was the crime. By 1967, six of the eighty police precincts accounted for more than a third of the felonies "against the person"—assaults, robberies, murders, and rapes.[30] All were in the areas already defined as "slum area" in New York: Bedford-Stuyvesant, Harlem, and the South Bronx. There were three in the southern and southeastern Bronx—the Forty-First, Forty-Second, and Forty-Eighth Precincts—where poverty was harshest in the Bronx. The Puerto Rican communities living there, already struggling with the loss of jobs and with a heroin epidemic claiming their younger generations, were also living in fear for their lives.

The parishioners of Athanasius and their neighbors in Hunts Point–Longwood had perhaps more reason than any other area to live in fear. The Forty-First Precinct, which covered Hunts Point–Longwood, reported the highest number of murders of any precinct in the city. Statistics painted a stark picture: More than 5,000 burglaries and grand larcenies, nearly 700 auto thefts, 2,500 robberies and assaults, 72 rapes, and 33 murders occurred there.[31] Every form of crime threatened every corner of the neighborhood in 1967, and the situation would get worse year after year.

Police explained that this precinct had high levels of unemployment, a larger number of young people than other areas, and severe overcrowding in the neighborhood buildings. The Forty-First Precinct was among the most populated in the city, with 160,000 residents, compared to areas such as Yorkville, where Connolly grew up, with 130,000.[32] Crime was on the minds of everyone in Hunts Point–Longwood, including the staff of Athanasius parish and the Sisters of Charity at the school.

In the school convent, they responded to the growing crime problem in different ways. Since the sisters had problems with burglaries, they called in a handyman to reconfigure the windows on their fourth-floor space so that they would open only eight inches high. Above that height, an alarm would go off, a technology innovation meant to scare off thieves. Then, Sister Ann Marie was called to come in to the Forty-First Precinct. The friendly Irish desk sergeant told her, upon arrival, that her used Volkswagen had been robbed. He then advised the disappointed sister that she should use a new technology, since the car's ignition had been broken:

> Sister, take this screwdriver and use it to turn on the car. Until you get a new key, okay?

For Lafferty, theft was not new, but she thought they had protected themselves pretty well with the convent window alarm, outsmarting the burglars. Now, she learned about car thefts and new uses for screwdrivers.

For his part, Connolly saw how much crime was affecting his parishioners. People were frightened to come home from work or attend meetings. He noted how two men who had early morning shifts for work, one at five o'clock in the morning and the other at two, spoke about the danger of walking or driving or subway trips to work in the dark of night. "You're still alive, eh?" one said to the other, as they laughed, after a meeting in the rectory. With the constant threat of crime, they could do nothing but earn a living, be extra careful, and keep their sense of gallows humor.

Then, after nighttime meetings, Connolly worked to take his car out to deliver the women back safely to their homes. It was not enough to drop them off at the front door, since trouble could be waiting in the stairways or halls.

Once, Connolly arrived at Lillian Camejo's Southern Boulevard building and instructed the rest of the group: "Remain in the car. I'm going to accompany her upstairs."

When he went upstairs with Camejo, he was wondering, *Will I get out of the building?* After he had dropped her off and came down the stairs, he saw some men standing in the lobby who looked to him like they were waiting for someone vulnerable to get into the elevator. Once he left the building, he quickly got into the car and prepared to hurry to the next building. Then a sudden noise shocked the passengers: *Boom!* A projectile crashed into the window shield, shattering the quiet anxiety of the passengers, but the window remained intact. It was a can of beer, thrown by one of the men whom Connolly and Camejo had probably interrupted during a deal.

As Connolly sped off, he asked the women if they were all right, and they assured him they were. But he began to think about them and about Camejo, particularly about their daily life. *These were heroic people*, he thought. *They were living in this atmosphere, day by day, seeing users wake up in the hallway in the morning, and the dealers and users trading cash and plastic bags. They must have been praying as they went in and out of the buildings, 'Please God, don't let them hurt me or my family.' But they had no place to go*, he thought. *This was their neighborhood, their parish, their building. They had to make it their home, where they would raise their family and build their community. What strong, good people!*

At that time, the streets could seem filled with tension. Little Korea, where he visited the murdered SRO tenant and gave him last rites, was an area that generated tension. A superintendent from a building in little Korea once asked Connolly to walk with him, in priest cassock, to calm things down, and he did that evening.

But on another night, he was walking near the elevated train station at Simpson Street and Westchester Avenue, when he heard the screeching wheels of the train curving along the tracks and a simultaneous *Boom Boom!*. He knew gunshots had been fired, and he then saw a man lying in the streets, writhing in pain. People had scattered and a car sped away, and then the people started to return to the scene and the man in the street. Out of nowhere, a siren screamed and a police car arrived at the scene, and two detectives jumped out of the car, with guns drawn, ordering everyone to back away. They looked at the man, and without speaking to a person, picked the man up and threw him into the back seat of the car before speeding off. Other police cars came in afterward and dispersed the crowd that was gathering at the location of the shooting. *That was the nature of* crime, Connolly thought: *It could happen at any moment on any corner and to anyone. Even to the priests.*

Even during the O'Brien era, robberies and burglaries took place in the church. When a worshipper wanted to pray for a particular person or a solution to a personal crisis, she often went to an alcove with the statue of the Virgin Mary or of Jesus Christ, lit one of several dozen candles below the statue, and placed an offering in a metal coin box. The coin box, however, was being regularly broken into in the later 1960s, as the drug activity increased, and thefts increased, including burglaries.

After several replacements of the box and the loss of several hundred dollars, the normally positive and friendly O'Brien had enough and took action. He purchased a new coin deposit near the last bench, built a durable pipe where the coins would go through down into a safe box in the basement, and had an alarm system installed that was attached to the basement safe box. The box was emptied every day by one of the priests and the collection coins were taken to the bank for deposit.

Then, one night while watching the eleven o'clock news on television, the priests heard an alarm bell.

O'Brien knew exactly what had happened.

"What the hell is the matter with you guys? The alarm! I spent five thousand dollars on that alarm! Someone's broken into the basement! Do something!"

So Gigante and Connolly jumped up, grabbed some item to use as a potential weapon, and ran into the backyard.

While running out, they yelled at O'Brien, "Call the cops!"

It was pitch black as they stood outside the basement door in their pajamas and with their makeshift weapons in hand as they waited for the burglar, or burglars, to come out with money in hand.

Maybe with a weapon, too, they thought.

The door opened, little by little, with the basement light growing from a sliver to an open flood, exposing a man with his hands out and up.

The burglar whispered to the priests, *"Por favor, no tienen que tener miedo, yo no voy hacer na'."* ("Please, you don't have to be afraid, I'm not going to do nothin'.")

Connolly did not see him holding anything in his hands. He thought, *The man got frightened when the alarm went off and was about to escape when they trapped him.*

Just then, two police officers came right behind them, running in the backyard. Everything was dark in the back, except for the basement light.

"Father, for God's sake!!" blurted out one of the officers, shattering the quiet tension between the priest and the burglar. His gun was pointed at the basement door where Gigante, Connolly, and the burglar stood, astonished.

"Put a black shirt on or something next time, Father. We were going to shoot you!"

Connolly was confused and afraid like everyone else. Later, he realized, *he could have been dead, shot like the man he saw lying on the street under the subway tracks. At any moment, at any corner, by anyone.*

Then there was the wave of car battery thefts which Connolly had to contend with. It was usually in the mornings when Connolly would discover what had happened. After several tries at turning the key in the ignition, Connolly would get no response from the car, except that "err-ugh, err-ugh," a motorized grunt that sounded as disgusted as he felt.

"Oh shit," he replied back to the car before getting out and looking to find the car parts store and search for a new battery.

After too many mornings like that one, Connolly was motivated to buy the latest protective device against thefts—chains that could tie down the hood so closely to the rest of the car that only the most agile, long-fingered, and determined car thief could do something with it.

As it started to lose residents, Tiffany Street, along with everything and every person located on it, was a potential target for theft. One building on the block was emptied out, so there were fewer lights and there was less activity on the street. Most people walked in the street instead of on the sidewalk to avoid getting mugged or, worse, to avoid getting attacked by someone inside the dark vacant building.

Connolly noticed this more often as he stepped out of his car at night, coming back home. He was motivated to make self-defense "pacts" with a neighbor from across Tiffany Street. "Let's work together" said the neighbor, who had been victimized by car thieves. Connolly agreed: "If you guys see anything, call us. If we see anything, we'll call you."

The "lookout" partnership was put to the test one night when Connolly received a call. Someone got into his car and stole a battery, and he was starting to walk quickly toward Intervale Avenue.

Connolly told Gigante and they said, "Let's go."

They ran down the stairs and out through the rectory door, past Tiffany Street, onto Fox Street, toward Intervale Avenue. The athlete-priests ran quickly, since the thief was also speedy. But while Connolly was fully dressed, running in his shoes and clerical garb, Gigante, who wasted no time, was running in his pajamas and sneakers. Seeing the thief run into the *Arco Iris* bar at Intervale Avenue near 163rd Street, they followed right in and stood in the middle of the bar, asking for the man who ran in. They received no answers and knew he had escaped or hidden with someone's help. They left in disappointment and even received some ridicule.

As they walked out, someone muttered, "¡Qué vergüenza, el padre Gigante corriendo detrás de un hombre y en sus pajamas!" ("What shamefulness. Father Gigante running after a man, and in his pajamas!")

It seemed that nothing they could do would keep the priests safe, not even their "guard dog." A Belgian Shepherd, a super-sized version of a German Shepherd, was the house pet, having been brought to the rectory as a small pup by Gigante, who named him Guaglióne (Italian for "little boy" and pronounced "wa-joan"), and he grew up with the staff. At full size, he was large, described by a local news reporter as having "the head of a lion." Loved by Connolly and Gigante and Anna, the cook, who later rejoined the staff, Guaglióne was hated by Byrne, who was frustrated at his barking attacks at clerics, workers, and others who visited the rectory.

One day, while everyone was seated doing their paperwork at the kitchen table and Anna was cooking, a local junkie ran into the room. This man was known in the neighborhood and tolerated by the priests, who remembered the time when he was high and threw a Molotov cocktail through a window into the rectory. Gigante and Connolly, who quickly put out the Molotov and fire, had him arrested, but they realized he was high and didn't press charges. So when he ran past the front office secretary and into the dining room this time, they looked up and thought, *Him? What now?*

"Hey man!" he yelled, looking around at all of them. "We're here!"

They stared at him.

"What are you doing here??" he asked them, without an explanation for his question. They did not ask for one.

"Get out of here!!" was the priests' joint response, and he ran out of the room and rectory.

After seeing this, Byrne furiously looked at Guaglióne, who never even raised his large head at the invader.

"Look at this," said Byrne.

"Here we are, our lives are being threatened by a crazed drug addict and the dog is sleeping in the corner. But he harasses the bishop when he comes for confirmation. He traps the Con Ed man, where they have to climb up the wall. All the members of the union, the faithful, he's attacking. But he doesn't attack the bad guys. What kind of a dog is this?"

Everyone knew Byrne was right. But they couldn't understand Guaglióne's actions, just as much as they couldn't understand the junkie interloper. They had too many things on their mind, and they had learned to accept Guagliòne and the junkie.

Connolly tried to pay attention to greater struggles. After all, they were contending with the unholy trinity—the epidemic of poverty, the epidemic of heroin, and the epidemic of crime—all striking the neighborhood in the same years, with one furious blow after another. Like any epidemic, they ate away at the health of the neighborhood, the people, and the parish. And even with all their extraordinary programs, the parish could not protect all their parishioners from the great toll the epidemics took on their health and their mental health, especially on the younger parishioners. When they struggled, Connolly, who had taught and played with hundreds of youth over the years to protect them and nurture them, struggled for answers.

Youth in Trouble

One was a teenage boy whom Connolly had gotten to know a little through the religious education programs over the years and the boy's regular visits to the rectory with other young people. Sometimes, when Connolly would see him and say hello, he seemed to be uncomfortable or even troubled. He couldn't always express himself well enough to let Connolly know what was happening in his life. Like others who came in the earlier migrations, he struggled with the English language as well.

"¿*Le molesta si hablamos Español, Padre?*" ("Do you mind if we speak Spanish, Father?")

Connolly said, "*No, no me molesta.*" ("No, doesn't bother me at all.") He was so pleased that the young boy trusted him and was confident enough in Connolly's Spanish to open up.

"*Mi Mama me dijo que soy travieso,*" ("My mom said I am wicked") the boy said about his mother, a well-known beautician from the neighborhood. Then he paused and said, "*Lo hice porque yo he hecho cosas malas.*" ("I did it because I've done bad things.")

Connolly was looking at him quizzically until he noticed that the boy's shirt was getting dark at the chest level. Dark red spots were appearing, and Connolly realized he was bleeding. As Connolly hurried to take off the boy's shirt and take him to the bathroom, the boy continued speaking in Spanish. He explained to Connolly that his mother said he was doing bad things in his life because there was evil in his heart. She told him that he had to get the evil out of his heart. The boy took the steps that his mother had recommended.

"*Trate de quitarlo de mi Corazón*," ("I tried to take it out of my heart") he said, explaining that he used a knife and began, but that it hurt too much.

After putting bandages on him, Connolly put a new shirt on him and hurriedly walked him over to the beauty salon near the rectory, where his mother was cutting someone's hair.

She saw the two and stopped.

Connolly walked right up to her with the boy and said, "You need to take your son to the emergency room. He's bleeding."

The woman looked at them dismissively. "I'm not going to do nothing," she said. "You take him to the emergency room. I can't do anything to save that boy."

Connolly challenged her. "You're not going to do anything? You're not taking him to the doctor?"

"No," she said.

"I'm not his father," said Connolly. "They won't treat him without permission from his mother or father."

Connolly gave a look at the mother, then the boy, and then he left, feeling helpless.

He never heard from the boy again.

On another occasion, Connolly found another lost young person, but under different circumstances. There was a smart, attractive, and pleasant seventeen-year-old girl who was also a regular visitor to the rectory. The oldest daughter of a mother with mental illness and an alcoholic father, she assumed the caretaker role for all her siblings. She ensured that her younger sister and fifteen-year-old twin brothers were registered in school and attending it. Also, she arranged for their medical appointments and accompanied them for those appointments. At the same time, she worked in a local *fábrica* (factory) while attending high school.

The pressure of living with these responsibilities was great for this girl, who was already living the life of the adult women in her neighborhood. Connolly first learned about her life when she made a visit to the rectory and explained her life situation to Connolly. The visit was followed by several others as Connolly tried to understand her situation and give her support by listening to and reassuring her that she would be all right. He did this while also trying to identify resources to help her. She became more concerned about the siblings not attending school and her not being able to sort things out while trying to hold onto her job and her own school participation and requirements.

"My mother and father can't do anything to get the kids to school," she told Connolly on several occasions.

One evening a call came in to the rectory for Connolly: The girl was missing. Connolly asked the caller, one of the siblings, where she might be. He said he didn't know but that she used to go to Pelham Bay Park a lot, all the way up in the northeast Bronx, by herself. Connolly went up to the park in his car, wondering what had happened to her and if she was going to be safe. He drove to different corners of the park, getting out of the car and walking around inside the park to see if he could identify a young girl, in the dark. After an hour or two of searching, he finally found her sitting against a tree. She was startled but relieved to see him. He asked the girl what she was doing there at this late hour by herself.

"I have to move," she said. "I can't do this anymore."

Connolly took her in the car and planned to take her home. However, he decided, as he was driving through the east Bronx, to take her instead to Jacobi Hospital. *She may be seriously depressed*, Connolly thought, *and no one at home would take care of her*. After an hour, Connolly saw a doctor in the emergency room to explain the situation. The doctor, who spoke with a German accent, seemed dismissive. After reluctantly speaking with the girl by herself, he continued to be dismissive.

He told Connolly, "Dees ees a religious problem," suggesting that she needed Connolly's counseling rather than medical care, or that she was doing too much out of a religious commitment or religious fear of punishment.

Connolly quickly and emphatically replied, "This is not a religious problem. It's not religion."

"She should go home," said the doctor matter-of-factly.

Connolly stared at him and challenged him, disturbed by the casual indifference.

"You let her go," Connolly said angrily, "it's going to be your responsibility, whatever happens to her!"

Startled and angry at Connolly, the doctor stopped, turned, and walked toward the administration desk and spoke to the staff. The girl was immediately admitted and given a room.

The next day, Connolly came back to see her.

He spoke to another doctor, a much nicer one than the previous one, about her condition. However, he didn't have many answers.

"You're not her family," he told Connolly. "She has to make the decision to be admitted for further observation and treatment, or we have to let her go."

After that conversation, he spoke with the girl and explained that he could not do anything else about the hospital situation, but that she should call Connolly or come visit him if she wanted to. Connolly left and never saw the girl after that day.

Of all the losses the parish was facing, none seemed to touch Connolly quite like those of troubled youth. There was the young boy with the bad heart, and there was the mother too young to be one. There were others, like those who called on Connolly to listen to them, to lift the weight of their world.

He thought about that: *There was no one at home that might even listen to them, much less support them or heal their troubled minds. They felt the ongoing punishment of the streets and the world—of the drug use and dealing and deaths, the robberies and beatings, and the losses of jobs by fathers and mothers. There was little mercy for young people. And these health institutions had little mercy for them.*

Connolly, Gigante, Adams, Lafferty, and Collins had brought mercy to these streets with Summer in the City, and then with the new organizations. But the streets had a nonstop punishing quality. Some of these young people—like this boy and girl—came to him when they knew they were lost. Others, who immersed themselves in the street life and drugs, were lost before they even had a chance to know it.

This single parish, with its shrinking but dedicated staff, was all they had to answer the unholy trinity, Connolly thought. The unholy trinity seemed to make everything in life an emergency for these families, many of whom were desperate, so every day the rectory was filled with people searching for help. However, no new staff or organizations were being sent up by the archdiocese to save the day and save these young people and families. The staff at Athanasius was used to the idea of being on their own, without resources from the archdiocese, except Connolly could not understand why or what mattered to the Church at headquarters. He so wanted to let the bishops, administrators, and others know: *These people matter. It's an emergency, every day, in every corner of this neighborhood, and you're not doing everything that we need to fight this unholy trinity. Don't abandon us.*

In the meantime, Connolly prayed for them all, especially for the young people, and for the strength and wisdom to guide those who came to him. And for more answers in the world, in the streets.

Youth for Each Other

As he walked around the streets one day, Connolly found an unusual but pleasant sight. In the middle of Fox Street, near Intervale Avenue, a large group of young boys and girls were sitting in a large circle, with a circle of teenage boys and girls around them. A few were speaking while the rest were listening in, with a man sitting and occasionally speaking.

Connolly went over to a couple of observers standing outside the circle and asked them, "What is this? Is this part of the PAL (Police Athletic League, a program for youth which had a community center on 156th Street)? Who runs this program?"

Within a few minutes, he was directed to a nearby, almost vacant building, where an art therapist was working at a makeshift office on the first floor, in an empty apartment. She introduced herself as Mary Oslovich, assistant to Doctor Ed Eismann, who was responsible for what Connolly saw.

"Can you take me to Doctor Eismann?" Connolly asked. "I want to know more about this."

Connolly learned how Eismann came to create this circle. Eismann was a former seminarian who changed career paths and decided to become a psychotherapist. He worked for Lincoln Hospital, which had been given a grant to create something called "community-based mental health services." A clinic was set up by Lincoln on Westchester Avenue near Intervale Avenue, with full-time professionals and the expectation of seeing many teenagers and youth. However, it saw only four patients over the first two months. With no youth coming from the neighborhood, Eismann simply decided to go out into the neighborhood to explore it and see what he could do. He sat on stoops and spoke with younger children and teenagers, in their small groups. With his open curiosity, he talked about what they did and liked, and about their conflicts and issues with families and friends. Eismann came back repeatedly to the same stoop, and more youth came, and he engaged them in further discussion, until a large circle grew naturally, eventually reaching 100 to 150 in number, which he then took to the middle of the street itself.

After several months, the federal grant funds for Lincoln's community mental health services had run out, and Eismann was told that he had to return to traditional clinical practice at the main hospital site if he wanted to continue working at Lincoln. At that point, Eismann thought, he could not return, and he decided to run this effort full-time independently, and with his own support. He called it *Unitas*, and he organized it as what he called a "therapeutic community."

Eismann developed *Unitas* at a time when the community mental health movement was gaining attention as the "third revolution" of psychiatry.[33] Placing the emphasis on the influence of a social network on an individual's life and mental health, community mental health became a leading approach to treatment in the 1960s. In using the social network or community, the community mental health approach focused on engaging both the functional and dysfunctional members of that community in the process. It used interventions and preventive practices to influence an individual's behavior, and not necessarily a change in his personality. Community mental health also called for a continuity of care for the individuals, and for all the caretakers to work in coordination with each other.

In *Unitas*, Eismann created the only street-based, youth-focused therapeutic community in the city of New York. Each day, children and teenagers came together at Fox Street as Eismann drove in and opened up a van full of balls and toys and games for the youth. Then, after an hour of play, about 75 to 100 children and teenagers came and sat down in a large circle, with Eismann being the first to sit.

Eismann would introduce and affirm the *Unitas* community and ask whether anyone had any problem they wanted to talk about. Then, with the spirit of empathy central to this approach, he proceeded methodically to get an explanation of the problem, then an expression of feelings from the person about the problem, and finally, he recommended solutions from others in the circle. If conflicts arose among circle members, they were

Unitas-trained caretaker Johnny and his "child." (Photo courtesy of Edward Eismann/Unitas.)

The Unitas circle heard and solved problems as a community. (Photo courtesy of Edward Eismann/ Unitas.)

addressed the same way, and the teenagers were asked to take an active role in both confronting the problem and making specific recommendations to carry out daily with the children and for each other.

With Eismann in the circle in a grandfather role, teenagers were trained to be the "fathers" and "mothers" while in the circle, as well as before and after "circle time." Also, one-on-one interaction between "parents" and their "children" took place each day, especially when city-funded summer program lunches were delivered. Caretakers spoke and played with their "children" while providing literal and emotional nourishment. Eismann continuously but positively challenged the caretakers to do two things: Take care of their charges and support each other in this work and in their lives each day.[34]

Connolly was highly impressed by the *Unitas* circle and approach, seeing it in action and hearing from Eismann. He wanted to be part of the program in some way, and Eismann explained that he needed to organize *Unitas* in a formal way, including a board. Connolly was invited to chair the new board of directors and to help raise support for it. He accepted the invitation and did more than just sit on the board.

Connolly asked for help from his priest friends, and Father Bob O'Connor responded.

O'Connor's cousin, Mary Ann Quaranta, was dean of the Fordham University School of Social Work at Lincoln Center. O'Connor introduced Connolly and Quaranta, and Connolly was enthusiastic in arguing for a "town and gown" relationship between the university and this innovative community mental health organization in a poor community. Quaranta was impressed when she met Eismann and Connolly, and her commitment to give financial and publishing support to Eismann and *Unitas* gave them the assurance that this program and community could continue. The children and their symbolic parents would continue supporting and reinforcing each other, and other new "symbolic parents" and children could follow each year to form new "symbolic families," which they did for decades to come.

Connolly saw Eismann's program as an extraordinary and yet natural solution to the neighborhood struggles. *There was no fanfare in the introduction of Unitas, even though it occurred in public, on the streets. It just caught on and naturally grew because it reached the young people where they inherently were and did not try to bring them into a strange institutional structure called a mental health center. In so doing, Eismann reached countless youth who would otherwise have been lost to the streets.*

Summer in the City had done something similar—it just made its presence in the streets and simply invited residents to play and make art and activity with strangers. People would respond to these efforts to engage them, Connolly saw, *as long as you stayed with them, lived with them. It didn't matter if there were teenagers or adults in a religious education program, or in a school playground, or in the streets for community therapy.* But bringing young people to the streets for therapy and for building a therapeutic community of symbolic parents and children was a special sign of hope for Connolly. *The boy with the bad heart and the mother too young to be one could have used this therapy.*

He thought about Frances Connolly, his mother, who lived with a depression so severe that it occasionally paralyzed her and the rest of the family. Connolly remembered, *as a boy, getting up at night, wondering if his mother was still in the house, or if she had gone walking around the streets, lost in a state of despair, as she occasionally did. Then,* he remembered, *going with his older brother Denis to St. Vincent's Hospital in Manhattan's West Village neighborhood. There, the two teenagers were discussing her conditions while she was hospitalized for intensive treatment and monitoring during a long stay at Reece Pavilion.* During those years, Connolly learned that his mother was receiving electroconvulsive therapy, or "shock treatment," as it was known, especially at Pilgrim State Hospital in Long Island.[35] Connolly had hoped that she would be fully healed and come back quickly to the family, but he learned from those conversations with the St. Vincent's doctors that this would be her lifetime condition, and she would need their support.

While his father loved and cared for her, Connolly knew, *Con was too busy providing for the five children, and he, like other immigrants of his generation, did not understand mental illness well. In those conversations with the St. Vincent's doctors, Neil and Denis were like Eismann's teenagers and the teenage girl whom he saved in Pelham Bay Park—the caretakers of the family.*

Priests for Each Other

Connolly found yet another reason to be on the streets, but this time it was to build the Church community, not a therapeutic one.

He was working together with the neighboring parish priests at St. John Chrysostom, near 167th Street in the West Farms area. Connolly had raised the pastoral issue in one of their social gatherings at Athanasius: Not enough men were involved in the church, either on Sunday or in regular parish life, such as societies and event committees and councils. Connolly and the others—Bill Smith, John Rossi, and Jim Welby in St. John, and Gigante and Byrne—decided that some event to focus on the participation of men would give them a significant visibility and, perhaps, a greater impetus to take an active role in each of the churches along with the women and young people.

The priests at Athanasius and John Chrysostom found common cause with other neighboring churches—St. Anselm to the south and St. Thomas Aquinas, north of St. John. All four parishes agreed to hold the "March of Men" on the feast day of Christ the King. Each parish devoted itself to weeks of promotion, especially at Sunday Mass and in their elementary schools, urging the men who attended Mass to attend the march and recruit their friends to it, and the other families to recruit their "absentee" husbands or fathers.

After all the promotions and preparation of the march, the day came. There were about a hundred men present in front of St. Anselm on Tinton Avenue, where the route began. Along each stage of the procession, on the street in front of each church, prayer and Scripture reading were followed by music and a special invocation. They picked up a hundred or two hundred men at each consecutive stop, waiting to join the procession, as well as some observers along the way, invited by the marchers. Each contingent led with its own readings, music, and special invocation, and consisted mostly of men, but also teenage boys accompanying some fathers. At the final procession point at St. Thomas Aquinas on Crotona Parkway, after gathering supporters over a two-mile walk, more than seven hundred men had become part of the March for Men.

As Connolly and the other priests looked on, they realized their collaboration was a success. The male participation carried over into future activities of the collaborating parishes. Each of the parishes would see more men in the pews after they had used the streets, the same streets which had been so cruel to many of their people, especially the younger men, the way Bob Fox had recommended, and the way Ed Eismann had used the streets—as their public forum, as their own place to build community.

This collaboration led to discussions between the staffs at St. Athanasius and St. John Chrysostom about collaboration, which led to an idea to solve their shortage of resources. Both parish staffs saw higher costs and fewer donations in the pews, and they recognized the talents of each priest in the two places. Their thought was that they could keep both parishes operating, but maybe act as if they were one church, with one person to handle a particular function related to the church and to their particular strength or personal interest. There were job recommendations for each priest: Gigante could handle all of the housing issues for both parishes; Rossi would address drug concerns and programs; Smith would handle liturgy; Byrne would manage finances; and Connolly would create and oversee religious education programs.

In this way, they could keep the parish identities for each place but act as one staff for both places. Also, they could come to preach and say Mass at each other's church and, in the process, build an identity with a larger community. With this proposed staffing arrangement, team ministry at Athanasius could grow into something greater, and create something unique in the area, maybe even in the archdiocese.

Institutional Pressure

However, at that same time they were considering this initiative, Connolly got a call from the Chancery office at the archdiocese: They offered him the position of pastor at St. John Chrysostom.

Connolly was surprised, as were the other priests, and the Seneca Chapel and Seneca Center Board.

"Oh, why don't you tell him no? Stay here with us," was the response at a Seneca board meeting where he brought up the possible promotion. Connolly and the board discussed all the Seneca projects going on, and he was convinced that he still needed to spend some time with the center to see some projects through to completion. But he prepared himself for the possibility of going to a new parish, where he could perhaps realize some changes he was considering after Vatican II and Summer in the City.

Connolly went downtown to Archdiocesan headquarters to meet with Vicar General Jim Mahoney to discuss the appointment and the possible timetable for making the change.

"You know," Connolly told Mahoney, "I'm not opposed to going."

"You would have to go in two weeks," said Mahoney in a sharp, businesslike tone.

Two weeks? Connolly was stunned that the archdiocese, which always took a long time to launch a new program, could ask him to leave his community in such a short time. *He could not just stop everything with so many relying on him.*

Connolly defended himself and used a financial example that he thought the archdiocese could understand: "I don't know if you know anything about what's going on, but we have a storefront, and we're getting a grant. It's necessary that I be there because I'm the contact person. We may not get the grant if I'm not present at the meeting. Please let me hold off until June."

"No," insisted Mahoney. "I need an answer right now."

"Well," said Connolly, not pleased with having an ultimatum issued like this. "In that case, no."

Mahoney issued a threat: "You might never get a parish in the diocese."

Connolly stood as firm as Mahoney in this quick standoff and refused to change his answer: "Well. That's okay with me."

After the brief but rapid exchange, the meeting ended, and upon shaking hands with Mahoney, Connolly left and headed back to his car.

As he drove away from Manhattan and over the Willis Avenue Bridge, reentering the southern part of the Bronx, he reflected on the meeting and the situation.

They did not know what was going on in Athanasius, as he had told Mahoney. Each year the Athanasius priests sent down a report on the parish, on the organizations, and on the new activities taking place, as did every parish in the archdiocese. But no one came up to see how the parish was doing or to provide any help for the priests. The administrators at the Chancery could not have imagined the toll of absorbing so many new immigrants at one time; and then the second toll of experiencing a rapid decline of parishioners, donations, and even parish staff; and the toll of dealing with the unholy trinity.

They didn't know about the arrangement for the parishioners to feed their priests, instead of having a parish cook, as they struggled to save parish funds.

Nor would they know about a new chapel in Hunts Point and special outdoor Masses, and the neighborhood services provided to sometimes desperate mothers and families.

Headquarters did not really know about the auto thefts and rectory and convent burglaries. Nor did they know about the Puerto Rican school parents who brought supplies to the school or the neighbors who alerted them to crimes.

Even in that brief meeting with Mahoney, all the bishop wanted to hear from Connolly was an answer on the appointment. No offer of help, no commitment of resources to handle the unlimited days of endless emergency, and no plans to find out what was really going on here. *It felt a little like that school ceremony day out on Southern Boulevard: a show of power, and a defense of a Catholic Church where laypeople answered to priests, and priests answered to bishops and cardinals.*

As he remembered the teachings of Vatican II, he thought, *This encounter with the Chancery was not the vision of Church he had embraced earlier, during that Christmas Eve Mass in the chapel and the celebration in the firehouse in Hunts Point. The bishop's ultimatum and threat were not what he expected in the Kingdom of God, or a new Church. His defiance of the appointment, as well as the ultimatum and the threat,* he knew, *put him in trouble with the people at headquarters, and he would pay a price for that, somehow. He did not care; he had to push back. He had to take sides. With Vatican II and with the Kingdom. With his people of God.*

Yet the fact was, this headquarters housed the Institutional Church which he still answered to as a priest of the Archdiocese of New York. He thought, *He could not be a priest without the institution. That archdiocese was the Church he belonged to and had just left, in an unfortunate misunderstanding.*

But, he also thought, *it was good to go back to Hunts Point–Longwood.*

Back to Lillian Camejo and her center filled with needy mothers and her building lined with beer-can-throwing drug dealers.

Back to the layperson-led chapel services and all the apartments that housed his Masses and Christian Base Community gatherings.

Back to Gigante, Byrne, Adams, Lafferty, and Collins, so immersed in the worship and education of their Puerto Rican parishioners and school families.

Back to the parishioners who did not leave the parish, because they could not afford to move out, or because they chose to participate as neighbors and to lead the societies and committees and councils.

Back to the school on Southern Boulevard, and the rectory on Tiffany Street, and the church building next door, and the new therapy program on Fox Street.

Back to the struggles and solutions in the world he belonged to, and the other Church he belonged to and understood. A Church of the People.

6

Organizing Priests

Hence it is very important that all priests, whether diocesan or religious, always help one another to be fellow workers on behalf of truth. Each one therefore is united by special bonds of apostolic charity, ministry and brotherhood with other members of this presbytery....

Furthermore, in order that priests may find mutual assistance in the development of their spiritual and intellectual lives, that they may be able to cooperate more effectively in their ministry and be saved from the dangers which may arise from loneliness, let there be fostered among them some kind or other of community life....

—Article 8, Section II, Priests as Related to Others,
in *Decree on the Life and Ministry of Priests*, 550

"Just the South Bronx"

On a cold winter day late in 1973, Neil Connolly opened the newspaper to find an unusual sight: a picture of himself. In the photo, which was part of the Archdiocese of New York's new ad campaign recruiting men to the priesthood, Connolly sat on an apartment building's stoop, speaking with a couple of young people. The ad copy read: "Father Neil Connolly isn't out to change the world. Just the South Bronx."[1]

Connolly had always tried to be a good priest. But by 1973 it was a surprise to him, both to be asked to participate in the campaign and, a little bit, that he was willing to do it. While promising greater freedom to go into the world and calling him to build a kingdom on earth, Vatican II had left Neil Connolly with unanswered questions, including one in particular: How would he, as a priest, take responsibility for the Church? Not just his church. The Church. Within a year of the closing of the council, that question came up and led to others, which forced him, again, to let go and to participate in a number of controversial activities in the late 1960s and early 1970s which seriously called his standing in the archdiocese into question. The question arose, as it often did, outside New York.

Priests Unite

On a cold November day in 1966, Neil Connolly and a couple of priest friends from the Bronx stood in a large room at McCormack Place, Chicago's major convention center. A large gathering of priests, over one thousand by Connolly's estimates, was assembled. They were there from every corner of the Archdiocese of Chicago, the largest in the United States, to take their first action: to present a sixteen-resolution platform from their new organization, the Association of Chicago Priests. The recipient would be Archbishop John Cody, considered the second most powerful Catholic clergyman in the country, after Connolly's own boss, the archbishop of New York, Cardinal Spellman. Having been voted into existence by over four hundred Chicago priests months before in a news-making event for American Catholics, the association was ready to lead on issues affecting its members' service as priests, both in the Church and in the world. But before moving to discuss these matters, the association wanted to alter how their archdiocese saw them as workers.

Before each other and before observers from the dioceses of St. Paul-Minneapolis, Milwaukee, Detroit, Bridgeport, and New York, they called for recognition of their lives as priests.[2] Their resolutions included calls for a personnel policy, a retirement policy and board, regularly scheduled pastor-assistant meetings to ensure communication within parishes, a structured in-service training program for graduates of seminary to truly understand the requirements of priesthood, and consultation before all parish assignment changes.

Everyone present and voting, as well as the observers like Connolly, knew how significant these measures were. Chicago, like all dioceses throughout the United States, had expected priests to be lifelong, unconditionally loyal, unquestioning soldiers. But Chicago priests, Connolly saw, did not just have questions; they had "resolutions," which would have been called demands by any other American workers. The "rank and file" gave full approval to the resolutions, as well as to the constitution of the association, "whose purpose is to assist the bishop by expressing and effecting the will of the priests of the diocese in parochial and diocesan matters."

Chicago's association organized itself after the Second Vatican Council and gave permission for priests' senates and associations to be created in dioceses throughout the world. These bodies would be expected to function according to the dictates and guidelines of the local bishop. During the next couple of years, priests' senates indeed appeared on the American horizon to serve the diocesan bishop.

But Connolly was attracted to the Chicago association because it was going to be something stronger than an advisory body. The Chicago priests had *not* organized as a bishop-sanctioned body, to advise when called upon. Instead, they had created themselves independently in a quest to solve their problems. They knew what struggles they were facing in the pews and what struggles they were facing beyond the church doors. As in New York, neighborhoods were declining as jobs left the city and whites fled from blacks, and the struggles for civil rights and fair housing were coming to the forefront. So, driven by struggle, this association meeting was not a ceremonial, cautious gathering, with everyone looking over their shoulders at diocesan leadership. Instead, it was a dynamic, boisterous, publicly organized action by priests. For these clergy, it was a question of finding their power amidst the unsettling changes of both Church and world. "The will of the priests"—that was the concept that attracted Connolly and his fellow observers.

Connolly was excited to see something so unique: a "new rising" of the Church, in which people would have a say about the structures of the institution and direct involvement in the governing of the Church. It was unheard of for most members of his Bronx clergy community to be at this kind of event, but Connolly was unusual. He had already attended conferences around the country related to post–Vatican II changes. He had heard lectures and animated discussions at Notre Dame and St. Louis universities about other experiences and ideas for Church life and activity and leadership. And he had often been excited at hearing of breakthroughs and departures from the Church he had grown up with. But it was the idea of "building the new" that appealed to Connolly, more than just "breaking the old." The Vatican II conferences, like this gathering of the Association of Chicago Priests, were looking to do just that. Build something new.

Looking out at the gathering of the association in that Chicago assembly room, Connolly thought about the individuals there. *Each one was a priest and had attended seminary, like he had. Even with all the challenges brought by that schooling, seminarians were all part of a fraternity and worked toward the same goal, to become part of the same great global institution and the same great global community of priests. They were all soldiers for the Church, the "front line," sent to save souls and proclaim the Word.* Connolly was reminded of that night he saw Ivan Illich, in Athanasius, when he had reflected on how that fraternity dissolved into individual parish priests' lives as they "soldiered on." In his South Bronx social gatherings, and in this day in Chicago, however, they became a community of priests again. Connolly wondered what would come of this demonstration of power and community.

He had never been in a room with so many priests at one time. There were certainly no priests' groups coming together in the Archdiocese of New York to declare an association for all New York priests. But Chicago showed Connolly what was possible, and he paid increased attention to priests' events occurring outside the Archdiocese of New York. Within the year, dioceses throughout the United States saw the formation of independent associations as well as official priests' senates. Vatican II's call to priests to have a voice in ecclesial, pastoral, and social issues enabled the organizations to take up all those issues. By fall 1967, dozens of priests' associations had taken shape in the United States, and a movement was gaining momentum.

On the way back to the Bronx, Connolly was asking himself: Is a separate Church taking shape? Would the organization of thirteen hundred priests in the largest archdiocese of the country create a separate structure for authority and decision-making in the Church? Also, would priests elsewhere ask for the same kind of voice in their archdiocese as these Chicago priests were doing? Or would they assert their authority in some other way and take other actions? What had the Second Vatican Council expected when they encouraged priests to come together?

And, Connolly wondered, what would he even think of that—a separate church, or a separate structure of authority? He didn't know. But, like the priests in Chicago, he felt pretty strongly that he didn't want the parishioners at Athanasius, who were struggling more each day, facing the unholy trinity of poverty, drugs, and crime, to be ignored by the archdiocese anymore. He started to think, *maybe I could generate attention for our parishioners through an organization like this, with our own agenda.*

An Area Called the South Bronx

Connolly was excited to bring news of the Chicago convention home to his fellow priests from New York. He would begin with his own priests' group, the South Bronx Catholic Clergy Association. Expanding on the socializing at Athanasius during the early 1960s, priests of about a dozen parishes of the southern Bronx had begun getting together on the third Sunday of every month at six thirty in the evening, taking turns visiting each others' rectories. But this group was not meeting directly with the cardinal, like his peers in Chicago were. Instead, they were assigned to Monsignor Gustav Schultheiss, a long-term priest who was well-liked in the borough, especially in his own parish of St. Raymond's in Parkchester. Schultheiss was vicar, or the representative of Archbishop Spellman, for the Bronx, and as such he occasionally attended the meetings of the South Bronx Catholic Clergy Association.[3] For Connolly, it was a way to hear what the priests in his area were concerned about, and it was a way to share ideas and experiences as priests.

Connolly already had personally gotten to know some of these priests during the 1960s. He had been with them at the Vatican II educational events down at archdiocesan headquarters, learning how to celebrate the new versions of the Mass and how to get parishioners to participate. Through the Spanish Apostolate, he joined them at the annual *Fiesta San Juan Bautista* at Randall's Island Stadium. They had gone to Mount St. Vincent College and diocesan headquarters for Summer in the City orientations and conferences. In addition, Connolly worked with the neighboring priests to organize parishes in cooperative public events such as the March for Men, attempting to create an area-wide Church community.

But in the association meetings, Connolly learned about how all these men were handling the work of running parishes, which was getting harder. Their experiences were disappointingly familiar. Sunday Mass collection baskets were becoming emptier as the months passed. Elementary schools, with more laypersons and fewer women religious teaching the students, needed more funds than tuition could handle. While they struggled to respond to the schools' needs, priests were seeing more people at the door asking for help with public assistance applications. Still other parishioners wanted help finding new jobs or new apartments to raise their families, and they often had a hard time understanding the language of the documents they needed to produce, or sign, or bring to an office or courthouse.

Similar stories of struggle were being told by all the Bronx priests, from St. Luke's and St. Jerome's parishes near the Willis Avenue Bridge to St. Pius and Immaculate Conception near the Third Avenue shopping district to St. Anselm's, St. John Chrysostom, St. Thomas Aquinas and, of course, St. Athanasius, along the elevated train stations near Longwood, Hunts Point, and West Farms.

The priests also discussed the other struggles, which Connolly was confronting as all the parishes became poorer. Drugs were being used and sold on more street corners, and more mothers and fathers of drug addicts pleaded for help from the parish priests. Treatment centers were not easy to find in the city, and priests sent parents to Catholic Charities, or to the one or two treatment centers they could think of, or to the hospitals. On the days they were not turning down drug addicts' requests for money, the priests were being victimized by break-ins at the schools and rectories. Some were even being robbed at knifepoint or gunpoint by desperate young men. They were becoming "streetwise," as much as they wished they could just be "church-wise," and so they shopped for burglar alarm systems and car-trunk locks and chains. Finally, stories of funeral Masses said for lost young men were punctuated with special regrets, because the dead men had been "CYO kids," or religious instruction program graduates just a year or two earlier.

After the first tentative months of the priests' meetings, other, newer parishes began to join association meetings from areas Connolly had only heard of in passing. But they were also seeing changes in their collection baskets and in the pews. All had to have a Spanish Mass and Spanish-speaking priests and sisters, trained in language and culture at Cardinal Hayes High School or in the Catholic University of Puerto Rico, to serve the new parishioners, run youth programs, and teach new students. From streets like Morris Avenue, University Avenue, Tremont Avenue, Featherbed Lane, Marcy Place, and Ryer Avenue, once all Irish or Italian or Jewish strongholds, new priests were coming to tell their stories of going Spanish and of becoming poorer. Like the migration and development forces that created the Spanish parishes in the Eastern Bronx, other similar forces created these new Spanish parishes in the 1960s.

After the mid-1960s, when it seemed *La Gran Migración* had finally settled in the Bronx, the migration process occurred again, but this time migrants flowed between neighborhoods in the Bronx. Those who had settled into the southeastern Bronx in the 1950s and early 1960s were finding new places in the southwestern parts of the Bronx.

In particular, Puerto Ricans settled in the cluster of neighborhoods around the world-famous Yankee Stadium—Highbridge, Grand Concourse, and Concourse Village—becoming, at 30,000, a fifth of the area's population by 1970.[4] North of that cluster were some other neighborhoods, near the Cross Bronx Expressway, a mammoth construction project which destroyed dozens of blocks in every Bronx neighborhood in its east-west path between 1948 and 1963.[5] This northern cluster of neighborhoods—Morris Heights, University Heights, and South Fordham—saw Puerto Rican settlers as well in the later 1960s. By 1970, the combined neighborhoods housed over 20,000 Puerto Ricans, or one out of every six people there.[6]

Following the migration patterns of the 1950s, large numbers of white residents began leaving those western neighborhoods in the 1960s. Mostly middle-income Irish and Jewish populations moved out, leaving many apartments available for the next migration. From Con Edison office workers and managers to lawyers and doctors, the white residents departed buildings that were known for their elegant Art Deco facades and lobbies, as well as walk-up tenements with simpler, traditional structures. They fled as the public housing developments and urban clearance events occurring in the eastern and southern Bronx, which they had only read about, brought those once-distant populations into their own neighborhoods. As they saw neighboring buildings begin deteriorating, their fears were heightened: fear of people of other races, fear of crime, fear of declining services, and a fear that the city was abandoning or destroying their areas, as the Cross Bronx Expressway upheaval demonstrated.

Thousands of these white households were given an opportunity for a new "neighborhood" with the opening in 1968 of a 15,000-unit cooperative housing development in a remote area of the northeast Bronx. Known as "Co-op City," it was the largest housing complex in the world at the time. As with the other urban renewal projects overseen by Robert Moses, the city's construction coordinator and planning commissioner, Co-op City was backed with union and government resources and was situated on "cleared" land. The 1965 groundbreaking work was on a parcel vacated a year earlier by a bankrupt amusement park known to patrons only as "Freedomland." Co-op City promised its new residents a different kind of freedom: not amusement, but freedom from the crime, deterioration, poverty, and racial integration that were finding their way into western Bronx neighborhoods. Its building accelerated white middle-class residents' flight from the southwest Bronx.[7]

In the meantime, Puerto Rican migrants to the southwest Bronx were still arriving while struggling to earn a living, as jobs also quickly migrated out of the city. As a result, new migrants came with lower incomes than those who left. In Highbridge/South Concourse, 14 percent of families lived below the poverty level by 1970, and that number would triple over the 1970s. In Morris Heights/South Fordham, as well, poverty became concentrated; one out of eight families were poor by 1970, and the number skyrocketed as well within the next ten years.[8] The buildings in those neighborhoods reflected the population changes as well, with 13 percent and 11 percent of the housing being overcrowded in the southern and northern areas of the west Bronx, respectively. With the overcrowding came landlord neglect, abandonment, and deterioration.

All of these shifts were felt in the parishes of the southwest Bronx. Puerto Rican Catholics came in and filled the pews at Sacred Heart (Highbridge), St. Angela Merici and Christ the King (South Concourse), St. Francis of Assisi (Morris Heights), Holy Spirit and St. Nicholas of Tolentine (University Heights), and St. Simon Stock and St. Margaret Mary (South Fordham). As long as the Irish also remained, priests often faced "culture wars," as the introduction of Spanish Masses, Spanish societies, and Spanish religious education programs frustrated the white parishioners. Priests bemoaned the culture wars, but they also endured them for practical reasons, as one pastor explained to Connolly at a Clergy Association meeting: "I can't alienate the white parishioners—they're giving me the money to run the parish."

In those association meeting discussions, Connolly came to discover that the Puerto Rican parishioners who were leaving Athanasius and emptying some of his pews had found refuge in the western parishes now joining the association. However, these soon began to see declines as well. The rapid changes for all the parishes in this expanded community of Puerto Rican Catholics took Connolly and his fellow priests on a roller-coaster ride that was far less entertaining than those "Freedomland" had once offered. Sunday attendance at these twenty-four parishes that became part of the association began in 1950 at 89,000 and reached nearly 95,000 a decade later. Then it quickly decreased to 80,000 in 1965, and 50,000 in 1968, before it reached a floor of 22,000 in 1975, a quarter of what it had been in 1960.[9]

As Connolly heard all these stories of rapid in- and out-migrations, he was worried, but at least he was convinced that these were the right priests for the Puerto Rican faithful. These priests, and the sisters in the schools and communities, had learned about Puerto Rican culture and learned to speak Spanish. They organized chapters of *Santo Nombre, Sagrado Corazón, Legión de María, Hijas de María, Carismático* and *Cursillistas*, and other groups that Puerto Rican parishioners could join and lead. In addition to Masses in Spanish, they celebrated the *Fiesta San Juan Bautista* and *La Virgen de la Providencia.* He was sure there was a *Misa del Gallo* (the "Rooster's Mass") at midnight of Christmas Eve in every one of those parishes. They counseled their parishioners and heard their confessions in their language. Like Connolly, they had gone Spanish.

As the priests from the western half of the area joined the ranks of the South Bronx Catholic Clergy Association, Connolly realized, *this whole area—the eastern and western parts of the Bronx up to Fordham Road—was speaking Spanish. And it was all being dominated by the "unholy trinity" of epidemics—poverty, drug addiction, and crime—that he and the staff at the parish, the school, and the organizations were living with. All of this was now the South Bronx. And he, Neil Connolly, was not just a priest of Athanasius parish, he was also a South Bronx priest.* As he was elected president of the South Bronx Catholic Clergy Association, he had questions about this new area and this growing community of parishes.

The first question came up for him, as it did with his sometimes over-whelming struggles against the unholy trinity at Athanasius: Why? Why do we have to face these struggles every day on our own? If this struggle had spread all over, why can't we challenge the unholy trinity? The arch-diocese had not given any more attention to the unholy trinity in these parishes as it had at Athanasius. Only the creative work of the Summer in the City parish staffs, along with some of the others, led to the formation of some parish-based service organizations to care for some of the people's needs—youth centers and family services centers.

Connolly thought, *If this were like Chicago, he and the others could present a set of resolutions to support the priests of the South Bronx and the parishioners of the South Bronx. We could present resolutions to get special programs to fight the epidemics of poverty, drugs, and crime. We would need to do some planning like the Chicago priests did. They had dozens of meetings and a large planning committee. Maybe he could include some of these priests and their parishes from around the archdiocese who were involved in Summer in the City and whom he had gotten to know—in East Harlem, Harlem, Lower East Side, West Side, and other places where Bob Fox was working. All these areas could vote on a constitution and present a set of resolutions to the cardinal, even if he was close to impossible to meet with. It had worked in the largest archdiocese, in Chicago. Connolly had seen it. Could it work here?*

Then, on December 2, 1967, those questions were dismissed and new ones arose when the New York Church lost its own leader: Francis Cardinal Spellman died.

A Bishop of Power

Spellman was the only leader of the New York Catholic Church Connolly and many of his fellow priests had ever known.[10] His dominant role in the American Catholic Church was made possible by his strong, long-standing friendship with Cardinal Eugenio Pacelli, who became Pope Pius XII in 1938. One year later, Pius appointed then-auxiliary bishop Spellman of the Archdiocese of Boston to succeed the prominent Cardinal Patrick Hayes as the leader of the Archdiocese of New York. He arrived as archbishop of New York on September 8, 1939, and attained global and national stature in the Roman Catholic Church over the next twenty-eight years. The significance of Spellman's tenure was demonstrated by the attendees at his Requiem Mass: more than a hundred bishops and cardinals and many luminaries of the local and national political and religious world.

Thanks to a friendship, Connolly and Gigante were lucky enough to join the dignitaries at the Mass. Father Bob McManus, who worked at a church on Soundview Avenue, was a friend of Connolly, who loved to play squash with him up in the seminary's athletic facilities. Many of Connolly's games with McManus, a lifelong athlete who suffered from diabetes, were suddenly interrupted when McManus called a break to inject himself with insulin. "Neil, let's take a break," he would say. "I gotta shoot myself." At one of those "shooting" breaks, during the week of Spellman's passing, McManus offered Connolly a unique opportunity: upfront seats at the funeral Mass. McManus, new coordinator of ecumenical programs for the archdiocese, was responsible for the goodwill gesture of obtaining premier seating at the funeral for the Protestant leadership of New York.

"Listen, you guys want good seats?" McManus said to Connolly. "I've got extra tickets. Come in with the Protestants; the top Protestant ministers are going. They'll have much better seats than you guys are getting." Intrigued, Connolly accepted, and so he and Gigante, in their formal clerical garb, marched with McManus and the Protestant leadership into St. Patrick's Cathedral. They sat close to the action, in the same pew as President Lyndon B. Johnson and members of his family and Administration. Later that day, he received a surprise call from home. Connolly's brother Denis, who saw the ceremony on television next to their mother, told Connolly that his mother was stunned to see her son sitting next to New York's Protestant leaders. A worried Frances turned to her oldest son and asked, "I wonder if Neil has lost his religion." The brothers had a good laugh.

Connolly was aware of Spellman's power both in the Church and in the world. Without a national decision-making membership body of bishops or elected national Church leaders to rein him in during his tenure, Spellman had had as much power as any American Catholic bishop or cardinal, and most thought it was more than any other. As the leader of the Archdiocese of New York, Spellman's see was in the media and financial center of the country, and it was the nation's second largest archdiocese after Chicago. Spellman had been on friendly terms with every United States president from Franklin D. Roosevelt to Lyndon B. Johnson, and he had conducted diplomatic missions for some of them.[11]

Spellman's power was also reflected in his military conservatism.[12] In the Vatican-appointed position of military vicar for the American Catholic Church, Spellman supervised more than two thousand chaplains throughout the world and made regular visits to American troops during the Second World War, the Korean War, and the Vietnam War. He staunchly supported the latter, even as his own Pope was urging peace negotiations in his world travels. His support for deterrence via nuclear weapons put him at odds with many priests, religious, and Catholic laypersons, including leading national dissidents and peace activists like Dorothy Day of the Catholic Worker Movement and Fathers Phil and Daniel Berrigan.[13]

Spellman did not tolerate labor-union challenges to his own position as an employer any more than he changed his position on peace and war in response to intra-Catholic criticism. In 1949, confronted by hundreds of cemetery workers and their supporters in their strike at the archdiocese's Calvary Cemetery in Queens, Spellman struck back. Ignoring decades of Catholic social teaching supporting labor rights and a living wage, he ordered the last-year students from St. Joseph's Seminary to replace the striking workers, dig the graves, and bury the dead. Pro-labor priests, including Father John Byrne, publicly condemned the strike-breaking action, and the archdiocese responded with demotions and transfers of dissenter priests.[14]

Following the standard set by his predecessor, Spellman had also expanded the archdiocese by building physical and social infrastructure on a grand scale. He raised and invested over half a billion dollars for capital projects including many new elementary schools, such as St. Athanasius. Catholic elementary school enrollments doubled to 179,000 in the Spellman era. Other educational facilities were built as the student population in high schools tripled to 50,000 and Catholic university students reached nearly 28,000 in number.[15] Moreover, Spellman built a vast social services network known as Catholic Charities, expanding it to two hundred social service organizations in the 1960s. In a city that was 47 percent Catholic, and a country of 47 million Catholics which had recently elected the nation's first Catholic president in John F. Kennedy, this Spellman-era growth enhanced the already formidable power of the institutional Catholic Church in New York.[16] It was this power which Connolly and fellow priests had lived under for years, and no one expected to change it.

But a group of people had already challenged Spellman's power and forced him to take action for them: Puerto Rican migrants. Spellman had assumed his position as archbishop after a period of decline in the Catholic population of New York. But that population grew from 1 million to 1.8 million, owing largely to the influx of 750,000 Puerto Ricans, the vast majority of whom identified as Catholics. As New York's Catholic leader, Spellman had no choice but to act when the new migrants repopulated his archdiocese. Although they were seen as an institutional challenge with a different language, a non-European ethnicity, limited economic resources, and no clergy from their community, the Puerto Ricans enhanced the Catholic share of New York and Spellman's rationale for expansion.

Yet for the first seven years of the Puerto Rican migration, Spellman's integrated parish plans for pastoral care were not implemented, and he was powerless to adequately respond to events. When he hired Joseph Fitzpatrick and Ivan Illich and instituted the Puerto Rico program and the Office of Spanish Catholic Action, Spellman reestablished control. This response to the migration created a new wave of priests, including Connolly, who embraced a new people and culture with needs that Spellman had originally not been ready for. The changes in the archdiocesan approach demonstrated that this institution was capable of being challenged by another force. Then, in December of 1967, when the powerful leader of the archdiocese passed away, an opening was created for another force to challenge the institution again. *Why*, Connolly thought when he heard the news, *can't we choose our own bishop and our own priests for our neighborhoods?*

A Democracy for Priests

Like John XXIII, Connolly and a few other priests thought it was time to "open the windows" and renew the Church, right here in New York. During the days surrounding Spellman's death, Connolly thought about the priests' gathering in Chicago the year before, and the courage they had shown in setting an agenda. He also thought about the South Bronx Catholic Clergy Association and the struggles they were facing as they went Spanish, continuing the program that began with Fitzpatrick and Illich and the Puerto Rico immersion summer almost ten years earlier. Connolly thought, *It was good to have the Office of Spanish Catholic Action and its special programs, but the parishioners and poor parishes needed more. They—even he—needed a leader who could understand what they faced and could work with them. After all these struggles in their parishes, his South Bronx priests needed a new kind of archbishop, one whom they could also support as much as he could support them.*

On the subway ride back from the Requiem Mass, holding onto the straps, Connolly and a few others were commenting on the event and Spellman, wondering about the future. Then, it finally came out. Someone suggested that they should appeal to the Vatican to let the priests of New York select their next archbishop.

"There's a precedent for it," Connolly said, remembering Church history and theology lectures on the topic of bishop selection and the early Church. He remembered a quote from St. Augustine: *If the people don't want me as their bishop, I will not go to that diocese.*

In addition to the petitions of the Chicago priests, Connolly heard of a demand for a different kind of democracy in the Church, also from the Midwest. In the Archdiocese of St. Louis, Missouri, and the Diocese of Green Bay, Wisconsin, priests lost their archbishops. Instead of following tradition and waiting for the appointment of their next leader by the Vatican, however, they demanded to be heard. In an action unheard of in the modern era, the two cities' priests' associations independently wrote petitions to the Vatican and to the newly formed United States Conference of Catholic Bishops, asking to have a direct say in the selection of their next bishop.[17]

Even in 1967, just two years removed from the end of the Second Vatican Council and with a spirit of change still in the air, these actions were considered revolutionary. Priests, who were directly responsible for carrying out the orders and teachings of the global Church at its most basic, local level, the parish, wanted responsibility for the Church at its central level. The petitions, though unsuccessful, became major news stories in the American Catholic media and caught the attention of Connolly and other New York priests. Whatever the results, one thing was clear: *The priests of Green Bay and St. Louis took action*, Connolly thought, *and so could he and other New York priests*.

"Why don't we write a letter or petition and get as many signatures as possible to elect the next archbishop?" said Connolly.

Peter Gavigan, another priest, responded, "It's happened in the past. Why don't we try it?"

They looked at each other and then nodded and said, "Yeah. Let's try it." Before their train dropped them off, they agreed to form a committee to launch a petition campaign and get every priest they could to support it.

A priests' meeting was called at Athanasius with the staff's friends from seminary and from the Spanish Apostolate network. A written statement and request were agreed upon. Individual committee members were assigned to gather signatures from segments of the archdiocese—the schools, St. Joseph's Seminary, the services institutions and agencies, and the parishes, by vicariate clusters. Connolly worked in the South Bronx with another committee member, while Ed Byrne, another member and friend, focused on the Lower East Side.

Reactions to the petition drive were mixed. Monsignor Austin Vaughn, an authority on Church history, confirmed that election of a bishop had historical precedent, but he refused to ally himself with this particular campaign. On the other hand, Monsignor Robert Browne, former spiritual director of the seminary, spontaneously provided his parish home in Irvington as a centrally located meeting site for supporters. Connolly was surprised at this show of support, and he was pleased by the welcome Browne gave to the priests at meetings.

Even in the South Bronx, the reactions were not universally positive. Connolly garnered many supporters, even among those who did not give it much thought but were just friendly with Connolly and other petition leaders. Some were enthusiastically in favor and quickly signed the petition. On the other hand, another priest viscerally opposed Connolly's effort. "Uh, who do you think you are, the Holy Spirit??" said the furious priest. "I'll take my direction from the Holy Spirit." He told Connolly the suggestion was outlandish and disrespectful: "No, you should go the way we always went."

The conflict intensified as Connolly and the members of the committee, which had grown to twenty-five, each gathered dozens of signatures and reached every corner of the archdiocese. Inevitably, word soon got back to the diocesan headquarters, and remarks about Connolly's involvement found their way to him in meetings and phone calls with committee members. "Neil Connolly, that arrogant bastard!" one diocesan official was reported to have said. "Who does he think he is?"

These encounters with the angry priest from his own South Bronx, and the priest who told him about hard criticism from the headquarters, raised another question for Connolly: *Will I risk losing my place in the priesthood fighting for a democratic Church?* Everything was moving so fast, especially since this campaign was conducted in the middle of the Christmas season, and they had to get their message to the Vatican before it acted, so there was no time to consult, or reflect.

Connolly knew his involvement was risky, but he thought the intensity of the negative reactions was surprising, and he did not expect it to be so personal. "Your name at the Chancery office is not very good, you know," someone else on the committee told him. And everything intensified when the broader New York world discovered both the petition and Connolly's role. At Emmaus House, a Catholic shelter for single homeless men in

East Harlem, Connolly attended a lecture about the modern Church and dissent. Responding to questions about the amount of individual opinion and dissent permitted within the institutional Church, Connolly stated that he felt free to express himself. But he was approached by a man who identified himself as a reporter for the *New York Times* and said he wanted to discuss the petition campaign.

"I know you guys belong to a movement to elect the next archbishop," he said. "I want to hear about it. Tell me what you're doing."

Connolly and Gavigan, who was with him, said, "No, we're not going to do that. We're not going to go to the press."

"Well, I know about it already. I'll write the story, or you can control the story." Connolly and Gavigan, feeling trapped, decided to give him some information, and the article came out on the front page of the *Times*.[18] The conflict between priests of the Archdiocese of New York became known to the world. The tension made Connolly realize that the stakes were higher than he had thought. The potential conflict between priests of the Archdiocese of New York and the decision-makers at the Chancery and the Vatican, as well as Connolly's name, now became known to the world. He realized he could be in direct trouble now with headquarters.

But Connolly was also reading about encouraging developments for a democratic Church occurring in the United States. More independent associations had been forming around the country over the last twelve months, and even a national layperson's association had been established to call for a "formal and positive share in the Church's decision-making processes."[19] Shortly after Spellman's death, the Association of Chicago Priests held a major conference for priests at the University of Chicago to discuss and affirm priesthood. Father Raymond Goedert, president of the association, had pointed out that over the decades, laypersons had gained increasing definition and a greater role in the Church, and Vatican II had given the bishops of the world a clear role and clear authority over their own dioceses. Then he made clear his and every American priest's pressing concern with his question: "Where, may I ask, does a priest fit in? . . . We priests love the Church. We love our priesthood. We are willing to suffer for the Church and our priesthood, to be patient while the study of our roles goes on—but onward, it must go!" One of Connolly's fellow priests from the 1958 summer program in Puerto Rico, Father Leo Mahon, was at the conference, and he also challenged priests and the state of priesthood in the post–Vatican II era: "The priesthood is not a function to be fulfilled, but a mission, as being a poet isn't a function."[20] With Mahon's reminder that he was responsible for fulfilling the mission of Vatican II, Connolly moved forward.

Connolly and the petition committee met one last time to plan the submission of the document to the Vatican. On the advice of Monsignor Bob Stern, who had studied for his doctorate in Rome for several years and knew its workings, the committee sent it by diplomatic pouch to ensure that it would not be intercepted before arriving at its intended destination. Stern provided final wording on the document, using the appropriate language to present the priests' position in a way that would be respectful of the Pope's authority and yet clear about the intentions of the signers. On January 15, 1968, the committee submitted a 750-word letter to Pope Paul VI, signed by 563 priests and signaling a widespread call for a greater role for priests in the global and New York Church. The *New York Times* reported on this event too: "'We wanted to express our opinion and be consulted,' said the Reverend Neil A. Connolly, assistant pastor of St. Athanasius Church in the Bronx and a member of the steering committee."

The petition acknowledged the contributions of Cardinal Spellman during his long tenure and highlighted his role in implementing liturgical changes, ecumenical initiatives, and the reorganization of Church structures, including the Priests' Senate, all undertaken in the spirit of Vatican II. Then it described the qualities which the priest signatories called for in a successor to Spellman: "Not only do we make remembrance of our late bishop and pastor, but we fervently call upon the Spirit of Christ to raise up for this Church a leader filled with this same Holy Spirit, with the greatness of heart and the skill of mind to inspire and lead, to strengthen and unite, and to plan and provide for the needs of God's people in this almost prototype of the modern city of man. . . ."

Finally, the memorandum called for an anti-institutional approach to the selection of that successor to Spellman—allowing a direct say for priests: "Also, conscious of the ancient traditions of the church and animated by the new vision of the council, may we presume to petition Your Holiness to be invited to place ourselves even more at Your Holiness' disposition in the complex and delicate matter of the possible restructuring of the church in this area and of the selection by Your Holiness of its new Shepherd. If it please Your Holiness, we should be delighted to share in any way in the preparation for these weighty decisions. If the possibility may be entertained, may we have the opportunity to express to Your Holiness our particular hopes and ideas and most prayerful and deep wishes for the future of our beloved city and diocese. . . ."[21]

No one heard a response to the petition from the Vatican or the archdiocese.

Then, in early March, a surprise announcement came: the Vatican had appointed auxiliary bishop Terence Cooke as the next archbishop of New York.[22] Connolly and the other priests on the petition campaign steering committee were frustrated that the institutional Church had ignored the wishes of so many priests. Their campaign for a meaningful role in the office that influenced their lives as pastors was done.

However, to Connolly's surprise, in March the priests took two other actions.

On March 14, 1968, priests who had been active in the Priests' Senate which convened during Spellman's last two years, and who were disbanded upon Spellman's death, came out with a document of their own. The self-proclaimed Interim Senate Advisory Committee presented the document, "A Memorandum of Priorities," before the archdiocese and the larger New York public.[23] The memorandum was another call for a direct role for priests in the selection of the leaders at archdiocesan headquarters: auxiliary bishops, vicar general, other vicars, chancellors, "and other officials whose office and jurisdiction affect the pastoral mission of the Church in New York."

It also called for a new system of governance in the archdiocese, including a diocese-wide pastoral council, to advise the new archbishop and serve as a model for parish councils to help govern each parish of the archdiocese. Such a council would include religious and laypersons as well as priests, an unheard-of arrangement in the conservative archdiocese, but one that several local parish staffs had tried to implement in some limited way. Finally, the committee called for an archdiocesan department to prioritize urban ministry and the issues of the world—civil rights, housing, and poverty—and to actively engage the Church in these issues. The Interim Senate Advisory Committee, like the Steering Committee Connolly helped organize, wanted the Church of New York to become a Vatican II Church in every aspect of its organization, activity, and life.

Then, in one final effort to change the direction of the archdiocese as it gained new leadership, another public document for change came out. A group of priests, including some of the Advisory Committee members, issued and endorsed a study of the archdiocese.[24] Conducted by Father Philip Murnion, then a Columbia University doctoral candidate in sociology, the study analyzed the archdiocesan organizational structure and its changing demographics and resources, and it concluded with a recommended merger of area dioceses.[25] It sought to bring together the resources of dioceses which had gained wealth and income during the expansion of suburban areas in New York—the Diocese of Brooklyn and the recently created Diocese of Rockville Centre in Long Island—with the one which had lost these, the Archdiocese of New York.

A merger would have meant an unusual reorganization for any diocese, even for one with the size and scope of the Archdiocese of New York. But Murnion and the priests who supported the study found that the post–World War migrations and changes in communities required this strategic response. Mostly, they felt, these events required that the Catholic Church see itself in a different way, especially with the pressure that a fast-changing world placed on the stability of the Church. They wanted New York's Catholic Church to thrive.

None of these actions by priests' groups was answered, and the Catholic Church in New York did not yield in its institutional ways. But Connolly saw all these initiatives and realized he and his friends had been right to stir things up. More than 560 priests wanted a different Church in New York than they had known for decades. New York City had changed rapidly; its surrounding counties had gotten richer while it was getting poorer, and there was a whole new set of people and issues the New York world had to face.

Other rapidly moving events motivated Connolly and his association colleagues to keep fighting for a voice. In February 1968, while they were waiting for a decision from the archdiocese and the Vatican, a national clergy group was being formed at a meeting in Chicago: the National Federation of Priests Associations.[26] The Federation, like the Association of Chicago Priests, a member, was going to deal with retirement and personnel policies, boards, the careers and lives of priests, and the relationships between priests and bishops and each other. However, this Federation was focused on the world as well as the Church, as Vatican II had urged, and would address the social issues of the day. Convening months after the summer 1967 inner-city riots, the Federation aimed to make sure the Church, through its national and local entities, would address the issues of civil rights, housing, education, and employment. Addressing the concerns of American priests after Vatican II, Father Peter Shannon said, "We priests, as individuals and as a group, have refused to assume the responsibility that is ours: to reshape the Church or better yet, to reshape the world."

Echoing Shannon's thoughts, Connolly made a decision after the petition campaign: He was not going to accept the Church any longer as just an institution. *For him, it was also going to be a Church of the priests. Connolly was no longer just "a priest"; he was a Vatican II priest, like all the others who had organized and petitioned and presented new priorities and recommendations. A Vatican II priest would not just follow the Church; he now owned it, just like the other priests who spoke up, and he was right to claim his ownership.*

Challenging a New Authority

The next of many significant new questions Connolly had to answer became: *Would he fight the institution over the power to choose pastors and priests for South Bronx parishes?*

As the new archbishop assumed power, there was some unfinished business that the South Bronx Catholic Clergy Association needed to address with him. While he was still auxiliary bishop, Terence Cooke had met with the association to discuss two items needing archdiocesan attention. The priests wanted to establish a requirement that all persons seeking baptism be required to attend a course in advance. Association members also wanted to have a say in the appointment of priests and pastors to parishes in the South Bronx. In that earlier meeting, Cooke accepted the proposal for a baptismal education requirement, which was not controversial. On the second issue, though, he recommended that the issue be "taken up with the new archbishop." No one had expected that Cooke himself would be that new archbishop.

In the event, Cooke declined requests for a follow-up meeting with the association. Undeterred, the association persisted. Connolly discovered that the newly appointed archbishop was at a national bishops' conference in New Orleans. Through an old contact of Cooke's from his two years at Athanasius, they reached him directly by phone and made the request again, and he reluctantly agreed to meet. Cooke knew Connolly wanted a meeting with the full association. However, he agreed only to meet with Connolly, and only at his own residence on Madison Avenue, leading the association to anticipate a confrontation.

Connolly went down to the residence with his friend Father Bob Banome of St. Joseph's, who drove him there. Banome asked Connolly before he entered, "Do you want me to go in with you?" Connolly, who felt he had to be solely responsible for the meeting, since that was what he had agreed to, declined. It was Connolly's first visit to the residence, an imposing, classic structure.

Cooke, joined by the new vicar general, Joseph O'Keefe, greeted Connolly with a no-nonsense approach, a deviation from his prior tolerant demeanor. It made Connolly worry, but he proceeded with his case. Connolly said, "I'm here as a representative of the South Bronx Catholic Clergy Association, and I just wanted to explain that there are certain issues that we have and wanted to discuss with you. And you said that you wouldn't meet with us."

Cooke replied tersely, "That's right, I said I wouldn't."

South Bronx Catholic Clergy Association would meet with new Cardinal Terence Cooke (*left*) and Bronx Vicar Gus Schultheiss (*center*). (Photo by Chris Sheridan. Courtesy of *Catholic New York*.)

Connolly, at a bit of a loss, said, "You know, Your Eminence, I'm under a little pressure here with you being the archbishop. I'm going back to a meeting of the entire association, of all the priests, and I just want to make sure to report accurately your quote that you will not meet with us."

He had hoped the importance of the meeting to a large body of clergy waiting for the decision would somehow persuade Cooke to reconsider his refusal.

But Cooke repeated, "That's right." He was emphatic.

Connolly paused, looked at him and said, "Okay."

The conversation ended with a shaking of hands and Cooke saying, "God bless you."

Connolly brought the news of Cooke's refusal to the next association gathering. "He said what?? He won't meet with us???" said Gigante. For him and for others in the meeting, it was time to escalate things and resolve this issue directly. "We'll make posters. Let's go down and picket the residence. He can't get away with this!!" But after some heated discussion, they agreed to hold off on the protests and instead send a letter and press again for a meeting. Cooke, sensing that the group would not back off their demands, finally agreed to meet.

The priests did not get any specific concessions from Cooke, but at least they had an opportunity to express their concerns and their rationale while Cooke listened. And the meeting did have an effect in the larger archdiocese: It created a stir among priests' circles, including in the seminary. Word spread far and fast through the grapevine. Connolly and many others regularly visited the seminary for its athletic facilities and as a getaway on their one weekday off. After a couple of hours of squash or basketball, Connolly would visit the steam room, a place for relaxation and conversation among priests. There, he overheard some comments about the meeting. "Did you read what *Inklings* said about the meeting between Cooke and those South Bronx priests?" (*Inklings* was a somewhat secret newsletter with an anonymous publisher who covered unofficial news, including gossip about priests and the hierarchy in the archdiocese, and it was distributed in priests' mailboxes in the seminary.) "Did you read that?" someone said. "Who are these guys, these young Turks? I mean, what disrespect for the archbishop of New York!"

Someone else countered, in a room where people could barely see each other beyond the steam. "Great. At least somebody's talking!" he said.

"You're bucking a certain line of authority; great!" said yet another person, as Connolly listened in attentively, in silence.

Connolly thought about the position he and the other members of the association had put themselves in. *By all priests, they were considered rebels against the Institution. Some accepted and endorsed this "rebellion," which was a lot less public than the original petition for an election or the other two priests' calls for action in March 1968.*

Others were unable to see Connolly's position: *Parishioners and priests and religious in the South Bronx were facing very hard times. South Bronx parishes needed priests who could understand them and work with them, and believe in the Vatican II approach, the Summer in the City approach, and in living with the struggles of poverty. The priests of the South Bronx were not aiming to make enemies with the Chancery or with other priests. They just could not accept things as they were.*

They also could not accept that any of their priests could be readily removed without their having a say. Steve Kelleher of St. Jerome's parish was being threatened with removal over positions he had taken, as a member of the Archdiocesan Marriage Tribunal, on the subjects of marriage and annulment. Kelleher's defenders were members of the association, who arranged for another meeting with Archbishop Cooke.

Connolly realized that these meetings with Cooke were coming at a time of increasing tension between clergy and their bishops throughout the United States, sometimes with harsh consequences for the priests. It was one thing for Vatican II to call for the whole Church, not just the Pope, to take responsibility; it was another thing to figure out what that meant on the local level for relationships between bishops, clergy, religious, and laity. Connolly read some of these stories of bishop-clergy tensions over power with great concern. In San Antonio, for example, Archbishop Robert Lucey touched off a firestorm when his archdiocesan priests' senate sought a meeting with him to discuss the relations between the bishop and his clergy. To make their point about the need for sharing of responsibility in the diocese, and the need for clergy to be heard, the priests' senate used a document prepared by Notre Dame University professor and award-winning theologian Father John McKenzie, who asserted that, after Vatican II, authority belonged to the whole Church, not just the hierarchy. Lucey responded to the senate president, Reverend Clarence Leopold, with anger, labeling the statement "heresy" and "nonsense": "The clergy and laity who will not believe the bishop shall be condemned."[27] This action would lead to protests and suspensions of priests in the Archdiocese of San Antonio and in its seminary.

It was not just priests who wanted "to reshape the Church" who were in trouble, either. Priests who had more involvement in the world were also challenged. In Buffalo, Bishop James McNulty ordered Father William Wartling to transfer from his inner-city, African American parish, St. Nicholas, because of his activism in a new community organization, BUILD, organized by Saul Alinsky to fight the city's power structure.[28] Wartling, a young white priest, refused the transfer, and a series of protests ensued after the bishop forbade the rebel priest from administering the sacraments to anyone in the parish. Similarly, in Ohio, Father Edward Murray was transferred from St. Peter's Parish in Ridgeville by Bishop Clarence Issenmann of the Cleveland diocese because of his participation in an organization focused on ecumenism and social action.[29] Despite the Vatican II message to be in the world, to support the poor and vulnerable, and to advance ecumenical interaction, a greater number of American bishops were increasingly carrying out the only Vatican II message essential to them: *The bishop has authority over his own diocese.*

And in the midst of an intensely heated debate over birth control, a topic of post–Vatican II concern in the Catholic Church all over the world, further protests occurred. On the one hand, bishops defended the Pope's 1968 encyclical maintaining the ban on birth control, and on the other hand, there were clergy and theologians as well as many laity who questioned it. Debates led to statements of opposition, which led to suspensions and vigorous protests. In Washington, D.C., for example, Cardinal Patrick O'Boyle suspended Father Joseph O'Donoghue for teaching alternative perspectives on birth control. This led to a "showdown" with dozens of other priests and laypersons of the Archdiocese of Washington.[30] It also created an atmosphere of protest, and assertions of power in response, throughout the country.

These stories once more raised a serious existential question for Connolly: Could he lose everything in his fight for support of the work and lives of priests? Could he lose his own priesthood, even as he fought for the right kind of priesthood? Would he risk it? For him, the answer continued to be yes. He had remembered to do what he learned in Puerto Rico and everywhere else he would face an uncertain future: Take his fears, pray for God's guidance, then let go and immerse himself.

In the midst of all these threats to clergy expression and organization, the members of the South Bronx Catholic Clergy Association asserted themselves at the headquarters of the new archbishop of New York. There they were joined by allies—other priests from outside the South Bronx who were supporters of Kelleher's modern thinking. There was Aldo Tos, a friend of Gigante and Connolly who worked often with them on pastoral and liturgical matters, even though he was based in the West Village parish of St. Joseph's. Tos agreed to be their spokesperson on this subject. In addition, there was Pat McCormack, a classmate and friend of Connolly's who was also considered more forward-thinking and who had a more direct, blunt conversational style.

Cooke expressed the Church's traditional views about the institution of marriage and about the Tribunal's role in sustaining those views when deliberating petitions for annulment and other actions. Tos questioned Cooke's views and, more broadly, his traditional approach to the Church in the post–Vatican II era. "You know, Bishop," he said, "you've got to change your image. The Catholic newspapers, they have pictures of you all over the place, and you're always with the 'blue-haired ladies'"—New York's elite Catholic donors. "I think we need a much more dynamic image of the Church than that."

Cooke, for his part, attempted to ingratiate himself with the priests, many of whom were sports fans, by using sports language, particularly making references to baseball. "Oh, you try not to make too many errors," he said at one point.

Then McCormack, reaching a boiling point, stopped Cooke from any more explanations with his own baseball reference, which silenced the meeting for a few seconds. "Yes, Bishop, but remember, many of the players are leaving the game."

While the meeting ended on a positive note, with Cooke promising ongoing dialogue, the essence of McCormack's warning shot stayed with everyone in the room: Priests were leaving the profession.

Priesthood: A Professional Crisis

For Connolly, the last question to be answered during this time was whether he *wanted* to bring more priests into this struggle.

The 1968 Official Catholic Directory, recording the activities and status of the Roman Catholic Church in the world in the year 1967, reported the first decline in the overall number of American priests since 1940. Even while the total population of American Catholic laypersons continued its constant increase, the body of priests ready to serve them was not growing.[31] The future of priesthood preparation was no more promising than the future of priests: There was a major decline in the number of seminarians across the country, from more than 45,000 in 1967 to 40,000 the following year. This was part of a trend that had begun a decade earlier, since the year Connolly himself graduated: the 1967 seminarian population in the United States was 10,000 fewer than the 1959 population.[32]

In the New York Catholic Church, the story was as bleak as it was elsewhere, as McCormack boldly reminded Cooke. There were 950 priests in the archdiocese in 1973, compared with as many as 1,100 in the 1960s. St. Joseph's Seminary, whose facilities had been vastly expanded in the Spellman era, saw the number of graduating seminarians decline from its high of 33 a year in Connolly's era in the 1950s, to 25 in the mid-1960s, to as low as 12 by the end of the decade. And in the place where it mattered most to Connolly and his peers, the Catholic parishes of the South Bronx were being served by 74 priests in 1975, a drop from 100 in 1965. As Connolly and the others attempted to stand firm in their challenges to Cooke, in their quest for a new Church, and a new way of living the priesthood in the world, the ground was shifting under their feet.

Nationally, the Church's hierarchy and its priests were looking at the problem from opposing sides. In the American Catholic battle to save, baptize, marry, and even bury souls in the faith, the "soldiers" were deserting. Even as the newly organized United States Conference of Catholic Bishops was staking out bold, forward-thinking positions in favor of civil rights, farmworker protests, and income support for the poor, it was issuing a pastoral letter decrying those who departed from the priesthood, calling those who asked to leave the ministry "derelicts."[33] On the other hand, the National Association for Pastoral Renewal called for bishops to examine the trend closely to see what could be done to change it.

In New York, the archdiocesan response was not to conduct a study or to issue a pastoral letter. Instead, in the media capital of the world, they engaged Madison Avenue. In 1973, a group of advertising and media professionals developed a clever message, a carefully crafted campaign to reach Catholic parents and Catholic high school boys and recruit more young New Yorkers: "The New York Priest: God Knows What He Does for a Living." The campaign featured a different priest in each of five ads, including Connolly, which is how he found himself in the newspaper yet again, this time with archdiocesan approval.[34]

Despite his issues with the Chancery and the old Church of the hierarchy, Connolly had agreed to be part of their campaign to recruit more young men into priesthood. As long as there was an opportunity to find others willing to build a Vatican II Church, he was ready to take it. Connolly knew that greater forces were at play, shrinking the army of priests who would build that Church. Even as it shrank, however, he fought to bring the right priests into the South Bronx. He believed that good members of the South Bronx Catholic Clergy Association "went Spanish" willingly. *They knew and embraced the Puerto Rican migrants as their parishioners and committed to their parishioners' lives and fates, even as those parishioners' households became increasingly poor. If there were fewer priests coming to replace them in the future, then they would have to develop new kinds of parishes,* Connolly thought. *Like operating two parishes with one shared staff, the project which he was starting to work on with the priests at St. John Chrysostom. Or a parish chapel led by laypersons, like the Seneca Center he built with Hunts Point Peninsula parishioners.*

Every new change in his life as a priest was a challenge to Connolly: Accept the Church as it was; leave the Church and try to change the world; or try to change both Church and world as a priest. He had committed himself to this life as a priest and would stay committed, even as others around him, including some of his classmates, left. But he was also not ready to accept the Church as it was, not after all these changes in the decade. *Vatican II told him that he and the people of God owned this Church, and that this church was supposed to go into the world and be part of its history. Some battles for the Church had just been fought by him and other priests who believed in Vatican II, but with few victories. There would be more battles, however, for a Vatican II Church. There had to be.*

But the world was also calling.

7

Social Action, Political Power

But where citizens are oppressed by a public authority overstepping its competence, they should not protest against those things which are objectively required for the common good, but it is legitimate for them to defend their own rights and the rights of their fellow citizens against the abuse of this authority, while keeping within those limits drawn by natural law and by the Gospels.

Those who are suited or can become suited should prepare themselves for the difficult, but at the same time, the very noble art of politics, and should seek to practice this art without regard for their own interests or for material advantages. With integrity and wisdom, they must take action against any form of injustice or tyranny, against arbitrary domination by an individual or a political party and any intolerance . . .

—Articles 74 and 75, in Chapter IV, "The Life of the Political Community," *Gaudium et Spes*, Pastoral Constitution on the Church in the Modern World, 81

March

At seven o'clock in the evening on December 16, 1969, Neil Connolly walked down 163rd Street from Southern Boulevard to Simpson Street, crossed the street, and then walked back up 163rd Street to Southern Boulevard. Joined by Pastor John Byrne, Father Lou Gigante, and three hundred parishioners and neighbors of Hunts Point–Longwood, he then walked the pattern again. At the center of their circle were four large metal cans filled with old pieces of lumber and debris, with flames flickering out of each. Everyone on the street chanted and sang for that same heat to be piped through their apartment buildings in the neighborhood. This was a parish protest—the first time Connolly had ever been in a church procession for a neighborhood problem. When Gigante invited him and Byrne to co-organize the event, he felt he had no choice. The bitter cold made clear there was a state of emergency. Still, this kind of marching was new to Connolly.[1]

Three years earlier, in the spirit of Vatican II and at a time ripe for new forms of worship, he and Gigante had led the Easter Eve Ceremony of the New Fire, bringing dozens of parishioners through the streets with candles to liberate them from darkness. Now, they needed fire to liberate them from the cold and from suffering endured at the hands of others. They were stopping traffic on a busy intersection, in the middle of the holiday shopping season, creating a disturbance and conflict with drivers and pedestrians. But this seemed just as right to him as the Ceremony of the New Fire. *Disturbing the world, calling for attention, and marching against acceptance of the status quo, were all right. Because the status quo meant suffering in the buildings housing the marchers.*

In the last few years, Connolly had already spent many days making calls about the buildings in Hunts Point–Longwood. Parishioners came to him after Mass, either in the chapel or at the main church, asking to see him about their problems. He often got on the phone to try to reach some of the government offices that might be relevant: the Department of Buildings, the Housing and Development Administration, the Bronx borough president, the neighborhood's city council representative, and the local congressman. There were not too many results from these calls. Connolly spent much of the time translating the complaints in Spanish for the agency staff, or asking the staff persons what could be done about this, or, very often, being put on hold. In the end, there were only promises to "look into the matter," or other numbers to try calling, or recommendations to call the landlord or the management company—certain to be a dead-end path.

Even in the last few weeks, when the temperatures were low and more buildings were freezing, no one seemed to change their response. Connolly learned that some inspections had been done by the Buildings Department staff, but conditions remained miserable. During some of his apartment visits in the Hunts Point Peninsula, family members walked around the apartments with blankets wrapped around them, while he kept his coat on. The increasing number of calls, along with more and more encounters in icy apartments, reminded Connolly again and again that he was not getting anywhere.

Please, he implored the landlords and the government agencies, *fill the boilers with heating oil, or repair the radiators, or fix the hot water tanks, or replace the broken glass on the living room windows, or get the exterminator to deal with the rats threatening their children, or replace the broken lock on the front door to keep out the junkies.*

In the 1960s, it seemed the entire city was becoming more powerless about its housing problems with each passing year. In 1969, more than 400,000 calls came into the City Central Complaint Bureau of the Office of Code Enforcement over broken heat, hot water, and other issues.[2] Requests to the Office of Rent Control to allow rent reductions for an apartment, which were permitted in cases of serious quality problems, tripled from 113,000 in 1962 to 387,000 in 1969.[3] With too few inspections conducted by Buildings Department staff and meaningless legal enforcement occurring in the courts, landlords had little reason to change their behavior. The authorized rent reductions did little to cut down the number of violations and the power of landlords just seemed to grow. "Despite valiant efforts," said a 1971 special city-commissioned report, "the city of New York has been unable to fully enforce the Housing Maintenance Code to stem the tide of housing deterioration."[4]

It was not just widespread neglect that was overwhelming the residents of the city; it was landlords' outright abandonment of buildings. Many of the negligent landlords being cited by the city were simply walking away from mortgages and operating responsibilities or selling them off. In Hunts Point–Longwood, for example, the two brothers who owned the building at 1029 Simpson Street, which had been gradually taken over by the young addicts known as the "Glue Angels," sold it to the building superintendent. They walked away from a $40,000 debt balance and left the already desperate nonaddict tenants to fend for themselves. Those remaining tenants eventually found a way to leave in the face of police and city inaction and with no help from the new owner. Like several others in Hunts Point–Longwood, the building had become vacant in 1970.[5]

The city government knew which buildings were—like 1029 Simpson—in "serious trouble," a classification for those with thirty or more violations. Of New York's 148,000 multiple-dwelling buildings, 17,000 fell into this category.[6] Officials predicted the future of those buildings in their report: "Abandoned and demolished buildings in recent years have been characterized by a large number of these violations before they finally disappeared from the market." Between July 1965 and 1968 annual demolitions of vacant apartment buildings increased seven times from 215 (1965) to 1,500 (1968).[7] But landlords were at war with tenants and their defenders. They

publicly fought rent control laws, blaming their own neglect and abandonment of their property on those laws. In October 1968, landlord groups
came together and publicly announced that they would abandon another
4,000 buildings, in addition to those already abandoned—estimated by
some at 12,000 buildings in 1968 in New York City.[8]

In the very cold winter of 1969–1970, this increasing neglect worsened
dramatically and a heating crisis swept through the city. With hundreds
of heatless buildings in the South Bronx that winter, Robert Abrams, the
newly elected Bronx borough president, declared a state of emergency.[9]
He called on the city government to enforce the building code and to provide heat directly in affected buildings. He lamented and denounced the
highly publicized freezing death of newborn Jose Luis Infante in a building
on 138th Street in the Mott Haven neighborhood. Abrams called for opening the vast, empty Kingsbridge Armory in the northwest Bronx to shelter
every affected South Bronx household in a heated building overnight. City
hall promised an emergency repairs coordinator, but nothing changed.

First came neglect, then abandonment: an ice
formation from a burst water pipe in an occupied
Hunts Point building doorway. (Photo by Mili Bonilla.)

As he marched that December night and rallied his parishioners, Connolly thought, *Maybe this was the way to go. The polite phone calls were not ending the suffering. News articles were not ending the suffering. The borough president and city hall were not ending the suffering.* While the people on the other end of the phone lines all seemed to accept the human costs of inaction, Connolly could not. *He had no ability to fix a boiler, or the funds to pay for it, or even the legal knowledge to sue the landlords. As a priest, he could pray, he could console, and he could even advocate with city agencies for vulnerable parishioners. Now,* he realized, *he could also march, he could protest, he could organize. After all, he had organized with priests for an election of the archbishop and for the new archbishop to negotiate with South Bronx priests. Now,* Connolly thought, *he should organize here, in the neighborhood, for the people. Not just parishioners, either. After all, he was marching with both strangers and parishioners, and that was where he needed to be—with all the people.*

And, he wondered, *what else could be done?*

Moral Power

Shortly after the protest, Gigante suggested that the parish staff should join an organization of clergy already working on housing issues in the South Bronx. It was an ecumenical group with some Episcopalians, Lutherans, Presbyterians, Baptists, and evangelical ministers, as well as some of the priests they already knew, like Gerry Ryan at St. Luke's and Joe Donahue at St. Anselm. Even some of the women religious from the Dominican Sisters Health Service and Catholic Charities and other organizations were in the group. Connolly thought, *This would be a great thing to join. Maybe they could do something about all these freezing tenants he had marched with. He had never been part of an ecumenical project or organization, but after Vatican II loosened restrictions on this kind of collaboration, there was no reason why not, and this was a chance to do it.* So, he joined the group: the Bronx Clergy Coalition.

The coalition was first led by Presbyterian minister Ron Ridgely. Within a short time, Ridgely brought in a layperson, Frank Handelman, a Jewish social worker trained at the University of Chicago who wanted to become involved in social issues in New York City.[10] The new group requested funds for organizing staff from the Campaign for Human Development, the foundation recently created by the United States Conference of Catholic Bishops (USCCB) to support social and economic justice.[11] Clergy and religious members, who had full-time jobs running community service organizations or ministering to their congregations, could not do the day-to-day work of research, organizing meetings, and planning actions. Ridgely and Handelman were approved by the coalition to serve those roles, and the coalition began work on its campaigns.

There were several issues to tackle, but the coalition was focused at first on the most important one to Connolly: emergency building repairs. Connolly learned more about this issue from the research done by Ridgely and Handelman. Like the other clergy and religious, he would be briefed by them, then publicly play the role of "moral authority." As a representative of many churchgoers, he would also collect copies of the newsletter published by the coalition, which discussed developments on issues important to them. At the end of Sunday Mass, he and Gigante announced the coalition's formation and urged parishioners to take a copy of the newsletter.

Their first action was to write to their representatives on the city council and ask them to pass a law that would compel the city government—either the Buildings Department or the Housing Department—to make emergency repairs in buildings with no heat or hot water, or with some other immediate need. When the repairs were done, the bill stated, the city could then assess the landlord for payment. But with no response from their elected officials, the coalition made a decision. The ministers would need to bring the issue of an emergency repairs bill directly and publicly to the city council during one of its sessions. If the council members did not hear or raise any motion to discuss the legislation, then the coalition would interrupt the meeting. As clergy and ministers, they would use their unique role as moral leaders to highlight the issue, but since standing up in meetings was not really in anyone's comfort zone, they would take an action that was: praying. Connolly, Gigante, and their colleagues reviewed and approved the prayer, and they agreed that Reverend David Wayne, a white Episcopal priest known as "Dave" to the coalition, would lead the group in it.

Connolly knew, from his conversations with Wayne in between meetings, that this action would be difficult for him. His mostly African American congregation, he told Connolly, was fairly conservative about church involvement in "matters of the world." They would look unfavorably at this kind of action being taken by their minister and would not want to be directly involved in lobbying or protest actions. Connolly thought, *He and Gigante were lucky to have a congregation that marched on 163rd Street. Dave was about to show courage, not just in the political world, but in his own church. The coalition ministers would need to support him.*

Two dozen coalition ministers went down to city hall wearing full clerical garb. As they walked in, some of the Bronx council members noticed
their constituent ministers walking in and greeted them. Councilwoman
Aileen Ryan asked Connolly why they were there, but it didn't seem wise
to disclose their plans. He said, "Well, we never saw a city council meeting
before, and we thought we'd come."

Ryan responded, "Oh, thank you for coming."

The council session began. After fifteen minutes it became clear to the
coalition ministers, sitting upstairs in the balcony, that emergency repairs
legislation would not come up in the meeting. They looked at each other,
nodded, and stood up.

Reverend Dave pulled out a sheet of paper and began speaking in a
loud voice: "Since no prayer was offered here today, and it has usually
been done at the beginning of a city council meeting, we will contribute
the prayer."

Everybody on the floor of the council chamber turned their heads
and looked up to the balcony. Dave read the "Litany of the South Bronx
Clergy on Housing," and using the call-and-response method, the group
participated.[12]

"Hear our prayer, O Lord, as we cry out for the human in which thy
people dwell—In your compassion help those forced to live amid inhuman conditions, especially in the South Bronx." As the Litany continued,
Dave reviewed the examples of poor housing conditions, and the clergy
responded, "Good Lord, Deliver Us."

Then the prayer began to focus on the government's role in the housing
crisis and asked for change. Dave called, "From all excuses, postponements,
and delays; from redundant investigations, inquiries, studies, and reports;
from referrals and reconsiderations; and from all subcommittees. . . ."

"Good Lord, Deliver Us," responded the coalition.

Call: "From the excuse that the city council has no power, but only the
mayor, that the mayor has no power, but only the State legislature; that the
State legislature has no power, but only the governor; that the governor has
no power, but only the Congress; that the Congress has no power, but only
the president; and from all buck-passing. . . ."

"Good Lord, Deliver Us," responded the coalition.

And, in a reference to the stark news-making event that was emblematic
of the brutal winter of 1969–1970, Dave called: "Remember the soul of
the child living on East 138th Street who died because of no heat in the
building. . . ."

"Lord, Have Mercy," responded the coalition.

At the end of the Litany, there was no noise below. No response, and no applause.

Then, Tom Cuite, a council member from Brooklyn, bellowed, "This is a day of shame in my life. I am a member of a Roman Catholic parish in Carroll Gardens. I see priests up there at this meeting. This is a disgrace. Today, as a Roman Catholic, I am ashamed."

The clergy were shortly surrounded by police, who pulled them out of the balcony and down to the office of Sandford Garelik, city council president. There they presented their concerns again, and Garelik promised to look into the legislation. He then summoned a staff photographer and asked the ministers, "Anybody want to take a picture with me?" Some did, but Connolly refused, thinking, *it's this "that's a disgrace." Why would anyone want to take picture with him?*[13]

The media attention from the public disruption drove the council to action. Legislation to establish and fund a citywide emergency repairs program was introduced and passed. Connolly and the other coalition members celebrated the victory. Connolly had been excited by the protest, but he was even more pleased that the action had produced results. *He had used his position as a priest before to get quick access to see a doctor, to represent a board before funders from the federal government, and to get a Catholic university to support a special therapeutic community for youth. But this time he had used it as part of a united front of clergy and religious and Protestant ministers to exert the power of moral authority. In this case, they were not just individual ministers caring for their respective flocks,* Connolly realized. *They were representing their cries for change against the unresponsiveness of the political world.*

Yet even as they celebrated, the clergy knew their new work had only just begun. Connolly and the others learned from Ridgely and Handelman that the victory would mean a new kind of campaign. Coalition members would need to monitor their own neighborhoods to see if the Buildings Department actually sent out inspectors and emergency repairs teams when called for. Besides housing repairs, there were other issues such as health care and public assistance that needed the coalition's attention. Moreover, their housing campaign was beginning to take on a citywide character as they formed coalitions with leaders on those issues from other boroughs.

Ridgely and Handelman were essential guides through all this. However, the coalition lost some momentum as they reached the end of their grant from the Campaign for Human Development. With no other funds to replace their salaries, Handelman went on to law school at Columbia

University and Ridgely returned to Virginia for a new ministry. The co-alition continued to meet, but some of its members were creating other organizations, including one for Black Baptists and another for Hispanic Evangelicals, and so those groups of clergy began disappearing from meetings. *They lost power,* Connolly realized, *when they lost their staff, who kept them organized.*

Connolly was thinking a lot about power.

He thought about *how powerless he felt when he was making those hours of phone calls for tenants at the rectory. However, it felt different when he was out on the street with his parishioners and Gigante and Byrne, chanting and yelling for changes. And the meetings with the co-alition, and the disruptive action in city hall, gave him a sense of power. He was doing something that could change things, make things better for the people in Hunts Point–Longwood. Using this organized power as a Catholic priest against the government's power was not a disgrace, as Cuite argued. The motivation mattered. His power was rightly used to end the suffering of freezing tenants. A priest could use organized, moral power in the world in order to stop suffering.*

Political Power

Then one night at the rectory, in one of their chats over Scotch and Tab and the nightly news, Gigante began discussing his frustrations with the emergency repairs campaign. He spoke about how powerless he felt in getting the attention of the city council members, the borough president, and others, to do something. There was a lot to be done, and the neighborhood was going to need major funding to be saved, or even to slow down the deterioration. But someone needed to fight for that funding and not accept the status quo. Then Gigante told Connolly and Byrne his news: He was running for Congress. There was a new open seat and he was going after it. He wanted Byrne and Connolly to support him and get the coalition's help because there were only about two months to campaign before the June primary.

This wouldn't be Gigante's first ever involvement in a local election or a battle for funding. He had participated in meetings organized by Father John Ahern when he led the cardinal's commission to support the War on Poverty. Ahern had urged South Bronx priests gathered at Athanasius to pursue federal funding opportunities and join the local anti-poverty boards. Those parishes, which had formed organizations such as Seneca Center and SISDA, would need to submit their requests for financial support to these boards. Everyone knew that it was important to get representation, so Gigante and Connolly submitted a candidate for their local board—John Wright from Casita Maria—and campaigned for him with no luck. Gigante also attended meetings of the board to make the case for Seneca Center and SISDA, and to challenge it when it seemed to favor organizations politically connected to one man: Ramón Vélez. Gigante was often in conflict with the Vélez-controlled board, but he wanted to stay involved to get support for the parish organizations. He even urged parishioners to attend the meetings and advocate for their organizations. That led to arguments in the public board forums, which took place at the Hunts Point Palace.

On one of those nights, Gigante and his supporting parishioners left the meeting and walked back to the church. Walking down Fox Street, Gigante and the men and women were surrounded by a group of men, and they were forced to fight their way out. They held their own, and before the police arrived, the "ambushers" fled. Everyone knew they had been sent by Vélez to intimidate the Athanasius group and stop them from challenging the board. When Connolly learned about this, he realized that the violence in the Hunts Point–Longwood neighborhood was not just coming from the drug dealers, like the ones who had thrown the beer can at his car that night he dropped off Lillian Camejo. *Violence was possible in the political world, something Ahern could not have prepared them for when he was promoting Catholic involvement in the War on Poverty. Some people and organizations*, Connolly thought, *really meant war. They did not fool around, not even with priests or church members. They were going to get power either with votes in the public meetings or with fists in the public streets.* This was what Gigante and Connolly faced as they threw themselves into a historic election.

In 1970, a battle took place with the creation of the new Twenty-First Congressional District, which included Hunts Point–Longwood.[14] Publicly described as "the Puerto Rican District," the Twenty-First Congressional District was created by the New York State Legislature, "drawn" into existence under the mandate of the 1965 Federal Voting Rights Act, which required fair treatment for racial and language minorities on all voting issues, including the creation of districts.[15] With no Puerto Rican representation in Congress from a city with a large Puerto Rican population, this new district had great significance. It was seen as an opportunity to give a national voice for Puerto Ricans, two decades after the beginning of the *Gran Migración*. It was also seen as an opportunity for the South Bronx, which had become such a poor area over those decades, to have a voice in Washington.

But Puerto Rican representation was not guaranteed by the geographic composition of the area, which attracted a diverse group of candidates. It included neighborhoods in the southern and southeastern Bronx, the eastern half of East Harlem with its large Italian population, and the westernmost Queens neighborhoods, including Greek and Italian Astoria. "Backroom" political negotiations in New York State created this unique district, which was also known as the "Triborough District" because all areas were connected to each other by New York City's Triborough Bridge. As a result, only 22,000 out of its 75,000 registered Democratic voters were of Puerto Rican descent.[16] However, much of the political and media discussion focused on two leading contenders who had been rivals for the support of Bronx Puerto Ricans for nearly a decade: Herman Badillo and Ramón Vélez.

Badillo was a lawyer and accountant who had risen through the political ranks of New York City.[17] He was the city's first Puerto Rican deputy commissioner, and he became the first Puerto Rican borough leader when elected to the Bronx Borough presidency in 1965. In 1969, he was the first serious Puerto Rican candidate for mayor, a position he coveted all his political life. Because of his strong name recognition, because the district was mostly in the Bronx, and because it was seen as the "Puerto Rican District," Badillo was seen as the front-runner.

Vélez, meanwhile, whom Gigante and Connolly had become familiar with because of the Poverty Board, was a social worker with a different approach to political power.[18] As founder and leader of a local political club, Vélez also built two important anti-poverty organizations in the southern Bronx, each multimillion dollar social service providers. Vélez grew both by obtaining federal funding, beginning with the War on Poverty. He used his political club and Puerto Rican community network to gain recognition as well as money, and he became a significant political force, especially in Mott Haven and Hunts Point–Longwood. That made him Badillo's chief rival for the new congressional district.

Three other non–Puerto Rican candidates with some electoral support were also in the race. An Italian lawyer out of Astoria, Peter Vallone was the only candidate from Western Queens.[19] He was the son of a politically well-known judge and the leader of the Astoria Civic Association. Also, the only African American in the race, Dennis Coleman, was a former Bronx state senator.[20] With an endorsement from black Congresswoman Shirley Chisholm, Coleman hoped to attract a large turnout from his ethnic community.

In the middle of this crowded field of candidates, Father Louis Gigante made his entrance. Connolly joined his friend at a press conference on April 16, 1970, at the area originally known as "Little Korea," in front of an abandoned car and semi-abandoned, garbage-filled apartment building on Fox Street near the Westchester Avenue train line. Gigante stated his case: "The politicians have abandoned us. . . . I know it's unusual for a Catholic priest to run for this high political office, but there is nobody running who will do the job of getting our people the help they need."[21]

The Gigante campaign established an office on 163rd Street near Intervale Avenue. Connolly visited the office nearly every day, talking things over with volunteers, discussing strategy with Gigante and his team. This included a friend, Al Giordano, whom Gigante had known since their days together at Georgetown, and who had advised Gigante when he ran for student body president. Connolly coordinated with both Giordano and Gigante, organizing an intensive outreach effort with their church contacts, especially among the Catholic priests they had gotten to know from the Catholic Clergy Association. Connolly made calls to priests and arranged for a visit by Gigante: "Hey, listen, do you have any meetings soon? How about letting Lou go there and explain what he's doing?" He also reached the active Protestant ministers of the Bronx Clergy Coalition to arrange for campaign visits. There was little time to waste, so every day and event was important.

Connolly was sometimes so active with the campaign, in fact, that outsiders assumed he was Gigante's campaign manager. He was even approached by the police with that assumption. One day, a detective from the Forty-First Precinct came to the rectory and asked to speak with Connolly. He politely asked Connolly, "I think you're Father Gigante's campaign manager, right?"

Connolly was very curious about his visitor, but responded, matter-of-factly, "No, actually, I'm not the manager."

"Well," said the detective, impatiently, "you'll see him. Listen"—and now he spoke almost in a whisper—"Please tell him—you can't have gunfire in the elections."

Connolly was startled. "What's happening?" he asked. "Who's shooting guns??" he asked, wondering what was happening to Gigante on the streets.

"Well," said the detective, incredulous, "you know along Bruckner Boulevard, they're putting up posters. Other people are taking them down, and then guns are going off. I saw it."

"Holy shit," murmured Connolly, still in shock, and not conscious of using a vulgarity in front of the detective.

The detective stared at him and then pointed his finger at Connolly, speaking slowly to make each word of advice count. "Calm down the troops, okay, Father?"

Connolly duly reported the discussion to Gigante, and they wondered how to control the violence. They guessed which campaign was responsible for taking aim at their campaign staff—after all, Vélez had had people sent to attack Gigante and his parishioners that night on Fox Street. Sure, the rivalry between Badillo and Vélez was intense and received the attention in *El Diario*, the largest Spanish-language newspaper in New York City. But the Vélez-Gigante rivalry had been serious even prior to the congressional campaign. It wasn't just the street brawl. At one Poverty Board meeting, in the middle of another heated forum about allocating funding, Vélez had walked by a seated Gigante, dressed in his cassock, and insulted him by calling him a *Maricon*, a Spanish derogatory slang term for a gay man. Gigante had quickly responded, throwing a punch at Vélez.[22] That was why the Vélez campaign was considered a principal suspect in the shootings. They just hoped that Frankie Gregory from their own campaign was not involved.

Connolly and Gigante had gotten to know Gregory, whom everyone just knew as "Frankie," over the years. He conducted crap games, or streetside dice gambling, but these were run out of East Harlem, not Hunts Point–Longwood, where he lived. Gregory was a strong, short, squat man with a reputation as a tough guy who befriended dealers and thieves from the street, and Connolly and Gigante initially avoided him. After spending some time with them, however, he became interested in the parish campaigns, volunteering with the Poverty Board efforts and SISDA, and then with the congressional campaign. What Gregory did outside of their view, they did not know about. They did not think it was a problem, but they were never sure. Connolly thought about Gregory when the detective visited, though, because Frankie always carried a gun, which could be seen bulging underneath his shirt at the waist.

But, Connolly learned, *there were things in an election campaign—even in one's own campaign—that could not be controlled. Not in the world, nor in the Church*. One day during the campaign, Monsignor Schultheiss, vicar of the Bronx, invited Connolly over to St. Raymond's rectory, his home, for dinner. Connolly respected Schultheiss, thinking of him as a generous man and a very good listener, despite his institutional demeanor. After a hearty dinner, Schultheiss asked, "Neil, can you stay a little longer?" After the parish priests left, Schultheiss sighed. "I was asked to call you over," he said, "because you know Lou better than anybody else. I was supposed to ask Lou to get out of the race. The archdiocese asked me to do that."

Connolly was shocked and asked, "Well, why?"

Schultheiss paused and said, quietly but clearly, "Well, all this family stuff is going to be all over the news and the radio—is he able to sustain this, to take this?"

"Yes," Connolly replied. "I had a long conversation with him about it. He expects it to come. And he told me he is prepared to withstand it. He said it will not affect this campaign."

"Thank you very much," said Schultheiss. "I'm not going to talk to him. I got enough information from you."

The conversation, brief as it was, was an acknowledgment that Gigante had a brother, Vincent, who was thought to be heavily involved and perhaps a leader in one of New York City's five organized crime families.[23] Though Gigante was not involved, his brother's activities would follow his campaign. Connolly, however, knew and trusted his longtime friend as a priest with a commitment to his parish, his neighborhood, and the needs of the poor. Gigante had joined Connolly in Summer in the City, in building a community organization, in creating a Vatican II parish, in bringing in a new drug rehabilitation program for teenagers, and in the daily challenges of serving poor needy families facing job losses and government bureaucrats. He had joined the petition campaign to elect an archbishop and, along with Connolly, endured the losses of parishioners and financial support. After eight years together, Connolly and Gigante were committed to their mission as priests, and this campaign was part of that mission.

Their efforts were then concentrated on turnout and mobilization of voters. They called parishioners, urging them to go out and vote on primary election day, which often had less participation than a November election. They had a team of callers at the rectory, as well as allies in other parishes. Connolly even reached out to the nuns cloistered in the Corpus Christi monastery in the Peninsula, driving them to the polling site himself on election day. With talk on the streets, meetings throughout the South Bronx, and phone calls and distribution of fliers, the campaign was a very exciting experience for Connolly, who was happy to see the genuine involvement of the people they knew.

On June 23, 1970, however, Gigante lost, his 5,691 votes taking third place to Badillo, whose 7,723 votes edged out the surprise second-place candidate Vallone, with 7,151 votes.[24] At a gathering of parishioners, neighbors, and other supporters that election night at Athanasius auditorium, the news was disappointing, but Connolly realized *he had never known such excitement. Not the excited fear he felt while chasing car battery thieves or hearing shootouts under the train station. No, this was an excitement full of*

Candidate Fr. Louis Gigante campaigning on streets with his entourage. (Photo by Chris Sheridan. Courtesy of *Catholic New York*.)

hope for the future of the parish and the neighborhood, and for the South Bronx. The people who had suffered within their freezing apartments and dangerous hallways might have a voice. And he realized that, as with the protest at the city council meeting, *for the few months of the campaign, he and Gigante were giving them that voice.*

Connolly and Gigante's project was part of a national trend beginning in the 1960s: Clergy and religious were now serving in elected office in the United States at all levels. Three Protestant clergy were already serving congressmen during Gigante's campaign. The city of New York was home to the most famous Reverend Adam Clayton Powell, Jr., of the legendary Abyssinian Baptist Church in Harlem.[25] Powell, the long-serving and controversial leader of the House Committee on Health Education and Labor, was known for his national advocacy for the inner city as well as for his battles for control of Harlem's anti-poverty funds.

The War on Poverty, which called for "maximum feasible participation," generated political participation by locally involved urban ministers, including Protestant clerics, Catholic priests, and Catholic sisters and brothers as well. Vatican II's call to bring "the Church into the world" motivated religious and priests to serve on community anti-poverty boards and school boards. In the South Bronx, Sister Alice Kerins of St. Anthony of Padua was elected to serve on the local school board, joining other religious and priests in New York City electoral politics. Several priests served in local offices in Massachusetts, while Sister Lucy Falcone, dean of women at Florida's St. Leo's College, also served as the mayor of her college town.

But 1970 witnessed a new phenomenon: Several Catholic priests ran for Congress.[26] Father Robert Drinan, dean of Boston College's law school, ran on an anti-war platform. Father John McLaughlin, associate editor of the Jesuit magazine *America*, ran for the U.S. Senate in his native Rhode Island. Father Joseph Lucas, a professor at Youngstown State University, ran for Congress in the city of Youngstown, Ohio, which had a sizeable Puerto Rican population. The issues of poverty and the Vietnam War were central to those campaigns and others as far west as California, and as far south as Georgia. But the only Catholic priest to run for Congress in New York State was Father Gigante.

Clergy campaigns for political office raised the question of the Church's role in the world, in the social and political arenas of the country. Although the Archdiocese of New York did not publicly comment on Gigante's campaign, the United States Conference of Catholic Bishops strongly urged its local bishops to discourage priests from direct political participation that involved seeking elected office.[27] During the 1940s, 1950s, and 1960s the American Catholic Church had not been shy about taking a public political stance on "Church" issues such as government support of Catholic schools and establishing a decency code for the film industry. In the 1960s, after Vatican II spurred the creation of the Bishop's Conference, it took on the issues of "the world." Priests, bishops, and even cardinals now spoke out on the Vietnam War and on race issues, civil rights, and the War on Poverty. But the idea of putting direct responsibility for all the laws of the land in the hands of a Catholic priest didn't just make non-Catholic Americans nervous. The institutional Church also questioned whether a priest-politician could still be loyal to the Church, especially in the situations that could involve a decision which ignored or contradicted Church teachings.

Another Campaign

With no doubts about either the rightness of his campaign or the value of political power, Gigante made another run in a couple of years. In 1973, when new electoral districts were created for the expanded city council, Gigante declared himself a candidate for the district representing Hunts Point–Longwood.[28] Connolly, who had seen Gigante build his political base after the 1970 campaign loss, was not surprised. They spent less time together in parish activities than they had before the 1970 campaign, because Gigante was devoting himself to building two organizations: the Bruckner Democratic Club[29] and a housing organization called the South East Bronx Community Organization, or SEBCO. But, as much as he had done during the congressional campaign, Connolly came to the support of his friend on the streets and in the church.

Connolly and Gigante tried to get support for the new campaign from Church headquarters and from their parishioners. They held a meeting with Cardinal Cooke to inform him of Gigante's plans. In the course of the meeting at the cardinal's residence, Cooke was friendly, but as in the South Bronx Catholic Clergy Association meetings, he was noncommittal and nonconfrontational.[30] As Gigante explained the need for genuine advocacy and reform against the increasingly desperate situation in Hunts Point–Longwood and the South Bronx, Cooke merely listened in silence. Gigante made no requests for approval, and Cooke granted none. At the end of the discussion, Cooke presented Gigante and Connolly with a book about developing laypersons. Everyone shook hands, and Connolly and Gigante went back to work on the campaign, realizing they were on their own.

In the streets and at subway stations, they handed out fliers and called on the passersby to come out and vote. "Vote for Gigante! Gigante for council!" Connolly would bark at the commuters.

"What's so good about him? What the hell has he done?" was the response of some commuters at the Hunts Point subway station, where hundreds of people poured in during the early morning rush hour. Connolly would speak to the occasional person who bothered to stop and explain that Gigante had been fighting for housing and neighborhood people for years. Some people were fascinated with the idea of a priest in office, and Connolly found some hopefulness in those conversations.

Others had their doubts, including some of the people in the church itself. Athanasius parishioners were sometimes heard commenting after Mass, "*Ese cura, esta perdiendose en la politica. La politica es sucia.*" ("That priest, getting himself lost in politics. Politics is dirty.") Nevertheless, Connolly and Gigante attempted to have discussions in the church after Mass was over to see what parishioners found wrong with the neighborhood or what they felt city hall should be doing to fix the neighborhood. Sometimes, to make the discussion very immediate and relevant for the people, Connolly just commented about the state of a particular building. The two priests hoped they could make the connection between the Church and the life of the neighborhood and thus involve the churchgoers in doing something about their living conditions.

On June 13, 1973, Gigante won the Democratic primary with a slight margin over the East Harlem candidate, Bill del Toro, which meant he would win the general election in November. Six months later, before he was sworn in as the new city council member for Hunts Point–Longwood and East Harlem, Gigante celebrated Mass at St. Athanasius Church on the Feast of the Epiphany. He held a ceremony after the Mass in which he pledged to the parishioners that he would work to serve and protect them.[31]

Connolly was happy for Gigante and that the neighborhood would have a strong voice in city government, four years after they and their ecumenical colleagues had disrupted that same government with their Litany. But he had questions, which he had begun asking Gigante and himself during the founding days of the political club which Gigante had built as well. *As priests of Vatican II, they could promote the involvement of laypersons in the world, just like they did in those special Masses, and in their march on 163rd Street, and even in Summer in the City. Maybe they could have promoted some of the club leaders like Jimmy Alston or Freddie Caraballo to be their candidate. It would have given the people from the neighborhood a belief in one of their own as a leader, and that they could be leaders too. People could be taught to speak up for themselves, to raise their voice against the unjust conditions they were enduring—not just at Mass, but in public, before the world.*

As he gathered with hundreds of parishioners that Epiphany day, Connolly looked at them and thought, *These people could become responsible for their Church and for their world, like they were at the Seneca chapel.* Vatican II told Connolly and all the members of the Church: *You are the people of God and you are responsible for your Church.* As the faithful listened to Gigante's pledge to protect them and lead them, Connolly decided, *The people of God should lead the world. We have to develop them. Somehow. That is why we are priests.*

Facing an Enemy

Ironically, Gigante served on the New York City Council at the same time as two of his opponents in the 1970 congressional race. Peter Vallone, the lawyer from Queens, was the city council member from Astoria, and he would rise up through the ranks. Meanwhile, next to Gigante's district, representing Hunts Point–Longwood was the Mott Haven District, now represented by his longtime rival, Ramón Vélez. One day, a delegation from Vélez's South Bronx Democratic Club visited the rectory at St. Athanasius to meet with Gigante and discuss their political agendas. Stunned to see them as he was leaving the rectory, Connolly remarked to them, "Isn't this interesting? One day you're at war with each other, and the next day you're here." Connolly was reminded that, for Vélez and his people, power was power, and loyalties and principles did not matter much. He wondered if the suffering of his neighborhood residents mattered to these visitors.

While Gigante strategized on the council, Connolly was focused on an important new project for Seneca Center: the creation of a community health clinic that would serve the Peninsula community. Working with a friend of his, Doctor Ben Reynolds, and a proposal writer from the Community Service Society, a service and policy organization devoted to poor communities in New York City, Connolly and the Seneca Center Board developed a proposal for comprehensive care. It would bring dedicated medical school graduates into a public service corps to staff the clinic, providing them with full loan forgiveness in return. It would make available timely appointments, full checkups, and treatments to address the actual health needs of the population. In doing so, it would resolve many of the issues plaguing the existing health care system for Peninsula residents.

The private hospitals which had served the Peninsula through the 1950s were gone by the 1960s. Lincoln Hospital, originally on Bruckner Boulevard, was relocated; still the closest public medical institution at its new site on 149th Street, it was further away from Hunts Point–Longwood. A municipal health facility, Lincoln was historically considered to provide abysmal care.[32] People were rumored to leave in worse condition than when they entered. Connolly remembered a resident who was stuck inside his car after it was hit by a truck near Bruckner Boulevard. Connolly was called to the scene to administer last rites, just in case. When Connolly asked the victim if he was all right, he responded, "¡Padre, por favor, no dejen que me lleven a Lincoln!" ("Father, please, do not let them take me to Lincoln!")

On dozens of trips accompanying sick parishioners, from emotionally troubled teens to alcoholic adults, Connolly had seen firsthand how hard it was to be taken care of in the South Bronx's emergency rooms. He had learned over the years that local clinics were no better, though. Attending a panel discussion of New York's health care systems, Connolly learned that hospitals and their "clinics" were really established to meet doctors' educational requirements, not patients' needs. Whether in hospital-affiliated clinics or stand-alone clinics, which served many poor patients a day and were thus called "Medicaid mills," people could not get appointments for months at a time. On the visit days, patients were made to wait for a long time and were then seen quickly with inconsistent and incomplete evaluations and treatments. *Seneca Center's clinic would change that, if they could get it funded.*

When Connolly submitted their proposal to the Federal Department of Health, the Seneca Center Board was told that they needed to submit the proposal along with the designated federally qualified health service provider for the area. That "recommended" partner for Seneca Center was the Hunts Point Multi-Service Center, the organization directed by a familiar South Bronx leader: Ramón Vélez. So Connolly would have to work out an arrangement with Vélez if their innovative proposal was going to even have a chance of consideration.

Connolly learned more about Vélez as he was preparing himself for their meeting.[33] After the federal War on Poverty was initiated, almost every social service and community initiative funded in Mott Haven, Melrose, and Hunts Point–Longwood answered to Ramón Vélez. An aggressive Puerto Rican social worker who had arrived in New York with the *Gran Migración*, Vélez capitalized on the fast-growing Puerto Rican presence in the southern Bronx and the political establishment's unresponsiveness to their poverty. He appealed to Puerto Rican national pride by founding the Puerto Rican Day Parade in 1958 and had controlled its operations and finances ever since.

A founder and leader of the South Bronx Democratic Club, Vélez fielded candidates for every local office, and ensured they won in any way he could, including intimidation. As a result, he controlled boards of the local government planning structures, forcing city government to use and recommend his organizations when it came to federal funding applications. With boards controlled by Vélez, the Hunts Point Multi-Service Center and Hunts Point Community Corporation evolved into multimillion-dollar service organizations with hundreds of employees. These employees, in turn, became loyal political campaign "volunteers" for elections in the neighborhoods served by those organizations.

Vélez was thought to have warded off any potential opposition to his funding and political control with violence. Gigante and his parishioners had had to fight that one night after an anti-poverty board meeting. And on another night, after a meeting on the Federal Model Cities program funding at a local school, another incident occurred. An opponent of Vélez was walking past the parking lot gate when a car rushed out of the lot, fatally struck the pedestrian, and sped off. No one was found guilty, despite an official investigation, but most suspected Vélez was behind the incident.

Connolly kept all this information in mind as he went to the headquarters of the Hunts Point Multi-Service Center in neighboring St. Anselm's parish. While he had met Vélez before in a public setting, Connolly was meeting with him one-on-one for the first time. Vélez was a short, obese, well-dressed, and clean-shaven man with a broad smile. His large office was filled with photos of himself alongside elected officials, including presidents, governors, and mayors, as well as awards, certificates, and plaques. He greeted Connolly warmly and said, "Oh Father Connolly, how are you? So marvelous to see you!"

Connolly discussed the Seneca Center and its proposal for the innovative health clinic to serve the Peninsula, an area in which Vélez's organization spent little time, except for a youth program next to the Seneca Center. Connolly thought Vélez was attentive and even supportive as he smiled, sitting back in a plush executive chair at his large desk, his arms resting comfortably on the arms of the chair. Excited about the possibility of implementing this Seneca Center solution, Connolly began to explore ways in which the clinic could operate in conjunction with the existing clinics of Hunts Point Multi-Service Center, whose clinics largely operated in the Longwood side of the neighborhood. But before he could lay out all of his ideas, Vélez interrupted him. He suddenly leaned forward to his desk and said, "Oh, sure, Father Connolly, sure. I'd love to be able to work together with you and be partners with Seneca." Then Vélez paused, and with a broad beaming smile, he lifted both hands to emphasize his point and explain his very important political arithmetic—arithmetic which had served him well all these years in the anti-poverty world: "But don't forget—my representatives on the board will be five, and yours will be four."

At that point, the meeting ground to a halt, as Connolly realized Vélez had no intention of give-and-take bargaining, or of permitting any kind of independence for Seneca to design and operate the center as it had planned in the proposal. "No, no, no," said Connolly politely, as he stood up. "Ramon, no thanks. I don't bargain that way." In that moment, Connolly realized, *the proposed public service clinic in Hunts Point Peninsula was never going to happen.*

Defending a Political Priest

The meeting with Vélez was not Connolly's last lesson on power. An incident took place during Gigante's term on the New York City Council which raised questions for Connolly about the Church and loyalty, and lay ownership.

Connolly knew Rafael Collado as Athanasius's very bright and faithful parishioner, whose parish history had gone from baptismal lessons under Connolly as an untrained Catholic school parent to taking on increasing leadership roles. These included organizing the apartment visits for the Christian Base Community scripture-reflection-discussion groups in the Peninsula. Connolly knew that Collado was not only an inspired leader, but also a very excitable man. Collado had expressed concerns to Connolly about "political enemies" of Gigante, who was still an active priest even during his term in the city council. However, Connolly did not know how concerned he was until one Sunday. After the main Spanish Mass, which was offered by Gigante, Collado came up to Connolly outside the church.

"You know, Father," he confided in an almost whisper, "I suspected today was going to be the day when the political enemies of Father Gigante would try to disrupt Mass." He continued, in an animated tone, "And I brought my boys along, and we have bats." He gestured to his sons, who were standing off to the side with their equipment. "I was not going to let that happen again. I went through some of these interruptions in Cuba. I saw stuff that took place there."

Connolly paused, astonished. He quickly replied, "No, Rafael, you can't do that. Please, don't ever do that again in this Church."

Collado apologized, and they went on to discuss other things. But the memory of the incident kept going through Connolly's mind for days. Connolly thought, *This man really thought he was doing God's work. He did not want to see the Holy Eucharist disrupted by the enemies of a priest, by people of the world who had nothing to do with the Church. There are people who love their Church so much and feel a direct personal responsibility for it, as if it were their own home. Would it be right to stand in front of one's own home and say, "Nobody's going to pass this way"? In the American Catholic Church, there was public discussion about a "just war" theory, and about nuclear deterrence, but nothing much was said about defending one's church. What about pacifism?* Connolly wondered. *In wars and areas under attack, is it better to just put one's hands down and turn the other cheek?*

Connolly even raised the issue during a course he was taking with Father Benedict Groeschel on the subject of spirituality, up at the seminary. He wondered about this parishioner, who loved his church and worked to develop a spirituality, to strengthen his relationship with God. *Could the desire to keep the holy place holy turn the wrong way and, in leading to violence, defeat the purpose with unholy actions?* The ways of the world could sometimes impose themselves on the ways of the Church. This use of violent power here would engage the Church with the world, but not in the way Connolly had wanted or Vatican II had envisioned.

Gigante's political involvement, in addition to leading to a potential conflict during Mass, led to another parish staff conflict with the Archdiocese of New York. The three priests left in the rectory—Byrne, Gigante, and Connolly—learned that Gigante was not going to have his name included in the official New York Catholic Directory as a priest of St. Athanasius. Gigante had been at the church for over a decade, and even as a councilman he continued to say Mass and serve the parishioners. Byrne and Connolly felt that this editorial action was a first sign that the parish might lose Gigante soon, perhaps by a transfer or some other diocesan action.

"I'll be considered a pariah in the diocese," said Gigante. "I don't want that to happen."

The three priests decided to go down together to the archdiocese and meet with the vicar general, Jim Mahoney, and confront him about this move. "He's not really acting as a parish priest any longer," Mahoney said.

"He is very much a parish priest," fired back Byrne, a veteran of battles with the archdiocese over labor issues and the 1968 Memorandum of Priorities, both of which had led to his own transfers. "Why don't you come up and visit the parish and see for yourself?" Byrne said with a challenging tone.

Mahoney didn't want to answer Byrne directly, instead looking for a technicality. "Well, he's not full-time as a priest," he said, referencing the political campaigns and his work in elected office.

Connolly responded with indignation, using a comparison to a well-known priest. "Well, what about George Kelly? He's spending a lot of his time at St. John's University. How is that any different?"

Connolly knew this was a delicate issue in the archdiocese, the question of Kelly's work. Kelly was a parish priest at St. Monica's on Manhattan's Upper East Side, but he was also a professor at St. John's University in Queens. Originally a progressive, pro-labor priest, Kelly shifted increasingly to the right in terms of Church thinking. In contrast to Vatican II and the Papal Encyclical *Divino Afflante Espiritu*, Kelly took positions which were increasingly critical of modern scriptural study. Connolly knew that Kelly was widely considered a controversial figure among priests and the archdiocese, and he knew that the archdiocese would not remove him from his position, for fear of generating attention for such a move.[34]

So did the vicar general.

Byrne said, "We want to hear from Cardinal Cooke on this," and the discussion ended shortly afterward. Mahoney dropped his arguments. Gigante's name remained under "St. Athanasius" in the directory.

They never heard about the issue again. But as Connolly thought about Collado's plan to defend the church, he thought about that meeting with Mahoney. *A lay leader was willing to stand up for his church and for the priest-politician and others who were part of his community. The Institutional Church, meanwhile, was ready to remove that priest-politician and keep the Church out of world conflicts.*

This was why Connolly had mobilized the petition campaign, and why Byrne had presented the Memorandum of Priorities a few years earlier: because the Church needed to support priests like Gigante and Byrne and himself, as conditions were worsening in the parish neighborhoods, and as power brokers like Vélez were flexing political muscle to stop a health center for the people of Hunts Point Peninsula. The three of them, as well as many other priests in New York, needed the Institutional Church to support those priests who had gone Spanish, who chose to follow Vatican II and be "in the world."

This was the history of humankind being played out, right here in Hunts Point–Longwood. If the Church was to be in the world, as Gaudium et Spes *called for, and be living in history with humankind, then this piece of humankind could not wait, and neither could this piece of the Church. The history of this parish and its service to its neighborhood and its migrant Puerto Rican people was marching on. The Church needed to march with this neighborhood, and with this people. The march had begun for him that December night on 163rd Street. He needed to continue the march as a priest in the world.*

8

⠿

South Bronx—Commitment and Abandonment

"For I was hungry and you gave me something to eat; I was thirsty and you gave me something to drink; I was a stranger and you invited me in; I needed clothes and you clothed me; I was sick and you looked after me, I was in prison and you came to visit me." Then the righteous will answer him, "Lord, when did we see you hungry and feed you, or thirsty and give you something to drink? When did we see you a stranger and invite you in, or needing clothes and clothe you? When did we see you sick or in prison and go to visit you?" The King will reply, "Truly, I tell you, whatever you did to the least of these brothers and sisters of mine, you did for me."

—Matthew 25:35–40, Bilingual Bible, Good News Translation, United Bible Societies.

Tiffany Street Rescue

On a warm evening in the summer of 1974, Neil Connolly stood in front of an empty apartment building on Tiffany Street and Southern Boulevard. The building across the street from the church had just survived a fire. It was the first time one of the neighborhood fires had come so close to Athanasius. Smoke was still in the air, and firefighters, some covered with soot, were pulling back water hoses along with axes and other equipment. Families were huddled outside talking to each other, then looking up and pointing to their former homes and the places where the fire had reached inside the building. They were shaking their heads but relieved that no one was injured. Connolly, standing next to the fire captain, saw that the whole building was burned and that no one was going back.

"We're kind of concerned about the people here," he said. "Where are they going to go tonight?"

The captain responded, "Father, don't worry about them. Many of them knew about this fire." Connolly must have looked surprised, because the captain clarified: "They were told that there was a fire going to take place tonight, so—" He turned to Connolly with a knowing look. "You make sure you're not in your apartment." Looking over at the huddled tenants near the fire truck, the captain finished: "They're hoping that they'll eventually be placed on a housing list."

Relieved that the tenants probably had already found places to stay that night, Connolly was still troubled. *Did people know? How? Was someone in the building responsible for this? Why would anyone do this to a building full of tenants, even if they were given advance warning? Why would they take away their homes?* The captain seemed to take this whole event in stride, as if he had been through this scene many times. Connolly knew he was from Engine Company 82. He had seen their truck more often in the neighborhood recently, or heard them, and he knew they were getting very busy.

In fact, these days there was nonstop activity in Engine Company 82, on Intervale Avenue, around the corner from the Forty-First Precinct in Hunts Point–Longwood. From that location, which also housed Engine Company 85, Ladder Company 31, and Tactical Control Unit 712, the firefighters of Engine Company 82 answered callouts to several hundred fires a year in the 1960s, but the number grew as the area became more crowded and poorer.[1] By the late 1960s, the number had reached a few *thousand*, and in 1971, they reported answering 9,111 fire alarms.[2] Connolly began hearing stories of fires in the area both from parishioners and from news articles and television shows. A firefighter from their company would later say that his was "the busiest firehouse in the city and probably in the world."

Connolly thought highly of these firefighters. *They were saving our buildings. These were the same buildings the Bronx Clergy Coalition has been trying to save with the emergency repairs campaign.* He also remembered the men at the firehouse in the Peninsula who had been so welcoming of the Seneca Center *parranderos* on those Christmas Eves a few years earlier. And he recalled reading about the firehouses opening in the South Bronx in the late 1960s[3] and about protests by a fire department chief over some closings of the same firehouses which the city carried out in 1972.[4] This had happened because Mayor Lindsay commissioned a Rand

Institute study, having been led to believe there were "inefficiencies" in the department. In 1971, Rand proposed closing a number of firehouses, including some in the South Bronx.[5]

Thinking about the closures, Connolly thought, *What a bad idea. With all the people who had to be saved here on Tiffany Street and Southern Boulevard, how bad would it have been if the firefighters didn't get to the building in time? They were probably so busy that their captain just took this incident in stride and moved on to get ready for the next one.* Seeing the firefighters get back on the truck, Connolly noticed the exhaustion, as they finished their battle with the fire. Then his thoughts turned to the neighbors he had just lost.

What about the housing list the captain mentioned? The building was destroyed inside, so no one was going back to this place. These neighbors, who had been across the street for all the years Connolly had been a priest at Athanasius, would now become migrants again. This old piece of the neighborhood was gone, for good. Their new neighborhood would likely be outside of Hunts Point–Longwood, just like it had been for the ones who left when the buildings were being slowly abandoned by landlords. But with this fire; it was different. Here, abandonment was sudden and complete, and it was noticed by everyone in the neighborhood. Connolly thought, *With more fires going on in Hunts Point–Longwood, fire services couldn't be cut here. That wouldn't be efficient; it would be dangerous.*

Crisis and Cuts

In 1974, Connolly heard more news about abandonment and cuts after a new mayor, Abraham Beame, took power at the same time Connolly's friend Gigante became a new Council member.[6] The city of New York was going through a fiscal crisis.[7] Federal funding for cities was declining under President Nixon, who issued a national moratorium on housing rehabilitation programs. When Nixon resigned, President Ford continued the same austerity program,[8]—a major shift from a decade earlier when Lyndon B. Johnson launched the War on Poverty, or a generation earlier when the federal government authorized the National Housing Act to counter "urban blight" with "urban renewal," the active destruction and replacement of poor neighborhoods.

Therefore, when New York City turned to the federal government to prevent the possibility of the biggest bankruptcy ever by a city, Congress and the president denied the funds. Connolly picked up a copy of the *Daily News* in June 1975 and read the headline, "Ford to City: Drop Dead."[9]

Three months later, the city government was "rescued" from the crisis by a $2.3 billion agreement between the New York State government, the New York City government, labor unions, and major banks.[10] The city government ceded control of its budgets to two new institutions: the Municipal Assistance Corporation and the Emergency Financial Control Board (EFCB). They raised new funds from Wall Street and, more importantly, for every New York resident, they controlled all spending for all agencies affecting life in the neighborhoods. The EFCB called for spending cuts, and over the next three years, these spread like an epidemic all over the city. The cuts severely affected poor neighborhoods, which had depended on government funds for housing, education, health, income, and even basic safety, as Connolly and the Athanasius team knew too well.

Every area of city services was hit with the cuts. In a school system serving a million children, 15,000 teachers were lost. In a health system which saw two million patients a year, $85 million was cut, and both Fordham Hospital in the Bronx and the network of fifty public health clinics in the city, serving 400,000 annual visitors, were shuttered. The Human Resources Administration, known as HRA, which was providing public assistance to more than one million poor New Yorkers, shed 2,500 workers. The Sanitation Department laid off 3,000 workers, leaving the streets at the dirtiest levels they had seen in decades. More than 5,000 police officers were dropped off the rolls, making the South Bronx streets, which were already struggling with heroin and related crimes, more perilous than ever. Finally, one out of five firefighters were laid off at a time when firehouses had already been closed, despite departmental warnings about the consequences for dense, overcrowded, and deteriorating areas like the South Bronx.[11]

And even as the subway system was announcing its own staffing cuts and fare hikes, a stark physical reminder was standing in the South Bronx. In 1973, the Bronx section of the elevated rapid transit line known as the "Third Avenue El" was closed.[12] The Third Avenue El, originally a Bronx-Manhattan subway line, had connected much of the Bronx to New York City's business districts through stations along Third Avenue, from Gun Hill Road in the north to Mott Haven in the south. It was a very busy line. Its closing, which followed the 1955 closing of the Manhattan portion of the line,[13] removed critical rapid transit access all through the central South Bronx neighborhoods. People who worked and looked for work downtown, in Manhattan, lost a vital lifeline to New York's economic engine. Despite the closure order, the train's structure stood untouched for four years as a visible relic, looming vacantly over the abandoned neighborhoods. It was a harsh reminder of the government's withdrawal from the South Bronx.

In some cases, these government actions led to fierce organized resistance. For example, in 1976 the proposed closing of Hostos Community College, a two-year bilingual institution in the city university system, led to strong protests. Having just been opened eight years earlier as a product of the Puerto Rican civil rights movement, Hostos was the only bilingual college in the city, serving 2,600 students, mostly from the South Bronx. With their school's existence at risk, the Committee to Save Hostos, including students, professors, and local activists who had organized on prior Puerto Rican and South Bronx community issues, carried on a sustained campaign of action. Including marches at CUNY's Manhattan headquarters, "teach-ins" on the streets of the Grand Concourse adjoining the college, and ultimately, a nonviolent physical takeover of the school facility, the campaign helped galvanize the community and generated media and public attention. Led by a young Bronx lawyer and Hostos professor, Ramon Jimenez, the Committee campaigned intensely and was able to keep the college open, a result which surprised and pleased Connolly.[14]

The Hostos campaign was significant. Against the overwhelming power of a government and financial cabal systematically cutting at every aspect of New York life, a group of students, ranging from single mothers to former prisoners, had joined with professors, administrators, and South Bronx and Puerto Rican community supporters to win a "David and Goliath" battle.[15] Connolly, observing, was convinced again that laypersons had the power to change things, to speak up for themselves, and to build an organized community. They had done it at the Seneca Center and in the *Movimiento Familiar Cristiano*. In Seneca they had told Connolly, "You cannot abandon us." Here, Connolly saw laypersons say the same thing to the powerful City University of New York and, ultimately, to the Wall Street and State leaders who oversaw the city budget.

You cannot abandon us in the South Bronx.

Connolly and Gigante had answered the call against abandonment with their organized actions and with the creation of community organizations, the Seneca Center and SISDA. And as he was continually finding out in these years, so had priests and sisters of other parishes in the South Bronx.

Commitment to Neighborhoods

Connolly and his fellow priests who had formed the South Bronx Catholic Clergy Association decided to expand it. Their new group, the South Bronx Catholic Association, included religious and laypersons from those parishes who had been working side by side with the priests.

The decision to include religious in the expansion of the association made perfect sense for Connolly, as they had always been an integral part of parish life. Religious were running and staffing the elementary schools, but they were also creating and staffing organizations in the parishes, as Sister Anne Marie Lafferty and Sister Trudy Collins, known as Sister Thomas, did at the Seneca Center and SISDA. They had also been involved in Summer in the City and directed projects within the parishes during Project Engage. They had participated in area poverty boards and Community School Board meetings, and some were even elected to those boards. In rare cases, religious even served officially as pastoral associates, or official parish staff members.

Through the South Bronx Catholic Association meetings, Connolly learned that these were very active parishes, building youth and social service organizations.[16] Many of them, like St. Anselm, St. Angela Merici, St. Francis of Assisi, and Christ the King, ran summer day camps for youth. In other cases there were year-round youth centers, such as those at St. Francis of Assisi, Christ the King, and St. Athanasius (SISDA). Every parish, it seemed, also had a group of Catholic Youth Organization (CYO) teams, especially in basketball and baseball. Adult educational institutions were supported too. Grace Institute, a vocational training organization for young adult women, was housed at St. Augustine, while the College of New Rochelle would establish a South Bronx campus on the top floor of the elementary school at Immaculate Conception.

Full-purpose community centers were opened up at St. Athanasius with the Seneca Center; St. Luke, with Cypress Community Center; and Sacred Heart, with the Highbridge Community Life Center. Seneca Center was not the only parish center in the South Bronx serving seniors and other vulnerable populations. St. Augustine, Immaculate Conception, and St. Joseph also ran senior programs or stand-alone senior centers.

Specialized health and mental health services were provided for troubled youth and adults as well. Athanasius had Unitas, led by Dr. Eismann, to serve the mental health needs of young people and teens. St. Joseph sponsored the Fordham Tremont Community Mental Health Center to serve both parishioners and non-parishioners in need of counseling and treatment. Those facing drug addiction problems were benefiting from St. Joseph's VIP Program, which provided counseling, social services, and meals to addicts. In the Mott Haven community, the Health Services Program of the Dominican Sisters of the Sick Poor provided a walk-in clinic for residents, a visiting nurse service for shut-ins, and other health services. Also, Group Live-In Experience (GLIE), a network of group homes and centers founded and directed by Sister Lorraine Reilly, addressed the problem of runaway teenagers and addicts from South Bronx neighborhoods.

Finally, even though they offered different sets of services to their parishioners and neighbors, all of the parishes with an organized service had one additional interest common to all: housing. While some in the West Bronx, such as St. Angela Merici, focused on organizing landlords to maintain their buildings, others, such as St. Francis of Assisi, St. Augustine, and Holy Spirit, were organizing tenants to pressure landlords. But in the southern and southeastern portion of the Bronx—the areas that had first "gone Spanish"—almost all of the parishes had developed an organization to build or rebuild apartment buildings.

Father Tom O'Connor established the MelMac organization at Immaculate Conception in Melrose.

Father Gerry Ryan created the George Hardy Houses at St. Luke's parish in Mott Haven.

Father Roberto Gonzalez formed the Pueblo en Marcha housing organization at St. Pius in Mott Haven.

Father Lou Gigante founded the South East Bronx Community Organization (SEBCO) to renovate buildings in St. Athanasius's Hunts Point–Longwood neighborhood.

Father Bill Smith created the Mid-Bronx Desperadoes housing organization at St. John Chrysostom parish in West Farms.

Father Bob Banome developed the Tremont Community Council at St. Joseph in Tremont to build housing as well as provide services.

Father David Casella created the Aquinas Housing Corporation at St. Thomas Aquinas in Tremont-Crotona.

Father John Flynn and Sister Connie Kelly created the Bronx Heights Housing Corporation at St. Francis of Assisi, in the area of Morris Heights.

Father Peter O'Donnell and Father Carlos Lopez Acosta created the Borinquen Housing Corporation at Sacred Heart parish in the Highbridge community.

Father Josu Iriondo created Coa Housing Corporation at Our Savior parish in the South Fordham neighborhood.

In building these organizations, priests and religious from those parishes were moving beyond their old job descriptions. At first, their work resembled what many other parish staffs of New York had done in their younger, usually Irish Catholic days: They mostly kept the youth busy to keep them from going astray or to help them avoid gang or drug violence. But when they saw so many other needs arising—meals and visits for seniors, public assistance for single mothers, counseling for drug addicts, and shelter for runaway youth—they stepped out into the world and brought the Church along with them. Everywhere they looked, their parishioners and neighbors were being abandoned, so they had to answer with commitment as fast as they could. But they could not keep pace with the abandonment of their neighborhood buildings.

Abandonment of Neighborhoods

In 1968, New York landlords abandoned 12,000 apartment buildings. City housing agencies took them over because of tax, financial, or operational violations. Within ten years, the total number reached 20,000, and in the following year, under a new city law, 24,000 more buildings joined the list of buildings under the management of the newly created In Rem Program of the city's Department of Housing Preservation and Development (HPD).[17] After neglecting its enforcement responsibilities for years, New York City government became the largest landlord in the city, with the poorest tenants at its mercy.

Landlords had been at war against tenants and their government overseers for decades. In the era after the *Gran Migración*, this war accelerated with public challenges to city hall over rent laws and other housing laws. One dramatic challenge occurred in September 1973, when a group of Bronx landlords brought a scale model of the borough to city hall steps, threatened to "burn the Bronx," and attempted to set fire to the model before police stopped them.[18] The symbolic protest was an ominous sign of power not seen before in New York City and of real actions that would be seen in the South Bronx as neighborhood after neighborhood was abandoned.

In the southwestern Bronx, as Puerto Rican migrants left Connolly's parish and neighboring parishes to find better living conditions, the banks were actively abandoning their buildings as they had in the southeastern area. From 1965 to 1975, during the migration of Puerto Ricans to buildings in the western part of the borough, bank mortgages for refinancing those buildings—a sign of private-sector commitment to an area's real estate—declined from 385 to 85.[19] Then, with the completion of the closing of seven firehouses ordered after the Rand study, along with the layoffs of hundreds of firefighters and inspectors, the stage was set for Bronx landlords to act. The rate of residential fires in New York City, which began climbing in the mid- to late 1960s, accelerated in the 1970s. From 1972 to 1978, the fires reached extraordinary levels, including in the South Bronx.[20] In 1974, there were already 12,000 fires for the year, or an average of 30 fires a day, in the South Bronx.[21]

The fire on Tiffany Street, which Connolly saw that summer evening, was just one of these. And, like the abandonment of buildings, the firehouse closings, and the city hall incident, the Tiffany Street fire and the vast majority of the fires in the South Bronx were not accidental. *Arson was the cause*, Connolly realized. *That's why the captain said the tenants knew.*

Connolly learned about the mechanics of and reasons for arson from articles coming out in the paper. Arson became an industry after states were required by the U.S. Congress to create FAIR Insurance plans to counter the loss of investment in inner-city areas after the riots of the 1960s. FAIR plans required that insurers fund buildings in high-risk areas so that landlords would continue maintaining their buildings.[22]

Instead of maintaining their buildings, many landlords "milked" them—collecting rent while spending little or nothing on services and heat.[23] When enough rent had been taken and the opportunity arrived, it was time to commit arson and collect on the insurance policy. Insurance companies asked few questions of the landlords when they evaluated the buildings for a policy. They overvalued the buildings and denied few claims after the fires. In the typical case, there was a team of collaborators: the landlord; the professional "broker" who arranged for the insurance claim and the arson action; the "torch" who set the fire; and finally, the insurance company adjuster—the provider of the cash from the insurance company which made arson a profitable act.[24]

Landlords profited from arson because, as astute South Bronx resident and economist Gelvin Stevenson wrote at the time of the arson epidemic, the insurance laws did not require that the proceeds go to the building or tenants. Investment in the neighborhoods, called for in federal legislation for FAIR plans, never materialized.[25] Insurance funds left the neighborhood, along with the landlords, and the tenants. The South Bronx, already a national epicenter of inner-city poverty, heroin, and crime, now faced another epidemic with national reach. Arson became the fastest growing crime in the United States in the 1970s.[26] Incidents reached 150,000 a year, costing $1 billion. Like the heroin epidemic of the 1950s and 1960s and the related crime waves, arson spread through inner cities across the nation, and the problem was not seriously addressed until much of the damage had already been done.

Urban planners and elected officials knew, just like Connolly and the South Bronx parish staffs, what the fires meant for the future of these buildings. The city began demolition of buildings it deemed unsafe in the 1960s and accelerated the demolition rate in the 1970s. Demolitions, having already occurred in the slum clearance projects during the 1950s and early 1960s, were familiar to New Yorkers. But the destruction was gaining pace, growing from an annual average of 950 buildings in the early 1960s to more than 1,500 a year during the early 1970s.[27] The "new clearance" was advanced further when, in 1975, as the arson epidemic spread through the South Bronx and other areas, Mayor Beame called for accelerated demolition of vacant buildings, citing 3,000 fires in vacant South Bronx buildings the year before.[28]

Connolly read about Beame's call in the papers and suddenly thought, *This is all going to go. The buildings on Fox Street, where Gigante announced his run for Congress. The Tiffany Street building he had seen evacuated.* The buildings where he had visited his parishioners, where they had fed him and the other priests during the Athanasius budget crisis. The buildings where relationships had been established and extended family and friend groups had once supported each other. *They are all going to go.*

He had to do something. Speak out. Organize.

Denouncing a Crime

Connolly reached out to some of the people he worked with at the Bronx Clergy Coalition. He had maintained contact with some of them during Gigante's two election campaigns, and they were discussing some of the housing issues affecting them all. They all agreed that the arson situation was reaching epidemic proportions. Not knowing what to do exactly, but believing there were crimes being committed, they decided to call for the authorities to conduct an investigation. They reached out to the Bronx command office of the New York Police Department and to District Attorney Mario Merola and Borough President Robert Abrams of the Bronx for answers.

Merola had reportedly established a police arson task force, which was headquartered at the Forty-First Precinct in Hunts Point–Longwood.[29] Connolly and the coalition were stunned to learn that the entire arson task force, for a borough with thousands of fires every year, consisted of a three-man squad. One of its members, who operated undercover to find the "torches" and their "brokers," as well as the crooked landlords, was a tall, heavy-set man with a shock of red hair. Connolly found the idea of this man being undercover almost comic. He even came across him at St. Athanasius church one day, sitting in a pew in the back while Connolly came out of hearing confessions. Connolly went over to him and whispered, "Everybody knows who you are."

The detective, a burly Irish redhead named O'Halloran in a sea of smaller Puerto Rican men and women asked, "Do I stand out very much?" Connolly sighed with amusement. The coalition would need to push much harder if this redhead was the best weapon they were given to stop the arson epidemic.

The Bronx district attorney sent a young staff member to meet with the coalition.[30] He gave a report on arson, but also on developments in the South Bronx which he thought the coalition might be interested in. The report discussed the South Bronx in physical, geographic, and economic terms. It conveyed the strong potential for enhancing manufacturing activity, because of roadways like the New England Thruway, the Major Deegan, the Cross-Bronx Expressway, and the Bruckner Expressway, as well as the proximity to airports. The report emphasized that the Bronx had some available development space and that more space could be created with clearance.

The coalition was stunned. *Look at this*, Connolly thought, as he realized why the city was letting these buildings, and even entire blocks, be burned down. The assistant district attorney provided more hints about the city's plans: Other reports had lists of board members of some major development plans and projects for the South Bronx area. They included some prominent elected officials for the city and the Bronx, but he could not reveal any names. A couple of days later, when Connolly reached out to the attorney for a follow-up conversation about the plan and the various projects, as well as their board members, he was greeted by a very anxious voice. "Please do not call me back," he whispered. "I can't talk to you. I have a wife and kids, and I'll lose my job."

Despite this investigative dead-end over secret, valuable information, the coalition pressed on, demanding action from Borough President Abrams. In June 1975, a larger meeting took place at the Bronx County Courthouse near Yankee Stadium, where both the Bronx president and the district attorney had their offices. It was a large, boisterous gathering with Abrams and Merola, the Bronx police commander and the Bronx fire chief, and the clergy leaders of more than two dozen churches. It was declared a founding "Blue Ribbon" commission meeting to raise the issues that would be investigated. But while Connolly and the clergy presented their concerns and demands for action, the fire department and police department staff began blaming each other's agencies for not being able to stop the arson. Finally, Abrams told the clergy in attendance, "District Attorney Merola and I, we'll handle the press on all this stuff, okay?" The coalition agreed, but almost immediately Connolly realized, *it was a big mistake, giving away the power of the media to these politicians. They wanted to control the information about what was really going on, and they were afraid of what he and the other clergy were going to say.*

After the neglect, the destruction and demolition were the last phase of the buildings in Hunts Point–Longwood. (Photo by Mili Bonilla.)

St. Athanasius, once surrounded by dozens of buildings, stands alone in the center of Hunts Point–Longwood. (Photo by Mili Bonilla.)

Abrams and Merola did agree to launch an investigation after the coalition pressed them further. In fact, the New York City government stepped in, as the Beame administration created a two hundred–member arson task force composed of police, fire, and district attorney staff. Under the direction of then-deputy mayor Stanley Friedman, who was also a Democratic party leader in the Bronx, the task force carried out its mandate to investigate suspicious fires in the city and conduct full investigations, execute arrest warrants, and take related cases to trial.[31] Even Cardinal Cooke, at the request of his Catholic clergy in the South Bronx, urged parishes to provide full cooperation and assistance to this citywide effort.

A couple of hundred people were arrested over the next few years as a result; in many cases, they were landlords and their "torches," who were paid a hundred or two hundred dollars to bring kerosene cans to the roof and set a building on fire within minutes.[32] But the scale and the epidemic nature of the arson was far greater than the city's actions and made it seem unstoppable. So Connolly and the coalition looked for answers on the federal level. They met with Paul Curran, U.S. Attorney for the Southern District of New York, to see if he could bring the power of the federal government down on the arson industry.[33] The call for action by the clergy spurred congressmen from the Bronx, including Herman Badillo and Mario Biaggi, to call for federal action as well.[34] Curran rejected these appeals for justice, arguing that there were no interstate or federal laws being violated. His response left the city and the South Bronx to fend for themselves and face the epidemic until it had run its course.

Building an Area Church: A New Community

While the Bronx Clergy Coalition was meeting with elected officials to protest the destruction of their neighborhoods, Connolly was working with the South Bronx Catholic Association to build their community. Coincidentally, in 1976, the archdiocese was subdividing the Bronx Vicariate—which during Connolly's time had been under Monsignor Schultheiss and then Bishop Patrick Ahern—into four vicariates, with one just for the South Bronx. This area alone was as large as Boston or Milwaukee, and people in the archdiocese felt it deserved added attention.

The South Bronx Catholic Association saw an opportunity to create a unique office, instead of having a priest who would be a part-time caretaker vicar, as the diocese had expected. Association members thought, Why not make it a full-time position, with greater responsibilities dedicated to answering the needs of parishes and communities in the area? In fact, the association took the vicariate position so seriously that it decided that its occupant should not be appointed but elected to the position, and that the association membership should choose him. The association set a meeting for a vote on the proposal for Ascension Thursday in 1976, announcing it to all parishes and individuals of the area. At the meeting, there were priests, religious, and laypersons from many of the parishes in the South Bronx. Then, at the next meeting, the association elected Neil Connolly vicar of the South Bronx.[35]

This was a challenge to the usual process of limiting a vote to the priests of the vicariate area, but the priests of the South Bronx accepted the new voting approach, with voting rights for all members of the association. When Bishop Ahern called for a priests-only election, Connolly replied, "Sorry, but we have already had our election. We are recognizing the results of the election by the Catholic Association." He knew this was not the way the archdiocese wanted things to be done, but he happily accepted the new job, and in the early summer he took part in a large Mass and celebration introducing the four new Bronx vicars at St. Helena's in Castle Hill.

Then Connolly, who wanted to be a leader for the entire area, set out to do two things: learn more about the area communities and parishes, and help them come together with a sense of mission and unity. He spoke with his friend, Father Phil Murnion, who regularly came over to Athanasius to find out what Connolly was up to. Murnion, who had been instrumental in creating those recommendations to merge the Archdiocese of New York with the neighboring dioceses in 1968, and who directed the archdiocesan office of Research and Planning, asked Connolly how he wanted to use this unique position of full-time vicar.

Connolly laid out his plan for his three-year term: He would visit every parish in the South Bronx; go to each rectory, convent, and school; and spend time with the staff. He wanted to ask them questions:

What are your dreams for the South Bronx?
How happy are you in your pastoral roles?
What are the ups and downs of parish life?

In the hierarchical system in which they were working, no one from the top of the hierarchy, from the headquarters in the archdiocese, had ever visited them to hear what they had to say, whether they had been around for five years or fifteen years, as priests or as sisters.

No one had heard what dreams they had or where they wanted to go in their life. No one was able to discuss their approach to CCD (religious instruction) or pastoral strategy, such as evangelization, or baptism. No one was able to discuss their struggles leading a parish or serving one. *With Connolly as vicar, they would.*

Over the next few years, Connolly indeed visited every parish, met with the priests and sisters, and heard about their activities, their lives, and their plans. He participated in key parish events and in the events of organizations created or sponsored by their parishes. Since he wanted the parishioners to know who he was, that there was a vicar for the whole community of Catholic parishes in the South Bronx, he also said Mass at each church. At the end of his first three-year term as vicar, Connolly used the assistance of his friend and one-time seminary classmate Bob Stern, from Our Lady of Victory parish, who had a keen mind for analysis and planning, to develop and complete a survey and report on what had been accomplished by the new vicariate office. As if to reaffirm his outreach strategy, the most outstanding response Connolly received from the survey was that everyone believed that the visits, along with the efforts taken to learn about the life of the parish and its staff, were the most important thing Connolly did as vicar.

Meanwhile, Connolly also worked with the association to develop a mission statement, one that would define their members as a people of the Catholic Church, but also as a people of the world, of the South Bronx. The association's leaders and local parish staffs eventually created six goals which members would pursue:

Strengthen ourselves spiritually, socially, politically.

Use the strengths of some parishes to show what can be done in a seemingly desperate situation.

Create an image of the South Bronx that, despite terrible human conditions, Christ, our only source of true joy and hope is alive because the Church is alive . . . this is what causes us to struggle in freeing ourselves from oppression.

Wipe away our own ghetto vision and tunnel vision by growing toward a more universal sense of church.

Penetrate the smoke-filled rooms of city politics by organizing ourselves as a political force.

Build bridges of reconciliation and communication among the various ethnic and racial groups.[36]

Pursuing this mission, the association undertook initiatives to create a South Bronx–wide community of parishes, religious communities, and organizations. They came together to discuss the special programs for parish life in one meeting, then for neighborhood life in another. People discussed pressing needs of the South Bronx, such as housing and health services. Gigante gave a special workshop on the art and science of politics and legislation and getting things done in government. Special orientation sessions were also held for new members of the South Bronx Catholic Church community to educate them on all the parish involvement in providing services and to help them understand the concerns and advocacy about government abandonment.

The association even held "Area Church Days." Each had a special liturgy. They celebrated camaraderie, but they were also an occasion to discuss the trends in the Church and the South Bronx. The group knew that they needed to think about creating their own community in the South Bronx, because the forces of economic and political power were not in their favor. Connolly and the other association members knew they needed to speak out about their mission and create a broader vision for the

South Bronx Catholic Association celebrates outdoor mass and commits to rebuilding community. (*Left to right*) Fr. John Flynn, Mili Bonilla, and Sr. Louise Mileksi. (Neil Connolly's personal collection.)

South Bronx. The local organizations they had created and served, along with the common bonds around an area church which Connolly helped them strengthen, would strengthen their commitment, even in these difficult times.

Life Cycle

The fiscal crisis and the subsequent budget cuts to New York's services hit the South Bronx so hard that it was difficult to sustain the neighborhoods at all, and the parishes did everything they could to face this large-scale abandonment. But the commitment of the Catholic Church in the South Bronx was not as powerful as the federal government, Wall Street, and city hall's desire to forget it. When the federal government froze housing funds and then denied the largest city in the country a way out of bankruptcy, the ability of the city to function was at stake. So was its ability to answer the needs of the poor, the ill-housed, the sick, and the dependent.

In fact, the powerful in New York City and in the United States were unwilling to rescue poor neighborhoods. Those who made decisions in the United States had their own concepts about cities, especially about the inner cities. Some of those concepts originated in the 1940s, but a few became prominent in the 1960s, and their application would be felt in the South Bronx. Those concepts were the basis for the urban renewal and public housing programs, which changed the location and look of slums all over the United States.

The most central concept looked at a neighborhood as having a "natural life cycle"—a period of time and a kind of process in which a neighborhood could change from a middle-income area with prime living conditions, full municipal services, and special residential amenities to a low-income area with poor living conditions, few public services, deterioration, and then abandonment.[37] After full abandonment, it would then be resurrected as a middle-income area with new investment of public and private resources. Urban planners advanced the natural life cycle concept within the federal Department of Housing and a variety of housing, planning, and real estate "institutes," and they justified the use of this and related concepts as scientific thinking.

Then, in 1966, the executive director of the real-estate-sector-funded New York organization the Citizens Housing and Planning Council first advocated a concept called "planned shrinkage."[38] Roger Starr called for the active removal of existing municipal services from a low-income neighborhood until it was so destroyed that it could be abandoned and replaced.

Starr advanced the concept again in 1976, during the height of the fire epidemic in the South Bronx, that time as the leading housing official in New York City government, with the power to execute his decade-old policy.[39]

In 1969, Daniel Patrick Moynihan, as urban policy advisor to then-president Richard Nixon, advocated for a policy of "benign neglect."[40] Under benign neglect, no additional government services would be provided to a neighborhood in decline. The effect on the neighborhood of benign neglect, while promoted as not enacting any deliberate harm, would be a longer and slower physical death.

As early as the 1960s, government and other institutional forces openly supported either benign neglect or planned shrinkage policies for the South Bronx. In 1967, a Fordham University study called for the demolition of 2,500 housing units in the South Bronx to create enough land to develop a manufacturing base.[41] In 1969, the Department of City Planning, in its master plan for the city of New York, called for the designation of the South Bronx for "urban renewal," as an area which could be "cleared" for industrial or residential development.[42] In his first term as mayor, John Lindsay advocated the demolition of 300 occupied residential blocks north of St. Mary's Park in Melrose and Morrisania to "remove blight" and construct new housing.[43] In the period when the Puerto Rican migrants were settling and resettling, moving into the eastern and then western parts of the South Bronx, planners were planning to move them again.

At first, Connolly did not fully understand the connection between the articles he read about the earlier plans of the 1960s, the inaction of the city council on housing deterioration, and the inaction on the fire epidemic in the 1970s. *How could the people in power allow this kind of suffering and not feel compelled to act as he and his fellow priests and sisters did in the parishes?* But things started to make more sense when the district attorney discussed large-scale developments proposed for the areas where the fires were consuming block after block. The parishioners and neighbors that were burned out of that Tiffany Street building, the firefighters, and even Connolly could not change what happened there or in the thousands of buildings that lost their history. They could not know what their neighborhood's future would be. No one except developers and elected officials would be included in planning that future.

But Connolly knew that the Church had been in the world of the South Bronx, and that he and his fellow workers had committed themselves to "struggles in freeing themselves from oppression." *They knew that some entity—the federal government or city hall—would move ahead with its*

*plans unless an alternative was presented. If they were going to do some-
thing now, to fight the plans of other people for the future of the South
Bronx, they would need to take another step: Create their own plan.*

What Must Be Done

After some discussions about the reports from the DA and the arson campaigns, the Bronx Clergy Coalition and the South Bronx Catholic Association came together and developed a proposal for the future neighborhoods
of the South Bronx. "What Must Be Done to Rebuild the South Bronx,"
their vision for the area, was built from their reflections on the past problems with federal government plans for poor areas.[44] Remembering what
had happened after the enactment of the housing program in the urban
renewal and public housing laws, they challenged the concept of clearance
and of large-scale developments. The proposal writers remembered how
the War on Poverty, Multi-Service Center, and Model Cities programs,
with a public mandate for local control, ended up in the hands of local
power brokers rather than community residents. Thus the clergy proposal
insisted on true local control during and after the rebuilding process.

"What Must Be Done" called for housing to be built and managed by
existing nonprofit church-based and community-based organizations who
knew how to develop and manage housing and who were committed to the
community on a long-term basis. It also called for every opportunity to be
given to residents to own the apartments where they lived. Also, it called
for the apartment buildings to be built at a human scale, unlike the tall
and dense buildings which were typical in public housing developments.
Community participation, the proposal stated, should extend to the actual
construction of this housing. There should be an apprenticeship program
for local residents of the South Bronx so that they would both be part of
the rebuilding and would obtain jobs in an industry historically limited to
white men. Finally, "What Must Be Done" called for the creation of an
industrial park that would hire local residents and provide apprenticeship
opportunities in those positions as well.

Understanding that this comprehensive approach would need substantial funding, members of the Bronx Clergy Coalition and the South
Bronx Catholic Association knew they would need federal support. So,
in the spring of 1977, they took their case to federal officials in New York
and Washington, especially after the arrival of a new administration under
President Jimmy Carter. Connolly and the others thought they would receive a favorable response from a Democratic administration which was

expected to finally support new housing and the development of cities again after years of Republican control under Nixon and Ford. Coalition members held meetings and conferences to move forward on this plan and to build support. Connolly thought, *They would be creating the community of the South Bronx that would meet people's needs, restore dignity to their lives, and change the direction the area had been going in. As this Church was growing with the people who made it go Spanish, it would write a different future from the one planners had in mind. It would include the people who were living here.*

On October 5, 1977, however, Jimmy Carter would disrupt their plans, undermine their expectations of support, and assert the institutional power of the federal government.[45] After delivering a message in New York City to the United Nations that morning, the president then made an unannounced tour through the South Bronx. He was joined by his new housing secretary, Patricia Roberts Harris, and by New York mayor Beame. Their first stop was the housing and community facilities of an organization called the People's Development Corporation on Washington Avenue in the Morrisania/Tremont area of central South Bronx. There, Carter stopped to learn about cooperative housing, workforce development, and a solar power project.

Afterward, Carter took the delegation, which picked up news reporters along the way, to a large vacant lot on Charlotte Street and Boston Road, in the West Farms Tremont neighborhood, to look around at other vacant lots. There he declared the site, and by extension the South Bronx, a national symbol of urban loss, and he announced that his administration would rebuild on this area to turn it around. Within a few months, Carter proposed a seven-year rebuilding plan for the South Bronx.[46] It promised a federal contribution of up to $1 billion. The plan would create 20,000 new apartments through the rehabilitation of vacant buildings, and 5,000 others through the construction of new apartment buildings and private homes, all to be built in select areas. The plan also would generate ten thousand new jobs through residential construction and industrial and commercial development. New construction was expected to take place in a concentrated area, to be known as a "New Town," containing cooperative and rental apartments. Some expected that the Charlotte Street area, visited by Carter, would be the center of the "New Town" development.

After that plan was announced in 1978, an elaborate structure was established to convert the Carter promise into an actionable plan. New York City's newly elected mayor, Edward Koch, would be given control at the local level, in conjunction with Secretary Harris. Harris designated

Jack Watson as the federal special liaison to city hall in the South Bronx plan. By April 1978, Herman Badillo, who had been borough president and congressman in the Bronx, and who had just been appointed a deputy mayor by Koch, was made chief city overseer of the South Bronx project.[47] A South Bronx Development Organization (SBDO) was created to implement the project's daily operations. Ed Logue, a former leader of economic development agencies in New York, Boston, and New Haven, was appointed to head the SBDO.[48] Finally, a South Bronx Coordinating Council, led by Robert Wagner, Jr., son of the former mayor and U.S. senator whose 1949 Housing Act advanced urban renewal and public housing in the United States, was appointed.

In this entire Byzantine collection of officials, boards, and elected representatives hoping to save his South Bronx, Connolly noticed, *there were no residents from the communities that were affected.*

The coalition decided to oppose the federal and city part of the plan. Connolly and the others feared the planned housing would not be affordable for their parishioners and neighbors. Most of all, Connolly feared, *this was ignoring all the components of the plan the coalition had created, their vision for the future South Bronx. No one was being given apprenticeships or jobs; there was no notion of human scale and ownership by low- and moderate-income people of the area. There would be no control for the community-based housing organizations that many parishes and other churches had established during the early 1970s.*

Community and tenant ownership was on Connolly's mind when, as a leader of the coalition and as South Bronx vicar, he challenged the federal and city administrations via an opinion piece in the *New York Daily News*, "A Sermon on the Streets":

> When the churches of the South Bronx ask the U.S. government to help the spirit of America take flesh in the brick-strewn barrios of Tiffany and Simpson Streets, it is only asking the great nation to be faithful to its belief in independence, to its Lincolnesque abhorrence of slavery and submission, to its Statue of Liberty acceptance of all kinds of people.
>
> The churches of the South Bronx don't want the people to sit any longer as passive participants while the super task forces, builders, and developers construct their live-in pyramids and tomb-like projects.
>
> There has to be something new in the sense of urban renewal.
>
> Government must allow people to design their own neighborhood,

to have input into the buildings that are being planned, and it must provide the means by which people learn the skills to organize themselves, to manage property and eventually own it. They must see that people—all kinds of people—treasure most deeply the things they can call their own.[49]

The coalition held meetings and an all-day conference at Fordham University to discuss broader-based strategies for challenging the federal plan. They also reaffirmed their original plans for true community sponsorship and management, for tenant ownership and management, and for community-based employment. But, since the funding and final say would have to come from the federal government, they wanted the Carter administration to hear the plan from them.

Through the influence of Cardinal Cooke, Connolly and his colleague, Father John Flynn, presented their plan directly to Jack Watson, the federal liaison, who seemed impressed with the recommendations. Watson, however, confessed that he could not bypass the local political structure and give the funds or the decisions about the funds directly to the coalition. The results of the meeting frustrated Connolly and the coalition, which decided to issue a public call for the city to hear their plan and act on it. They scheduled a press conference on October 27, 1978, a year after Carter's Charlotte Street visit. Connolly was prepared to be one of the four leading spokespersons at the press conference.[50]

Yet before the 27th, calls went out from city hall. Badillo reached the leaders of the coalition and member congregations, which had contracts with the city of New York for senior services, youth programs, social services, and housing management. They were told that their contracts were going to be in jeopardy at budget time if their pastors or ministers showed up at the press conference. The messages reached the ministers, and the ministers reached Connolly and the other coalition leaders. The press conference was called off, and so was the campaign to challenge city hall on the South Bronx redevelopment plan.

City hall won this battle for power over the future of the South Bronx. Connolly, who, nearly a decade earlier, had found a way to challenge city hall over emergency repairs for his parishioners and neighbors, was not able to do a thing this time. Even as a member of a larger coalition, which included laypersons and religious as well as clergy, Connolly was powerless. Badillo knew these ministers, lay leaders, and religious from twelve years serving the Bronx, so he knew they understood their neighborhoods well. Connolly realized, *the same Badillo who had campaigned for Bronx borough president and congressman and mayor as a champion of Puerto Ricans was not going to champion any plan outside of city hall control, outside of his control.*

The residents' powerlessness would be visibly demonstrated during the late 1970s and 1980s in the images and stories of the South Bronx disseminated nationally. It would also be reflected in the population and geographic changes to the area. The areas that were first occupied by the people of the *Gran Migración* were those hit first by deterioration, abandonment, fire, and then demolition. The clearance that overtook these areas was different from the clearance of the Urban Renewal era. There were no government decrees about selected sites, no wrecking balls, and no new construction afterward. But the results were similar: More than 6,000 vacant lots were created by the end of the 1980s.[51] Three hundred thousand fewer people lived in the six districts that had become the South Bronx at the end of that decade.[52] The area Connolly had known all his South Bronx life, Hunts Point–Longwood, lost buildings which once occupied 29 percent of its land. Once spilling out from every building from 149th Street to Simpson Street to Lafayette Avenue, the neighborhood population was reduced from 94,000 to 34,000.[53]

But even in the middle of these vacant lots and buildings, Hunts Point–Longwood endured. St. Athanasius's community of parishioners was smaller than the 8,000 served a little over a decade ago, but it stood. *They were still a community*, Connolly realized, *with its parish societies and the SISDA organization and the Seneca Center built ten years ago.*

A Voice in the World

Twenty years after setting foot on Tiffany Street, Connolly stopped being a leader of one community, a shepherd for one flock. He was now a priest for all the parishes in the larger Church, what he liked to call the "Area Church," the Church that had gone Spanish throughout all these neighborhoods and committed itself to the needs of its people. The staffs at those parishes stayed, even through the abandonment, the arson, and the demolition. In the face of benign neglect, they chose active commitment. In the face of planned shrinkage and of plans crafted by power brokers, they created their own plan.

The battles over the abandonment and arson, Connolly realized, *were like the battles over emergency repairs years back. He and the members of the Bronx Clergy Coalition had implemented the process he had learned in Movimiento Familiar Cristiano—see, judge, and act. He saw the wide-*

spread abandonment and arson and judged that there were crimes to be stopped, and he took action—calls for investigations and task forces to stop the crimes.

When arrests took place, but the crimes didn't stop, they asked questions, like he had on Tiffany Street: Why did this happen? What would happen to the buildings and lots? They saw, judged, and acted again. This time they saw others had plans for the South Bronx, and his people were not to be included in them—the priests, the sisters, the laypersons of the parish, and all their neighbors. That was the way he judged things—people were not going to own their future, or their living conditions, or even their location. No one was listening to them, the way he had listened to the parish staff and laypersons as their new vicar.

He had given them a voice with those visits, and he wanted to give them a voice in their parishes and neighborhoods. When he fought for "What Must Be Done to Rebuild the South Bronx," he was a prophet, a voice for all the people in the world. The Church needed to have a voice in the world, Connolly thought. But if it was going to be heard well enough in the world, this Church was not just going to be him or just the priests or sisters. Laypersons would be needed to give this Church a voice and chance in the world. His prophetic voice would need to be turned toward his Area Church, to urge its people to build as a larger community, to find the only true source of joy and hope.

He did not know exactly how to build in the face of all this destruction and abandonment. But he remembered his parish days with the Seneca Center and the Movimiento Familiar Cristiano, when the laypersons he had worked with were very willing and ready to take ownership of their Church and their world if given a chance. And he remembered something else about Seneca. It had started when the people came together and said to him: Let us start something new.

Let us do it together.

9

***

New Ministers

The apostolate can attain its maximum effectiveness only through a diversified and thorough formation.... In addition to spiritual formation, a solid doctrinal instruction in theology, ethics, and philosophy adjusted to differences of age, status and natural talents, is required.... In regard to the apostolate for evangelizing and sanctifying men, the laity must be specially formed to engage in conversation with others, believers, or non-believers, in order to manifest Christ's message to all men.

—Chapter VI, Formation for the Apostolate, *Apostolicam Actuositatem*, Second Vatican Council, December 1965

A Need for Teachers

Neil Connolly's world was getting bigger, as his activism now took him to city hall and his ministry spanned the South Bronx. But in the summer of 1977, during his first full year as South Bronx Vicar, he was still living at his longtime home, St. Athanasius. Returning from a meeting on the coalition's South Bronx plans, he arrived at the doorstep of the rectory to find a man sitting sprawled across the entrance. He was drunk, bruised, and moving erratically when Connolly greeted him. He went inside, and the others said he had asked for Connolly.

It was nine thirty, and Connolly was exhausted after a long day, but he persuaded the man into a cab. Almost as soon as they left the rectory, Connolly regretted the offer to take him to Jacobi Hospital. Not only was he tired, but all through the ride, the drunken man made derogatory remarks about the black cab driver and even cursed at him. The same behavior carried over into the hospital emergency room, and Connolly had to guard him for two hours as he waited for medical attention. Finally, a nurse took the man back to an exam room, and the triage nurse, who had greeted them at the front, spoke to Connolly.

"Father, can I ask you a question?"

Connolly turned, relieved that the man was no longer his problem. "Sure, what is it?"

"Well, I feel like I have been a faithful Catholic raised in a good Irish Catholic family. And I have been educated pretty well for my profession." Connolly nodded, and she continued, "And you were educated for many years in learning about theology and faith and church history."

"Right," Connolly responded, wondering where she was going with this conversation.

"So why don't I know this?" the nurse asked.

Connolly paused and asked, "Well, what do you mean?"

"Why don't you priests teach laypersons what you learned—in seminary?" she finally asked.

He looked at the Irish Catholic nurse and said nothing. She looked back at him with a confident and yet polite smile. "That's a good question," Connolly finally said, knowing that she already knew that. "I don't know. But I will think about it." After all his efforts to counsel and advise laypeople on their questions, in a hospital or a rectory or an apartment, this woman had left him without any real answer. *She was asking him about his priesthood*, he realized—*about what he should be doing as a priest with laypersons. Not* for *laypersons, like the man he had just brought to the hospital.* With *laypersons.*

It was a brief encounter, but a fruitful one. It made Connolly think yet again about what laypersons knew and should know: about theology, and scriptural interpretation, and Christianity. He remembered the Vatican II documents which discussed laypersons' roles in the "updated" Church and in the world. *Lumen Gentium* referred to the Church as a living body of all the baptized Christians, as "the people of God," who all had a responsibility for being and building the Church. *Gaudium et Spes* had called on the Church to be active in the world, and to shape the history of humankind toward a just and loving community, led by faithful laypersons as well as religious and clergy. And a special document, *Apostolicam Actuositatem*, "The Apostleship of the Laity," called for the "formation" of laypersons in the teachings of the Church in order for them to apply those teachings in the Church and the world.[1] Following the strong involvement of laypersons in the Catholic Action and Liturgical Movements, Vatican II affirmed laypersons' legitimate place in the Church and called for them to be fully prepared in its teachings in order to live them and share them with the world.

It was a year later, in 1978, as he was waging the battle over the future plans for the South Bronx, that Connolly learned the answer to the nurse's question from his fellow priest, Father Bob Stern.

Stern, who, like Connolly, had gone to the Puerto Rico program, and who had guided the priests in the petition to the Vatican for the election of Spellman's successor, was the featured speaker one night at the South Bronx Catholic Association meeting. Along with a couple of other association members, Stern described a program he and some others had been operating for over a year at Our Lady of Victory parish. They were offering a couple of courses to laypersons, covering the history of Christianity and the New Testament. They had been preparing people to understand those topics and explain them to others within and outside the church. Stern said each course was being taught to prepare laypersons for leadership roles in their church. He called the program of courses *El Instituto de Formación Laica*.

Stern's presentation opened the eyes of the association members. Up to this point, most of them had been involved, like Connolly and Gigante, in two kinds of urban ministry. They had all been building community organizations to serve neighborhood needs and to connect their Church to the world. Also, as ministers to the largely Puerto Rican population of the South Bronx, they had been going Spanish for years, providing sacraments and education, and counseling and supporting societies and movements that involved and affirmed their Puerto Rican parishioners.

But as much as they wanted to fight the abandonment of the South Bronx, sustaining this ministry would be a struggle. They did everything possible to prepare newcomers for life and ministry in the South Bronx, but after a couple of years they found that fewer new people were coming to join the parish staffs and their religious communities to serve the South Bronx neighborhoods. In fact, the future of this urban ministry was at risk, because the future of ministry in the American Catholic Church was at risk.

If Connolly had begun to notice in the late 1960s that more of his fellow priests were leaving the ministry, by the late 1970s the loss was enormous. The priests and women religious who kept parishes and schools going were leaving at just the time when the church needed more leaders. The number of diocesan priests in the country, like Connolly, declined from 37,272 in 1970 to 35,627 in 1980, while the number of newly ordained priests went from 805 to 593. Meanwhile, the number of American women religious also shrank from 160,931 to 126,517 during the same period.[2] However, the Catholic lay population continued unfettered growth during the time, growing from 47.9 million to 50.5 million, creating increased demand for more parishes and more parish leaders. These conflicting trends led to an unprecedented and unexpected anomaly in the United States: *priestless parishes.*

The number of American priestless parishes grew from zero in 1965, the last year of Vatican II, to 1,051 in 1985, or 5 percent of all parishes.[3] Through the 1970s, as vocations continued to decline, the Institutional Church was in crisis and facing a series of existential questions.

How was it possible that all the local and national vocation recruitment drives were not stopping the decline?

What was the Church going to do to stop the growth of priestless parishes?

How were those parishes being managed without a priest?

Who was saying Mass, and how did decisions get made for liturgy and sacraments and related activities?

Finally, could the Church take on a different leadership structure, or a different kind of leader, to manage those parishes?

If the parish was the most fundamental unit of the Catholic Church, and no priest could be there for the parishioners, could a different kind of leader or group of leaders plan parish life and administer the sacraments?

Where would the answers come from if the Institutional Church had not provided them?

At the grassroots, one solution was offered in the Midwest. In Kansas City, a parish priest created a summer training program for a position called "pastoral associate," a person who would assume some of the planning and management duties of a pastor. That person would be trained and authorized to function in a team ministry setting with priests, women religious, and other associates. Within a short time, several similar programs surfaced. The next couple of years saw rapid growth in pastoral associate training programs. Dozens of parishes were using the graduates—mostly women religious—proving that the position of pastoral associate was needed to fill the gap in parish staff leadership.[4] At the same time, women religious demonstrated something unsettling to the Institutional Church: Having managed elementary schools, orphanages, parish-based programs, and service organizations for centuries, they were more than ready to manage parishes.[5]

Connolly thought about the staffing situation facing the ministers—religious and clergy—in the South Bronx Catholic Association. He thought about this new program Stern was operating, and he thought about the parishioners he had worked with at Athanasius. This approach Stern was using, working to develop the skills and roles of laypersons, wasn't that different from what Connolly had done with the Puerto Ricans and Cubans he had worked with before. Paul and Angie Martinez had proven they could be leaders in the Movimiento *Familiar Cristiano*, as did the other twenty-two Movimiento leaders. With support, they could "see, judge, and act" and organize events that broke isolation in Hunts Point–Longwood. Moreover, Aida Rodriguez, Ray and Nati Colón, Lillian Camejo, and a dozen others could mobilize the church and neighborhood people to create a Seneca chapel and a full-service community center for a neglected area. Even the initially reluctant Rafael Collado, through his conversion to active parishioner and his direction of the Christian Base Community reading-reflection meetings, proved his readiness to take responsibility for the parish. These parishioners, along with the many Puerto Rican leaders of societies, Summer in the City projects, and Cursillo and Carismatico groups, or the organizers of the Fiesta San Juan Bautista, were proven leaders. They had earned and deserved a greater role in the parishes.

They knew it, too, and they knew something else: There were few Puerto Ricans or Cubans among the priests and religious serving them in the South Bronx, or even in the Archdiocese of New York. And with the trends in the seminaries and religious communities continuing, there was little chance that more priests and religious from Puerto Rican backgrounds would fill parish rectories and convents.

In Stern's program, Connolly saw the potential for continuing to change the role of laypersons, but he realized that *it would mean another change. For him. He would need to surrender his control of the parish and his place within the parish. Occasionally he did so, within the Athanasius rectory and within the Summer in the City program, as a member of a team. He made decisions and set priorities with others—laypersons, priests, religious and board members, and even with Catholic Clergy Association and Clergy Coalition members*. In a new Church, if this lay leadership program were to become a full training program, Connolly envisioned himself becoming a different kind of priest in a different kind of parish. This was the vision Stern offered, and what he would teach Connolly and others: what this new kind of parish might look like.

Robert Stern

In 1969, Monsignor Robert Stern had become the new director of the Spanish-speaking Apostolate under Cardinal Cooke.[6] Frustrated with the social action and community-oriented focus which the Apostolate took, Cooke had just let Monsignor Bob Fox go. He insisted that Stern focus the Apostolate instead on pastoral issues affecting Hispanics.

Stern, like Connolly, had begun his priesthood in the Puerto Rico immersion program, and afterward he served Puerto Rican parishes in the West Side and Lower East Side neighborhoods of Manhattan. He pursued doctoral studies in Rome during the same years as Vatican II, so he was directly exposed to the revolutionary discussions taking place there. Also, while on summer break from those studies, Stern accepted an invitation from Father Pedro Richards, an Argentinian priest who led the Christian Family Movement in Latin American, to visit the Movimiento leaders there. Stern's subsequent journey through ten countries inspired him and left him convinced that laypersons were fully capable of leading the Church.

Stern took the experiences of his trip, of the developments at Vatican II, and of Puerto Rico, and applied them to his new Apostolate assignment. He invited Father Edgard Beltrán, a Colombian priest, to teach workshops on Vatican II and on themes such as the "people of God" concept of the Church. The workshops were for priests and laypersons in parishes that had "gone Spanish," and Connolly and his parishioners at Athanasius were energized by them.

Then, at Beltrán's recommendation, Stern began organizing an *encuentro* ("encounter"), a conference including the Spanish-speaking Apostolate of the Archdiocese of New York and the Hispanic Ministry offices of the surrounding dioceses: Bridgeport, Connecticut; Newark, Camden, and Paterson in New Jersey; Brooklyn; and others. The first Regional *encuentro* was organized to define and address the pastoral needs of Hispanics within and between those dioceses, recognizing the fluidity and continuous nature of the Puerto Rican migration in the region. The Northeast Regional Center for Hispanics, headquartered at the Archdiocese of New York, was formed as a result. Also, the first National *Encuentro* was organized after the success of the Regional one, and this event was attended by more than one thousand laypersons from across the country. The *encuentro* experiences confirmed for Stern and many others that Hispanics wanted an important role in the Church.

Meanwhile, Stern had organized several committees of laypersons, religious, and priests to develop a pastoral plan which the Apostolate Office could deliver to Cardinal Cooke. Such a plan, it was thought, would help the archdiocese better meet the needs of its mostly Puerto Rican faithful in all areas. The committees each focused on one of seven areas: liturgy, catechetics, apostolate of the religious and priests, community and ecumenical relations, and training and involvement of laypersons for roles in the Church. Month after month, Stern staffed the committee meetings and also brought together a coordinating committee to ensure communication of ideas and plans. Meetings and committees were led by laypersons, religious, or priests, depending on the expertise and interest of the leader rather than the title. It was a dynamic and yet structured effort, and after two years, a final plan for ministry to Hispanics in the Archdiocese of New York was ready for presentation.

The members of the coordinating committee asked Stern if they could present their results directly to Cooke, a request Stern happily approved. In 1973, the laypersons on the committee led the presentation and asked the cardinal to approve the plan. Without making a commitment, the cardinal then received another request from the committee lay leaders. With so much at stake in the outcome of the plan, the lay representatives asked for a leadership role in implementing their proposed plan. Cooke perceived the last request as a threat to his authority as leader of the archdiocese, and he immediately rejected both the plan and the leadership role request. The participants, and their two years of effort, were abruptly dismissed. Cooke dissolved the Office of the Apostolate shortly afterward, and after an inquiry by the media about this meeting and the cardinal's decision, he immediately sent Stern on a three-month "sabbatical."

The cardinal was sending a different message about ministry to the Puerto Rican faithful than that originally conveyed twenty years earlier, when the Spanish Apostolate was first created to serve migrating Puerto Ricans. It was also different from the message of Vatican II that all those baptized in the Church were the people of God. As it turned out, the question of finding future leaders for the Church would not be answered by the Institutional Church. Instead, one answer for the South Bronx would come from the people of God themselves. Stern would have a role in the next attempt as well.

Stern pursued a parish assignment after his forced sabbatical, but he asked to be in the South Bronx, and in a different kind of parish setting. After years in conversation about the potential benefits of using team ministry to run a parish, Stern and some fellow ministers decided to work together as a team. Together with two religious—Sister Nora Cunningham

Fr. Bob Stern, co-founder and director of the nation's first Catholic lay ministry organization, the South Bronx Pastoral Center. (Photo courtesy of Fr. Robert Stern.)

and Sister Muriel Long—and two other priests—Father Peter Gavigan and Father Neil Graham—Stern applied to the archdiocese to work on the parish staff at Our Lady of Victory.

Located in the central Morrisania area of the South Bronx, Our Lady of Victory was a small parish impacted heavily by abandonment and arson. The archdiocese was giving it minimal attention, so Our Lady of Victory proved an ideal place to develop a team ministry approach. The five ministers went to work planning activities to support parish groups and actively engage the people in parish life. In fact, the parishioners were so engaged that they began raising questions about their team of ministers. They were happy to be leaders in their societies and local chapters of Cursillo and Carismaticos, but they were also struggling a little with non-parishioners in discussions about the Church. It was difficult explaining their faith or their Church history, or discussing scripture with others, because they did not know much about them. *Could the ministers*, they asked, *teach them about these subjects?*

So, in 1977, Stern and the team responded by offering a ten-session course during the season of Advent on the subject of the Old Testament. Twenty-five people took up the offer and completed the course, to the parish team's delight. However, the laypersons did not stop there. They asked for more education, so the team created another course on the New Testament for the Lenten season. With an equally strong response to this class, Stern and his colleagues realized they had started something promising.[7]

They decided to teach the first two courses again for others in the parish, and to create a couple of new courses as well. Now called *El Instituto de Formación Laica*, the program of courses covered a wide range of topics: Old and New Testament, History of Christianity, Catholic Teaching, and others. The team also offered a couple of courses in communication skills, such as public speaking and group discussions and decision-making. All five ministers were involved in planning and teaching courses with the aim of addressing the original need raised by their lay leaders: being able to communicate and present the teachings of their Church with others. By 1978, the program was humming. "The courses were not just about parishioners learning scriptures," Stern explained to the South Bronx Catholic Association, "but about them becoming Christian leaders."

When Connolly and the association heard Stern's presentation, they were so impressed that they asked the ministry team to offer this program to the whole South Bronx. They wanted all their parishioners who were interested to be able to learn about these topics and more. Connolly asked the team to give up being Our Lady of Victory staff and to, instead, make a full-time commitment to a South Bronx–wide program. As Vicar of the South Bronx, he promised to raise funds for them from Cardinal Cooke, and he got $50,000 for this purpose. With Father Gavigan remaining as pastor at Our Lady of Victory, Stern and the rest of the team agreed to leave their responsibilities for Our Lady of Victory and to become full-time staff of their new organization, the South Bronx Pastoral Center.[8]

Word spread, and the innovative center gained shape and direction as it gained early interest among parishes in the South Bronx. In their inaugural 1978–1979 academic year, the center faculty of ten teachers (other priests and women religious quickly joined) taught 129 enrollees, who came from seventeen parishes in the South Bronx and two from the North Bronx. The only comprehensive lay formation program in the United States, the Pastoral Center brought new possibilities to Puerto Rican laypersons wanting a leadership role in the Church of Vatican II.

South Bronx Pastoral Center

From the first evening of that presentation, Connolly was actively engaged in the South Bronx Pastoral Center. As Vicar of the South Bronx, he was able to report on its developments regularly to the cardinal, who continued to provide funds to the center. Also, he served as chair of the center's board, and he worked with Stern and the staff to recruit other clergy and religious who could support and guide its direction. Maybe most importantly for him, Connolly became a center faculty member, joining a group of people—priests, religious, and even laypersons—who had committed to pass on their formal training to the people of God they had served over the years. He taught a course on the scriptures, and another in public speaking.

The public speaking class was a special joy to teach. Connolly discovered the ability of people—both strangers and some students whom he knew from Athanasius—to make speeches. Some were naturally more extroverted, and they were comfortable "on their feet." But Connolly saw others overcome a sense of inferiority through this course, and he felt a particular personal satisfaction at seeing the course liberate them from that sense. Each participant, whether an introvert or extrovert, learned to write an outline. Then they learned to write a speech, and then deliver it. In the process, all his students learned to speak with passion and clarity, and they began to have much more faith in themselves. *With these skills*, Connolly thought, *they could become leaders in small and large public settings, and they could give direction to the Church and the world, much as he had.*

Over time, as he entered the school building of Our Lady of Victory every week and saw the classrooms occupied with participants, Connolly understood how big the Pastoral Center was truly becoming. From its modest beginnings in an Advent class in one parish, it had grown quickly into a college-style school with three different programs of study available for different purposes: the Core Formation Program, the Specialized Ministry Program, and the Parish Services Program.

The Core Formation Program was the first and most popular, growing out of the original requests from the parishioners at Our Lady of Victory. Out of the first five *Instituto* courses came a full four-year schedule of twelve courses designed to fully prepare laypersons for a comprehensive understanding of their faith and Church—Catholic Teaching, the Old and New Testament, the History of Christianity, and History of the Catholic Church. Also included were courses in public communications, group decision-making, and group dynamics, which enabled students to explain and apply their knowledge to parish meetings and councils and community forums. Finally, the team added a course called "Challenges of the Inner City," which used visual and discussion tools developed in Summer in the City to help laypersons observe and analyze the conditions and needs of their neighborhoods.

The Specialized Ministry Program was intriguing to many of the center's students because of its unusual focus. It offered a series of courses that allowed laypersons to perform or assist in one of several sacraments in the parish. Courses in Eucharistic ministry, catechetical ministry, baptismal ministry, lector ministry, and even bereavement ministry covered both the theological and procedural aspects of each area. Connolly saw this particular program as having the potential for transforming parish structures and enhancing parish growth. *Specialized Ministry Program graduates could become an army of lay ministers ready to serve their parishes. Priests could be freed up from shouldering all responsibility and allow laypersons to be more involved in the sacraments and in the life of the parish. With so few priests available in any parish in the South Bronx, others might find desperately needed relief from their busy schedules and find other ways to build parish life.*

Finally, the Pastoral Center offered a Parish Services Program that customized training to fulfill the requests of a particular parish. Unlike the other two programs, which brought students to a central location, this one met students where they were: in their local parishes. Parish Services included the subject matter of some of the courses offered in Core Formation or Specialized Ministry, but in a format which best suited the local parish. In each course which was offered on-site, the content and schedule was specified by the parish staff or pastor. Customized courses included subjects ranging from improved parish planning to establishing an effective parish council to preparing a baptism ministry team (to take over the parish's baptism program from the priests). One parish even experimented with creating and training a team of part-time laypersons functioning as the pastoral team, in place of a traditional team of priests.

Connolly saw all three programs in action and discussed them at the Pastoral Center Board meetings, offering his feedback along with other board members, as Stern and his team proposed and built new course offerings. Over the next few years, the center grew: by the 1983–1984 academic year, thirty-eight different courses were offered. The number of students grew from 129 in the first academic year to 900 by that fifth year. Knowledge-hungry laypersons came to this seminary for the people from thirty-nine parishes, up from the original seventeen in the first year.

Co-founders Muriel Long and Nora Cunningham, and lay trainer Luis Brigantty, at the Pastoral Center. (Photo by Chris Sheridan. Courtesy of CATHOLIC NEW YORK.)

Moreover, over half of the participants came from parishes outside the South Bronx, including the North Bronx, Upper Manhattan, New Rochelle, and Yonkers. The Pastoral Center even developed partnerships with two Catholic colleges, the College of New Rochelle and Fordham University, which offered adult education degree programs to graduates of the center.

For Connolly, Stern, and the other board members, it was promising that laypersons at the center were not limited to the role of student. There were also lay representatives on the board of directors and on an advisory committee which recommended courses and other programming. Finally, there were lay faculty members, including a few of the graduates of the twelve-course Core Formation Program.

These graduates were part of the original *Gran Migración* who had arrived in New York with limited formal education but assumed active roles in their parishes and pursued their educational opportunity at the Pastoral Center with full commitment.[9]

Ready for Lay Ministers?

As he saw all this growth take place at the Pastoral Center, Connolly learned that accomplishments brought success. With broad support from laypersons from around the archdiocese, the center was reaching far beyond the little rectory of a parish in the South Bronx where it started. Because it was allowed to grow without interference by the Institutional Church, and because it met a great need for knowledge among Puerto Rican laypersons, it had expanded significantly.

But the lack of archdiocesan institutional support for the very idea of lay ministers who might join or even replace priests meant that the Specialized Ministry Program graduates, on returning to their parishes with new skills, might not actually find a new role. If the pastor of a particular parish was not given permission by the archdiocese to hire or use the new baptism ministers, for example, then there would be no baptismal ministry teams employed at the parish, and the ministers would have no place to use their newly acquired skills. The question remained: *Was the archdiocese—and its pastors—ready for this new kind of layperson, who did not sit in the pews but instead was a church minister?*

The United States Conference of Catholic Bishops gave slow, halting responses to the growing crisis of priestless parishes and the urgency of creating new ministry options. In 1980, fifteen years after the Vatican II documents *Lumen Gentium* and *Apostolicam Actuositatem* gave laypersons a clear claim to leadership in the Church, the U.S. bishops issued their own document, *Called and Gifted*.[10] It asserted that laypersons had a claim to Church leadership, but it fell short of authorizing them to take managerial or sacramental ministry roles in parishes. Even the Vatican gave no strong direction for the American Church: Its new 1983 Code of Canon Law recognized the existence of priestless parishes, but allowed laypersons to manage those churches only as a last resort.

No one in the Institutional Church said out loud that laypersons, with the right preparation, could lead a church.

Eventually, the same kinds of grassroots Church leaders who had generated experiments such as pastoral associate formation programs in the Midwest would come up with other solutions involving laypersons. Various parishes began training laypersons and using them as lay ecclesial ministers, who performed some of the roles usually reserved to priests.[11] Trained much like they were at the South Bronx Pastoral Center, lay ecclesial ministers around the United States took on baptismal, bereavement, and music ministries, and they continued to take on the roles of lector and

Eucharistic minister, which they had had in the mass since the late 1960s. And in a growing number of educational institutions, the position of Pastoral Life Coordinator—a layperson responsible for planning and operating a parish alone or in a team, functioning like a pastor—was introduced. These institutions, seeing the "signs of the times," developed full courses of study for those laypersons willing to take on the administrative responsibilities of a parish.

But Connolly did not see these kinds of positions, which he read about with excitement and hope, and which he was helping his Pastoral Center students prepare for, being established actively in his own South Bronx Church. He realized that, *even among his priest friends in the South Bronx, those who had stayed as priests and fought to salvage some part of their parish and neighborhood, the desire to change the world, stayed right there: in the world. Making the changes coming out of Vatican II, using the language of the people and going Spanish with the people, and even fighting to elect their own bishop, were all changes to the Church they could live with. But*, it seemed to Connolly, *some of his fellow priests were troubled by something deeper, in seeing the Pastoral Center prepare laypeople to become ministers: the question of their own identity as priests.*

All their lives as adults, with all the changes in the South Bronx, and in Vatican II, the only thing that was constant in the past twenty years was their role as priests. They were responsible for sacraments and for counseling and for ensuring the survival of the Church they were entrusted with. No one had changed that, not even during the revolutionary period of Vatican II, when every document and every educational conference told Connolly and every other priest—you will remain in your role as priests.

But, Connolly realized, *he and Stern, and maybe a few other priests on the faculty at the South Bronx Pastoral Center, were ready to change their role after all these years as traditional priests of a traditional Church. The priest he had planned to be when he left St. Patrick's Cathedral in May 1958 was not the same as what he had decided to become over the years, and what he was now ready to be. The priest who left Puerto Rico in the summer of 1958 learned from the jíbaros that he was going to be a priest wherever the Church was, wherever the believers were, even in the back of a colmado. The priest who went into the Peninsula streets learned to cofound a church he directed with the laypeople, to say Mass in the street, and to reflect in people's apartments. This same priest was pleased to learn from Bob Stern and his team how to develop laypersons for the future Church. That was the role he would learn to play as a priest: as a teacher and developer of laypersons, to become leaders in the future Church.*

Even though he and Stern and the others struggled to get their fellow priests to accept the new ministers, Connolly realized something else as he read about the Hispanic communities growing in the U.S. Catholic Church. Hispanics themselves would have some answers to the lay leadership question, the same one which the nurse had asked him in the emergency room.

As the fastest-growing part of the American Catholic population, Hispanics were becoming more important. But the American Catholic Church was not going to produce as many Hispanic priests as they needed to address their pastoral needs, and so their roles as lay leaders would become a bigger necessity. This, in turn, raised the question: How would the Church develop that leadership? That question led to another potential source of answers, which Stern had initiated with Father Beltrán: *encuentros*. Out of the original regional and national *encuentros*, Hispanic ministry centers and apostolates sprouted independently in various parts of the country. Some of those centers, in turn, generated Hispanic lay leadership formation centers, such as the Mexican American Cultural Center in San Antonio, Texas, and the Southeast Hispanic Pastoral Institute in Florida.[12] In the past, seeds of change had often been planted in such national Catholic gatherings in the past—the Liturgical Movement, the Christian Family Movement, and the National Federation of Priests had all sprung from these kinds of events. Now, Connolly thought, *perhaps the Church's best hope might come from those encuentros or other national gatherings. He had learned much from the national gatherings and was open to learning more.*

Learning New Ministry

It was at the same time Connolly was first learning about the *Instituto de Formación Laica* that he was given the chance to learn about other priests like him in the United States. His friend Father Phil Murnion had been interested in Connolly's work in the South Bronx since the priests' petition campaign in 1968. It was Murnion who had completed and submitted the report to reorganize the Archdiocese of New York, just weeks after Connolly and the others sent their petitions to the Vatican. Murnion, like Connolly, wanted to create a Vatican II Church, and he stayed in touch with him throughout the other initiatives of those years, including the Bronx Clergy Coalition, the South Bronx Catholic Association, the creation of the vicariate, and the fight for community plans for South Bronx housing. Wanting Connolly's program to deeply involve the Catholic Church in the world of the South Bronx to gain national attention, Murnion gave Connolly a national forum. He recruited Connolly to join the board of his organization, the Catholic Committee on Urban Ministry (CCUM), based at the University of Notre Dame, in South Bend, Indiana.[13]

CCUM was cofounded and led by Father John Egan, the leader of the Federation of Chicago Priests, whom Connolly had met at their exciting 1967 meeting.[14] Egan, known as "Jack" to most, had a long history of social action initiatives in Chicago, which started as far back as 1939. In that year, as a young parish priest, Egan worked with the famous community organizer Saul Alinsky to build an organization, Back of the Yards, which brought together mostly Catholic workers in the stockyards to fight for better living conditions.[15] Alinsky, emphasizing the essential role churches could play in building a powerful enough organization to "fight city hall," began a long-term collaboration with Egan to get other areas of the Chicago archdiocese to fight for people's neighborhoods. As a result, other organizations resembling Back of the Yards grew and engaged in active pressure campaigns to get policy changes from the notoriously corrupt Chicago government.

While successful during three decades in getting the Institutional Catholic Church of Chicago to commit its resources to those organizations, Egan was less successful at keeping a positive relationship with Chicago's authoritarian Cardinal Cody during the 1960s. After becoming an outcast in the Archdiocese of Chicago, Egan searched for an opportunity to bring together priests and sisters who, like him, were committed to justice for the urban areas of the country. Within a short while, after Father Theodore Hesburgh, Notre Dame's president, opened up the University as Egan's next home, he created that opportunity by founding CCUM in 1967.[16] Over the next decade, the committee brought hundreds of those priests and sisters—the "urban ministers"—to discuss their efforts to build organizations around urban and national issues, such as the farmworkers' movement, the anti–Vietnam War movement, and even movements on Church issues such as women's ordination. Yet even with this wide range of topics, the semi-annual conferences at Notre Dame always returned to the issues Egan originally took on in Chicago—organizing neighborhood churches to make government and businesses accountable.[17]

These conferences addressed the role that priests and sisters could play in taking on this organizing work. So did another CCUM activity: the Institute for Social Ministry, an intensive program of short-term courses given every summer at Notre Dame. Institute sessions effectively recruited priests and sisters from cities and suburbs around the country to join the growing league of active ministers in the United States.[18] Both the conference and the institute were reported on regularly in the *National Catholic Reporter*, the media vehicle read by socially conscious Catholic ministers and laypersons like Connolly, which helped them understand and debate the issues of the Church and the world.

When Connolly was given the opportunity to be part of CCUM's activities, he jumped in eagerly. He did more than attend conferences himself: He brought priests and laypersons from the South Bronx also. The second educational opportunity CCUM offered Connolly was at the Institute for Social Ministry, where he was not a student, but a teacher. One summer, he was given the chance to "co-teach" with a nun on the issues facing ministers in the inner city. While she discussed the analytical components of the issues and the way churches could respond, Connolly played the role of "color commentator," offering stories about urban issue campaigns.

Some of the ministers in the one-week course were from outside major cities, and the class included students from all around the country, so few of them immediately understood Connolly's descriptions of New York City and the South Bronx. In discussing the many arson fires, he described the "pumps" on every street corner that were being used as fire truck after fire truck rushed to save buildings from destruction. "What is this term 'pump' that you're using?" someone would ask, as others nodded. At these moments Connolly would suddenly realize that, as much as he felt a common bond with the people in the classroom over their justice work, it took quite a lot to explain his circumstances and even to do something as simple as translate the local slang term for "fire hydrant."

This was proven again when a student, a sister from the South, asked about the South Bronx Catholic Association's plan, relayed in "What Must Be Done to Rebuild the South Bronx," to create smaller, less impersonal housing than the twenty-story public housing buildings he and so many others had gotten used to.

"Weyul, just how haah are these heah new apartment buildin's you're speakin' about, Father?"

"Well, they would be about four or five stories high," Connolly replied.

"Gosh!" answered the excited religious. "In mah part of the country, where we come from, that's haaaah!" Connolly and the class laughed at her comments; they all enjoyed hearing and sharing about the variety of ministry experiences they had throughout the country.

During the late 1970s Connolly regularly came back from the CCUM conferences, which took place on Notre Dame's beautiful and historic campus, to a South Bronx where buildings and neighborhoods were experiencing extensive abandonment and destruction. Yet he was inspired by the people he met at CCUM, by the stories and concepts he heard, and by the reality that he was not alone. He remembered, from the days of conferences after Vatican II, that other priests and religious were opening up their Church to a new way of understanding scriptures, sacraments, and the roles of laypeople. Connolly knew that he was not just a South Bronx parish priest but part of an American Catholic community that was transforming.

In the CCUM, he had discovered a national urban Church community, one in which priests and sisters teamed up in fierce campaigns over many urban issues—segregation, urban renewal, poor housing, government abandonment, and others. Knowing and meeting these champions of their neighborhoods, and of the Church's role in those neighborhoods, gave him *animo*—new spirit—to go back and battle for his South Bronx.

Fighters and Builders

For all that he saw going on in the country through the lens of the CCUM conferences and the Institute for Social Ministry, it was his fellow board members that were maybe his best sources of wisdom. Connolly attended CCUM board meetings in Washington, D.C., and at Notre Dame to help organize the upcoming conferences and institutes. But during the meetings and post-meeting dinners, he became friends with a group of people who had led interesting ministry initiatives in their own lives.

Besides Phil Murnion, another New York priest on the board was Father Henry Browne, known as "Harry" to his friends.[19] Harry Browne was an accomplished scholar of Catholic labor history who had built and maintained the labor archives at the Catholic University of America in Washington, D.C. Also, Browne had been a pastor at St. Gregory's parish on the Upper West Side, an area which faced the pressures of urban renewal. In the 1950s and 1960s, Browne became a fierce defender of the parish and the neighborhood during its battles over government plans to "clear" entire blocks for major middle-income housing developments. During the 1960s and 1970s, Browne was joined on the staff by Jay Dolan and Murnion, two priests who would both become national figures in the American Catholic Church, and he built a reputation for being a priest of the people.

Connolly saw Browne as the typical pro-labor Catholic priest: salty-tongued with a great sense of humor, clear about his working-class roots, and ready to do battle with the enemies in powerful institutions, be it corporate America or city hall. Watching Browne in action made Connolly realize how differently priests could approach inner-city issues. One time, in New York City, Connolly attended a conference on poverty which included the Vicars of "inner-city" areas in New York, along with Cardinal Cooke, religious and labor leaders including the Teamsters' Jimmy Hoffa, and experts in poverty. The sessions all addressed the question of how to change the living conditions of the poor and of their neighborhoods.

Browne and Bob Fox, creator of the Summer in the City program, embodied the central debate among the attendees. In an open debate with Browne, Fox emphasized the importance of relationship-building and community-building as the prerequisite to any kind of social change. Browne challenged that, arguing that any changes made in the living conditions of working-class Americans would be brought about only by using the Church as a "power base" in direct and active conflict with corporate and government power. Browne had no patience for Fox's community-building approach. Fox, who saw the Church as a servant of the people, saw the beauty and potential in all people, and he felt that the Church's role was to build that potential, no matter who the person was. "You know what's the matter with you, Fox?" yelled a frustrated Browne halfway through the debate. "You see Christ in cockroaches!"

Connolly reflected on his own years of priesthood after watching this debate between two of his good friends, men he admired greatly. *He had been spending a good part of his life building up communities, small and large, to make sure people were included and involved and recognized. Movimiento Familiar Cristiano and the Christian Base Communities, and Summer in the City—they were all organized and supported by him in the role of "servant priest." The South Bronx Catholic Association was created to build a community of parishes throughout the South Bronx, and with the association he also played a servant role—helping to organize it, to shape its agenda and involve its members. Every one of those communities was meaningful to the people who were brought together, and they became stronger as they came together.*

They did not change the living conditions of the people, though—not by themselves.

But ever since the South Bronx Catholic Clergy Association had launched its petition campaign to elect their archbishop, Connolly knew, *priests could fight for something they believed in, and they should fight. It was absolutely right to fight for the buildings and tenants in Hunts Point–Longwood. He was right to join the Bronx Clergy Coalition and mobilize to disrupt the city council hearings, to get their concerns heard and their living conditions changed. The Church had to use this disruptive power*

*against the city government, the same way student protesters were using
their power against the government over the Vietnam War, and the way
civil rights movement disrupted luncheonettes and boycotted bus systems.*

*The Church had power and could use it to achieve justice. If that meant
fighting another power, then that was acceptable as well—as long as the
battle was engaged and undertaken with respect and dignity for people.*
Connolly thought to himself, *I have learned how to build communities
and relationships. That is part of my life, my identity as a priest—I am
a builder of community. Fox taught me—and so did the laypersons of
Athanasius, especially the Hunts Point Peninsula leaders who helped build
the Seneca Chapel and Seneca Center. Fox was right, he thought, that the
Church should be in the world as a community builder. But Harry Browne
was right, too.*

Once, at Notre Dame over dinner and a drink, Browne confided in
Connolly about his frustrations in the neighborhood battles over urban
renewal and affordable housing. "All these Irish Americans, they were
poor," said Browne. "We built buildings for them, and their lives got better.
Then they move out, they go to Westchester County, and they become
Republicans. And they vote against all inner-city renovation." Browne felt
that the Church had fought intense struggles for justice and changed the
neighborhood, but it hadn't taught that vision of justice or the struggle for
it to the people of the Church.

Oh, Connolly realized, *it's about the people. Even if the Church fights
for justice, it must be the people who lead and fight. Now he would need to
follow the lead of Browne and the CCUM urban ministers and use Church
power to fight for change. But if he did not want to be disappointed like
Browne, he needed to find a way to do it while also developing laypeople.*

Harry, Larry, and Marge

Three other board members had an answer for Connolly's new challenge.

One was Harry Fagan, a former retail marketing manager for the
Cleveland *Plain Dealer*. An active lay Catholic with little patience for
"do-gooders"—those who wanted to do good in the world for every cause
without any plan—Fagan developed a practical, hands-on approach to
organizing communities around problems of the world in their own neighborhoods. Along with his wife, Sheila, Fagan emphasized a process that
first involved research, then a way to define an issue, and, finally, a plan
of action to solve it. They devised a curriculum around this method and
shared it with a group of seventy-five leaders from different parishes in

Cleveland, who then mobilized 7,500 parishioners into action campaigns. As his accomplishments became known, Fagan became a leading authority on community organizing and was hired to be the director of the Cleveland Diocesan Commission on Catholic Community Action. He was then recruited to be a CCUM board member and faculty at the Institute for Social Ministry.

The second was Father Larry Gorman, a Chicago-based priest who was the director of CCUM's Institute for Social Ministry.[20] Gorman, who directed the deacon preparation program for the Archdiocese of Chicago, was also a teacher at the institute. His presentations focused on the social justice themes in the Old and New Testament. At CCUM conferences, Gorman also taught a course on a new topic to the American Church: liberation theology.

Finally, another member-teacher from Chicago was Dominican Sister Marjorie Tuite, who was chairwoman of the Social Concerns Committee of the National Assembly of Women Religious.[21] Tuite was an active champion for the ordination of women as priests in the 1970s and 1980s. As a faculty member of Bellarmine College in Chicago, she educated women religious in a pastoral formation program to run parishes with others on staff when

Sr. Marjorie Tuite, OP, CCUM Board Member and national trainer in power analysis. (Photo courtesy of Kathleen Osberger.)

Harry Fagan, CCUM Board Member and national trainer in community organizing. (Photo by Chris Sheridan. Courtesy of *Catholic New York*.)

few such programs in the United States were doing so. Tuite's talents and vision, as well as her blend of intense courage and humor, were widely recognized even in a male and clergy-dominated American Church. They led to her positions on the faculty and board of CCUM.

Tuite, Fagan, and Gorman did not just teach individual courses at the institute—they also taught together. Using the themes which they focused on during their individual courses, the three created a "road-show" presentation. Designed to reach all Catholic ministers and laypersons as well as religious and clergy, the presentation made the case for parish involvement in organized social action. Moreover, the program was targeted at laypersons, asking them, along with ministers, to become involved in the social justice agenda of the parish. Connolly was able to hear the full presentation at a special CCUM workshop, and he was amazed.

Tuite called on her audience to develop an understanding of power, especially the power relationships in society and its institutions. She noted that individuals often live or work under hierarchical institutions which give most of the power to a few individuals at the small top of the "pyramid," as she called it, and little power to the rest of the individuals at the broad bottom. The hierarchies had decision-making structures which refused to address the needs of most people; the goals of those at the top were at odds with those of the mass of individual stakeholders. These hierarchies created relationships of inequality or of indifference among individuals, with everyone acting on their own and often in direct competition with each other for scarce resources.

The solution to such hierarchies, inequalities, and indifferences, Tuite argued, was for the people at the bottom of the hierarchies to break out of their isolation and come together as equals across race, gender, religion, nationality, and other lines. In doing so, they could solve problems and meet needs with accountability to one another and to common goals, and with united action around those goals. Her most important point was that people needed to see the world they were living in, understand their relationships to each other and to the societal institutions that shaped their lives, and embrace the fact that they were not powerless to create change.

Fagan, for his part, articulated the principles of community organizing and of social action, and he discussed the steps involved in good organizing campaigns.[22] He followed up on a part of Tuite's presentation, which outlined the critical difference between social service and social action. Social service met the needs of an individual, and the agent of social service would thus do something *for* someone else. In a social action situation, individuals would come together around an individual need that was common to many, identify the condition and institution creating that need, and work with each other to have the institution change that condition. Parish-based social action committees, Fagan argued, could focus on social action and generate social change. By identifying the institutional policy they wanted changed and by building up community support for that change, they could make conditions better for a good number of people in the community.

Gorman's presentation, which focused on theology and social action, caught Connolly's attention in particular. It made the connection between scripture, Catholic social teaching, and the practice of social action by the parish. Citing the Book of Exodus, Gorman explained the Jewish people's struggles for freedom from slavery under kings and emperors. He referred to the prophets, such as Isaiah, and their calls for justice for the people. Gorman also discussed the Gospel message, which emphasized the liberation of the poor and oppressed and charity for the poor. It was not enough for a Christian to care for the suffering of a fellow human being; one also had to address the social causes of the suffering.

Connolly came away from this presentation with several conclusions. *First,* he thought, *this was the way for the Church to be in the world, to*

CCUM Board Member Neil Connolly receiving national leadership award, with friend and CCUM co-founder Fr. Phil Murnion (*seated*). (Archives of the University of Notre Dame.)

fight the fight Harry Browne wanted to win: to bring the Church in as an agent of change and power in the world, but with the people sharing the understanding of power, the method of organizing and the theological foundation for social action. Also, his own fights for justice in the South Bronx were righteous and genuine, but they were not the fruit of this prepared approach. There was a belief among the Bronx Clergy Coalition and the Catholic Association that their battles were just and rooted in Christian understanding of justice for the poor. But they hoped their moral authority and demands would lead to change by the city government without a full-scale plan of action and a full use of power.

Church-Based Organizing

What Connolly heard from "Harry, Larry, and Marge" was a call for ministers to build a social action organization—one that practiced church-based community organizing. Ministers like him could not just build organizations like Seneca, SISDA, and the other organizations built by the South

Bronx Catholic Association ministers—the priests and women religious—
all over the South Bronx. They had to build a broad base of churches led
by laypersons who could fight battles for the future South Bronx, but with
organized power and moral authority. This method was being learned and
practiced in the United States, and now it needed to be brought to the
South Bronx.

Saul Alinsky built a series of such organizations over several decades
using this approach. In Chicago, he and Jack Egan, among others, had
built the Back of the Yards Council, the Woodlawn Organization, and the
Southwest Community Organization into major, powerful groups. In San
Antonio, Alinksy's dynamic Mexican American organizer, Ernie Cortés,
created Communities Organized for Public Services (COPS). In Buffalo,
the BUILD organization took on the establishment over the treatment
of the city's black community. All of these groups and many others were
started by the Industrial Areas Foundation (IAF), founded by Alinsky to
advance the organizing approach he had developed, which was focused
on understanding and utilizing power and on "confrontation toward
negotiation."[23]

The IAF was just the beginning of the church-based community organizing approach in the country. Across the United States, newly created
groups used a similar training approach and organizational framework.
The Midwest Academy was developed in Chicago by Heather Booth, an
organizer trained in the approach of Alinsky. Also in Chicago,[24] Shel Trapp,
a former priest and Alinsky organizer, originated the National Training
and Information Center.[25] In San Francisco, Father John Baumann, a
Jesuit priest, established the Pacific Institute of Community Organization
(PICO) to organize in California and the Western United States.[26]

These groups' organizational models were somewhat different from the
IAF and from each other. However, they all built around the "organization
of organizations" approach, knowing that churches were central organizations themselves in any urban or suburban residential area. The church
was respected and trusted by the local community residents, having provided assistance over the years. The church was also a source of "troops"
for any potential battle with government, business, or landlord/real estate
types. Finally, the church was considered a holder, arbiter, and promoter
of values such as fairness, dignity, and community and mutual support. The
challenge of organizing churches was to turn this authority, goodness, and
charity into an army ready to "go to war."

After learning about the practice of church-based organizing, Connolly
decided he was ready for another role as a priest. It was the same role he

had taken on as a faculty member at the South Bronx Pastoral Center and at the Seneca Center a while back. He would teach what he had learned to laypersons and then let them take ownership of their lives and their future. Unlike the Bronx Clergy Coalition days, he would not be leading the fight against city hall over the conditions of his people in the South Bronx. The people who lived every day with that suffering would need to lead. Before, he had learned to develop laypersons to lead in the Church, as the nurse had asked him and as Stern had taught him to do. Now, he would develop laypersons to lead in the world.

It was time to build another kind of ministry among laypersons. Social justice ministry.

10

People for Change

He stood up to read the Scriptures and was handed the book of the prophet Isaiah. He unrolled the scroll and found the place where it is written:

> The Spirit of the Lord is upon me,
> Because he has chosen me to bring good news to the poor;
> He has sent me to proclaim liberty to the captives.
> And recovery of sight to the blind,
> To set free the oppressed
> And announce that the time has come when the Lord will save His people.

—Luke 4:17–19, Bilingual Bible, Good News Translation, United Bible Societies

Mission Teams

On a warm Saturday in the spring of 1978, fifteen people gathered in the auditorium of St. Athanasius Elementary School for an all-day workshop. Priests, religious, and laypersons from the South Bronx Catholic Association had come to hear a three-part presentation by Father Larry Gorman, Sister Marjorie Tuite, and Harry Fagan. The message of the presentation for the audience was compelling and yet a little daunting: *You can change the South Bronx. Using scripture and Christian history as your foundation, you as Church members can challenge the World to be just. Organizing social action committees and researching institutions, you as Church members can tell your government to fix neighborhood problems. Also,*

239

understanding how institutions in power divide people without power, people can come together and create a change in power relationships.

Everyone in the room was enthusiastic and curious but unsure about the next step. Then, at one point late in the afternoon, Connolly observed as one woman, a tall, outspoken parishioner from St. Peter and Paul, stood up. Connolly had long admired her for being a strong participant in the association, and for her help in his effort to bring the presentations from the national forum in Notre Dame to a school in the South Bronx. After hearing Tuite's presentation about institutional power over people's lives and the need to change those institutions, however, the woman was very skeptical and challenged a surprised Tuite. Frustrated, she loudly called her out. "Yes, but just how do you do that? How do you make those changes? This is the South Bronx, Sister. We are overwhelmed with the poverty!"

Tuite smiled from in front of the whiteboard, put down her marker, and walked slowly and confidently toward the woman. "You have to be able to risk," she said, as if she were confessing her own approach to life. "You have to be able to take a stand, you have to be able to do this!" As Tuite looked around at the participants, she continued, "You just can't go back and wait for somebody to do this for you." She turned again to her skeptic. "Get out of your dependency. You can do something in the world. You have power. You are a human being!"

Connolly and the audience were startled by the vehemence of the exchange, but he was not surprised by Tuite's message. She and her co-presenters, after all, had shared bold concepts and interpretations and techniques. Connolly had hoped they would inspire these members of the Catholic Association as they had inspired him at Notre Dame. Even while they were still fighting against overwhelming City Hall forces for the future of the South Bronx, the association wanted to build a force greater than themselves. So did Connolly, who did not want to give up hope. He did not want to accept the truth of a remark once made by his friend John Flynn, recently returned to the Bronx after a mission in Venezuela. In the middle of a conversation about "What Must Be Done to Rebuild the South Bronx," Flynn said to the South Bronx clergy, "I think you're so used to the smell of smoke that you don't think there's any other way to live here."

Connolly wanted to generate some positive discussion. But Tuite's challenge was bluntly personal—not just for the laywoman who had interrupted her discussion of power, but for Connolly and his association. *If you want the change, you can create the change,* she was saying to them. *Each of you better change your attitude about your own power. Change your attitude about your relationships with others and your ability to change institutions.* Connolly felt she was speaking to him personally: *If you want to change the conditions of the South Bronx, change your mind about your power and the people's power.*

After "Harry, Larry, and Marge" finished, Connolly and the association members agreed to promote their workshop to the rest of the South Bronx, to every parish that was ready for it. They sought to employ local culture, using the format of the event most likely to attract people to the local parish—a *misión*. In the largely Puerto Rican parishes, *misiones* typically involved an intense multiday period of presentations by an outside preacher, usually from Puerto Rico, to charge up parishioners and recruit non-parishioners. Several times at Athanasius, Connolly had observed Father Pedro Junquera, a dynamic preacher who created an elaborate, impassioned, multimedia sermon for each night of his *misión*.

Connolly knew this approach would give this social justice "mission" its best chance for success. So he and two dozen association members agreed they would get trained as members of mission teams and make their own presentations. Each mission team would be brought in by an interested pastor who would promote their presentation beforehand as a *misión para la justicia social*. They arranged for five weekends of intensive training by Gorman, Fagan, and Tuite.

Trainees specializing in the "Faith and Social Action" presentation spent their weekends with Gorman, learning to explain the scriptural foundations for social justice, both Old and New Testament. Those who wanted to share the principles and techniques of organizing campaigns were prepared by Fagan. Finally, those who were most galvanized by Tuite's presentation on the analysis of institutions and power relationships worked with her. At the end of the intensive training period, the new cadre of mission teams was ready to spread this three-part message. As Connolly sat in on all three presentations, to be ready to supplement any of the teams, he realized: *Wow, this new thing is going to really happen here in the South Bronx.*

Once their preparation was completed, the leadership group for the new mission project decided to begin with a *misión* at St. Anselm's. With all the mission team trainees in attendance, the first presentation was delivered before an audience of more than two hundred people. Most of them were parishioners attracted by an event promoted for weeks at Sunday Mass by Father Joe Donahue and others as a "Mission for Social Justice." Also, there were other members of the South Bronx Catholic Association from neighboring parishes who were curious about this new association initiative. Finally, there were even elected officials present: State senator Joseph Galiber and Bronx borough president Stanley Simon.

As Connolly stood in the back of St. Anselm's school auditorium watching the team at work, Galiber walked over to greet him and surprised him with a question: "You guys are bent on doing something with all these people?" Connolly replied that this was just a presentation, but he realized that this large a number of people mobilized in one place was enough to make a political powerbroker somewhat concerned. Galiber and Connolly were both realizing something: *There was power in that auditorium.*

A couple of months later, the mission team initiative moved on to the neighboring parish, St. Athanasius, where Connolly had first arrived twenty years earlier. Again, there were more than two hundred participants, all excited about the mission of social justice and wondering what was next. There was also a guest speaker, invited at the last minute: a woman named Dolores Rodriguez from the Industrial Areas Foundation organization based in Los Angeles. Rodriguez, in town for other reasons, was recruited to say a few words about the importance of building an action organization. After giving some brief remarks, the Mexican American Rodriguez addressed the audience of Puerto Rican laypersons with a challenge in their shared language: "*La actitud de el pueblo es que no se puede.* When people take on a new church project, they say, 'It's too much, I can't handle it.'" She concluded emphatically, "I am begging you please. Don't say, *No se puede!*"

After the successful mission, all of the mission team trainees remained at the school and went up to the convent on the top floor to celebrate. They ate snacks and enthusiastically reflected on what they had just done and what their next steps would be. With Pio Mendez playing guitar and a Maryknoll brother from the neighborhood playing a Bolivian *sicu* (wooden pipes played like a flute), they sang and clapped and danced. As it got late, Connolly and a few others were hungry and decided to go up to an Italian restaurant, Dominic's on Castle Hill Avenue, a local favorite. Not sure if they would still be able to eat there, Connolly called and inquired about whether the kitchen was still open and whether the restaurant could serve a party of twenty-nine.

"Twenty-nine? You said twenty-nine, Father Connolly? Come!" said the manager. "Of course, we can take you!" It was a good evening for Connolly and his friends and a good end to a meaningful day. He was about to embark on a new stage of his priesthood and take a new step for the Church he envisioned: *the source of justice and hope in the World.*

Building an Organization

Within weeks, Connolly and the Catholic Association members formed a committee for the new organization. A team of people worked to write a proposal, led by Connolly and Flynn on the narrative and Father David Casella of St. Thomas Aquinas on the budget and financials. They worked with the Institute for Human Development, the same group that had helped Connolly form the Seneca Center ten years earlier. Institute staff sharpened it into a crisp, comprehensive proposal for funding and helped the mission team members organize themselves into a board of directors. Connolly became chairperson of this new social justice initiative. Since it was going to focus on the laypersons of the South Bronx parishes, they called it South Bronx People for Change.

Fortunately for the new organization, they had a strong source of funding within reach. The Catholic Campaign for Human Development, the entity created by the United States Conference of Catholic Bishops in 1967, was actively funding community organizing projects just like People for Change. The campaign had long been familiar to Connolly, ever since it had funded his Bronx Clergy Coalition ten years earlier. Also, he had just been appointed to the campaign's local board by his old friend Monsignor John Ahern, from the days of the Puerto Rico summer program, the Family Services of Catholic Charities, and the War on Poverty. So he would be able to make a case for People for Change, even if he could not vote on it. Everyone on the board was equally familiar with Connolly and his work with the Catholic Association in the battles for the South Bronx. And the South Bronx itself had reached a level of national notoriety and reputation for urban neglect that evoked sympathy from many Americans. A fellow campaign board member told Connolly, "Listen, if there's any place in the United States that should be getting money, it's the South Bronx!" In December 1979, People for Change was awarded the maximum grant of $100,000.[1]

If organizing a board of directors and finding funding had been relatively easy, the next step—finding the right staff—became a challenge. Assuming they were going to need a nationally recognized, capable organizer who understood church-based community organizing, Connolly searched at national Church gatherings, such as the National Pastoral Life Center events organized by Phil Murnion and the Catholic Committee on Urban Ministry (CCUM) conferences, but he had no luck. Harry Fagan, who was connected to the national network of community organizing groups, asked around too but found no applicants. According to Fagan, the U.S.

organizing community was concerned that the South Bronx had no real church-based organizing history. Also, he reported, the South Bronx was seen as almost damaged beyond repair.

Connolly thought, *They see us like a fighter who goes down for the count, gets up, gets knocked down, and then gets up again. The same sympathetic national image that evoked such strong support from his Campaign for Human Development Board colleagues was scaring away the agents of social change.* Connolly made his next appeal for staff to the nationally renowned Bedford-Stuyvesant Restoration Corporation in Brooklyn, thinking they would know how to rebuild a battered New York community. With their decade of experience and early support from Robert F. Kennedy and the Ford Foundation, the sophisticated "Bed-Stuy Restoration," as it was known, was a potential source of real wisdom for Connolly. But they rejected collaboration with the new organization in the South Bronx, pointing out that their blocks in Bedford-Stuyvesant were full of private houses with strong potential for improvement, and that the homeowners would have a stake in saving their neighborhoods—unlike the South Bronx, with its many apartment buildings and burned-out lots.

At first Connolly was discouraged by all this feedback. Then he decided that, as the Pastoral Center demonstrated, *the solutions would have to come from within his South Bronx Church community. The fighter would have to get up. Again.*

People for Change, which, so far, was just a board of directors, learned about some younger local parish leaders who were interested in social action and community organizing and had heard the mission team presentations. Nelson Rodriguez, an experienced administrator and active parish leader at St. Joseph's in Tremont, where Connolly's friend Bob Banome was pastor, applied for the position. A tenant association leader and a member of the local community board, Rodriguez also had Banome's support. Then there was Wilson Martinez of St. John Chrysostom parish, an activist teacher and ex-seminarian who had expressed an interest in social justice. Rodriguez was hired as the lead organizer and executive director, and Martinez as the first organizer.

A special local recruit for Connolly was Mili Bonilla, who had been by his side as his vicariate special assistant for the past two and a half years. A fourth-year student at Hunter College when she began, Bonilla became known to Connolly from her days of participation in Bronx Clergy Coalition meetings, having been recruited by Father Joe Donahue, her pastor at St. Anselm. Connolly thought she showed a strong interest in organizing and in the South Bronx. In addition to helping Connolly administer the vicariate office at Athanasius, Bonilla also attended the Catholic Association meetings. She had presented with the mission team and helped write the proposal for People for Change. When Connolly talked to her about her future plans, Bonilla mentioned that she was planning to go overseas, to a project in Venezuela.

Surprised, Connolly said, "Oh no. You can't go."

"Why not?" said Bonilla.

"I wanted you to join the staff of People for Change as an organizer," Connolly said.

Also surprised but intrigued, Bonilla put off her travel plans and joined the staff as well.

Around this time, Connolly also finally succeeded at landing a national recruit, one especially important for his interest in the faith component of social action. Marjorie Tuite mentioned a Jesuit priest she knew from Chicago, a doctoral student at the Graduate School of Theology at the University of Chicago named Dean Brackley. Tuite had discussed the South Bronx project with Brackley and she mentioned the conversation to Connolly during one of their CCUM get-togethers at Notre Dame. Connolly went back with Tuite to Chicago and they met with Brackley at the Jesuit residence in Hyde Park.

The three talked for hours about their personal histories and their own dreams of change in the Church and in the World. The two priests realized they had a lot in common. After hearing about Connolly's plan to hire an organizer-theologian for his staff, Brackley declared himself not only interested, but enthusiastic: "I would really love to be part of that."

Connolly, for his part, thought Brackley would help People for Change become a unique organization, even among church-based organizing groups. For all of their involvement of churches, none of those organizations made the church's faith and theological discussions an integral part of its activities and program. *People for Change would*, Connolly decided, *and Brackley would help it.* Brackley settled into his new apartment in the Hunts Point Peninsula community, co-establishing the Jesuit Community in the South Bronx with his colleagues Father James Joyce and Father Joseph Towle, former and current directors of Social Ministry for the New York Province.

Forming Local Chapters

People for Change had a small central staff, but its main purpose was to organize and train local chapters in every parish in the South Bronx.

Connolly knew that support for creating a chapter, known as a parish social action committee, depended on the pastor. So he set out as vicar to recruit each pastor who might be ready to approve this development. In each case, with the "blessing" of the pastor secured by Connolly, a mission team presentation was organized and attendees would form the new Social Action Committee. Parish chapters were soon created in St. Anselm, St. Athanasius, St. John Chrysostom, and St. Luke on the eastern side of the South Bronx. Then Sacred Heart and St. Francis of Assisi joined from the western part of the South Bronx, and Our Lady of Victory, where the Pastoral Center was headquartered, also came on board. With pastors who were true believers in the new initiative, or in Connolly himself, the organization was ready to involve laypersons.

Connolly observed something interesting during his recruitment of pastors. A number of the priests he had been close to, who believed in the Church's involvement in the World, and who had been engaged in Summer in the City and its many offshoots, did not want to be so involved in People for Change, or even did not want to be involved at all. Banome at St. Joseph, Smith at St. John Chrysostom, and his friend Gigante at St. Athanasius had built sizeable housing development organizations through the 1970s and now had political connections with those who decided housing contracts.

Connolly thought, *They must have thought that the connections were the best solutions to housing and neighborhood problems. If so, they were not willing to take a serious risk that their parishioners might challenge the "powers that be." Maybe they were also uncertain about having laypersons showing leadership, after they, as priests, had spent many years leading them.* It made Connolly realize that not everyone shared his vision of the Vatican II Church, where laypersons would lead the Church and the World. He thought, *Some were "power priests," focused on "political power," not "people priests," focused on developing people power.*

Those "power priests" had helped their parishes survive the South Bronx's abandonment by taking action and building organizations that did a lot of good for people in their neighborhoods. Without those organizations built by priests and religious, survival might have been impossible. Seneca Center itself had made such a difference for his parishioners and neighbors in the long-neglected Hunts Point Peninsula. *But he had cofounded and comanaged Seneca Center with laypersons as leaders, as board members and managers, and it worked. Couldn't the "people" become leaders of those organizations? Maybe this new experiment with People for Change would help answer the question.*

The parish Social Action Committee, which was created after each mission team presentation to a parish, was the basic organizing unit in People for Change's program. A staff member was assigned to train and support a committee in the techniques and principles of organizing. Each committee was taught the "see, judge, act" approach. A committee would need to "see" what the conditions were in their neighborhood and make a decision about which of the many conditions that seemed to have an impact on them and their neighbors they should focus on. In order to make this decision, committee members would need to "see" if there was a lot of impact on the other members of the community. They would also need to identify what aspect of the condition could be changed and what it would involve. That was how the committee would "judge" what it had "seen." Once selected, the issue—a broken traffic light, an abandoned playground—would become the committee's focus, and they would "act," or carry out, a campaign to solve the problem or change the condition.

Following the process recommended in Fagan's organizing manual, *Empowerment*, the committee and staff member moved from "Problem" to "Issue" to "Action."[2] For an issue to be a good one, it had to be three things: *specific*, *urgent*, and *winnable*. There had to be a *specific* playground that was abandoned, and there had to be a *specific* institution which was responsible for that playground, and a *specific* person who made decisions about the playground. It had to be *urgent*, meaning that a broad group of people and organizations supported doing something about the issue. Finally, it had to be *winnable*—a situation that could be successfully changed within a reasonable time period. If they won a victory, then they could show others in the community that they had "people power."

Social action committees were also trained by the organizing staff in another key principle: "People Plus Knowledge = Power." It would be good to identify a decision-maker and an agency to do something about the playground in their neighborhood, but committee members needed to find out: *How could the playground be rebuilt? What would it cost to design and build it? Would there be a budget for this rebuilding? How did that get approved?* Each committee would need to research the issue by calling local officials or reading government information in the libraries of their local community boards. To succeed with the "people" part of the equation, they would need to collect signatures of parishioners on petitions and solicit support letters from community organizations and elected officials. With this record of support and with the research, they could have real "people power"—the power to change the institution's decisions about their playground.

Committee members were also taught to set agendas for their own meetings, and for any meeting or event they were going to organize. This included the marches or rallies they would have to organize to pressure the decision-makers to respond to their issues and demands. Every effort was made to teach committee members that they could get things done and conditions changed if they had a plan to reach their goals, the endgame in the campaign.

Pretty often, they realized that as basic and achievable as their goal might be, such as having a playground rebuilt, it was not the goal of the responsible institution. That meant, inevitably, that the committee would find itself in conflict with the institution. Conflict was a difficult subject for these Christians, who had been raised to "love one another" and resolve or avoid conflict. But the training they received in the mission team presentations, their own ongoing reflections on scripture and justice, and their sense of indignation at being ignored or rejected by the institutions over something important to them made them come to grips with the reality: *Conflict was part of any organizing campaign.*

The committees came to understand that conflict was going to occur not because they were "un-Christian" or disrespectful. Conflict arose because they wanted respect, and the new Christian teaching had convinced them that Christian love was manifested both in charity and respect for all. If the institution would not act on its own to respect the needs of the people it was supposed to serve, then the most Christian act the committee and the people could take was to change the institution's ways to ensure respect for all.

Local Campaigns

The committees were the leaders in each parish, and they met weekly or biweekly to define their issues, plan their next recruitment effort, and read and reflect on a passage from scripture. Some parishes were Spanish-dominant and others English-dominant, and still others had both English and Spanish committees. They tackled a variety of issues, as each neighborhood presented different conditions. In St. John Chrysostom, the committee pressed the Bronx Buildings Commissioner to invest in the seal-up of a vacant building on Hoe Avenue, in the hopes of salvaging it for future rehabilitation. The St. Anselm Social Action Committee wanted the MTA, New York's mass transit agency, to rehabilitate the Jackson Avenue subway station, which had been damaged a few years earlier by a fire. Still another wanted a vacant lot filled with garbage and used by local junkies to be

St. Anselm's Social Action Committee leader Aida García Martinez (*center, with microphone*) speaks out at the beginning of a march for safety in John Adams Houses. (Photo by Mili Bonilla.)

cleared out and gated, then rehabilitated into a neighborhood playground. And several committees were fighting to stop the crimes of street drug dealing and related violence, so they were focusing on getting the local police precinct commander to assign and deploy police and make arrests.

In St. Athanasius, where Connolly still lived but not as a full-time parish priest, the police protection issue commanded a great deal of attention, but it quickly evolved into another issue. Safety concerns in the Hunts Point Peninsula became so strong that even police were not ready to conduct foot patrols in certain areas for one basic reason—the streets were too dark. Members of the St. Athanasius Social Action Committee researched why there were so many broken streetlights. With their pens, clipboards, and notepads, they counted the nonworking lamps in each block in their neighborhood and came up with a list of more than one hundred. They identified the city's Department of General Services (DGS) as the responsible agency and found that DGS had a contract with only one lighting company for all of New York City's streetlights. With few resources and so many lights with problems, poor neighborhoods like Hunts Point–Longwood were being neglected. It was a revelation for committee members.

The committee found an initial ally in their quest to brighten up the dark streets in Assemblyman John Dearie. A Bronx elected official, Dearie held assembly hearings on the city's lighting contracts system and neglected neighborhoods. After attending the hearings, committee members found out that the city would change the system and issue five separate contracts, one for each of its five boroughs. They had hoped that DGS would act on their petitions to repair their one hundred broken lights, but the streets remained dark. The committee, frustrated with the lack of respect for their safety, decided it was time for confrontation. A delegation went down to the headquarters of DGS near City Hall to meet with Commissioner James Capalino.

The plan was to make a direct plea for his attention to Hunts Point. They sat down with Capalino and presented him with the petitions and letters of support for the replacement of the streetlights they had gathered, as well as the detailed list of locations for the one hundred lamps out of order. Since the commissioner didn't seem to be expressing a full willingness to act, they took another step. A Social Action Committee member stood up, walked over to the commissioner's shiny glass-topped executive desk, and pulled out a large piece of metal from a shopping bag. It was a piece of the base of a street lamp taken from the Peninsula, and it made a loud banging noise when it landed on the desk. Everyone was startled by the noise, including the commissioner, who jumped back against his chair. The commissioner was persuaded at that moment both that the problem was real and that the committee was serious. Within weeks, work crews from the Welsbach Electric Corporation, the contractor DGS selected for the Bronx streetlights, were on the streets of Hunts Point–Longwood, replacing the lamps on the committee list.

Committees from other parishes followed in the footsteps of the Athanasius committee, running campaigns and taking public action. They also agreed that these nonviolent actions, even if they disturbed social order and created conflict with institutions, were consistent with their faith. Regardless of their actions, committee members prayed and spoke of the validity of their actions as just. They staged marches, organized rallies, and held public meetings. Public housing tenants marched around the grounds of the John Adams Houses, calling for Housing Authority police to take protective measures against assaults in the elevators, as St. Anselm committee leader Aida García Martinez called on the Housing Authority to meet residents' demands. On Bruckner Boulevard, at a busy intersection leading to the Hunts Point Food Market, the major center of produce distribution in the northeast United States, Luis Rodriguez led a march of neighbors and parishioners from St. Athanasius calling for traffic lights and stop signs to end accidents. At Woodycrest Avenue, and on the streets of Highbridge, Carmen Guzman, Chickie Torres, and Rosa Valencia led a march for police protection, calling on the precinct commander to deploy police against drug dealing.

One committee even took on the issue of firehouse closings, which had played a central role in the epidemic of fires that had swept the South Bronx all decade. The Immaculate Conception committee, led by Marty and Francine Rogers and Mary Meade, knew what a threat the community would face with the proposed closing of Fire Engine Company 41. In addition to the petitions and letters of political support, committee members took public actions to make the issue visible in the community. After staging regular marches in front of the firehouse, they took another step when the fire commissioner announced the imminent closing. Rogers and staff member Mark Colville conducted a "sleep-in" at the firehouse, closing the doors and preventing the removal of vehicles and equipment. This act of civil disobedience generated more immediate attention, as a lawsuit was filed by attorney Pedro Garcia, from the neighboring St. Anselm Social Action Committee, which stopped the closing in the middle of a mayoral election. Within weeks of the election of new Mayor David Dinkins, the order to close was reversed, and Fire Engine Company 41 was restored to full service.

An Area-Wide Organization

After a year of action, Connolly and the Board of Directors of People for Change were confronted with an internal issue on the staff. Administration and finances were not being managed well, and the director seemed to be treating staff unequally. Connolly learned about these interpersonal conflicts through confidential discussions and about missing reports through the Catholic Campaign for Human Development. After a board meeting, he called in two management professionals: his cousin Ed O'Sullivan, and a colleague, Ed O'Reilly. Both were experienced in conducting management evaluations of other organizations for the Port Authority of New York. After several months of investigation and interviews, a report issued by the two men to the board forced it to make a difficult decision: the firing of their first hire, Executive Director Nelson Rodriguez.

As painful as the move was, Connolly realized it was the right thing to do. He had admired Rodriguez and even began to consider him a friend as well as a fellow "warrior" for justice. But he realized that it was more important to assure the survival and integrity of the organization, and that survival depended on a stable and committed staff that could work together. The work of organizing was hard enough, and he remembered that, without staff, the Bronx Clergy Coalition had eventually lost its power.

Despite their efforts to straighten out and stabilize the staff and budget, People for Change did lose a couple of staff who were loyal to Rodriguez; feeling betrayed, they resigned immediately in protest. The remaining staff eventually selected Tom Amato, who had been a Maryknoll lay missioner in Nicaragua before joining People for Change as an organizer, as their new director, and the organization regrouped. The internal shake-up, while initially demoralizing and a blow to their progress, woke up the staff and the board to the need to continue their growth so that they could make a difference in the larger South Bronx area.

After the crisis was over, an opportunity for that South Bronx–wide organization growth came from outside New York. Ed Dunn, a Franciscan brother from California, had heard about People for Change through church-based organizing networks on the national level, and he wanted to share his own organizing experiences. For a few years, Dunn had worked with the Pacific Institute for Community Organization (PICO), a church-based community organizing group based in Oakland and founded by Jesuit priest John Baumann. Dunn volunteered to share some of the techniques he had learned at PICO for recruiting parishioners and others, and a process for identifying larger issues. Dunn also knew how to organize an organization-wide convention. He guided the staff to mobilize new recruits and stage a convention.

On April 25, 1981, the first South Bronx Unity Conference took place at the auditorium of St. Anselm's Elementary School. With 350 people in attendance, representing delegations from seven different parish chapters of People for Change, the organization had reached a new milestone. The chapters were not acting as isolated social action committees; they were presenting their issues for consideration for a vote by other delegates. Spokespersons addressed the delegations and asked for the votes of the entire assembly. Sanitation, housing, transportation, crime, and other issues were presented and considered. Ballots were distributed and completed, and the choices were tabulated before the final session. In the end, improved police protection was chosen as the top issue, and the members of the delegations committed themselves to support that issue on an area-wide level, in addition to their local issues.

A people's convention in the South Bronx led by co-chairs Louise Mileski and Esperanza Oliveras at the PFC Unity Conference, April 27, 1986. (Photo © Maria R. Bastone, 1986.)

Invited to be the keynote speaker, Connolly marveled at the large gathering of people. Saying, "Our work has just begun," he thought about the work that had gone into bringing church-based community organizing into the South Bronx. The project rejected by both leaders in Bedford-Stuyvesant and the national organizing community was blossoming. An area-wide identity, like the one he had experienced as a member of clergy group advocating for the survival of South Bronx buildings, was taking shape again before his eyes. *This time,* he realized, *it was the laypersons alongside the clergy and religious—the people of God. And with a political-style convention, with issues, platforms, delegations, and votes for priorities, the people were speaking. They were declaring, "We as the people of God, as the people of the South Bronx, have been neglected too long. We will be heard, because we have acquired People Power."*

By this time, local campaigns were underway to address the crime issue in many parishes. Connolly saw one manifested in a meeting at the Athanasius Elementary School auditorium with the commander of the Forty-First Precinct. To set the stage and tone for the meeting, the commander sent detectives ahead to explain to members of the St. Athanasius Social Action Committee how they wanted the meeting to go. When the precinct commander arrived, he went to the front of the auditorium and shouted, "We're going to start now."

At that moment, as he was about to speak, a committee member stood up and said, "Captain, we always pray before we go into a meeting. In the name of the Father, and of the Son, and of the Holy Spirit. . . ." Solemnly she and two hundred others present made the sign of the cross and bowed their heads, as did—automatically—the captain and the detectives. Connolly realized the commander was furious, as the leader took control of the meeting away from him. Throughout the meeting the commander was asked to make commitments on the demands presented by the committee leadership, and they marked his responses on a poster board that had the list of their demands. They posted a rating of his responses, marking them "General answer" or "No commitment" or "No" throughout the evening. At the end, they gave him a "C-Minus" rating and called on him and the precinct to come back and discuss the safety issues again. Embarrassed, the commander left with his entourage.

Connolly realized that, in this neighborhood where crime and drugs had frightened many out of the neighborhood and left the remaining people feeling powerless, this was a show of organized power that many would not have imagined possible. There was much work to be done, and they had achieved few commitments that night, but they were making an impact in standing up for their agenda.

But the conflict created that night with the commander became the subject of gossip among parishioners, and it reached even a staff priest, who was upset. This priest, on assignment at the parish, heard a report on the meeting from a parishioner he saw on the street. The angry parishioner said that the Social Action Committee leader had "shown no respect for the police commander" and that the committee members were "a bunch of Communists." Connolly listened respectfully, but in great frustration, as the priest challenged both the presence of People for Change and Connolly's support for the committee.

"You know, you really shouldn't have a group like that. I mean, to be disrespectful of the police?"

Not caring to be diplomatic, Connolly responded with *animo*, "Father, whose side are you on, the people or the police?"

But he realized that the priest did not understand organizing, or conflict, or even the concept of "power to the people." Even the parishioner who had complained, he was sure, would not have understood that one could be respectful to an institutional leader while still holding him or her accountable to the community.

This was not the only time People for Change disconcerted an institutional authority. Connolly observed a similar kind of meeting happen in Morris Heights. There, the Social Action Committee of St. Francis of Assisi was challenging police captain Jones of the Forty-Fourth precinct. Again, the captain was expecting to run the meeting of 150 people. As the committee respectfully but firmly handled the captain's responses to their demands, however, he became increasingly frustrated and upset to the point where he was earning the nickname "Jumpin' Jones" among the people in the audience. Detectives who were supposed to maintain a calm demeanor were laughing at his reactions to the demands while trying to conceal their faces.

Then, almost out of nowhere, with no prompting, one of the committee members, an old Irishwoman named Mary Cummings, walked up to the captain and gently took a button from her coat and pinned it on the captain's jacket. It read "Kiss Me I'm Irish." The agitated Captain Jones stopped, smiled, and calmed down, and he pleasantly finished the meeting. Connolly enjoyed the moment, as did everyone in the audience.

Cummings, the "Irish sweetheart," was one of a few Irishwomen left in Father John Flynn's parish. Flynn referred lovingly to Mary and her ever-present friend, Margaret Murphy, as the "leftovers." They were part of a senior population that was unable to leave Morris Heights and Hunts Point and other areas in the South Bronx during the flight of many middle-class white residents in the 1950s and 1960s. Connolly admired how well Flynn was able to keep the "leftovers" feeling welcome in a now largely African American and Puerto Rican neighborhood. Cummings's action, while not planned, proved the wisdom of Flynn's long-term "strategy."

In the meantime, the area-wide Police Committee created by the South Bronx Unity Conference was able to secure a meeting with the top police official in New York City. With a set of demands to present concerning the activity of drug dealers in important areas of the South Bronx, the Police Committee wanted to make it clear to Commissioner Robert McGuire that they wanted safer streets. All their research made it clear that the commissioner was the key decision-maker they needed to see.

Down at Police Headquarters, only a limited number of people were allowed to go upstairs to participate in the meeting. These were the lay representatives of the seven parishes as well as their pastors. On the strongly held principle of People for Change that laypersons needed to take a direct role in representing their conditions and their issues, the laypersons took the lead in the meeting. The pastors, meanwhile, stayed silent, following a deliberate plan to force the commissioner to focus on the committee leadership, and not to rely on the comfort and familiarity of speaking with his Irish peers in their clerical collars. Despite having rehearsed their presentations and political responses, the lay leaders were nervous, and it showed at times. But they methodically delivered their presentations and engaged the commissioner in the discussion. At the end, the commissioner thanked all of them and promised that they would see action.

After they left the room, the commissioner greeted Connolly, whom he had gotten to know through a couple of friends. "So good to see you, Father," McGuire told him. Then, unsolicited, he told Connolly, "This is the most authentic meeting I have had with any group from the South Bronx. The people spoke for themselves. It was not the politicians, and it was not other people yelling and screaming. Congratulations."

Committee members were relieved and elated about the meeting. They had learned to speak directly to the most powerful official in the city impacting their safety and the safety of their South Bronx. As powerful as he was, he was made much more human to them in this face-to-face encounter. As they did in their local public meetings with precinct commanders, they overcame their fear of challenging the powerful.

New Leaders Emerge

As other South Bronx Unity Conferences were organized over the years, the People for Change leaders worked on other issues. The organization engaged in one campaign over the issue which had defined the history of the South Bronx: housing. An area-wide Housing Committee focused on obtaining a commitment to fund the rehabilitation of vacant city-owned apartment buildings throughout the South Bronx. The committee called for a halt to the continuing demolition of those buildings and developed a list of buildings which they targeted for priority funding.

In the course of this campaign, they reached another stage of growth: They joined forces with two citywide organizations: the Association of Neighborhood Housing and Development (ANHD), a housing policy and membership organization, led by Bonnie Brower; and the Union of City Tenants, a group organizing tenants in occupied city-owned buildings throughout poor neighborhoods, led by Jon Forster and Tom Gogan. A multiyear, citywide Housing Justice Campaign led by ANHD called for a multibillion dollar investment by the administration of Mayor Ed Koch and his housing commissioner, Paul Crotty.

But the Housing Committee of People for Change also took matters into its own hands when they wrote to Crotty asking for a meeting to discuss a South Bronx housing rehabilitation program. After follow-up calls went unanswered, the committee decided to take direct action. A thirty-member delegation representing the Social Action Committee from each parish decided to go down to the headquarters of the Department of Housing Preservation and Development at 100 Gold Street in Lower Manhattan. They told the receptionist that they were from the Housing Committee of People for Change and that they wanted to see the commissioner. When told he was not there and that there was no certain time for his return, committee members declared that they would wait until he arrived. The waiting room had a seating capacity for about six persons, so most of them stood. Soon visitors coming off the building elevator on the second floor were finding the reception area crowded and difficult to navigate.

As time passed, committee members acknowledged that they were not getting attention, despite their requests to the receptionist and the trouble they were causing for other visitors. Anticipating that this kind of "wait them out" situation might occur, the committee had decided that it might need to "supplement" their action with some show of faith—literally. The time had come, and they began to read from scripture and then recited the three prayers often said while praying the rosary—the "Our Father," the "Hail Mary," and the "Glory Be"—over a dozen times. They read from another passage of scripture, and again repeated the prayers a dozen times. After several rounds of this "pray-in," they began singing songs such as "We Shall Overcome" and "This Little Light of Mine."

The pray-in extended into the lunch hours, when dozens of employees exited and entered through the waiting area. Office gossip from these lunch hour entrances and exits appeared to circulate quickly, because in the early afternoon, the door to the office opened quickly, and an exasperated, sweating man identified himself: "I am the commissioner's chief of staff. The commissioner is not here." As the delegation defiantly continued their pray-in, he blurted out, "What do you people want?"

They told him. Within a week, Housing commissioner Crotty came with a delegation from his office up to the South Bronx. The delegates who had conducted the "pray-in" and others awaited him in front of a large, orange, chartered school bus. They greeted the commissioner, and the whole group boarded the bus, which took them to all the neighborhoods of the South Bronx represented by People for Change. At indicated stopping points, leaders showed the commissioner which vacant buildings they had identified as priorities for rehabilitation. At the end of the trip, the commissioner pledged to respond to their priorities list, and the buildings

Fr. John Flynn and Rev. Jim Fairbanks prepare the housing commissioner for a bus tour of South Bronx buildings in need of rehabilitation. (Photo by Chris Sheridan. Courtesy of *Catholic New York*.)

became part of the mayor's newly announced $2 billion citywide housing rehabilitation program.

What influenced the commissioner, in part, was the area-wide identity which People for Change had developed. As a politically savvy bureaucrat who had once campaigned for city council and was an appointee of a politically astute mayor, Crotty had estimated the numbers of the many voters and elected officials represented in the neighborhoods he toured. Elected officials at different government levels and from all areas of the South Bronx were aware of People for Change through their campaigns on local issues. Most committees had gone to the city, state, and federal elected officials for their neighborhood to seek their support letters for an issue after establishing community support through petition drives. In organized rallies and public meetings with commissioners and commanders, committee members called on their elected officials to appear and publicly state their support. At "Candidates' Nights," People for Change leaders pressed candidates for local office to support their issues in front of audiences of hundreds. For the committee members, these encounters were a chance to demonstrate their leadership—their understanding of the issues, their ability to speak to their experiences and the priorities of the people—in the face of political leaders. For Connolly, they were a show of laypersons leading the Church in the World, as had been called for in Vatican II.[3]

To support the lay leaders and build an area-wide identity, the organization developed some tools for communication. People for Change sponsored the production of a slideshow, created by two women artists, to tell the stories of People for Change members and campaigns, and used it to recruit member parishes and individual members. The organization also created a newspaper detailing the work of the committees and area-wide campaigns, which was distributed every three months to all the parishes and schools and local organizations. Maybe most importantly, a comic book, *People Power*, was created by staff theologian and popular education expert Dean Brackley, along with local resident and illustrator Joe Gonzalez. *People Power* communicated the principles of power taught by Marjorie Tuite and inspired people to organize in their building, block, or community. Committee members circulated *People Power*, which was published in English and Spanish, to the people in their parishes and communities.[4]

People for Change, at its core, was a direct-action organization led by trained and experienced laypersons. They became leaders for social change in their neighborhoods and in the South Bronx. A number of them also joined the board of directors, one selected by each committee to represent them. As Connolly got to know them in South Bronx Unity Conferences, local activities, and board meetings, he developed an appreciation for the new leaders. They were a much different social action community for him than the Bronx Clergy Coalition or the South Bronx Catholic Association had been. *In fact,* he realized, *they were much like the people at Seneca Chapel and Seneca Center, who built those entities with him years ago.*

This new group was an inspiration to him:

Carmen Guzman, Chickie Torres, and Rosa Valencia of Sacred Heart;
Margarita Garcia Villarini, Luis Rodriguez, and Tania Osorio of St. Athanasius;
Aida García Martinez and Pedro Garcia and Esperanza Oliveras of St. Anselm;
Rafael Lopez, Genoveva Santiago, and Ana Vélez of Our Lady of Victory;

Mildred Johnson, Kathy Affronti, and Hilda Sanchez of St. Francis of
Assisi;

Nereida and Guillermo Soler, Hugo Trivino, and Carmen Silva of St.
John Chrysostom;

Danilo Reyes and Steve Darrup of Our Savior;

Luz Catarineau, Luz Padron, and Maximino Rivera of St. Pius;

Sharon Joslyn and Mary Kay Louchardt of St. Luke;

Martin Rogers and Francine Rogers and Mary Meade of Immaculate
Conception;

Sandy Ramirez of Christ the King;

Maximino Soler and Jose Machin of St. Thomas Aquinas;

Jose Santos of St. Angela Merici.

These leaders combined efforts in different ways to involve their parishioners and their chapters with the larger organization. They were advancing
the agenda of church-based organizing envisioned by the mission team
presentations which Connolly had brought to the South Bronx, the seed of
People for Change.

Connecting Faith

Connolly's original vision for People for Change also included the development of lay leaders who understood the connection between faith and
social justice. That was why he eagerly accepted Dean Brackley from Chicago: to help incorporate the element of faith into the organizing agenda.
The planning and "problem-issue-action" campaigns and the pressure
tactics would give laypersons control over the policies of institutions. That
was a central understanding of the mission.

However, there was also Connolly's strong belief that faith itself was
an empowering agent. He had written about it in the mission statement
of the Catholic Association, and he thought often about faith's liberating
power. It would allow South Bronx people to break out of the conditions
of oppression, of subjugation and of poverty, and say, like Martin Luther
King, "Free at last, free at last, thank God Almighty we are free at last!"

Brackley, who worked as a parish organizer like all other staff, also
worked on special projects to help Social Action Committee members
relate their actions to scripture at local committee meetings or actions
like rallies or public meetings. In addition to the *People Power* comic
book, Brackley worked on a major project with Connolly: a South Bronx

Viacrucis. Again incorporating a culturally familiar activity used in the Church in Latin America, including in Puerto Rico, this time a street procession reenacting the Stations of the Cross, this project would involve all parishes in the South Bronx. But in a departure from the traditional Viacrucis, this one would strike the theme of social justice.

Promoted at South Bronx Catholic Association meetings and in the local Social Action Committee meetings, the Viacrucis would occur on the Sunday before Palm Sunday to avoid any schedule conflicts for local parishes. It was decided to hold the event on the Grand Concourse, the broad boulevard that was probably the most prominent street in the South Bronx. Beginning at Tremont Avenue, the procession would make fourteen stops down the Concourse, and end in front of the Bronx courthouse, a building with legal, political, and historical symbolism for the South Bronx. Letters and calls went out to all the parishes, and the planning of the event involved People for Change lay leaders, clergy, and women religious of the South Bronx, with the guidance of Brackley and the assistance of another active theologian, Sister Valorie Lordi of the community at St. John Chrysostom.

They also worked with a police captain from the Bronx Borough Command, who recommended them to a transportation company owned by a friend. At no cost, the friend provided the organizing team with a long flatbed truck which could hold several people. Each stop would involve a dramatization of the station's event—Jesus Falling Down for the First Time, or the Placing of the Crown of Thorns—and that dramatization would occur on the flatbed, or truck platform. The platform would also serve as the podium for the reading of the scripture, and of an original written reflection on the specific station and its relation to a social condition affecting South Bronx communities. Select parishioners were trained to perform the dramatization, in full costume, and musicians were recruited to perform songs at stops and in between.

On the day of the Viacrucis, some people assembled early at East Tremont Avenue and the Grand Concourse. When they began the procession, there were a few hundred, but the event quickly picked up others. Speakers used their reflection at each station to denounce the many injustices which were plaguing and creating the conditions of suffering in the South Bronx: poverty, deteriorating housing, and vacant buildings, poor treatment at the area hospitals, the unemployment afflicting many, and the scourge of crime and drugs which permeated the neighborhoods. The people proclaimed these injustices as the sufferings endured by the

PFC Viacrucis culminates at Bronx County courthouse, an important seat of political power. (Photo by Chris Sheridan. Courtesy of *Catholic New York*.)

people of the South Bronx at the hands of institutions in power. They also proclaimed the potential for liberation, much like Jesus' resurrection, in the form of a just and equal society in the country.

By the final stop, over one thousand people stood with the group as Connolly gave a final blessing. The joy and hope of that day was felt by all the participants. As observers looked on and even joined the procession, the Viacrucis was strengthening their love of community and their belief in social justice. The procession helped Connolly realize how unique a religious event it really was, and how unique an organization People for Change really was. No direct-action organization in the United States had yet staged a Viacrucis linking scripture and the conditions facing the poor. No church had done it to express the common conditions of the whole South Bronx. Connolly felt that this event helped over a thousand people connect the messages of scripture and the cries of the people for social justice. The suffering of South Bronx people was put on public display and publicly given meaning both for those who suffered, and those who may have caused the suffering. The event affirmed both Church power and people power in the World.[5]

PFC staff on retreat. (*Front row, left to right*) Katie Clyde, administrative assistant; Fr. Dean Brackley; and Tom Amato and Angel Garcia, organizers; (*back row*) Mili Bonilla; Nancy Brennan, intern; and Tom's wife, Kris, and son, Nate. (Photo by Mili Bonilla.)

Connolly believed that this *Church standing on the Grand Concourse was a Church with the Poor, and a Church of Justice for the Poor.* After he blessed the crowd, he realized, *the two liberations—the liberation expressed in the Gospel message and the liberation of creating a just society through social action—those were the things he was working for as a priest, every day. To enable those liberations—that was becoming his purpose as a priest.*

11

⠿

Another World, a Larger Mission

He answered, "Love the Lord your God with all your heart and with all your soul and with all your strength and with all your mind," and "Love your neighbor as yourself."

"You have answered correctly," Jesus replied. "Do this and you will live."

But he wanted to justify himself, so he asked Jesus, "And who is my neighbor?"

In reply Jesus said:

> "A man was going down from Jerusalem to Jericho, when he was attacked by robbers. They stripped him of his clothes, beat him and went away, leaving him half-dead. A priest happened to be going down the same road, and when he saw the man, he passed by on the other side.
>
> "So too, a Levite, when he came to the place and saw him, passed by on the other side.
>
> "But a Samaritan, as he traveled, came where the man was; and when he saw him, he took pity on him.
>
> He went to him and bandaged his wounds, pouring on oil and wine. Then he put the man on his own donkey, brought him to an inn and took care of him. The next day he took out two denarli and gave them to the innkeeper. 'Look after him' he said, 'and when I return, I will reimburse you for any extra expense you may have.'
>
> "Which of these three do you think was a neighbor to the man who fell into the hands of robbers?"

The expert in the law replied, "The one who had mercy on him."

Jesus told him, "Go and do likewise."
—Luke 10:27–37, Bilingual Bible, Good News Translation, United Bible Societies

Ministry Challenged

"I don't understand," a religious brother told Neil Connolly after one South Bronx Catholic Association meeting. "You're the vicar of the South Bronx, and you are taking these trips to Central America. Why don't you stay here in the South Bronx? Don't we have enough problems of our own?"

Connolly looked at him, surprised and disappointed. After all, Connolly thought, this man was a minister who had taken religious vows as a Catholic brother. Brother to all, Catholic to all. But every conversation with him was an adventure: Over the years he had been as capable of berating and attacking Connolly's positions as he was of supporting them.

So, Connolly fired right back. "You have to remember, we're Catholic. Catholic is a word that means 'universal.' We don't restrict ourselves to any one country, and we are not prisoners of any kind of culture or nationalism or anything like that. But we are in common union with our brothers and sisters suffering in these countries."

The sharp exchange left Connolly frustrated with this local minister of the Church and many of the others who had found their place in serving the poor of the South Bronx and in building their communities through organizations. But they were forgetting the teachings of Vatican II, he thought. They were losing the vision of *Gaudium et Spes*, which directed the Church to be "in the world" and to cultivate the Kingdom of God on earth. He thought he was losing his ability to keep those teachings uppermost in the minds of his peers, those who were responsible for the Church, like he was. *We were responsible for the whole Church*, Vatican II said. He had been preaching that message for years, and yet it had still not been accepted by everyone. He needed to preach it again, but in a different way to a different audience.

His frustration prompted Neil Connolly to write an opinion column in *Catholic New York*, which often had a guest column for any priest who wanted to share his thoughts on Christianity, the Catholic Church, or matters of the Church and the world. Before and during the same years he was learning to be a teacher of lay ministers and lay organizers in the world of the South Bronx, Connolly had also been enlightened by experiences undertaken outside that local world. These experiences had awakened him to a larger Church, and a larger world, and therefore, to a broader, more demanding vision of priesthood than he had known even in the demanding conditions of the South Bronx. Connolly's involvement in this greater priesthood had prompted that brother to challenge Connolly, and Connolly decided he needed to answer the challenge.

He would explain himself and his mission as a priest, reflecting on his journey to expand the Kingdom of God on earth. Over the last couple of years, the part of the Kingdom which he was cultivating had grown: from the People of God whom he knew and served in the South Bronx to the People of God in Latin America.

Learning about Latin America

Connolly began his column:

> The words of Jesus about lighting a fire and receiving a baptism are not soft words. They refer to the fact that people will have to make a decision about accepting Him or not.

Those words brought Connolly back to the 1960s, when he had had to make a decision. For all the work he did in his first ten years of "going Spanish," of immersing himself in the lives, the well-being, and the culture of the Puerto Rican people, he had not learned much about Latin America. Over the years, he saw priests coming to help with Spanish-speaking parishioners at Athanasius, mostly from Spain and occasionally from places like Ecuador. But he did not get any first-hand knowledge of Latin America, outside of Puerto Rico, until he was ten years a priest.

In August 1968, Connolly was invited by his friend Bob Banome from St. Joseph to take a trip to Ecuador and the Amazon. Even though they were going to explore the country and a part of the famous rainforest, they were also going to visit a fellow priest. "You know," said Banome, "I have a friend, don't know him very well, but I have met him. He is kind of an exciting guy. Educated in Paris, and he does interesting work down there in Ecuador. He could help us once we get down to Quito, to see a little bit of Quito."

Once down in Ecuador, Connolly and Banome met up with Father Juan Pozo, a Jesuit priest with La Compañia ("The Company"), a name sometimes used in referring to the Society of Jesus, but also the name of the principal church in Quito established by the Jesuit order. In that meeting, Pozo explained a new education program he was operating as part of a larger Latin American Church initiative. After Vatican II was concluded, the Consejo Episcopal Latinoamericana (CELAM, or the Latin American Bishops' Council)[1] opened up and operated pastoral schools of theology for priests in countries throughout Latin America.

These schools, Pozo explained, represented an opportunity for priests to receive a different kind of education than they obtained in traditional seminaries. Already-ordained priests were invited to return to school to learn about new fields such as anthropology, as well as new approaches to catechesis, the teaching of the Catholic faith and doctrine to children and adults. Guided and inspired by Vatican II teachings, the schools helped promote its fundamental concepts, such as the "people of God," and encouraged active development of lay leaders in the Church.

Pozo guided his two guests through Quito and surrounding towns, including Ambato, where an earthquake had leveled an entire town. Then he offered an unusual side trip: "Let me take you to one of the schools." In a little while, Banome and Connolly were in a classroom, listening to a lecture about anthropology. The lecture amazed Connolly with its depth and its ability to connect the social reality to faith and to the mission of the Church. He was also impressed with the presence of other priests eager to learn about social science issues and their relationship to the Church. Connolly thought, *This was a dynamic school, and,* he realized, *it came from a dynamic priest: Pozo.* He and Pozo each sensed a kindred spirit in the other. Connolly realized that Pozo knew, like he did, of Vatican II's great potential to change the Church.

Then his new friend surprised Connolly with an invitation. "I want you to come to this school," said Pozo.

Connolly, stunned, replied, "I can't come."

As a Jesuit, a member of a tight-knit global religious community, Pozo was well informed about the work of his peers and of the diocesan regulations under which they operated in different parts of the world. He understood some of the inner workings of the North American Church and the rules regarding sabbaticals. Despite knowing that, he was undeterred in his goal, confidently giving Connolly several reasons why his proposal would work:

"You qualify. You've been a priest for ten years. You know Spanish. And I want you to come." After Connolly refused again, Pozo persisted, looking for an opportunity to connect the new Latin American teaching approach and agenda to a North American priest who might bring the approach back to the United States and perhaps replicate it there. Then, Pozo suggested a compromise as Banome watched the back-and-forth curiously. "Come here for a year, or at least six months," he said.

Saying, "We've got too much work back in the United States," Connolly anxiously said, finalizing his answer, knowing he had passed up a special opportunity. After leaving Pozo and the school, Connolly was still feeling inspired. Banome was right about Pozo—he was a very exciting guy, undertaking something impressive—building a new Church through a new kind of teaching. *It's amazing,* Connolly thought. *This man is alive with Vatican II and he is teaching it to the people here in the jungle.* It reminded him of the lessons he had learned during his summer in Puerto Rico ten years earlier, when he found a living faith among the people in the *campo,* both in the hilltop chapel and in the *colmado.*

Wherever the faith was and the believers were, there also was the Church. There was also where he needed to be, as a priest. But that was also why he had to refuse this new chance to be in the campo: *because a new community of believers was taking shape in the Seneca Chapel and the Seneca Center, and the people were going to build that community with him. Connolly needed to be there, in the little corner of Hunts Point–Longwood, where the believers were, to build a church and face the problems of that world.*

The Latin American Church: Medellin

Ten years later, Connolly's opinion continued:

> The cross and the nails, the blood and the sweat, are much more likely.
> Jesus decides with a great deal of anguish that He will live faithfully the mission His Father has given Him, no matter what the cost.

Despite his decision in 1968 to return to the South Bronx, Connolly kept thinking about that offer and the teaching of new theological approaches to those priests. Always a student of theology, Connolly was fascinated by the concepts and teachings which came out of Vatican II. When he returned to New York from Ecuador, Connolly read about an extraordinary event that discussed new Church teachings and happened just three years after Vatican II.

In the same summer of 1968, while Connolly and Banome were exposed to the new Vatican II school, there was a second gathering, like Vatican II, taking place in Medellin, Colombia.[2] More than 130 bishops of Latin America, under the auspices of CELAM, came together for a three-week conference. Their goal was to address the social situation in Latin America and the role of the Catholic Church in it.

With an inaugural address by Pope Paul VI, the Medellin conference was the result of extensive preparation by bishops and clergy during a period of much study after Vatican II. In several countries, research and study centers were using the social sciences to examine the economic and political factors behind the conditions of widespread poverty. The thinkers of these centers attributed the conditions to Latin American dependency on the United States, and the dependency of the poor on the elites in Latin America. Through discussions around the themes of education, ministry and social action, development and integration of Latin America, and the mission of the Catholic university in Latin America, they generated several documents that would provide critical direction for the Latin American Church going forward. Three Medellin documents in particular defined the most important concerns: *Justice*, *Peace*, and *The Poverty of the Church*.

The document known as *Justice* called for the formation and support of Latin American peasant organizations and women's groups.[3] It also called for these organizations to unite around policies which were just, including land redistribution. Emphasizing the need for continuous social education as part of pastoral activity, the bishops urged all sectors of society to be trained. Also, *Justice* encouraged the formation of small faith-based communities to enable this education. Finally, it called for broader political participation, to allow those who were marginalized to be brought into Latin American political processes.

The second document, *Peace*,[4] made some key points. It recognized that the tensions within Latin America were rooted in political and economic inequalities. In each country on the continent, CELAM declared, inequalities existed between the rich minority and the vast majority who were poor. But these tensions and inequalities also prevailed between countries in Latin America. "Peace," as an answer to this situation, was a phenomenon described in three ways: as a work of justice to resolve those intranational and international tensions; as a permanent activity to be taken up by all of society; and as the fruit of love, of true support for the dignity of all humans. Finally, the bishops addressed the issue of violence, both physical and institutional, by recognizing it as a result of injustice and inequality and by calling on the Church to answer it with social action and education.

The final major Medellin document, *Poverty*,[5] was the bishops' effort to reflect on themselves and their Church. In it, the bishops acknowledged that the Church had been perceived by the poor in Latin America as rich and as deliberately ignoring their needs. It also declared that poverty was an evil, a social phenomenon created by humans and contrary to God's will. It recommended a "poverty of the spirit," an opening up to God for the needs of life. The bishops urged themselves and their clergy to adopt this poverty of the spirit, as Jesus Christ did, in order to assume the living conditions of the poor. Poverty of the spirit, they asserted, would lead all the ministers of the Latin American Church—bishops, priests, and religious—to denounce the conditions and causes of poverty throughout the continent, including the social, economic, and political powers governing life for the poor.

After the Medellin conference ended, the approved documents were distributed throughout the Church in Latin America and North America, as well as the rest of the global Catholic Church. As Connolly read these documents in Catholic news publications, he realized that the world had changed once again, as it had with Vatican II. He had never seen documents calling for such bold action by Catholic clergy.

Reflecting upon his meeting with Father Pozo and the documents of Medellin, Connolly wanted to know more and to get more involved. Over the course of the next decade following the Ecuador trip, Connolly read actively about these priests from Latin America, especially those involved with Medellin. He was intrigued by those who became involved in their countries' struggles for justice, like Camilo Torres, a Colombian priest whose story was followed in the *Catholic News* and *National Catholic Reporter*.[6] Torres was a brilliant university professor who wrote about his work with the communities of the Colombian poor and then about his work with *la guerilla*, the rebel army.

"We have to change these living conditions," Torres stated, citing his reasons for involvement with an armed group. He wrote that he was terribly torn between the economic and political injustices going on in Colombia, on the one hand, and the criticism he received for his involvement with the people from the bishops of his own Church, holding him back from taking action in defense of his people, on the other hand. Connolly was saddened when Torres wrote, "To be totally honest, in my conscience, I can no longer stay as a priest in the Church." Shortly after leaving the priesthood for full-time involvement with *la guerilla*, Torres was killed in battle.[7]

Connolly thought about the Medellin concepts of priesthood and Church, and the real-world choices of priests like Camilo Torres. *Priests were urged to face the ways of the world—the political and economic inequalities—with prophetic actions. He had not considered himself a prophet. Nor had he considered himself someone with a prophetic voice or role. But there was clearly a need for the poor to be served with dignity and for the Church to address their poverty with urgency. That was why he had campaigned for a new archbishop and a new archdiocese to give urgent attention to the needs of the poor.* But the full implications of these documents, the Church of Latin America, and the world of Latin America, for Connolly's priesthood in the South Bronx, would need time to be understood and appreciated.

A Visit to Central America

Connolly's opinion column continued:

> He also predicts that those who try to live as He did will pay a price. The catechists and leaders of Christian communities in Central America today know all about that.

In writing those lines, Connolly remembered a second trip. In 1980, he had been invited by his friend Dean Brackley, staff theologian at People for Change, to a lecture at Fordham University given by a Jesuit priest from Nicaragua, Alvaro Arguello. Arguello, a liaison between the new Sandinista government and the Catholic Church, gave a report on the status of the country and the relationship between society and Church under the changes brought about by the recent revolution. Afterward, Brackley introduced Connolly to his fellow Jesuit Arguello, and they began a long conversation about the Church and social change, and the South Bronx and Nicaragua.

Were they able to organize down there? Connolly asked.

Arguello replied, "Well, we haven't been able to do what you have been doing. We have a different construct in society, in terms of government relationships." Then he added, "I'd love it if you came to Nicaragua. Why don't you come this summer? This way, we can talk more, and we can learn from you."

Connolly had to reply cautiously: "Okay, maybe we can come. Let's see." But he realized, *This is my opportunity to see for myself what was going on with Latin America and with the Church down there.* He recruited his friends John Flynn, who had spent a few years in Venezuela, and Ed Byrne, from the Lower East Side parish of St. Mary's, who had also done missionary work in Venezuela. They both had experience traveling and living as priests in Latin America, and that would be reassuring to Connolly, who had only been to Puerto Rico in 1958, to Ecuador and the Amazon in 1968, and to Mexico for vacation a couple of years back. But this trip, he knew, would be different.

In July 1979, Sandinista movement rebels had overtaken the capital of Nicaragua and thrown out the military government of Anastasio Somoza

Debayle.[8] A few religious priests who had been supportive of the rebellion against the decades-long dictatorship were given leadership positions in the new government. Father Ernesto Cardenal[9] became the Culture Minister for the country. Also, Father Miguel D'Escoto Brockman, a Maryknoll priest and supporter of the Sandinistas, was selected to be Foreign Minister for Nicaragua.[10] The addition of these two to the new cabinet showed how important a role religious communities and a significant part of the Catholic Church had played in the change in government.

Over the last few years, Connolly had read about the many local and U.S. religious communities working with the poor to build up their communities, whether in rural or urban areas of Nicaragua. Over four decades, Capuchin Fathers lived in rural Zelaya with the poor and worked with them to build 265 basic Christian communities, 30 agricultural extension clubs, communal dining halls, chapels, and 186 rural schools.[11] Meanwhile, in the capital of Managua, Maryknoll sisters organized with urban slum residents, teaching them their rights, which led to campaigns demanding better transportation services and lower water rates.[12]

As with other community-led efforts to build peasant organizations, schools and radio stations for adult education, and cooperatives, the Somoza government, which had ruled Nicaragua for decades in every sector of society, denounced those efforts. But Somoza went further, as his National Guard terrorized the residential and religious communities with beatings and killings and the destruction of the projects. It would not be until the Sandinista takeover that such communities would have a chance to be created again, after thousands of Nicaraguan people paid the price for organization against a brutal government. Cardenal pointed out, in a public awareness campaign to build U.S. support for the cause of the Sandinistas: "My commitment is to the poor. Because of this, I am struggling with people. I must be in this struggle, even at the risk of my life."[13]

Down in Nicaragua, Connolly and his two friends went to visit the Universidad Centro Americana (UCA), the Jesuit university where middle class families sent their sons and daughters to study. Dean Brackley knew some of the Jesuits down there and was able to secure accommodations for the three visitor priests in a neighborhood called Opus Trece, where Sandinista supporters lived. On another day, they were scheduled to meet with Larry Pezzullo, U.S. ambassador to Nicaragua and a family member of Flynn.[14] During the day, they walked around their neighborhood and saw a large street festival taking place, with many people painted in black. Revelers were celebrating the feast of Santo Domingo, a black patron saint, and so they were made up to look like him.[15]

Standing in the festive crowd, the priests heard "*Vamos atacar a los americanos!*" (Let's attack the Americans!) Connolly and his friends froze, as they were surrounded by a group with buckets of paint, who then smeared them all over, to make the three white priests look as black as they did. A little while later, with the celebration still in play, they left, knowing they had a formal event in a short while with Pezzullo at the embassy. They cleaned themselves off at a local gas station, where they took off most of the paint. Facing a long trip back to their place and running out of time, they decided instead to stop at the UCA to finish cleaning up. They were welcomed by a priest at the UCA residence and asked for his help. After showering, they asked for some clean dress clothes for the event.

The priest said, "Yes, we might have some *guayaberas*," the Latin American buttoned shirts traditionally worn like a jacket at formal events. Unfortunately, there were only two, and Byrne and Flynn got theirs first. Connolly was left with nothing but a tee-shirt. He complained, "I can't go out like this to a diplomatic reception. I still have the smell of gasoline!" But he had no time to go back home and no choice but to go "as is." They finally met with Pezzullo and his wife at the reception, and after Flynn explained why they were dressed as they were, they relaxed. Connolly and the others spoke with a representative from the Cuban mission and shared authentic Cuban cigars with him. They also met with a representative from the presidential campaign of Ronald Reagan, a candidate whose conservative ideology, they knew, threatened serious trouble for many, including the people of Nicaragua. But they had too little time to have a genuine conversation with Pezzullo, to learn about the Nicaraguan political reality, so they came back the following night for a meal and conversation.

At the end of the meal, it was very late, and they needed to go back in the ambassador's limousine, since they lacked a car, and there was no mass transit available at that time. The priests knew it was not a good thing to be arriving late at night in a Sandinista *barrio* in an American luxury car. Neighbors might see three white men leaving a limousine in an expensive car and make unfounded assumptions. But they had no choice, and they took the ride back home. The following night, they went out and returned home on the bus. After they got off and began walking back to their house, Byrne whispered, "Don't look back, but there's a car right behind us. It's a Volkswagen, with the lights turned off."

Afraid, they heeded Byrne's warning and hurried a little, hoping to get home without trouble. Just as they arrived at the house, four soldiers stepped out of the Volkswagen with submachine guns and put the priests against the wall. "¡*Quiero ver los pasaportes!*" yelled the leader. But not knowing the new national laws required everyone to carry a passport, they had all left them at home. While Connolly was trying to come up with an explanation, Byrne turned to them: "What do you mean passports? We're not doing anything wrong! We were just walking!"

Connolly barked at Byrne, "Shut up, please! They have us against the wall!"

Meanwhile, Flynn said to the soldiers, "¡*Mira, temenos los pasaportes aquí, en esta casa!*" ("Look, we have our passports here, in this house!")

But the soldiers remained quiet, their guns raised. Connolly pleaded with them to ring the bell: "*Por favor, toque el timbre.*"

The soldiers finally complied, and an older priest, Padre Julio, answered. Interestingly, Padre Julio, their host at the residence, was not a Sandinista supporter, but the visitors knew he had taught many of the Sandinista soldiers in earlier school days, and he was someone they regularly visited for counseling, even during the war. So they thought their crisis would be resolved when the soldiers saw Padre Julio. But when their host opened the door, he saw the guns and ran to the back. Eventually, however, the soldiers relaxed, and the priests were allowed to go in and retrieve their passports.

After seeing them, the suspicious leader asked, "¿*Y porque no firmaron los pasaportes?*" ("And why didn't you sign the passports?")

"*No sabiamos que habia que firmarlos,*" ("We didn't know we had to sign them,") Connolly answered.

Still suspicious, the leader asked, "¿*Y porque han viajado tanto por Latinoamerica? Y porque ustedes hablan español?*" ("And why have you traveled so much through Latin America? And why do you all speak Spanish?") They explained their way out of both issues, and they were let go, after a scary few minutes that seemed like hours to the priests. Connolly thought, *The soldiers must have suspected them of being CIA, especially when they returned in that limousine in those unusual, un-clerical street clothes.*

The day after the assault, Connolly and his friends went to meet with Father Miguel D'Escoto Brockman, Byrne's good friend from Maryknoll mission activities together. Now the Foreign Minister of Nicaragua, D'Escoto got an earful from his friend Byrne about the government soldiers' actions.

"Get these Sandinista soldiers off our backs!" said Byrne, and he explained what happened.

D'Escoto apologized, and then he discussed the background to the revolutionary takeover. He told them the story of being "on the run" with a comrade named Borge. D'Escoto had been living in exile in the United States when he decided to return and support the Sandinistas. He joined up with Borge, and they had to run away once Somoza learned D'Escoto had secretly returned to the country. Both were traveling from one safe house to another and staying overnight, before moving on to the next one. Borge, a tough, smart man, was essentially his bodyguard, but he also prayed and reflected every night with D'Escoto before going to sleep.

They relied on the families sheltering them, and when soldiers came near, on several occasions, the host families would dance, talk, and otherwise distract soldiers in the front of the house. In the meantime, D'Escoto and Borge escaped through the back to the next safe house. Local families were organized in their communities and made those escapes possible, but they also faced the dangers of confrontation with soldiers. D'Escoto explained how he counted on their sacrifices as Connolly, Flynn, and Byrne listened with amazement to these stories of life and death, simple heroism, and community among true believers.

They then went to meet with three others before heading back to the United States. Lorraine Hooper, an American layperson who was active with solidarity efforts to build support in the United States, explained how important the American efforts were to the Sandinista cause. Bishop Miguel Obando y Bravo, the leader of the Archdiocese of Managua and Nicaragua's best-known representative of the Institutional Church, explained to Connolly how he had changed his views from Sandinista supporter during the rebellion to government critic after they took over. Finally, Alvaro Arguello, the Jesuit who had first invited Connolly to the country, explained the situation was still delicate, with a government that was still taking shape and that needed time to enact programs to benefit society. Arguello had the serious responsibility of organizing the *Instituto Historico* of Nicaragua, a project to ensure that the memories of victims of the Somoza regime would be preserved and given a meaningful place in the new Nicaragua.[16]

Arguello, however, also had a humorous side. The day after their long evening of conversation, which was peppered with snacks and Nicaraguan rum, Arguello saw them and smiled—"*Ustedes trataron de picarme anoche, pero yo no fui picado.*" ("You guys tried to get me drunk last night, but I was not drunk.") Kidding aside, Arguello told them that he was, in fact, grateful that Connolly accepted his invitation in the Bronx and that they had visited. He stressed the importance of sharing the stories of their experiences with the Church back in the United States, in order to get support so that the right kinds of developments could take hold and succeed at this early stage in the new Nicaraguan society.

Connolly had many questions after the trip, questions about the world he had just visited. *What kinds of changes had been achieved in the lives of the people, beyond no longer fearing the power of Somoza and his regime? Those Santo Domingo Fiesta revelers—were they finding better opportunities for their families, or for themselves? What of the soldiers who assaulted them? Were they still in a state of emergency or conflict? What were they expecting would happen to the country they had just taken control of? All the students they met near the UCA—why were they not more hopeful? They were certainly able to pursue their studies in peace, and the Jesuits seemed to be free to teach them.*

The one thing that was clear, including from D'Escoto and Arguello, was that there was a very uncertain future for everyone in Nicaragua, but there was a future.

And the Church—what of the Church there?

Obando y Bravo and a group of Jesuits were suspicious and unsupportive of the Sandinistas, although maybe it was because they had hoped for more. On the other hand, Arguello and D'Escoto, who were aligned with the Sandinistas before and after the takeover, were taking an active role in governing the new country.

While Gigante had run for Congress and dozens more clergy and religious were holding office, Connolly had not thought it was possible for clergy to have such a direct governing role. He also wasn't sure what he thought about clergy being involved with armed guerillas, like D'Escoto or Cardenal or Camilo Torres, and supporting the use of violence. Connolly certainly had not wanted his parishioner to use those baseball bats at Mass to defend Athanasius against the henchmen of political kingpin Vélez. But he also did not approve of Vélez's tactics or the violence of the drug dealers and criminals.

These circumstances in Nicaragua were nothing like he had seen though: An entire country's government had changed. What does a priest do then? He was certainly impressed by D'Escoto and Arguello and their belief that society could change for the better, and that the Church as a people might be able to ignite that change.

A New Approach to Theology

This involvement of the priests in the Nicaraguan revolution had taken root in Medellin, Connolly knew. For years, as he followed more closely the goings-on in Latin America, Connolly marveled at the Church's potential. The Latin American Catholic Church was in a unique position to influence the lives of its people, greater than the North American Church could expect. More than 90 percent of the continent's 320 million people considered themselves Catholic.[17] About the same percentage was considered poor, as the continent also exhibited a great disparity between the "haves" and the "have-nots." For centuries, the Church had lived with, and often benefited from, this inequality and did little to challenge the existing power structures.

However, after the Second World War, the Church was forced to begin reconsidering its position, as the United States and military governments acted decisively to take greater control of the rich natural resources on the continent. Local wealthy elites controlled much of the land, and they also acted in support of the centralized military power in each country and its use of violence against the poor. With greater levels of brutality made possible by more efficiently lethal technology, new military governments generated and sustained physical terror not seen before by anyone, including detentions, torture, rapes, and killings on a grand scale.

The continent's biggest country, Brazil, became the focus of Catholic attention in the United States as well as Latin America. The 1964 military overthrow of the government occurred at the same time that new socially critical bishops were emerging in Brazil and presenting their claims for change in Vatican II.[18] Many of these bishops were facing persecution even while challenging the military repression: Dom Hélder Câmara, Bishop Pedro Casaldaliga, Cardinal Aloisio Lorscheider, Cardinal Paulo Arns, and others.[19] Vatican II gave the Brazilian bishops, and those of other Latin American countries facing military repression, a forum to challenge the status quo and to appeal for global support from other Church leaders.

Unfortunately, Camara was more often chastised than supported by the Vatican as the military exercised greater power over all institutions. To the dismay of the central Church, Camara and his peers in the Latin American Church had adopted a new approach to theology, first postulated and discussed in 1968 at Medellin.

Connolly first learned about this new theology with the English-language publication in 1971 of *A Theology of Liberation*, written by the Peruvian priest-theologian, Father Gustavo Gutiérrez.[20] A graduate of Louvain University in Belgium, known for its progressive teachings, Gutiérrez developed *A Theology of Liberation* from presentations made in Medellin. According to Gutiérrez, there were three ways of looking at liberation from a theological perspective.[21] First, "liberation" could be seen, on a basic level, as the goal of oppressed and poor classes, groups, and nations to free themselves of dependency from others. Second, "liberation" was the continuing history of humankind working to achieve a better society, of realizing humankind's potential. Finally, "liberation" was to be seen as a gift, presented by Christ the Savior, to bring Christians away from sin and toward salvation, to humanity's final Communion with God.

Gutiérrez and others advocating for this new kind of theology advanced the education of the poor, most of whom were illiterate, as an essential step to liberation. Gutiérrez favored *concientización* as both the method and goal of popular education.[22] This concept was described in another book that was popular in Latin America: *Pedagogy of the Oppressed* by Paolo Freire.[23] Freire, a Brazilian educator, demonstrated that by allowing the poor and oppressed to learn about their immediate world around them, and the conditions in which they were living, they could develop literacy most effectively. In the process of becoming literate, Freire argued, they could also become liberated.

The oppressed, according to Freire, would first learn to move from a "naive awareness" of life based on the past and on their cultural myths to "critical awareness" to raising questions about their interests. Then they would learn to confront and analyze problems and to develop solutions to their conditions. *Concientización* involved a rejection of the consciousness instilled in them through decades, or even centuries, of domination by the upper classes, educated classes, and government institutions. Those persons made newly educated and aware, as a result of *concientización*, would take steps to transform the current world and build a better one.

With *concientización* as the fundamental tool for educating and liberating the poor of Latin America, Gutiérrez declared, the Church would take action. He urged the Church, which had been a dominant institution in Latin America for centuries, to play a new role in Latin American countries through several actions[24]:

> Prophetically denouncing unjust social structures by making every effort to criticize the institutions, corporations, and governments imposing oppressive conditions upon the poor
>
> Raising awareness of evangelization by educating the faithful to follow the liberation messages of the Old and New Testaments
>
> Addressing poverty by implementing a simple lifestyle, with a commitment to the poor, free from the centuries-long trappings of privilege and prestige enjoyed by the Church and its ministers
>
> Recognizing the inadequacy of structures of the Church, which were hierarchical in nature and did not allow for laypersons to have a voice
>
> Changing the lifestyle of the clergy by immersing them in the life of the poor and involving more laypersons in the direction of the Church.

Connolly learned about Gutiérrez's ideas in the 1970s and was intrigued, but he was too focused on the needs of the South Bronx at the time to give them his full attention. However, he learned about other developments in this theology of the new Latin American Church throughout the 1970s. In addition to Gutiérrez, Connolly read about other priests exploring, writing, and speaking about liberation theology: Juan Luis Segundo, a Jesuit from Uruguay; Leonardo Boff, a Franciscan from Brazil, who wrote *Ecclesiogenesis*, which Connolly read and enjoyed; and Jon Sobrino, a Catalan Spanish Jesuit based in El Salvador.[25]

There were also liberation theologians in the United States. Among them was Sergio Torres, who escaped imminent execution during Pinochet's regime with the help of his bishop and Maryknoll priests after working on social justice initiatives in Chile.[26] Torres, who was now a parish priest in New York's Washington Heights neighborhood, helped organize a major conference in Detroit, "Theology in the Americas," one of several efforts to discuss liberation theology and its application to the U.S. Catholic Church.[27]

Connolly learned that the conference surfaced differences in the approaches to liberation theology between the North and Latin Americans. All of the Latin American theologians were also active in parishes and communities in their home countries. Their experiences with the education and organization of the poor defined and redefined their theological views. Most of the North American theologians were teachers, but in the world of higher education—university professors at respected Catholic universities in the United States. Many priests and religious who understood the roots of liberation theology in Latin America thought that these theologians, with little involvement in the lives or neighborhoods of poor parishioners, had less life experience to shape their views.

When Connolly read about these discussions of liberation theology in the United States and their strong interest in bringing dignity and well-being to the poor, he became more and more interested. The conferences and articles made him think more about the work that he and the Catholic Association members were carrying out in the South Bronx. Connolly thought about the ministers in the Latin American Church motivated by this new theology and the documents of Medellín. These priests, religious, and laypersons seemed to be doing work *with* the poor, much like the ministers in the South Bronx parishes and parish organizations.

Connolly also thought about the basic Christian communities and the Seneca Chapel community he had worked to create in collaboration with the laypersons, much like those in Latin American countries. In Brazil alone, for example, the church ministers had developed nearly eighty thousand such basic Christian communities.[28] When he looked at all this work being done in the South Bronx Catholic Church, in the spirit of Vatican II, and compared it to Gutiérrez's calls for the Church to live with the poor, he realized, *Oh, that's liberation theology. We have been practicing this here.*

At the same time, he realized, there were harsh consequences for the actions of the followers of Medellin and liberation theology in Latin America. The elites, and often the military, persecuted all the ministers—priests, religious, and laypersons—who promoted and practiced *concientización* and discussed new ways of looking at society. As in Brazil, where even bishops were targets of government action and violence, other countries witnessed this kind of persecution of their own communities exploring *concientización* and promoting new Church association with the poor. Even the once-conservative bishops in Chile[29] and Colombia[30] were targeted as military governments expanded their repressive reach to many sectors of the Church.

In the United States, the conflicts with the government were not violent, but the experiences of the South Bronx Catholic Association over the future plans for the South Bronx showed that government was also very forceful in its actions to eliminate the opposition. Connolly found himself at odds with the politicians who stood by while the neighborhoods of the South Bronx were "cleared" by arson fire. Prophetic calls for investigations into the fires, and then for a community-based South Bronx plan, were dismissed by government officials and institutions in power. Connolly had wondered what that new Church was like in Latin America. He wondered about the conflicts that that Church was facing and how the ministers in the new Church lived with those conflicts. He wondered how this new theology was being lived down there.

A Different Visit to Central America

Connolly's opinion continued:

Maximilian Kolbe knew about it and so did King and Romero.

As he wrote this line, Connolly thought about those who gave up life and death for a ministry in pursuit of justice, and those who faced those risks to their life each day. He remembered how, when he had another opportunity to visit another part of Central America, he had pursued it. This time the invitation came from a friend who was a U.S. missionary.

Early in the 1960s, there were twelve thousand missionaries from the United States working in Latin America, many of them from orders of women and men religious.[31] Over the decade, a growing number of them lost faith in the promises of development for Latin America embodied in the Alliance for Progress program begun under John F. Kennedy, the first Catholic president. They realized that few benefits of these programs would actually reach the poor, whom they were serving, and so they refocused on living with the poor and carrying out the principles of Vatican II. They developed collaborative efforts with local religious and clergy who were truly committed to serving, educating, and engaging the poor by creating grassroots projects. Particularly after dictatorships spread throughout Latin America, those projects became targets of extreme repression, and the people who were associated with them became victims of government persecution.

In Guatemala, there was a connection between the U.S. missionaries and the South Bronx. In 1980, Connie Kelly, a Sister of Charity who served in St. Francis of Assisi parish with Father John Flynn, was working in a community in San Cristobal Cucho, in the Diocese of San Marcos, Guatemala. Kelly was a veteran missionary; she had already worked in Chile before the Pinochet military regime was established in 1973, and she and other missionaries were forced to flee in 1975.

Guatemala was a country which had lived under military rule for decades after its elected president, Jacobo Arbenz Guzman, was overthrown in 1954 with covert American support.[32] A civil war intensified in the early 1980s.[33] Kelly found that most of Guatemala's people lived in poverty, and they also suffered under violent government repression during that civil war. Native and U.S. religious, clergy, and laypersons were subjected to persecution, from the kidnapping of conservative bishop Casariego to the killings of hundreds of lay catechists.[34]

Connolly and Flynn went to Guatemala, both to visit with Kelly and to get an understanding of the country's situation. Kelly arranged for their first stop to be a restaurant, in a place not far from the airport. This first stop, however, was startling and surreal: a full-grown lion was sitting in a cage in the open space next to the restaurant entrance. After overcoming their shock, they went through the entrance to an outdoor garden, where Kelly introduced Connolly and Flynn to two men. Both, it turned out, were supporters of the opposition, and they discussed the difficult situation they were in. One was a priest, and the other was a layperson, but they both had something else in common, which Connolly noticed after looking at them quizzically during their conversation: They wore masks, so as not to be identified.

As the conversation progressed, the priest turned to Connolly and gave him an envelope with some papers in it. Speaking in hushed tones, he said to Connolly, "In your country, these papers would be like comic books.

They are harmless. But in our country you'd be put in prison for having or using these. Would you please take these papers out of the country for us?" he asked.

Connolly looked at the priest and at Kelly and decided the documents were harmless to carry, so he agreed to the request and put them in his suitcase. They proceeded to a retreat house, which also served as a postulate for young Guatemalan women who were candidates for sisterhood. The house was situated on a mountaintop. It was a popular destination for religious retreats because of the tranquility of the natural surroundings and the extraordinary view. Guatemala's bishops had just met there, including Mario Enrique Ríos Montt, brother of the notorious and widely feared president of Guatemala, General Efraín Ríos Montt.

After a nice conversation and visit with the religious candidates, Connolly and Flynn went with Kelly to go back to their own community in Cucho. They borrowed a jeep from one of the nuns who ran the house. Before they left, she gave Connolly some advice. "You should know that this road you will be on is full of bandits who are from the opposition, and of *bandidos soldados* (bandit soldiers) from the government army. Either group will rob you."

"Don't tell your driver," she continued, "because he'll be so nervous that it won't be good." Flynn, who liked to drive stick shift cars, had enthusiastically volunteered to drive the group and was already sitting in the jeep, ahead of the other two and another nun.

Once they were on the road, one of the nuns suddenly said, "You see what's happening?" Traffic was building up, and so the pace slowed down. The cause was a boy who came onto the road on a cart pulled by oxen, which slowed every other vehicle.

Then the other nun said, "Watch this. This is not happening accidentally. Something is going to happen."

As they went around a mountain curve, they saw snipers perched around the mountain areas, their machine guns pointed at the road. The delegation in the jeep looked at the snipers, who looked back at them, but nothing happened, and so they moved forward. But Flynn, driving while looking at the snipers, did not know what to do, and he suddenly went into reverse.

The passengers were startled, and the nuns told him, "Don't do that! Get the clutch right and go forward!" A panicked Flynn followed their orders and changed direction. Eventually, they left the road without incident and arrived a while later at Kelly's home.

The following day, after a good night's sleep, Connolly came down for breakfast. At the kitchen table, he read the cover pages of the local newspapers. A headline startled him: *"El sobrino del coronel asesinado"* ("The Colonel's Nephew Assassinated"). This incident, he discovered, took place on the road they were traveling, a short while after the time they were there. Connolly realized, *The traffic was slowed down by that cart, and it was slowed so as to give the snipers the best opportunity for a clean shot.* He remembered exchanging looks with the snipers, and he was glad they were seen clearly and not mistaken for anyone else. *At the same time*, he realized, *he and Flynn and Kelly and the other nun were this close to death.* The fear he experienced there was unlike anything he experienced in Nicaragua and even in the South Bronx.

They had a more peaceful time on another day when they went to meet with Bishop Alvaro Ramazzini. At forty-three, Ramazzini was a young bishop, and Connolly learned that he was another leading proponent of liberation theology and the Medellin approach in Latin America. Kelly introduced Connolly and Flynn, and they all went out for a lunch at a local seafood restaurant overlooking the Pacific Ocean. They enjoyed a great meal and conversation and learned about the work being done by the diocese for the poor, and the activities taking place in the South Bronx and the North American Catholic Church. When the bishop learned they were going swimming, he asked if he could join them. "Sure," they said. For all of his official importance, Ramazzini was a simple man who was able to enjoy himself with his visitors at the beach. Connolly appreciated this unique moment of peace, nature, and companionship with friends, especially in comparison to some of the frightening moments he had experienced.

After returning to the United States, Connolly was relieved and glad he had been able to see the country and his friend Connie. For Connolly, this was so much of a different experience for him than the visit to Nicaragua. *Everyone was aware that there was a constant threat of warfare breaking out. Their lives were shaped by it—when and where to travel, who to speak with, and about what topics. The priest who had aligned himself with the opposition caught Connolly's attention. Connolly delivered the package to its destination without knowing the contents. What had he done that drove him to this secret meeting and the transaction with Connolly? The Church was in a constant state of threat because it was a place of refuge for the people. So was everyone associated with the Church, including American missionaries like Connie, with access to the greater society, the media, and the American government supporting the Guatemalan government.*

Even though he knew she was smart enough to get around safely, Connolly worried for Connie and the other nuns. *They were brave*, he thought,

Connolly (*left*) with Kathy Osberger (*foreground, right*) and colleagues at CCUM Conference in 1977. Osberger and Connolly joined with others to organize the South Bronx Committee in Solidarity with Central America.

to practice their faith and build their communities in such a constant state of danger. Connolly would pray for her, and he would do something to support her and the people.

Spirituality and Struggle in the South Bronx

Back at home, Connolly and a few others in the South Bronx Catholic Association had decided to form a reflection community of their own after hearing about the importance of reflection to the ministers in Central America and the proponents of liberation theology and Medellin principles.

In People for Change, and in the Christian Family Movement, reflection was supposed to accompany action so that people could be more certain they were taking the right course of action. They were also seeking inspiration and guidance, from scriptures and from the Catholic thinkers and writers, about why they were involved in struggles for a better world. *It was not enough just to act without reflection and prayer, just as it was not enough to reflect and pray without action to change the world and institutional powers around them.*

With this reflection group, Connolly was returning to the part of his priesthood that he was struggling with, as a very active priest of the world: his spirituality. At Athanasius, a few years into his ministry, Connolly had come to realize that he was so busy that he often neglected his own prayer life. At the seminary, of course, he had been given several scheduled times in the day to pray in quiet. But left on his own, operating in his own parish, with the constant demands of the world, he had to force himself to stop and make time for prayer. It was very hard to return to the life of quiet prayer-reflection while also being an activist priest and creating other religious activities to engage parishioners, like the apartment Masses and Christian Base Community reflection groups.

But he needed to have personal, private prayer and reflection. For him, this was a serious need—to be sure that he was listening to and following God. After all, he had been raised that way. Growing up, Connolly had seen his father kneel at the bed and pray time and again to get support and help for his struggles, raising the family, caring for his sick wife, and working.

Then Connolly had a breakthrough one day, away from the parish. He was up in Dunwoodie on one of his "Tuesday group" retreats—he took off Tuesdays and joined with his priest friends for socializing, sports, and reflection. As he was thinking about his campaigns, his community-building, and the counseling and hospital visits, Connolly came to understand that prayer came into all the work that he did.

He thought, *If I am serving the mission of the Lord, it is because God is directing me. Knowing that the source of my energy, my creativity, and my life is God, and that I am not number one, that would mean that I have been guided, and I am being guided, not just in my personal life, but in my life with the people, by God. My mission is my prayer.*

In returning to that spiritual foundation, Connolly came to another understanding about prayer: *I am an individual building my own personal relationship with God, but I am also part of a community, so my prayer life also has to be part of the people's prayer life.* Connolly thought, *Priests don't often share their reflections with other people, whether it is with laypersons, religious, or even other priests. But God wants us, as priests, to be in communication with Him, through our communication with people. The priests and pastoral team should be able to pray together in the rectory, and they should be able to use their prayer time to share their faith. They should also use every opportunity for scriptural reading and then small group discussion, as well as prayer, with the people.*

So, after working through this struggle over prayer, Connolly also formed a community of reflection among his close friends and fellow ministers. They decided to come together weekly, for what one of the group members called "Beer and Bible Fridays." This group did not just share his interest in theology; they shared his vision for the Church in the South Bronx and for the Church in the wider world. They also shared his vision for the cultivation of the Kingdom of God, justice, and dignity on earth.

The group included Kathy Osberger, a layperson who graduated from Notre Dame University and spent a summer in San Miguelito parish in Panama with Father Leo Mahon, then a year and a half in Chile. After coming to join the St. Athanasius staff in 1977, Osberger ran the Seneca Center and later became the Director of Religious Education at St. Athanasius. She lived in the neighborhood and shared an apartment with Mili Bonilla in the old convent on Bruckner Boulevard, which had once housed the Charity Sisters and then the Odyssey House drug program. A proponent of South Bronx Catholic unity, Osberger was active in the South Bronx Catholic Association. Engaged in social justice issues, she helped advance the Bronx Clergy Coalition agenda for a community-controlled housing future for the South Bronx. She was also a trainer, cofounder, and promoter of the project that would become South Bronx People for Change, and she was an active supporter of the St. Athanasius Social Action Committee.

Connolly's community also included Sister Louise Mileski. A member of the Sparkill Dominican religious order, Mileski was Director of Religious Education at St. John Chrysostom, which had collaborated with Athanasius on many efforts over the years. A Long Island native, Milekpi had worked in St. Louis, Missouri, for a number of years before coming to the South Bronx in the 1960s. Active with the South Bronx Catholic Association, Mileksi was also a trainer, cofounder, and promoter of the South Bronx People for Change project. She became a supporter and member of the Social Action Committee at St. John Chrysostom and was a longtime board member and leader of People for Change.

Connolly also valued his longtime friendship and collaboration with Father John Flynn, the pastor at St. Francis of Assisi parish. After working at St. Raymond's parish in the Parkchester neighborhood in the East Bronx, Flynn went to Venezuela for a few years, working with the poor in a "sister parish." Upon his return to the United States, Flynn settled in the South Bronx, becoming the pastor at St. Francis. His community building efforts led to the creation of a community center, a day care center, the Morris Heights Neighborhood Improvement Association, and the Bronx Heights

Neighborhood Association, helping to organize tenants. As Housing Committee Chair of the Bronx Clergy Coalition, he teamed up with Connolly to promote the community-controlled housing plan for the South Bronx. He was also a trainer, cofounder and board member of South Bronx People for Change. His strong interest in lay leadership even led him to form a pastoral team at St. Francis. As a prolific writer, Flynn contributed several articles to *Catholic New York* and the *New York Daily News*, sharing his belief in the South Bronx, in social justice, and in the Latin American Church of the People.

Finally, Connolly's community also included People for Change's staff theologian, Dean Brackley, who had invited him to meet Fr. Arguello for the talk that led to his trip to Nicaragua; Lourdes Costa, a Salvadoran woman who received immigration assistance from Brackley as she sought refuge in the United States; Father Gerry Ryan, from St. Luke's Parish; and Father Peter Gavigan, from Our Lady of Victory Parish.

Central American Solidarity

Connolly's opinion article continued as he considered the challenge of taking on society's ways:

> It is not easy to be honest in a world of inflated charge accounts, to practice charity of speech when it's considered funny to cut down people of other races and nationalities with cute jokes and degrading euphemisms, to lead on issues of justice and peace when many believe that economics and government policy are outside the orbit of morality and to do so is to meddle in politics.

Through news articles in the mainstream media and the Catholic media, and through associates of Osberger and others who had been to Latin America, Central America remained a regular part of the conversations of the reflection community and others in the South Bronx Catholic Association. Another Central American country, El Salvador, would come to Connolly's attention, and events involving the Church in the world of El Salvador eventually compelled him to act.

In the 1970s, El Salvador was the most densely populated nation in Central America, a poor, largely rural people dependent on a coffee industry controlled by a few elites and the military.[35] With decades of conflicts dating back to the 1930s, it entered into a full-scale civil war in 1980 between the government and the Farabundo Marti National Liberation

Front (FMLN).[36] As in Nicaragua and Guatemala, tens of thousands would be killed, and the Church and other suspected supporters of the FMLN were major targets of government persecution.

Oscar Arnulfo Romero, appointed archbishop in El Salvador's largest city, San Salvador, in February 1977, was a leading Church figure whose original, moderately conservative views were impacted by the conflict.[37] He became alarmed at the killings of several priests, including his good friend, Jesuit Father Rutilio Grande, a month after Romero became archbishop.[38] As more priests, religious, and laypersons were killed, Romero called out for peace and an end to government brutality. Denouncing injustice as contrary to the will of God, Romero appealed for international support—to U.S. President Jimmy Carter,[39] to the Latin American bishops at their 1979 gathering in Puebla, Mexico, and even to the Vatican, which scolded him for his public actions.[40] A radio commentator on events in the country and the need for better living conditions, whose Sunday homily was transmitted live every week, Romero appealed to the military via radio on March 23, 1980, imploring the soldiers to stop using violence and put down their weapons.[41] On the following day, Romero was assassinated by government forces, shot while saying Mass in a hospital chapel.[42]

Then, eight months later, while driving back on the road from the Camalapa airport, four U.S. Catholic missionaries—Ursuline Sister Dorothy Kazel, Maryknoll Sisters Maura Clarke and Ita Ford, and Cleveland-based Maryknoll lay missioner Jean Donovan—were stopped, raped, and assassinated by several Salvadoran national guardsmen.[43] The December 2nd attack turned out to have been deliberately planned at the highest levels of the military. The missionaries had been targeted, like other U.S. and Salvadoran Church workers, because they had been living and working with the poor. They had also become outspoken advocates for the poor, and one had just returned from a trip to a conference in Nicaragua, which had just had its own military government overthrown. The assassinations of Romero and the four women shocked many Catholics and others around the world, including activists in human rights, anti-war, and other organizations.

Opposition to U.S. involvement in Nicaragua, El Salvador, and Guatemala began mobilizing after Romero's assassination, and it intensified after the four women were killed. The United States Conference of Catholic Bishops' Latin American representative, Father Brian Hehir, began testifying in Congress against the repression in the late 1970s, and he increased his lobbying after these incidents.[44] At the grassroots level, a national organization, the Committee in Solidarity with the People of El

Salvador (CISPES), was formed in October 1980, and its activities intensified after the murders of the four Americans.[45] CISPES chapters took to
the streets with marches, rallies, and civil disobedience. They disrupted
the Salvadoran president's motorcade to the United Nations, blocked or
shut down government buildings in Los Angeles and Chicago, and even
blocked access to the Pentagon.[46]

CISPES was joined by other organizations, including Maryknoll and the
newly formed Witness for Peace, a Catholic advocacy organization with
members from many of the religious orders who worked in Latin America.
In the South Bronx Catholic Association, Connolly and a few others began
discussions about what role they could play to promote peace and justice in
Central America. After seeing the formation of solidarity groups following
the assassinations of Romero and the four women missionaries, Connolly
and a few others decided to form their own group.

Solidarity in the South Bronx

Jesus wasn't trendy and did not divinize the status quo.
    He knew the mind and will of His Father, and when he preached
that to the authorities and bigots and pretentious of His day, He was
killed.
    We cannot say what kind of price will be exacted from us.

As Connolly wrote these words, he remembered the series of actions his
own community had taken on Central America. The South Bronx Catholic
Committee in Solidarity with Central America was formed not only to learn
more about what was taking place in Central America, but also to organize
pressure against the U.S. involvement in the region. Most of their actions
initially involved participation in national efforts organized by CISPES.
They attended rallies, marches, and educational events in New York City.
Connolly and the others also took part in a National Day of Action, going
on a bus trip to Washington, D.C., with other New Yorkers. Moreover,
to get congressional support to stop funding military governments in El
Salvador and Guatemala, they met with their congressman, Robert Garcia.

The South Bronx Catholic Committee also wanted to get the archdiocese involved in the issues of U.S. support for the Salvadoran and other
military governments in Latin America. They wanted the archbishop to
speak out on the killings of priests, religious, and laypersons, and the
suffering of the mostly Catholic people of Central America. Connolly

wondered, *Isn't anyone going to say anything about the killing of nuns in Central America, or of Romero, a fellow archbishop?* Then, they finally heard of some official action being taken by the Institutional Church—a Mass of Remembrance for Romero to be held at St. Patrick's Cathedral.

Connolly contacted Father James Rigney, who was responsible for administration of St. Patrick's, to advise him that the committee would be handing out leaflets outside the Cathedral for the hundreds of expected churchgoers that Sunday. In the material, they called on Archbishop Cooke and on New York City's Catholics to take a stand and call for U.S. withdrawal of support for El Salvador and Guatemala military.

The committee also focused their attention on the New York embassies for these Central American governments. On one occasion, they went to stage a demonstration at the Guatemalan Embassy in midtown Manhattan, to protest the U.S. government support of Guatemala's repressive regime. They had learned to generate press attention, so the word reached a number of people quickly. On the morning of the action, Connolly received an anonymous call at the Athanasius rectory: "Call off the demonstration or we'll call it off for you."

Concerned, Connolly made a call to the Forty-First Precinct, reporting the death threat, and the precinct provided him with an escort car to trail his own car, which Connolly thought would protect them for the duration of the event. However, as he drove out of the Bronx and toward midtown Manhattan, the escort car stopped, to Connolly's astonishment. He was on his own.

At the meeting site, in front of Our Savior Church on Park Avenue, he met up with his friends and fellow demonstrators. Flynn, who had talked to him about the threat earlier that morning, asked him about the escort car.

"What happened to your protection?"

"He stopped in the Bronx," Connolly answered, as he shrugged his shoulders.

Then, before they handed out candles to light and begin the demonstration, a man walked over to him and said, "I'm your police protection, Father."

It came at just the right time, as one of the protesters shouted, "Let's go to the Embassy!" and the whole delegation followed him across the avenue. To Connolly's relief, the event went off safely.

The committee conducted religious and educational events in addition to protests and lobbying. Connolly concelebrated a Mass on the anniversary of Romero's death, at Our Lady of Pity Church. Also, the committee invited Father Brian Hehir of the Bishops' Latin America office to give a talk on the situation in Central America at St. Joseph's Seminary, as a way to reach both current and future priests from the Archdiocese of New York. The event had a mixed audience response: Some faculty and current priests enjoyed the presentation, but none of the seminarians were allowed to attend, per orders from the administration. Connolly, hoping to educate the next generation, was still grateful to Hehir.

For Connolly, even with the challenges of trying to fight against a militaristic, pro-war administration in Washington, *what was important was that he was taking action. He was joining with others who had known the suffering poor in the South Bronx. Together, they were declaring their common bond in both the suffering and, some day, the resurrection with their Catholic brothers and sisters throughout the world.*

Fr. Neil Connolly (*right*) meets Brazilian Bishop Dom Helder Camara (*left*), Latin American Church icon, in South Bronx. (Photo by Chris Sheridan. Courtesy of *Catholic New York*.)

A Larger Mission

Connolly finished his opinion piece for *Catholic New York*:

> St. Paul tells us we are in the race.
>
> We have been part of it since baptism.
>
> We can expect it to be tough, but the great thing is that we are guaranteed a prize greater than any price, if we keep our eyes on Jesus.[47]

The opinion was more than an answer to that challenge posed by the brother about his spending time in Central America. For Connolly, it was a statement of support for the new way of the Catholic Church in Latin America. It was an affirmation of the principles of Medellin and liberation theology and the Comunidades de Base, which he had created and cultivated for a few years at the Seneca Center. It was an acknowledgement that, like the original Christian communities organized by Paul and others, people were putting their lives at risk for their faith. Whether it was Torres in Colombia, or Romero and Ford, Clarke, Donovan, and Kazel in El Salvador, or the countless catechists, their work to cultivate the kingdom and seek the perfection of justice on this earth—the prize which Connolly felt drawn to—was paid for by their lives. As a priest of the Catholic Church of the world, Connolly declared, he was part of that work in Latin America.

Yes, there were real life-or-death consequences to a committed ministry. Connolly likely had escaped those consequences when he turned down the invitation from Pozo. He and his fellow priests certainly escaped them in Nicaragua and in Guatemala. But now, in the South Bronx, in the United States, he was part of the global Church and its ministry to the poor and victims of injustice, and he had to keep his commitment to solidarity with the poor, even if the conditions in his life and priesthood changed.

And conditions would change.

Chapter 12

New Leadership

Happy are those who know they are spiritually poor; the Kingdom of heaven belongs to them!

Happy are those who mourn;

God will comfort them!

Happy are those who are humble;

They will receive what God has promised!

Happy are those whose greatest desire is to do what God requires;

God will satisfy them fully!

Happy are those who are merciful to others;

God will be merciful to them!

Happy are the pure in heart;

They will see God!

Happy are those who work for peace;

God will call them His children!

Happy are those who are persecuted because they do what God requires;

The Kingdom of heaven belongs to them!

—Matthew 5:3–10, Bilingual Bible,
Good News Translation, United Bible Societies

Letter to an Archbishop

In the winter of 1984, Neil Connolly was at the monthly meeting of consulters at the archdiocesan headquarters. This group, which included all the vicars of the archdiocese, such as Connolly, met to review and take action on physical properties belonging to the archdiocese. When he was a parish priest at Athanasius, consulters had come to inspect and take action on the convent on Bruckner Boulevard, which he and Gigante were secretly using for the Odyssey House drug program. In this new role, with the serious financial responsibility in his own hands, Connolly was more careful. But on this day, he and the group had a more serious responsibility than usual: making improvements to the cardinal's residence on Madison Avenue.

The consulters were facing a special challenge with this project: the upgrade of the entire electrical system, which was deemed essential by their inspector team, would need to be done soon. The time-sensitivity of decisions was heightened by the expectation of a new occupant: John J. O'Connor, newly appointed by the Vatican to be archbishop of New York, would be arriving in a couple of months for his grand inauguration in May.[1] As the leader of New York's 1.5 million Catholics, a position which had always been associated with prestige and power in New York society, the archbishop always occupied the ornate residence on the block adjoining St. Patrick's Cathedral.

Like any other old building in New York, it had systems that required occasional work and sometimes major work. This particular renovation, however, would require tearing up part of the plumbing system, which had just been completely replaced throughout the residence during the term of Cardinal Cooke, who passed away in 1984 after a period of illness.[2] Everyone in the meeting realized, without looking at the budget proposal, that this two-system project would cost more than a million dollars, maybe a few million.

It made Connolly uncomfortable, both because of his long history in the South Bronx and because of his more recent travels in Latin America and contact with the Church there. Oscar Romero, after all, had lived in a small bedroom in a humble convent for the last few years of his life. Sensing the apparent willingness to accept the costly action among his peers, Connolly impulsively made a suggestion. "I think," he said, "it would be a great sign if he were to move into Harlem or the South Bronx and live there temporarily until the building were fixed later on. I don't think such a move would be so expensive."

There was no immediate response for a few seconds. Just silence. Finally, someone replied, "Well, he's a new person coming in and we want to welcome him, and we don't want any negative stuff. Let's just give him whatever he wants. Let's give him a nice package." After some nodding of heads around the room, the meeting moved on to other topics.

Even without a formal vote taken, Connolly knew there was no support for his position. So he decided he would write directly to O'Connor, who would remain bishop of the Diocese of Scranton, Pennsylvania, until the inauguration. Connolly sent a letter with the same arguments and recommendations he had made at the meeting: that O'Connor live in a poor community for a while. In the era of the Reagan administration, one which had exacerbated already difficult living conditions for poor communities like the South Bronx, Connolly was even more aware than usual of the great divisions being created between the wealthy and the poor in America. These divisions became more visible and stark in New York City with a growing population of homeless people on the streets of Midtown Manhattan and an increasing presence of soup kitchens for people whose food benefits were being cut by the federal government. His instinct was telling him, *supporting such spending on a luxurious residence like the cardinal's would not seem right, especially in these times.*

After all, he had learned from Gutiérrez's *Theology of Liberation* of the call for a "poverty of the spirit"—for the Church, including the clergy and bishops, to shed the symbols of power and wealth, which had led the poor to believe the Catholic Church was as rich and powerful as the elites in Latin American society. Gutiérrez and the bishops of Medellin had called for the Church to truly understand the poor by living with them and by using their prophetic position to denounce poverty and its institutional causes.

Connolly had seen how difficult it became for his colleagues in the South Bronx Catholic Church community to answer this call, as they endured deep federal government budget cuts to their housing, senior, youth, and other service organizations. But Connolly and all the ministers—clergy, religious, and laypersons—had answered the call and willingly adopted a spirit of poverty, living among the South Bronx people and ministering to their spiritual, educational, and social needs. He also saw how American institutions such as media cultivated the myth of "welfare queens," public assistance recipients living in luxury off hardworking Americans' taxes.[3] During the Reagan era, such institutions were making it more acceptable to blame and denounce the poor rather than society for poverty or inequality and therefore cut housing and other assistance.

This new federal approach to the poor was being implemented just four years after President Carter had initiated his own approach, promising a rebuilding of the South Bronx, and fifteen years after President Johnson had promised an end to poverty with his own program. Given this newly hostile approach to the poor, Connolly felt that the message of Gutiérrez and the Medellin bishops—to live as Christ did, with the poor—was crucial for the Church not only to preach, but to live out. He was asking the new archbishop to do just that in the meeting and in his follow-up letter.

As he put his letter in the mail for Scranton, Connolly remembered another letter he had sent when a new archbishop was to be selected for New York. At that time, sixteen years earlier, an entire generation of priests was ready to challenge the ways of the Church, to demand a direct voice in deciding the future of their archdiocese. This year, there was no such petition to the Vatican for an election by priests. Nor was there a new Memorandum of Priorities or a Strategic Reorganization Plan for the archdiocese to be offered up to a new archbishop, as there was in March 1968. *In this case*, Connolly thought, *he stood by himself, representing, in spirit, the wishes of a few dozen priests, sisters, and laypersons in the South Bronx for a renewed commitment by the Church to the poor.*

Connolly never received a written response to his letter, so he moved forward on his other responsibilities as vicar. However, he was expected to see O'Connor soon enough because of an official requirement under canon law, the rules and regulations of the global Catholic Church. At the inauguration ceremony in May, following the official protocols of such an event, Connolly joined the other consulters immediately behind the first group in the procession—the bishops, auxiliary bishops, and high-ranking officials at the chancery. After the participants in the first group were officially introduced to the newly inaugurated archbishop, the consulters were brought in for presentation by the vicar general to their new leader. When Connolly's turn came and he stood before the archbishop, O'Connor stopped.

"I know who you are," said O'Connor, as he looked at Connolly with a seriousness that he also felt in the handshake. "You're the one who wrote the letter."

Connolly affirmed that he was the author, and then, after a second, O'Connor moved on to the next consulter introduction, as the inauguration continued. He did not know what to think of O'Connor's remarks, or of O'Connor himself, since all he knew was what he had read in the papers and heard from his priest friends. John O'Connor was perceived as a "military man" by the public and by New York's Catholics. A chaplain in the U.S. Navy since the Korean War, he had reached the rank of admiral. O'Connor was educated at the School of Foreign Service in Georgetown University, where he obtained a doctorate under the tutelage of Jeane Kirkpatrick, who was defining and defending Reagan's vigorous hawkish approach to foreign relations, including Latin American policy.[4]

The one encouraging aspect of O'Connor's background, in Connolly's view, was his lineage: His father, like Connolly's father, was a lifelong labor union member. *So it was possible*, Connolly thought, *that with this family lineage and with his experience in a working-class Diocese of Pennsylvania, O'Connor might show some sympathy for the basic needs of working-class people.*

Connolly had already had concerns about the man who appointed O'Connor to the Archdiocese of New York: Pope John Paul II.[5] The first non-Italian to be elected Pope in modern Church history, the former Cardinal Karol Wojtyla of Poland was an advocate of workers' rights and of more just economic and political systems in the world. He wrote three encyclicals advancing workers' needs and rights: *Laborem Exercens, Solicitudo Rei Sociales*, and *Centesimus Annus*.[6] All sustained the Church's position that workers and their families should be treated with fairness and dignity in economic and other terms. A more prolific globetrotter than even his predecessor Paul VI, John Paul II went to New York City in October 1979, one year into his papacy, and visited the South Bronx, with Connolly and the association members joining tens of thousands of spectators.[7]

But in matters of the Church, the Pope was a traditionalist. He seemed to forgo the teachings of Vatican II, which encouraged the "people of God" view of the Church and gave equal responsibility to laypersons, religious, and priests for its direction. He rejected appeals for the Institutional Church to ordain women for the priesthood, for example, and barred the distribution of the Eucharist by women religious, including during his visit to New York. Much to the dismay of the politically involved clergy, John Paul II also forbade involvement of clergy or religious in elected office.[8]

Also, the supporters of the New Latin American Catholic Church and liberation theology felt betrayed by the new Pope's removal of bishops sympathetic to their causes.[9] Because of his Eastern European background, John Paul II was deeply concerned about Communism, and he was inclined to reject any teaching about the poor that seemed to suggest Marxism. With the active involvement of Cardinal Joseph Ratzinger, his chief theologian and keeper of doctrine, John Paul II rejected not only Stalinist-style Communism but also the Church vision that Connolly and his fellow ministers had lived by and worked for every day in the South Bronx.[10] Because of the Pope's leaning toward more conservative Latin American bishops, Connolly reasoned, O'Connor's term should be seen as a discomforting message to him and his peers: *You may call for change in the world, but you may not change the Church.*

South Bronx Tour

Once settled in his new (and expensively renovated) residence and head-quarters, O'Connor decided that he wanted to see his entire archdiocese. That meant a tour would be set up for the cardinal to visit each Vicariate in the region, including the South Bronx. Since it was essentially up to the vicar to organize the tour, it was going to be Connolly's responsibility to lead O'Connor, organize the various stops along the tour, and arrange for a dinner at the end of the day.

Handling the cardinal's schedule was his secretary, a young priest whom Connolly found very amiable and eager to plan the day. Originally from the South Bronx, the secretary recommended a series of stops that seemed more nostalgic than realistic. Connolly rejected the recommendations, tell-ing the secretary, "The cardinal should really see the South Bronx as it is today." The schedule would be full and busy, but fortunately for everyone, the tour took place on a pleasant summer day. It was also extraordinarily easy to navigate: With a small army of police officers stationed at all of the stops, in many of the neighborhood streets, all the streets that were on the route were cleared of any traffic. So the cardinal's limousine moved quickly through the South Bronx.

At first, Connolly took him to visit with Bob Banome and his people at St. Joseph's, meeting with a variety of housing and social service orga-nizations it sponsored. After a series of other stops with other Catholic Association member organizations, the entourage moved on to visit Con-nolly's friend Gigante and the SEBCO housing organization, which he had devoted himself to on a full-time basis after his city council term was over in 1977. O'Connor was well-received by Gigante and the SEBCO staff, and he was impressed by the housing which was already built, as well as the maps and blueprints for the planned housing developments for Hunts Point–Longwood.

At the end of the tour, Connolly decided to take O'Connor to the Cor-pus Christi Monastery in the Hunts Point Peninsula, where a religious order of contemplative nuns lived and worked. They spent much of their daily lives in prayer, including prayer for increased vocations in seminaries and novitiates, and in work on the monastery grounds, cloistered from the industrial and residential world of the Peninsula, and from the rest of the world. It was a nice, quiet place to end the tour, especially after a busy day of meetings with people from the organizations and parishes and hearing a multitude of presentations.

Connolly saw the visit as a timely opportunity to discuss an important issue that was not on the cardinal's agenda for getting informed about his Vicariates: the state of Central America. Once appointed archbishop, O'Connor became a member of the Central American Committee for the United States Bishops' Conference. Since that committee was about to embark on a tour of Central America, Connolly, as a member of the South Bronx Catholic Committee in Solidarity with Central America, wanted to engage O'Connor in conversation. Connolly's greatest concern was the committee's projected visit to Nicaragua, which was still working to build its new government but was constantly under threat from the war-hungry Reagan administration, driven by Kirkpatrick. He decided he needed to share what he had seen during his trip with Flynn and Byrne and ensure that O'Connor at least heard the perspectives of others besides those of Archbishop Obando y Bravo, who had the less optimistic view of the Sandinistas and their plans for the country.

Connolly had not fully made up his own mind about what he thought of the current situation, with the Sandinistas in power. He knew that many of the wealthier citizens had left the country, which might make economic matters challenging, but he also observed a lessening of the great inequalities between rich and poor. Connolly had not seen extreme poverty during his tour, or extreme wealth as there had been before, or the brutal repression which had been a regular occurrence in the country. So Connolly tried to present the fullest possible view of the country based on what he had seen himself and on what he had read and heard from Brian Hehir and others.

Connolly had hoped that the quiet setting of supper at the end of a long day would give him the opportunity to have the cardinal's full attention. He spoke of his own experiences and impressions and then, with a calm conclusion to the impromptu lobbying effort, pleaded with O'Connor: "The only thing we are asking is that when you speak to Bishop Obando y Bravo, just understand that there are other opinions on the part of other Church members, and so you might want to hear some of those." As he had done during their first encounter in the inauguration ceremony, O'Connor looked at Connolly for a brief moment and said nothing. Then, at the end of the supper, he left and thanked the nuns for their hospitality, and Connolly for the tour.[11]

Connolly knew that this position he was communicating, of keeping an open mind to the revolutionary government, put him in conflict with virtually every person in the hierarchy at the archdiocese, and probably even at the Vatican, which had publicly chastised the priests in the Nicaraguan government for their political involvement and for their support of liberation theology. However, Connolly thought, *He had had this unique opportunity to bring his own experience to the attention of O'Connor, and so he had to take advantage of it. Even if he was signaling some sympathy with people dismissed by the Institutional Church leaders as "Communist," he was able to speak from his own experiences, which many of the critics did not have. Just like the Latin American clergy, who lived with the suffering poor every day, as he did in the South Bronx, his views of the world and his faith and theology were shaped by that experience of suffering. It was important, as Vatican II had said, for the Church and its priests to be in the wider world, to see the world, and to live in the world, to see what the people lived with.*

What he saw in both Nicaragua and Guatemala helped him see how important it was to be with the people, as they tried to improve their lives and put an end to their suffering. He had to speak for those people in the Santo Domingo parade, and the university, and for the masked opposition leaders in the Guatemalan restaurant, and for Connie Kelly and Alvaro Ramazzini, who were in danger every day. Their voices needed to be heard by the powerful in the North American Institutional Church, including O'Connor.

A Letter to the Clergy

In 1985, Connolly was about to complete his third term as vicar of the South Bronx, and he was thinking about the future. After the tour of the South Bronx organizations with the cardinal, he began to think about changes going on in the parish staffs and in the larger area which needed special attention. He had learned that there were a couple of pastors recently appointed to South Bronx parishes who were not able to relate to the Puerto Rican parishioners and their Catholic traditions. They did not embrace the "people of God" theology of the Vatican II Church, and they were not interested in the development of lay leaders. After he and the South Bronx Catholic Clergy Association had specifically appealed to Cooke for the appointment of priests who were willing to "go Spanish," and to live the Vatican II way, as Connolly and his peers had done, they were instead getting traditionalists with pre–Vatican II beliefs.

Unhappy with these pastors, Connolly decided as vicar to intervene, and he asked the archdiocese to find replacements for those South Bronx parishes. The archdiocese did not accept his recommendations, and Connolly knew his campaign was not appreciated at headquarters. But he would have to raise those and other appointment issues with the new archbishop and with his fellow priests.

First among these other issues, Connolly was concerned about his friend Bill Smith, who was being transferred out of St. John Chrysostom after twelve years of service. Connolly had worked closely with Smith and the St. John Chrysostom staff for years, and he had personally felt a particular kinship with those who had "gone Spanish" and remained in the priesthood, like Smith. Smith challenged the application of the archdiocesan rule limiting pastors to two terms in a parish, and he asked Connolly to advocate for him. He cited the example of Larry Lucas, who had been allowed to stay on much longer than two terms as pastor at Resurrection Parish in Harlem. Smith believed Lucas, as one of the few black priests in the archdiocese, was getting special treatment because of his nearly unique relationship with his Harlem parish. Knowing that the ranks of priests who had "gone Spanish" were dwindling, Smith argued, in his heavily Puerto Rican parish, he should get special consideration like Lucas's.

But their situations were not really similar. Lucas, who often spoke publically about issues involving race and the Catholic Church and larger New York City issues, was not without some power. He had been a quiet seminarian, as Connolly recalled, one class behind Connolly at St. Joseph's. However, he became outspoken shortly after, beginning in the civil rights era, and was often quoted in the newspapers on matters involving racial inequality in New York City and in the Archdiocese of New York. On the other hand, Connolly found Lucas, who was always an amiable colleague to him, to be too traditionalist about the Church and about Catholic theology itself. Lucas felt the opposite about Connolly. At priest gatherings and ceremonies, even in friendly discourses, Lucas challenged Connolly's thinking about Church as the "people of God." "You're going to tear this Church apart, the way you are. Way different than the way most people think." These traditionalist views allowed him to be left alone by the archdiocesan hierarchy. Lucas did publicly raise the issues of racial exclusion in the Church in his book *Black Priest, White Church*.[12] However, in part because of his willingness to not challenge the Institutional Church's ways regarding the roles of laypersons or women, Lucas had more influence about his place in the Church than Bill Smith could imagine.

Connolly's other appointment concern was about the future of the South Bronx Pastoral Center. After seven years as executive director, his friend Bob Stern was about to leave to pursue another ministry. So there was a need to conduct a search, and as chair of the board at the Pastoral Center, which had evolved into a true South Bronx institution, he wanted the clergy to have a say in its future. Connolly had hoped, since there were a large number of women religious involved in teaching and preparing programs of study at the center, that one of them might be seriously considered as a candidate for director. He thought, *Sisters Louise Mileski and Valorie Lordi, for example, who had taken leadership roles in the Pastoral*

Pastoral Center graduates another lay minister, with new Cardinal John O'Connor, South Bronx Vicar Connolly, and lay leader Brigantty. (Photo by Chris Sheridan. Courtesy of *Catholic New York*.)

Center and in People for Change, and who were formally trained in theology, were great candidates, worthy of consideration and acceptance by religious, laypersons, and, yes, clergy of the South Bronx. Connolly knew it was not going to be an easy discussion, but he thought the clergy of the South Bronx should at least have it.

Connolly wrote a letter to the South Bronx clergy, calling for a special meeting. In his letter, Connolly noted that the decisions about the Smith issue and the Stern replacement belonged to the Personnel Board of the Archdiocese of New York. However, he wrote, there were no plans being reported to the South Bronx Vicariate, and he thought it was important for the priests of the South Bronx to make some recommendations to the personnel board. After all, Connolly thought, *Vatican II had called for consultation with the priests and other members of the church on diocesan matters.* He sent off the letter, and he learned that it somehow reached the cardinal's desk. *Some priests in his community*, he realized, *did not like the idea of consultation.*

There was no answer to the letter. But a short time later, in a surprise development, Connolly was offered an opportunity to become a pastor in a new parish. The cardinal's vicar general, Joseph O'Keefe, called Connolly with the offer of St. John's Parish in the Kingsbridge neighborhood in the

Northwest Bronx. He did not know if this move by the archdiocese was related to the letter, but he wanted to clarify and settle things first on his two issues before making any decisions on a new place.

Connolly knew a little about St. John's, which he had visited one time, to say a Mass as a favor to a priest friend. It had a large school, and there was a Central American community arriving in greater and greater numbers there, with needs for services he had once been very familiar with. After saying that Mass, which took place in the basement, he spoke with some of the new parishioners. They explained how they were getting used to the new ways of the country, and the new Church, but they were concerned about not being welcomed. They told Connolly what they had asked the former pastor: "Why do they have a Spanish Mass in the basement, instead of the main Church?"

Connolly realized that this church was somewhat like Athanasius must have been in its early days of change from an English-speaking to a Spanish-speaking church. He also realized that, between resolving the potential "culture wars" in the parish activities and managing the school's time-consuming administrative challenges, which would fall on a pastor, St. John's was not the right next step for him to take. There would be so much parish work that he would effectively stop being the vicar he had been for almost nine years.

He called the vicar general with his decision. To Connolly, O'Keefe was friendly and well-respected, but a powerful figure who served as the cardinal's "right-hand man" on personnel matters and on the management of parishes. Rejecting an offer from O'Keefe would be considered a rejection of the cardinal, at the beginning of his term, but Connolly decided he was not ready. He told O'Keefe that he had thought about it and appreciated the offer but decided, "No thanks."

The genial O'Keefe sounded solemn when he replied. "You know, you will be the first person to say no to Cardinal O'Connor."

Perceiving the threat of some counteraction, Connolly remained defiant. "Then it's a historic moment."

He did not want to seem disrespectful, but Connolly was once again feeling frustrated with the archdiocese. It seemed that the archdiocese did not want to know about what was going on in the Vicariate, did not want to discuss its future, and was only interested in pastor assignments. *What was going on down there?* Why did the cardinal tour the South Bronx, if he did not want to act on Connolly's concerns about traditionalist pastors who couldn't relate to the Puerto Rican parishioners? *Was that tour just for show?*

After the letter to Cardinal O'Connor and the call with O'Keefe, Connolly received new messages from the archdiocese, which he perceived as warnings. Bill Smith came back from a visit to the cardinal and, at a South Bronx clergy meeting, announced that O'Connor had said to him, "Please tell Neil Connolly that I'm not mad at him." Everyone in the meeting room, especially Connolly, was stunned and confused by the message. O'Connor had not said anything else, Smith said. But Connolly thought the cardinal's words suggested the exact opposite of their literal meaning.

Then, Connolly heard from a priest friend named John Oleaga, who was living at Blessed Sacrament rectory with Connolly's good friend Bob O'Connor. Oleaga was serving as a Hispanic clergy representative to the Presbyteral Council, the group of priests in the archdiocese created in the Vatican II era to advise the cardinal on important diocesan matters. At the council meeting, Oleaga said at supper one night that he heard a comment from the cardinal: "In this diocese, there is a Vicariate that's out of control." Connolly was not only surprised but confused. He could not understand what would lead anyone to think his Vicariate was out of control. *It was he, in fact, who wanted to get people together and plan for the future, to come up with organized, meaningful recommendations from the clergy. That was what he was supposed to do as a vicar*, he thought.

Wasn't it?

Having heard these two "messages" from the archdiocese, Connolly called Vicar General O'Keefe to ask him about the situation and his own relationship with the cardinal and the chancery. "I don't understand this," he said. "I'm getting all these remarks. Is there someone upset with what I'm doing? Because no one's talking to me."

O'Keefe calmly replied, "Oh, I wouldn't worry about that."

Connolly paused, not knowing how far to take the conversation, and then he ended the call with an "okay." He knew, however, that things were not "okay" and that these messages coming from the cardinal, in addition to the attempted transfer to St. John's parish outside of the South Bronx, were all indications that this new archbishop was not on Connolly's side. More importantly for Connolly, however, it meant he would not be on the side of the South Bronx Area Church, the South Bronx Pastoral Center, the South Bronx People for Change, or even the vision behind all of them. It seemed that the work of the Vicariate was in danger, and Connolly thought, *Maybe he was the problem. Maybe the diocesan disagreements with Connolly were getting in the way of support for the Vicariate projects and the Area Church.*

Connolly took his concerns to a clergy meeting. "I don't think we are carrying out the ideals we had when we started this whole thing," he said and proposed that he return to pastoral work while another priest was elected as vicar. But the other priests were startled. They told him there was really nobody to replace him, and it would take another few years to groom a successor. Connolly accepted this, after some discussion, and agreed to stay on for one final term as vicar. But after the meeting broke up, John Flynn took him aside.

"Remember, make sure," said Flynn, looking at him and speaking quietly and slowly, "when you go home tonight, write a letter to the cardinal and let him know that you want to stay on. With these rumors that are circulating, there's a chance that you might be out of this job if you don't act."

Connolly knew Flynn was right and that there was a small window of opportunity. He wrote his third letter to O'Connor, this one saying, "I am still interested. I want to stay on as vicar of the South Bronx."

Official News

About two months later, Connolly was on retreat, as he was every few months, with his friends Ed Byrne, Bob O'Connor, and Peter O'Donnell. They were taking a lunch break from the prayer and discussion session when a retreat house manager came over to tell Connolly that he had a phone call in the administrative office building next door. Connolly excused himself and went to accept the call.

It was O'Connor himself on the line.

"Neil, I'm so sorry that I'm interrupting your retreat, but I am appointing you the pastor of St. Mary's on Grand Street, in the Lower East Side."[13]

For Connolly, the news was unbelievable. Like something that fell from the sky and crashed into his life. It was like a bolt of lightning—he was being taken out of his South Bronx, the place he had come to know over the last twenty-seven years and had committed his past and his future plans to. This time it was real.

He had no response for the cardinal, on the other end of the line, other than to say, "Goodbye."

When he returned to his friends, still in disbelief, they asked him what was wrong.

"Boy, I'm just kind of overwhelmed," he said. "Cardinal O'Connor just told me that I was appointed the new pastor of St. Mary's on Grand Street."

Byrne, who was the outgoing pastor at that church and was planning to become pastor of an upstate parish after many years, exclaimed, "That's great!"

Connolly solemnly looked at him and the rest of his friends and said, "Well, I'm not so sure I feel great about it."

The reactions back in the South Bronx community were similar: shock and anger and rebellion. John Flynn, the other board members at the Pastoral Center and People for Change, and his reflection community were all stunned. Some, like Mili Bonilla, Kathy Osberger, and a few other friends, responded like the organizers they had learned to be: "We're not going to take this! We're going to organize protests on this!"

Connolly expected that. After all, he and they had spent so much time learning to fight powerful institutions: not only protesting for heat and emergency repairs, but fighting for election of the next archbishop, among many other actions aimed at both the government and the Church. Yet, although part of him wanted to wage this fight, to build further on the work that he and the association members had done, Connolly was caught in an identity crisis. After all, there were many things he still wanted to do as a vicar. He wanted to continue building an Area Church. In fact, he wanted a situation like the one he had begun to plan years ago with his fellow priests at St. John Chrysostom—one set of priests shared by two parishes. In such an arrangement for an Area Church, all the clergy of the South Bronx would work together to preach and serve a community of parishes, rather than just be a pastor of one.

In organizing such an arrangement, they would avoid the crisis Bill Smith faced, of being sent away from the parish he called home all his priestly life. He would not have been just a pastor for one parish, having only two terms to complete before serving another parish. Instead, priests of the South Bronx could collaborate with each other across parish lines, belonging to a community of parishes. They could also engage the religious and laypersons they had come to know, by putting them into the leadership roles of new pastoral ministers after completing training at the Pastoral Center. There was much community-building still to be done, and that was why he had agreed to become a vicar: to build a community. And he had just promised the South Bronx clergy that he would continue as their vicar.

Connolly's termination as vicar had another, more personal impact for one person. Connolly had become aware of a priest in the South Bronx who was in an intimate relationship with a woman. Connolly thought very highly of the priest, both as a decent man and a very good priest to his parishioners and to others in the South Bronx Catholic community. A couple of people had spoken to Connolly about the priest and his situation, and about the rumors being circulated about the relationship. Some accused Connolly of not doing anything about either the relationship or the priest's status in the Church. When the news of Connolly's transfer spread among the South Bronx Catholic Association members, the priest went to meet with Connolly. He was in tears.

"Pardon me," he said to Connolly, "if I'm the reason you were kicked out of the South Bronx."

Connolly reassured him. "No, that's not true. Nobody ever brought that up to me in the archdiocese." He consoled the other man and urged him to do what was right for him as a priest.

This meeting reminded Connolly of his own decisions about priesthood, beginning with the one he had taken in St. Patrick's Cathedral twenty-seven years before. *As a priest, he had promised "obedience and respect to the Ordinary of New York"*—that is, the archbishop. *Although this new archbishop had been in office for only one year, Connolly, with all his years as a priest, would have to follow his orders, and O'Connor had ordered him to leave the South Bronx. If he did not, then what would become of his priesthood, of his own identity as a priest? Would he have to leave the Church? Many of his peers would not accept him, and he would no longer be able to be part of that original community he had committed to. When several of his friends and seminary graduates ended up leaving the priesthood over the last few years, he had stayed on.*

A priest was the role he had chosen when he entered Cathedral Prep, at the age of twelve, to help others in need. The more he thought about it, the more he realized, *this feeling had not changed.* So, despite the severe frustration he felt, Connolly decided he would remain a loyal priest and follow O'Connor's transfer orders. *But,* he vowed, *he would still be a priest who spoke his mind and who declared the truth, within the Church as well as within the world.* He would make clear to the powers at the archdiocese, when the opportunity came up, how he felt about this reassignment, just as he had when he wrote the cardinal how he felt about excessive spending for that Madison Avenue residence.

His chance came pretty soon. Before his departure in June, all the newly named pastors of the archdiocese were called down to meet with the cardinal. Twenty priests were gathered together with O'Connor, O'Keefe, and a few others in the hierarchy. The cardinal began the meeting by announcing the names of all the priests in the room in alphabetical order, with their new parish assignments mentioned as well. The announcements were relatively basic and pro forma until he reached Connolly's name and assignment. O'Connor began complimenting and praising Connolly: "What a wonderful guy he is." "He speaks Spanish and has done such good work."

To Connolly, this all felt like O'Connor was issuing the *coup de grace*, a final complimentary gesture just as he was delivering the "death blow." Then, realizing what he had done by focusing on Connolly and ignoring others, O'Connor went back to the other new pastors and paid them compliments as well. Afterward, as the meeting concluded without much fanfare, O'Connor mentioned that he would be available to speak in private with anyone who wanted to discuss their new appointments. Connolly was not expecting this opportunity, but his instinct was telling him, *I have to take advantage of this moment and let him know how I feel*. Connolly went over to O'Connor after the meeting and asked for a private discussion. *Even if he was going to accept orders*, Connolly reasoned, *he was going to speak his mind*.

"You know," Connolly said, wasting no time in the private session, "I thought, at least, that you would have invited me in before the change and sat down and talked to me about this. After all, I was nine years there as vicar. This was a different job than any other vicar job in the archdiocese. It was a new thing, an experiment to serve the people. We took this seriously. We even sent you an evaluation because we did evaluate that work. I think it was positive and—"

"You stop right there!" interrupted an angry O'Connor. "Who do you think you are? I'm the cardinal! I am the bishop of New York." He continued his tirade. "You're not the bishop! And yet you were trying to appoint these people to their positions." O'Connor looked at Connolly as he pointed his finger toward himself, "I'm the one who makes the appointments."

Connolly was being accused by the most powerful Catholic in New York of insubordination, of usurping his power. He was as infuriated as O'Connor, and he was not going to be silenced. This time, he would defend his actions, even without his allies by his side. "Excuse me," he interrupted. "But no one was trying to make appointments. We saw a lack of planning for priests and parish personnel. We were trying to look ahead, and see what the circumstances were, and see who there was in the South Bronx that could offer the kind of leadership that Bob Stern offered. So we thought that that would be a commonsense thing to do, without any gesture of taking the power unto ourselves."

O'Connor fired back, making the dispute a larger, more personal one. He said that he had done so much for Connolly in terms of praise, and that Connolly had not done the same for him.

They both remained quiet for a short while.

Finally, Connolly broke the tension with a final suggestion. "Well, Cardinal, you're the archbishop of New York, and I know we have to work together, so why don't we shake hands?" Connolly stood up and shook hands with O'Connor, and left the office to go back to his South Bronx, to his home.

There were still efforts being organized locally to resist the cardinal's action. Connolly's friends and colleagues urged him to stand up against the order, but he finally told them, "If you want to organize protests and pickets, that's fine. But I'm not going to be part of it." As a result, two delegations held separate meetings with the cardinal: one, a group of South Bronx and other clergy, and the other, a broader group of clergy, religious, and laypersons from the South Bronx Catholic Association.

The grassroots Church of the South Bronx, Connolly realized, *was showing it was becoming a dynamic community on its own. Without his presence.*

Preparing for the Next Role

After much prayer for guidance, Connolly realized that he had to not just accept the cardinal's decision, but to be open to it. *To let go again.*

Eventually, he went down to St. Mary's Church to meet with the parish leadership, and he was surprised to learn that a great deal had been involved in the process of selecting him as pastor. This appointment, it turned out, was more than just the cardinal's assignment of him to fill an open position that was, not coincidentally, outside the South Bronx.

As the people he met with at St. Mary's explained to him, there was an active group of lay leaders and religious who, faced with the departure of their pastor, Ed Byrne, wanted to take action. They had come together in a reorganization of parish groups and activities and roles, and they redefined their mission and agenda. Leaders also described the qualities and values of the person they wanted for their next pastor. Since they had already been working effectively with several religious in the parish, the group was open to being led by either a woman religious or a priest. They emphasized that they wanted someone who would work with them and would respect their roles in the management and direction of the parish.

As pastor, Byrne, speaking on the leadership group's behalf, invited the Personnel Board of the Archdiocese of New York to meet with the group at the rectory. At the meeting, the parish leaders interviewed the personnel board representative and explained their criteria for an acceptable pastor. They asked the representative about people who might fit their criteria and about the archdiocesan selection process. Based on that, and based on their discussions with Byrne, they also held a meeting with the cardinal to express their concerns and their criteria for acceptable candidates. Finally, they asked for the archdiocese to select from a list.

Byrne, for his part, created a list of the candidates whom he knew and who also would meet the criteria: Bob Stern, Bob O'Connor, and Neil Connolly. Those names were approved by the leadership group and then submitted to the archdiocese on their behalf. Connolly was pleasantly surprised by this story and to learn about the parish leadership's process. He knew his friend Byrne believed in developing laypeople and team ministry. Connolly understood, as did Byrne, that the Church had an active role to play in the conditions of the world and that it had to support the poor and work *with* the poor. As a Maryknoll missioner, Byrne was an advocate of the new approach of the Latin American Church to commit itself to the poor and to the U.S. Church's support of the oppressed. *Most importantly, Connolly thought, he practiced the Vatican II principles in his own parish, giving a role to the "people of God" in the future church. St. Mary's offered a promising new start,* he thought.

A couple of weeks later, however, Connolly received a call from the cardinal's secretary. "The cardinal wants to see you," he said. "At your convenience. When you are able to meet."

After arranging the date, the secretary added, "He'd like to see you at the seminary." There was always a dedicated apartment for the cardinal at St. Joseph's Seminary for the occasional getaway from the busy New York City schedule, or for special gatherings, and the cardinal had planned to be up there on the date scheduled with Connolly. Connolly was wondering whether there would be any more of the tension which took place down in the archdiocese, although the tone of the scheduler seemed very accommodating.

On the day of the meeting, O'Connor was dressed in his full ceremonial attire and ready to greet Connolly at the front steps of the seminary.

"You wanted to meet with me, Cardinal?" Connolly asked.

"Oh yes, yes," O'Connor replied as he accompanied him to his apartment. His tone was hard to read.

They sat down and looked at each other, and finally the cardinal began the discussion by asking, "How are you feeling?"

Not sure what to say, Connolly gave a polite "Good."

Finally, the cardinal said, "I want to apologize to you. I didn't realize that you had been involved in so much. My impression of you was that you were someone who had just been involved in housing." Then he said, "I want you to know that you don't have to go to St. Mary's. You can stay in the South Bronx."

Connolly was stunned. O'Connor was a bigger man than he had thought, in showing both the willingness to apologize and the seriousness of the apology. This was an unusual act for Connolly to witness, an act of humility from a powerful man. He wasn't sure what motivated O'Connor, or if the meetings or protests had anything to do with this offer to let him stay.

Regardless of whether his people's organizing had had an effect, O'Connor had still apologized, and he was trying to make peace with Connolly. Finally, Connolly replied, "Well, I've already gone down and visited with the people at St. Mary's, and I've decided I am ready to go." He thanked the cardinal for his offer and his apology and went back home.

His thoughts were now turned to the future. As he prepared to become a parish priest again, Connolly thought about a conversation he had a year earlier with a mentor, Father Leo Mahon.[14] Based in Chicago, Mahon was one of those experienced priests present in that 1958 summer program in Puerto Rico, and he was, to Connolly, a breath of fresh air, with his open ideas and his spirit and beliefs. Connolly had met him again in Chicago thanks to Margie Tuite, who was friends with Mahon. Tuite brought the two together again a few years after People for Change began operating, and Connolly and Mahon shared stories about their community-building efforts. While in Panama, Mahon had worked to build a theology school for laypersons to become ministers, without the twelve-year preparation priests underwent in the United States. Like the South Bronx Pastoral Center, the school sought to prepare laypersons to assume full ministerial responsibility over the Church, which would be actively engaged in the world. To Connolly, it seemed like the Pastoral Center and like that amazing little school he encountered in Quito, Ecuador, where Father Pozo was teaching priests to help form a new approach to Church and pastoral activity.

At the end of the inspiring dinner and discussion, Mahon left Connolly with a few words of advice. "Neil, remember this," he said. "Never imagine obstacles that people will place in front of you. Sometimes you might say, 'I don't know if I can make this move, because the bishop might not want me to, and nobody told me I could do that.'" He looked at Connolly again and said, "Go ahead and do all the things you want to, until you are stopped."

Tuite nodded and smiled.

They both knew Mahon was right.

Mahon and the others he met that summer in Puerto Rico were truly priests, Connolly thought. He had sensed that, even there in the classrooms at *La Universidad. They did all the things they wanted to do until they were stopped. They were committed to the people's needs, and they saw, in full, the people's dignity. They lived and worked with the people, and prayed and reflected and fought alongside them for a better world.*

They saw that the Church was where "two or three are gathered in my name"—in a Panama ministry school; or in the colmado *confessional in the* campo *in Jayuya; in the candlelight procession for peace during the East Harlem riots; in the Fiesta San Juan Bautista on Randall's Island; in*

Enjoying the freedom of a swim on a Nicaraguan beach. (Photo by Mili Bonilla.)

a Hunts Point apartment reflecting on the Gospel according to Luke and its meaning for the people of Seneca Avenue; in a circle of teenagers and younger children on Fox Street confronting life's pressures with each other; in the classroom at Our Lady of Victory, teaching people to become baptismal ministers; and in the housing commissioner's waiting room conducting a pray-in.

Seeing that the Church could be in all those places, and that those places were where a priest needed to be, was what made them priests.

Living with that vision of Church every day was what made them true priests.

Connolly had developed that vision, too, and he prayed every day that he could live that vision, because living that vision would make him a true priest. Being a true priest was all he had ever wanted when he entered Cathedral Prep, and that was all he had wanted when he entered the South Bronx.

As he entered a new world and a new life, that was still all he would ever want.

ACKNOWLEDGMENTS

First, thanks to Neil Connolly, who not only led the remarkable life, which is partially revealed here, but also put up with six years of telling the story, revising the story, and tolerating my learning process. He became immersed in the formalization of stories, many of which he had shared with people throughout his life.

Then I want to thank Professor Mark Naison for giving me the opportunity to introduce myself to Fordham University Press and for promoting the written works of his students over the years.

Of course, I am grateful to Fred Nachbaur, Katie Sweeny, and Kate O'Brien, Eric Newman, Will Cerbone, and the good team and board at Fordham University Press for believing in this project and making this publication possible.

Working with the Fordham team, Mildred Sanchez provided a keen eye and thoughtful attention through the copy-editing phase of production.

Of course, many thanks to my own sharp, thoughtful, and knowledgeable editor, Catherine Osborne, who made the writing significantly better and allowed the messages to get through. She did this with niceness, smarts, and encouragement, even from as far as Mexico—all while also a professor, national conference organizer of the nation's leading thinkers in Catholic history, and a Catholic Worker member.

A special acknowledgment to the late Monsignor John Ahern, Lillian Camejo, and Sister Ann Marie Lafferty (Lord rest their souls, as Neil

Connolly would say), who spent time with me sharing their part of the South Bronx world in that shared time with Connolly.

There were a number of readers who made this text better:

Denis Connolly, Neil Connolly's brother, who also shared his insights on the person he grew up with and whom he called his "best friend."

Mili Bonilla, Neil Connolly's "right hand" in the fledgling Vicariate experiment, his first real organizing recruit and long-term core of the People for Change staff, and a very good photographer, whose pictures permeate this book and made this project better. Her continued, lifelong organizing work is a model for others. From my childhood days at St. Anselm's to the organizing trenches of People for Change to today, you have become a good friend who made me appreciate more the kind of person Neil Connolly was.

Kathy Osberger, his close friend and ally from the South Bronx days who ran the Seneca Center in Hunts Point, and who read a couple of versions of the manuscript and gave some detailed insights of those days. She also took the time to add a couple of nice photos while carrying on her solidarity work and beginning new lay leadership programs with immigrants making "good trouble" in Chicago.

Sister Louise Mileski and Sister Valorie Lordi, also close friends and allies from the South Bronx days, who are theologians and leaders in both the South Bronx Area Church and People for Change and its work in the world. They continue to teach the next generation of young people at St. John Chrysostom.

Angel Diaz and Sister Mary Ellen Ryan, who worked on the unique staff with Neil Connolly and Father Bob O'Neill at St. Mary's Parish on the Lower East Side and, in Sister Mary Ellen's case, at St. Frances de Sales as well. Both gave great insight into the priest he became after the South Bronx phase of his life and promoted this story with vigor. As a champion on the radio and of the people, Angel "breaks the waters" and continues to share Connolly's life story with people near and far.

Sister Veronica Mendez, who actively collaborated with Neil Connolly at St. Mary's and provided national leadership in the RCIA and other programs.

Father Phil Kelley, who knew Neil Connolly and led the people of St. Frances de Sales on 96th Street with him. He continues to do so with an extraordinarily good parish team, which has, among other things, carried on Connolly's name with the parish Pop-up Theology Neil Connolly Lectures, a series of talks tackling the major social issues that the Church can and should face.

Reverend Jim Fairbanks, of the United Church of Christ and long-term advocate of the South Bronx, who campaigned as part of several ecumenical coalitions for justice with Neil Connolly on so many issues in the South Bronx while serving on staff with Reverend Wendell Foster.

To Reverend Jim Joyce, who lived in the South Bronx with Dean Brackley and Joe Towle and has given himself to the Jesuit causes of social justice ministry and educating the next generation of leaders. (Go Regis.)

To Frank Handelman, who contributed the Bronx Church Coalition materials and knowledge as part of the original staff in the first round of battles for housing in the South Bronx.

To Eileen Markey, journalism professor and author of *A Radical Faith*, who has helped in reviewing text, reviewing responses, and providing me with various opportunities to promote this project. She also provided my wonderful editor.

To Margaret Groarke, a Manhattan College professor who both preaches (in person and in writing) and practices organizing for change in the Northwest Bronx, and who gave good guidance on a couple of versions and put me in touch with Eileen.

To Brad Hinze, Fordham University Theology professor and chair, who also preaches (in person and in writing) and practices the connections between theology and social justice in the Northwest Bronx.

To Father Claudio Burgaleta, S.J., who lived in the South Bronx Jesuit community, provides valuable ministry at St. Peter's University in Jersey City, and has worked to tell the story of Father Joseph Fitzpatrick.

To Wilson Martinez, part of the original People for Change team and an advocate and deacon in the Bronx and teacher at De La Salle Academy. He continues the push for Church community and teaching the next generation.

To Mark Colville, Catholic Worker leader in New Haven and one-time People for Change organizer and civil dis-obeyer. He is now challenging the system of nuclear weapons as part of the Kings Bay Plowshares 7.

To Martin Rogers, one-time People for Change leader with the people in Immaculate Conception, who also civilly dis-obeyed and challenged the closing of firehouses and is continuing to build community and fight the good fight in the South Bronx.

To Joan Boyle, a friend who believes and actively practices the messages of Vatican II and the Call to Action movement, commits herself to Resistance and Justice daily, and is just a good cheerleader.

To Reverend Michael Caine, friend, who leads the Old First Reformed

UCC Church and community in Philadelphia, and who has stood up for justice there and, in earlier days, in East Harlem and Brooklyn.

To Gelvin Stevenson, who shared his organizing and economist's knowledge of the South Bronx and organizes efforts on environmental and other issues.

To Roger Hayes, Joseph Muriana, Bill Reilly, and Gregory Jost, who shared their experiences and understanding of insurance and bank disinvestment in the South and Northwest Bronx as directors, housing organizers, and analysts in the Northwest Bronx, leading the fight to save their neighborhoods through the Northwest Bronx Community and Clergy Coalition.

Special thanks to Dr. Ed Eismann, founder and longtime director of the Unitas therapeutic community featured in this story, for providing the essential content, background, and vision behind Unitas, and for the amazing photos of just a few of its special members.

Special thanks to Monsignor Robert Stern for being both a reader and essential contributor to the story, for taking the time to interview with me to help me understand the struggles of ministry of those important years, for sharing his vision of the Vatican II Church as a Church of the People, and for implementing this in the South Bronx Pastoral Center.

Special thanks to Monsignor Thomas Shelley, long-respected historian of the Church in New York and in the United States, for taking the time to read the manuscripts through several of its iterations and giving me some key advice throughout, helping to significantly reshape it as a viable story, and for being the prodigious storyteller of the Catholic Church's presence in New York and in the United States.

Special thanks to Gwendolin Herder, a lifelong publisher and head of Crossroads Publishing, who was a friend to Neil Connolly since her days as a parishioner in St. Mary's and has given me amazing, essential guidance in preparing this manuscript at its various stages. She helped me really frame the question of Connolly's essential question of who he wanted to be as a priest and gave me her publishing expertise.

Special thanks also to two "super-readers" who put up with *every* version of the manuscript:

George Horton, Director of the Office of Social and Community Development of the Archdiocese of New York, who appreciated Neil Connolly for his friendship and his commitment to a true Church and a just world. He is a very decent human being and friend.

Elaine Soffer, who has been a dear friend for a long time and has, even in her most critical evaluations, always been so unimaginably good about this project. Her community college students have had a teacher with heart and commitment.

Thanks to John Woods at *Catholic New York*, the Archdiocesan newspaper, for assisting me in my research and for providing several photographs to support the stories of the South Bronx and the Catholic Church in the 1980s.

Finally, to the good people at the libraries that served as my faithful resources over the years:

Kate Feighery of the Archdiocesan Archives at St. Joseph's Seminary, Yonkers; the staff of the Fordham University Library at Rose Hill Campus, Bronx; the staff of the Mid-Manhattan Library, New York Public Library; and the staff of the Research Library, New York Public Library, including those of the archives, periodicals/microfilm, and maps rooms. You did not know it, but you made these trips to these vast libraries such pleasant steps on this research journey.

NOTES

1. Puerto Rico

1. "Graduates for the Archdiocese of New York from St. Joseph's," *The Catholic News*, May 31, 1958, 15.

2. "Saint Joseph's Seminary (Dunwoodie)," Wikipedia, accessed June 3, 2014, http://en .wikipedia.org/wiki/Saint_Joseph's_Seminary (Dunwoodie).

3. Jay P. Dolan "The Catholic Ethos," in *The American Catholic Experience: A History from Colonial Times to the Present* (Garden City, NY: Doubleday, 1985), 221–240.

4. Lawrence J. McCaffrey, "Irish Catholics in America," in *Encyclopedia of American Catholic History*, ed. Michael Glazier and Thomas J. Shelley (Collegeville, MN: The Liturgical Press, 1997), 696–705.

5. "Going My Way," (1944), Plot Summary, Internet Movie Database (IMDb) https://www .imdb.com/title/tt0036872/plotsummary?ref_=tt_stry_pl#synopsis; "Boys Town" (1938), Plot Summary, Internet Movie Database (IMDb), https://www.imdb.com/title/tt0029942 /plotsummary?ref_=tt_ov_pl.

6. "Bus Strike Voted to Start Monday," *New York Times*, March 4, 1941, 21; "Buses Run Again as Walkout Ends," *New York Times*, March 23, 1941, 35.

7. Two oral history statements describing military activities of Cornelius Connolly in the Irish War for Independence, transcribed and stored on the "Military Archives" page of the *Oglaigh na hEireann (Defence Forces Ireland)* website, accessed December 2, 2019, http:// www.militaryarchives.ie/collections/online-collections/bureau-of-military-history-1913-1921, as follows:

—Bureau of Military History, 1913–1921, Statement by Witness, Witness: Cornelius Connolly, Lissenhuig, Skibbereen, County Cork.

—Bureau of Military History, 1913–21, Activities of Skibbereen Battalion, Cork III Brigade, IRA, 1917–1921 and Brigade Flying Column.

8. Brian Hanley, "Irish Republicans in Interwar New York," *Irish Journal of American Studies Online*, no. 2 (Summer 2010), accessed June 17, 2014, http://www.ijasonline.com/BRIAN-HANLEY.html.

9. "About Pilgrim Psychiatric Center," Office of Mental Health website, accessed August 18, 2014, https://omh.ny.gov/omhweb/facilities/pgpc/; "Pilgrim Psychiatric Center," Wikipedia, accessed July 15, 2020, https://en.wikipedia.org/wiki/Pilgrim_Psychiatric_Center.

10. "Fifty-Two from Archdiocese to Study in Puerto Rico," *The Catholic News*, May 31, 1958, 15; Robert L. Stern, "Formation for the Pastoral Care of Puerto Ricans," in *Bienvenidos, But . . . The Archdiocese of New York and Ministry to Hispanics, 1952–1982* (New York: Roman Catholic Archdiocese of New York, 1982), 21–22.

11. Pontifical Catholic University of Puerto Rico, accessed June 3, 2014, http://en.wikipedia.org/wiki/Pontifical_Catholic_University_of_Puerto_Rico.

12. Jaime R. Vidal, "The Great Migration," in *Puerto Rican and Cuban Catholics in the U.S., 1900–1965*, ed. Jay P. Dolan and Jaime R. Vidal (Notre Dame, IN: University of Notre Dame Press, 1994), 54–69; Ana Maria Diaz-Stevens, "The Stone and the Pitcher: Gospel Reality vs. Institutional Self-Interest," in *Oxcart Catholicism on Fifth Avenue: The Impact of the Puerto Rican Migration on the Archdiocese of New York* (Notre Dame, IN: University of Notre Dame Press, 1993), 14–18.

13. Virginia Sánchez Korrol and Pedro Juan Hernández, *Pioneros II: Puerto Ricans in New York City, 1948–1998* (Charleston, SC: Arcadia Publishing, 2010), 11.

14. Thomas J. Shelley, "From the Start—For 200 Years, the Church of New York's History Has Been an Immigrant Story," in *Archdiocese of New York: The Bicentennial History, 1808–2008* (Strasbourg: Éditions du Signe, 2007); J. J. Lee and Marion R. Casey, eds., *Making the Irish American: History and Heritage of the Irish in the United States* (New York: New York University Press, 2006); Thomas J. Shelley, "Twentieth-Century American Catholicism and Irish Americans," in *Making the Irish American: History and Heritage of the Irish in the United States*, ed. J. J. Lee and Marion R. Casey (New York: New York University Press, 2006), 574–608; Dolan, "The Catholic Ethos," 221–240.

15. Robert L. Stern, "National Parishes for the Spanish-Speaking," in *Bienvenidos, But . . . The Archdiocese of New York and Ministry to Hispanics, 1952–1982* (New York: Roman Catholic Archdiocese of New York, 1982), 3; Jaime R. Vidal, "Rejecting the Ethnic Parish Model," in *Puerto Rican and Cuban Catholics in the U.S., 1900–1965*, ed. Jay P. Dolan and Jaime R. Vidal (Notre Dame, IN: University of Notre Dame Press, 1994), 73–87; Vidal, "Ethnic Parish Model," 73–87; Robert L. Stern, "The Policy of the Integrated Parish," in *Bienvenidos, But . . . The Archdiocese of New York and Ministry to Hispanics, 1952–1982* (New York: Roman Catholic Archdiocese of New York, 1982), 17.

16. Jaime R. Vidal, "Implementing the Vision," in *Puerto Rican and Cuban Catholics in the U.S., 1900–1965*, ed. Jay P. Dolan and Jaime R. Vidal (Notre Dame, IN: University of Notre Dame Press, 1994), 92–101; Ana Maria Diaz-Stevens, "The Missionary Impulse and the Basement Churches," in *Oxcart Catholicism on Fifth Avenue: The Impact of the Puerto Rican Migration on the Archdiocese of New York* (Notre Dame, IN: University of Notre Dame Press, 1993), 104–109; Robert L. Stern, "The Coordinator of Spanish Catholic Action," in *Bienvenidos, But . . . The Archdiocese of New York and Ministry to Hispanics, 1952–1982* (New York: Roman Catholic Archdiocese of New York, 1982), 10.

17. Vidal, "Implementing the Vision," 101–107; Stern, "Pastoral Care of Puerto Ricans," 21. Harvey Cox, "Appreciation: A Prophet, a Teacher, a Realistic Dreamer," NCR Online, National

Catholic Reporter, accessed May 11, 2016; "Ivan Illich," entry in Wikipedia, accessed August 20, 2014, http://en.wikipedia.org/wiki/Ivan_Illich.

18. "Joseph Fitzpatrick," in *Encyclopedia of American Catholic History*, ed. Michael Glazier and Thomas J. Shelley (Collegeville, MN: The Liturgical Press, 1997), 513; Lawrence Van Gelder, "Rev. Joseph P. Fitzpatrick, 82, Fordham Migration Expert, Dies," *New York Times*, March 17, 1995, https://www.nytimes.com/1995/03/17/obituaries/rev-joseph-p-fitzpatrick-82 -fordham-migration-expert-dies.html"fordham-migration-expert-dies.html; Vidal, 88; Robert L. Stern, "The Puerto Rican Migration," in *Bienvenidos, But . . . The Archdiocese of New York and Ministry to Hispanics, 1952–1982* (New York: Roman Catholic Archdiocese of New York, 1982), 7.

19. Vidal, 101–107; Stern, "Pastoral Care of Puerto Ricans," 21; Floyd McCoy, "Catholic Church in Puerto Rico," in *The Encyclopedia of American Catholic History*, ed. Michael Glazier and Thomas J. Shelley (Collegeville, MN: Liturgical Press, 1997), 1180–1185.

20. Aida R. Caro Costas, "The Outpost of Empire," chap. 2 in *Puerto Rico: A Political and Cultural History*, ed. Arturo Morales Carrión (New York: W. W. Norton and Company, 1983); Aida R. Caro Costas, "Towards a Plantation Society," chap. 6 in *Puerto Rico: A Political and Cultural History*, ed. Arturo Morales Carrión (New York: W. W. Norton and Company, 1983).

21. Luis Gonzalez Vales, "The Challenge to Colonialism," chap. 7 in *Puerto Rico: A Political and Cultural History*, ed. Arturo Morales Carrión (New York: W. W. Norton and Company, 1983); Arturo Morales Carrión, "1898: The Hope and the Trauma," chap. 8 in *Puerto Rico: A Political and Cultural History*, ed. Arturo Morales Carrión (New York: W. W. Norton and Company, 1983).

22. Arturo Morales Carrión, "The Wilsonian Era in Puerto Rico," chap. 10 in *Puerto Rico: A Political and Cultural History*, ed. Arturo Morales Carrión (New York: W. W. Norton and Company, 1983).

23. Caro Costas, "Towards a Plantation Society."

24. Census of Population: 1960, Volume 1, Characteristics of the Population, Number of Inhabitants, General Population Characteristics, General Social and Economic Characteristics, and Detailed Characteristics, Part 53: Puerto Rico, U.S. Department of Commerce, Bureau of the Census; Caro Costas, "Towards a Plantation Society"; "Operation Bootstrap," Lehman College, Department of Latin American and Latino Studies, Puerto Rico History, accessed October 15, 2014, http://lcw.lehman.edu/lehman/depts/latinampuertorican/latinoweb/Puerto Rico/Bootstrap.htm.

25. Carrión, "1898"; Arturo Morales Carrión, "The Plight of the 1930s," chap. 12 in *Puerto Rico: A Political and Cultural History*, ed. Arturo Morales Carrion, (New York: W. W. Norton and Company, 1983).

26. Emilia Badillo Joy, "The Sugar Industry of Puerto Rico," *Puerto Rico en Breve*, www.preb .com/apuntes5/sugarind.htm accessed July 18, 2017; Carrión, "1898."

27. Carrión, "Plight of the 1930s"; "Operation Bootstrap," Lehman College, Department of Latin American and Latino Studies, Puerto Rico History.

28. Carrión, "Plight of the 1930s."

29. "Operation Bootstrap (1947)," Puerto Rico Encyclopedia, Fundación Puertorriqueña de las Humanidades, https://enciclopediapr.org/en/encyclopedia/operation-bootstrap-1947/; "Operation Bootstrap," Lehman College, Department of Latin American and Latino Studies, Puerto Rico History, accessed October 15, 2014, http://lcw.lehman.edu/lehman/depts/latin ampuertorican/latinoweb/PuertoRico/Bootstrap.htm; Arturo Morales Carrión, "The PPD

Hegemony (1944–1969)," in *Puerto Rico: A Political and Cultural History*, ed. Arturo Morales Carrión (New York: W. W. Norton and Company, 1983); César J. Ayala, "The Decline of the Plantation Economy and the Puerto Rican Migration of the 1950s," *Latino Studies Journal* 7, no. 1 (Winter 1996): 61–90.

30. "35% of Puerto Rican Women Sterilized," The Chicago Women's Liberation Union, The Herstory Project, Archive, http://www.cwluherstory.org/health/35-of-puerto-rican -women-sterilized; Kathryn Krase, "History of Forced Sterilization and Current U.S. Abuses," October 1, 2014, Our Bodies Our Selves, accessed October 28, 2019, http://ourbodiesourselves .org/book-excerpts/health-article/forced-sterilization/; Carrión, "Plight of the 1930s."

31. Virginia Sánchez Korrol, *From Colonia to Community: The History of Puerto Ricans in New York City* (Berkley and Los Angeles: University of California Press, 1983), 84–117.

32. Ana Maria Diaz-Stevens, "Island Within the Island: Faith and Institution in Puerto Rico," in *Oxcart Catholicism on Fifth Avenue: The Impact of the Puerto Rican Migration on the Archdiocese of New York* (Notre Dame, IN: University of Notre Dame Press, 1993), 44–52.

33. "Porto Rico," *Catholic Encyclopedia*, accessed August 19, 2014, http://www.newadvent .org/cathen/12291b.htm; "A Brief History of Religions and Religious Beliefs in Puerto Rico," Puerto Rico Encyclopedia, Fundación Puertorriqueña de las Humanidades, Grupo Editorial EPRL, September 20, 2010, accessed August 20, 2014, http://www.enciclopediapr.org/ing/print _version.cfm?ref+081003002; McCoy, "Catholic Church in Puerto Rico," 1180–1185.

34. Diaz-Stevens, "Faith and Institution," 44–52; "Brief History of Religions"; "Catholicism in Puerto Rico," The Teodoro Vidal Collection/Religion, National Museum of American History, http://amhistory.si.edu/vidal/about/?id=4.

35. Diaz-Stevens, 44–52; "Brief History of Religions."

36. "Historia Chea," Congregación Misionera de San Juan Evangelista Hermanos Cheos, accessed July 18, 2017, http://www.hermanoscheos.org/index.html; Edward Louis Cleary, "Hermanos Cheos: Lay Preachers Who Preserved Catholicism," Providence College, February 19, 2009, accessed August 21, 2014, http://ssrn.com/abstract=t346413.

2. The New Parish

1. "Injured Boxer Remains in Critical Condition," October 25, 2012, http://www.boxinggyms .com/news/marciano_vingo1950/marciano_vingo.htm; *The Boxing News/The Poughkeepsie New Yorker,* January 1, 1950.

2. "Population of New York, by Counties: 1950 and 1940," U.S. Census, 1950, Department of Commerce, Washington, D.C.; "New York State; Area and Population of Counties, Urban and Rural: 1960 and 1950," 1960, U.S. Census, Department of Commerce, Washington, D.C.; "Table 1—New York City; Characteristics of the Population by Census Tracts: 1950, Bronx Borough," U.S. Census, Department of Commerce, Washington, D.C.

3. "Table P-1, New York City, General Characteristics of the Population, by Census Tracts: 1960, Bronx Borough," U.S. Census, Department of Commerce, Washington, D.C.

4. "Table P-1, New York City, General Characteristics of the Population, by Census Tracts: 1960, Bronx Borough," U.S. Census, Department of Commerce, Washington, D.C.

5. "Table P-1, New York City, General Characteristics of the Population, by Census Tracts: 1960, Bronx Borough," U.S. Census, Department of Commerce, Washington, D.C.

6. "Housing Act of 1949: Summary of Provisions of the National Housing Act of 1949," Committee on Banking and Currency, United States Senate, U.S. Government Printing Office: Washington, D.C., 1949; "A Study in Contradictions: The Origins and Legacy of the Housing

Act of 1949," Alexander von Hoffman, Harvard University, Housing Policy Debate, Volume II, Issue 2, Fannie Mae Foundation, 2000.

7. "Report on New York City Slum Clearance Program Under Title I of the Federal Housing Act of 1949," September 30, 1958, Robert Moses, Chairman, Mayor's Committee on Slum Clearance; Wayne Phillips, "Scandal Charges Buffet Title I Projects in City," *New York Times*, July 1, 1959, 23; Steven V. Roberts, "Decisions Nearing on Urban Renewal Projects Planned Under Mayor Wagner," *New York Times*, May 3, 1966, 29; Wayne Phillips, "Unorthodox Title I Procedures used by Moses Create Disputes," *New York Times*, June 30, 1959, 1.

8. "National Housing Act of 1934," accessed November 2, 2019, https://www.encyclopedia .com/economics/encyclopedias-almanacs-transcripts-and-maps/national-housing-act-1934; "Housing Act of 1937," Wikipedia, accessed November 11, 2015, https://en.wikipedia.org/wiki /Housing_Act_of_1937.

9. "Project Statistics, June 30, 1962," New York City Housing Authority, New York, 1962, Gerald J. Carey, General Manager; "New York City Public Housing, 1934–Present," Presentation by Tania Branquinho, Elena Conte, Alyssa S. Gerber, Chirstopher Korwel, Alexis Rourk, Sabrina Terry, Pratt Center for Community and Economic Development, Brooklyn, https://nyspexchange.files.wordpress.com/2010/06/4-100318-nyc-publichousingpresentation final11.pdf; Richard Rothstein, "Race and Public Housing: Revisiting the Federal Role," *Poverty and Race*, December 17, 2012.

10. "Report on New York City Slum Clearance Program under Title I of the Federal Housing Act of 1949," September 30, 1958, Robert Moses, Chairman, Mayor's Committee on Slum Clearance.

11. Megan Roby, "The Push and Pull Dynamics of White Flight: A Study of the Bronx Between 1950 and 1980," *The Bronx County Historical Society Journal* 55, nos. 1 and 2 (Spring/Fall 2008): 1–55; "How We Got Here: The Historical Roots of Housing Segregation," The Future of Fair Housing: Report of the National Commission on Fair Housing and Equal Opportunity, December 2008, accessed November 2, 2019, https://www.naacpldf.org/wp -content/uploads/Future-of-Fair-Housing__Economic-Justice__.pdf.

12. Roby, "Push and Pull Dynamics," 1–55.

13. "How We Got Here."

14. Roby, 1–55; Sydney Gruson, "Our Changing City: New Faces in the Lower Bronx," *New York Times*, July 11, 1955, 25.

15. "City Aide Calls One-Room Homes in 700 Old Buildings Slum Evils," *New York Times*, November 16, 1959, 37.

16. "Table 1, New York City, Characteristics of the Population by Census Tracts: 1950, Bronx Borough," U.S. Census, Department of Commerce, Washington, D.C.; "Table H-2, New York City, Year Moved into Unit, Automobile Available and Value of Rent of Occupied Housing Units, by Census Tracts: 1960, Bronx Borough," U.S. Census, Department of Commerce, Washington, D.C.; "Table P-1, New York City, General Characteristics of the Population, by Census Tracts: 1960, Bronx Borough," U.S. Census, Department of Commerce, Washington, D.C.

17. "Table H-2, New York City, Year Moved into Unit, Automobile Available and Value of Rent of Occupied Housing Units, by Census Tracts: 1960, Bronx Borough," U.S. Census, Department of Commerce, Washington, D.C.; "Table 2, New York City, Characteristics of Housing by Census Tracts: 1950, Bronx Borough," U.S. Census, Department of Commerce, Washington, D.C.

18. Judith Greene and Kevin Pranis, "Gangs in New York City," *Gang Wars: The Failure of Enforcement Tactics and the Need for Effective Public Safety Strategies,* Justice Policy Institute

Report, July 2007, chap. 1, 15; "Racial Tension Up in East Bronx Area," *New York Times*, April 24, 1947, 30, col. 1; "New York—Nits vs. Stompers," *New York Times*, *Week in Review*, sec. IV, June 4, 1950, 2.

19. McCandlish Phillips, "Violence on Rise among Girl Gangs," *New York Times*, July 17, 1961, 23, col. 1; Murray Schumach, "The Teen-Age Gang: Who and Why," *New York Times*, September 2, 1956, sec. VI, 7, col. 1.

20. Ira Henry Freeman, "Few Gang Battles Laid to Race Bias," *New York Times*, August 19, 1956, 80.

21. "3 Hurt in Battle at Coney Island; 12 Held After Free-for-All—High Bail Is Set for 8 in Orchard Beach Case," *New York Times*, June 25, 1957, 60; "Bronx Judge Says P.A.L. Unit Knew Gang Planned Beach War," *New York Times*, January 8, 1958, 22.

22. "Violence Trails Teenage Gangs," *New York Times*, April 28, 1958, 15.

23. The full-page advertisement was posted with 162 organizations as signatories, including St. Athanasius R.C. Church, Bronx; see also "We Too Fight Delinquency," Puerto Rican Self-Help Community Program, *New York Times*, September 23, 1959, 16.

24. Alfonso A. Narvaez, "Clubs in City Substitute for Puerto Rican Plaza," *New York Times*, March 23, 1970, 43; "We Too Fight Delinquency."

25. Gertrude Samuels, "Number 1 Project for the City," *New York Times*, June 29, 1958, sec. VI, 10; "City to Add Police in Summer Spots," *New York Times*, April 28, 1958, 15, col. 5.

26. Samuels, "Number 1 Project," 10.

27. Robert Rice, "Who You Are and What You Think You're Doing," *New Yorker*, December 23, 1961, accessed January 30, 2015, http://archives.newyorker.com/global/print.asp ?path/djvu/CondeNast/NewYorker/1961; Samuels, 10; Ira Henry Freeman, "Youth Board Saw Gang Tension Rise," *New York Times*, September 23, 1959, 30; Greene and Pranis, "Gangs in New York City," 15.

28. Samuels, 10; Rice, "Who You Are."

29. Rice, "Who You Are"; Freeman, "Youth Board," 30.

30. "Places That Matter: Hunts Point Palace," accessed June 17, 2014, http://www .placematters.net/node/1243.

31. "Puerto Rican Settlement House Is Moving to Bronx Next Year," *New York Times*, November 19, 1961, 125, col. 4.

32. Bill Bullivant, "New St. Athanasius School Schedules October 5 Opening," *Catholic News*, September 30, 1965.

33. "Reverend Charles Coughlin (1891–1979)," *The American Experience: America and the Holocaust/People and Events* (Public Broadcasting System), accessed September 30, 2014, http://www.pbs.org/wgbh/amex/holocaust/peopleevents/pandeAMEX.html; "Charles Coughlin," Wikipedia, accessed June 3, 2014, http://en.wikipedia.org/wiki/Charles_Coughlin.

34. "Guide to the Louis F. Budenz Papers," Providence College, Phillips Memorial Library/ Special and Archival Collections, accessed November 2, 2019, http://library.providence.edu /spcol/fa/xml/rppc_budenz.xml.

The *New York Times* regularly published announcements of the annual Holy Name Society Communion Breakfasts sponsored by various Manhattan parishes, usually in springtime. Breakfasts typically sponsored a keynote speaker, and Louis Budenz was one of them. An internationally recognized Catholic laypersons' organization, originally all-male, with active chapters in the New York City police, fire, and corrections departments, the Holy Name Society dates back to its founding in 1571; see also "History of the Holy Name Society," accessed November 2, 2019, http://www.nahns.com/Website/AboutHNS/HistoryHNS.htm.

35. Father Bruce Nieli, "A Return to Catholic Action," *U.S. Catholic: Faith in Real Life*, http://www.uscatholic.org/articles/201506/return-catholic-action-30210; "Canon Joseph Cardijn (1882–1967)," *Catholic Authors.Com: Your Guide to Catholic Literature*, accessed March 6, 2014, http://www.catholicauthors.com/cardijn.html.

36. Robert McClory, "Can the Old-Movement Spirit Power the New Francis Movement?," *NCR Today*, March 12, 2014, accessed January 13, 2015, http://ncronline.org/blogs/ncr-today /can-old-movement-spirit-power-new-francis-movement.

37. Jocist Movement and CFM; Meirad Scherer Edmunds, "See-Judge-Act: How Young Christian Workers Renewed the Church," *Salt of the Earth*, accessed January 13, 2015, https:// d3n8a8pro7vhmx.cloudfront.net/cfmusa/pages/109/attachments/original/1452567834/jocist.pdf ?1452567834; "History," Christian Family Movement, accessed January 13, 2015, http://www .cfm.org/history.html.

38. "St. Francis Hospital (New York City)," Find Glocal, accessed November 2, 2019, http:// www.findglocal.com/US/New-York/1487317631518329/St.-Francis-Hospital-%28New-York-City %29; "St. Francis Hospital," The New York City Chapter of the American Guild of Organists, accessed November 2, 2019, http://www.nycago.org/Organs/Brx/html/StFrancisHosp.html.

39. Robert L. Stern, "The San Juan Fiesta" and "The Expansion of the Fiesta of San Juan Bautista," in *Bienvenidos But . . . The Archdiocese of New York and Ministry to Hispanics, 1952– 1982* (New York: Roman Catholic Archdiocese of New York, 1982), 11, 20, respectively; "40,000 Puerto Ricans Here Join in Fiesta of Their Parton Saint," *New York Times*, June 16, 1958, 25.

40. "Historia de la Devoción a Nuestra Señora Madre de la Divina Providencia," Puerto Rico en Breve/Nuestra trayectoria historica y cultural, accessed October 31, 2019, http://www.preb .com/amen/vprovide.htm.

41. Robert L. Stern, "New Directions," in *Bienvenidos But . . . The Archdiocese of New York and Ministry to Hispanics, 1952–1982* (New York: Roman Catholic Archdiocese of New York, 1982), 11–19.

42. Monsignor John Ahern, in interview with author, Old St. Patrick's Cathedral, New York, January 14, 2015.

3. A Changed Church, a Changed Role

1. Xavier Rynne, "Letter from Vatican City," *New Yorker*, October 21, 1962, 1–13.

2. R. F. Trisco and A. Komonchok, "Vatican Council II," in *New Catholic Encyclopedia*, ed. Catholic University of America (New York: McGraw Hill, 1967), 407–418.

3. Rynne, "Letter from Vatican City," 1–13.

4. Rynne, 1–13.

5. Rynne, 1–13.

6. R. F. Trisco, "John XXIII, Pope, BL," in *New Catholic Encyclopedia*, ed. Catholic University of America (New York: McGraw Hill, 1967), 932–938; Rynne, 1–13.

7. Rynne, 1–13.

8. Rynne, 1–13.

9. Rynne, 1–13.

10. P. Gransfield, "Paul VI, Pope," in *New Catholic Encyclopedia*, ed. Catholic University of America (New York: McGraw Hill, 1967), 26–33; Xavier Rynne, "Letter from Vatican City," *New Yorker*, July 20, 1963.

11. Xavier Rynne, "Letter from Vatican City," *New Yorker*, May 11, 1963; Xavier Rynne, "Letter from Vatican City," *New Yorker*, November 30, 1963.

12. Xavier Rynne, "Letter from Vatican City," *New Yorker*, September 28, 1963.

13. Edward P. Hahnenberg, "Constitution on the Sacred Liturgy," in *A Concise Guide to the Documents of Vatican II* (Cincinnati, OH: St. Anthony Messenger Press, 2007), 16.

14. Xavier Rynne, "Letter from Vatican City," *New Yorker*, January 9, 1965.

15. Xavier Rynne, "Letter from Vatican City," *New Yorker*, January 9, 1965.

16. *Sacrosanctum Concilium* ("The Holy Council"), Constitution on the Sacred Liturgy, Promulgated by His Holiness Pope Paul VI, Vatican Council II, December 4, 1963; "Catholic Worker Movement," in *Encyclopedia of American Catholic History*, ed. Michael Glazier and Thomas J. Shelley (Collegeville, MN: The Liturgical Press, 1997), 413–417.

17. *Unitatis Redintegratio*, Decree on Ecumenism, Promulgated by His Holiness Pope Paul VI, Vatican Council II, 1964.

18. *Orientatum Ecclesarium*, Decree on the Catholic Churches of the Eastern Rite, Promulgated by His Holiness Pope Paul VI, Vatican Council II, 1964.

19. *Nostra Aetate*, Declaration on the Relation of the Church to Non-Christian Religions, Promulgated by His Holiness Pope Paul VI, Vatican Council II, 1965.

20. *Dei Verbum*, Dogmatic Constitution on Divine Revelation, Promulgated by His Holiness Pope Paul VI, Vatican Council II, 1965.

21. *Divino Afflante Espiritu* ("Inspired by the Holy Spirit"), Pope Pius XII, September 30, 1943.

22. *Christus Dominus*, Decree Concerning the Pastoral Office of Bishops in the Church, Promulgated by His Holiness Pope Paul VI, Vatican Council II, 1965.

23. *Lumen Gentium*, Dogmatic Constitution on the Church, Promulgated by His Holiness Pope Paul VI, Vatican Council II, November 21, 1964.

24. "Chapter I: Ecclesiology," *Lumen Gentium*, Dogmatic Constitution on the Church, Promulgated by His Holiness Pope Paul VI, Vatican Council II, November 21, 1964.

25. "Chapter II: People of God" and "Chapter IV: Priesthood of the Faithful," *Lumen Gentium*, Dogmatic Constitution on the Church, Promulgated by His Holiness Pope Paul VI, Vatican Council II, November 21, 1964.

26. John Cogley, "United Nations: The Pope as Ancient Prophet," *New York Times*, October 6, 1965, 4, col. 1, 3; "Text of Pope Paul's Speech at U.N. Appealing for an End to War and Offensive Arms," *New York Times*, October 6, 1965, 6–7; John Cogley, "Pope Announces Jubilee Year Stressing Role of the Bishops," *New York Times*, December 7, 1965, 9, col. 3.

27. Edward B. Fiske, "Catholic Bishops Map Wider Role," *New York Times*, April 11, 1967, 42, col. 4; "Text of Bishops' Pastoral Statement on Peace and Vietnam," *New York Times*, November 22, 1966, 18, col. 2–3.

28. "The Bishops and the Farm Labor Dispute," American Catholic History Classroom; American Catholic History Research Center and University Archives, accessed December 5, 2019, https://cuomeka.wrlc.org/exhibits/show/chavez-higgins-site/documents/-the-bishops-and -the-farm-labo; Marco G. Prouty, "César Chávez, the Catholic Bishops, and the Farmworkers' Struggle for Social Justice," promotion on University of Arizona Press website, accessed December 5, 2019, https://uapress.arizona.edu/book/cesar-chavez-the-catholic-bishops-and-the -farmworkers-struggle-for-social-justice.

29. John Cogley, "Catholic Religious Seek Modern Role," *New York Times*, June 19, 1966, 71, col. 1; Daniel Callahan, "Sister Jacqueline Becomes Miss Grennan and Dramatizes a Crisis in Catholic Education," *New York Times*, sec. IV, 4, col. 3; Diane Winston, "How a Group of California Nuns Challenged the Catholic Church," The Conversation, December 6, 2017, accessed December 5, 2019, http://theconversation.com/how-a-group-of-california-nuns -challenged-the-catholic-church-83944.

30. Cogley, "Catholic Religious," 71; Amy L. Koehlinger, "Demythologizing Catholic Women Religious in the 1960s," *Journal of Southern Religion*, http://jsr.fsu.edu/Volume10 /Koehlinger.htm; "How Nuns Changed Everything: A History of Catholic Sisters of the Midwest," Sisters of St. Benedict/St. Mary Monastery (Illinois) website, accessed December 5, 2019, https://www.smmsisters.org/who-we-are/sister-stories/88/how-nuns-changed-everything-a -history-of-catholic-sisters-of-the-midwest.

31. *Perfectae Caritatis*, Decree on the Appropriate Renewal of Religious Life, Promulgated by His Holiness Pope Paul VI, Vatican Council II, 1965.

32. Edward B. Fiske, "Catholic Laymen in Chicago Unite," *New York Times*, April 2, 1967, 30, col. 2; "Catholic Laymen to Form Long Island Group," *New York Times*, May 6, 1967, 20, col. 1.

33. John Cogley, "Membership in Glenmary Nuns Curtailed by Cincinnati Prelate," *New York Times*, September 25, 1966, 72, col. 3.

34. "Bishop Bans Folk Music throughout Texas Diocese," *New York Times*, February 21, 1966, 10, col. 8.

35. "Catholic Laymen in Dallas Parish Start a Protest," *New York Times*, May 29, 1967, 22, col. 4.

36. Austin Wehrweiss, "Second Milwaukee Priest Told to Quit Public School Boycott," *New York Times*, October 21, 1965, 30, col. 1.

37. John Cogley, "Vatican Reproves Cleric on Coast," *New York Times*, August 10, 1966, 84, col. 1.

38. George Dugan, "Priest in Jersey Stripped of Duty," *New York Times*, September 14, 1967, 49, col. 1.

39. *Gaudium et Spes*, The Pastoral Constitution on the Church in the Modern World, Promulgated by His Holiness Pope Paul VI, Vatican Council II, 1965.

40. Msgr. George Higgins, "Schema 13 Will Be Drastically Revised," *Catholic News Service Vatican II Anniversary*, "Vatican II: 50 Years Ago Today," dedicated to a review of events and developments as they occurred at Vatican Council II, November 20, 2014, accessed December 5, 2019, https://vaticaniiat50.wordpress.com/2014/11/20/schema-13-will-be-drastically-revised/; Edward P. Hahnenberg, "Constitution on the Church in the Modern World," in *A Concise Guide to the Documents of Vatican II* (Cincinnati, OH: St. Anthony Messenger Press, 2007), 58.

41. "About NCR," accessed November 6, 2019, http://ncrnews.org/advertising/Media_Kit .pdf.

42. "Chapter I: The Dignity of the Human Person," and "Chapter II: The Community of Mankind," *Gaudium et Spes*, The Pastoral Constitution on the Church in the Modern World, Promulgated by His Holiness Pope Paul VI, Vatican Council II, 1965.

43. "Section 1, Economic Development" and "Section 2, Certain Principles Governing Socio-Economic Life as a Whole," in "Chapter III: Economic and Social Life," *Gaudium et Spes*, The Pastoral Constitution on the Church in the Modern World, Promulgated by His Holiness Pope Paul VI, Vatican Council II, 1965, 70–78.

44. "Section 1, Economic Development" and "Section 2, Certain Principles Governing Socio-Economic Life as a Whole," "Chapter III: Economic and Social Life," *Gaudium et Spes*, The Pastoral Constitution on the Church in the Modern World. Promulgated by His Holiness Pope Paul VI. Vatican Council II. 1965.

45. "Section 1, Economic Development" and "Section 2, Certain Principles Governing Socio-Economic Life as a Whole," "Chapter III: Economic and Social Life," *Gaudium et Spes*, The Pastoral Constitution on the Church in the Modern World. Promulgated by His Holiness Pope Paul VI, Vatican Council II, 1965.

46. *Rerum Novarum,* Encyclical of Pope Leo XIII on Capital and Labor, May 15, 1891, accessed November 6, 2019, http://w2.vatican.va/content/leo-xiii/en/encyclicals/documents/hf_l-xiii_enc_15051891_rerum-novarum.html.

47. James Martin, S.J., "Fr. Corridan: Karl Malden's 'Waterfront' Inspiration," *America,* July 1, 2009, accessed December 5, 2019, https://www.americamagazine.org/content/all-things/fr-corridan-karl-maldens-waterfront-inspiration; Wolfgang Saxon, "John M. Corridan, 73, the 'Waterfront Priest,'" *New York Times,* July 3, 1984, sec. B, 8.

48. "Chapter III: Man's Activity throughout the World" *Gaudium et Spes,* The Pastoral Constitution on the Church in the Modern World, Promulgated by His Holiness Pope Paul VI, Vatican Council II, 1965, 37–38.

49. "Eddie Condon's," Wikipedia, accessed June 1, 2014, http://en.wikipedia.org/wiki/Eddie_Condon.

4. Summer in the City

1. "Text of President Johnson's Economic Report on the Nation's Economic Progress and Trends," *New York Times,* January 21, 1964, 16, col. 1–8; "Text of President Johnson's Special Message on Poverty Presented to Congress," *New York Times,* March 17, 1964, 22, col. 1–5.

2. "Text of President's Message on Housing and Community Development," *New York Times,* January 27, 1964, 16, col. 1–8.

3. "Main Programs of the War on Poverty," *Congressional Digest* 47, no. 1, January 1, 1968, 2, Obtained via EBSCO March 23, 2015.

4. "Main Programs of the War on Poverty," *Congressional Digest* 47, no. 1, January 1, 1968, 2, Obtained via EBSCO March 23, 2015.

5. A. H. Raskin, "Generalissimo of the War on Poverty," *New York Times,* November 22, 1964, sec. IV, 39.

6. Natalie Jaffe, "Poor to Convene to Pick Leaders," *New York Times,* July 28, 1965, 13, col.1

7. Charles Mohr, "President Spurs Poverty Fighters," *New York Times,* December 13, 1964, 60; "Civilians Enlist in Poverty War," *New York Times,* January 17, 1965, 43, col. 4; Paul L. Montgomery, "Poverty Program Is Ready to Begin," *New York Times,* July 3, 1965, 7, col. 5.

8. Jaffe, "Poor to Convene," 13.

9. Fred Powledge, "Politicians Eye Antipoverty Plan," *New York Times,* November 28, 1965, 139;

Joseph A. Loftus, "Election of Poor May Be Ended, Shriver Tells House Committee," *New York Times,* March 9, 1966, 24, col. 3.

10. Fred Powledge, "$52 Million in Aid Due for City Poor," *New York Times,* November 25, 1965, 51, col. 1.

11. John C. Devlin, "Hunts Point Follows the Pattern of Poverty," *New York Times,* March 23, 1964, 33.

12. "Catholics Planning Activities for the Poor," *New York Times,* May 3, 1965, 18, col. 4.

13. George Dugan, "Fight on Poverty in 35 Parishes Here Set by Cardinal Spellman," *New York Times,* May 6, 1965, 32, col. 7; Author Interview with Monsignor John Ahern, in interview with author, Old St. Patrick's Cathedral, New York, January 14, 2015.

14. Dugan, "Fight on Poverty," 32; "Poverty Requests," *New York Times,* June 9, 1965, 26, col. 1.

15. Monsignor Robert J. Fox, "Keynote Address," Summer in the City Orientation Weekend (Document), Mount St. Vincent College, June 1, 1966.

16. Fox, "Keynote Address."

17. Fox, "Keynote Address."

18. Fox, "Keynote Address," 9.

19. Fox, "Keynote Address."

20. Fox, "Keynote Address," 11.

21. Fox, "Keynote Address," 11.

22. Mary Cole, *Summer in the City—Monsignor Fox's Program* (New York: R. J. Kenedy, 1968.)

Fox, "Keynote Address."

23. Homer Bigart, "Looters Invade Manhattan; East Harlem Stays Calm," *New York Times*, July 27, 1967, 1; James Stevenson, "Reporter at Large: The People, All the People," *New Yorker*, July 29, 1967, 141–151.

24. Hope Macleod, "Man in the News: Msgr. Robert Fox—A Living Link Between Slums and Suburbs," *New York Post Magazine*, 2, April 27, 1968; Robert Carroll, "5,000 from Where It's Better Fight Slum Dirt," *New York Daily News*, April 27, 1968, 2, col. 1.

25. Robert L. Stern, "Project Engage," in *Bienvenidos, But . . . The Archdiocese of New York and Ministry to Hispanics, 1952–1982* (New York: Roman Catholic Archdiocese of New York, 1982), 31.

26. Lillian Camejo, in interview with author, Camejo Residence, Bronx, New York, August 13, 2015.

27. Edgard Beltrán receives "Virgilio Elizondo Award" from the Academy of Catholic Hispanic Theologians of the United States at the V National Encuentro of Hispanic Latino Ministry," event website, https://vencuentro.org/edgard-beltran-receives-virgilio-elizondo-award-from-achtus/; Hoffman Ospino and Rafael Luciano, "How Latin America Influenced the Entire Catholic Church," *America*, August 21, 2018, accessed November 7, 2019, https://www.americamagazine.org/faith/2018/08/21/how-latin-america-influenced-entire-catholic-church.

28. "Christian Base Communities," Encyclopedia.com, accessed November 7, 2019, https://www.encyclopedia.com/humanities/encyclopedias-almanacs-transcripts-and-maps/christian-base-communities.

29. Dr. Paul Davies, "'Ecclesiogenesis': Base Ecclesial Communities in Contemporary Perspective," All Nations—Training for Mission website, accessed November 7, 2019, https://encountersmissionjournal.files.wordpress.com/2011/03/ecclesiogenesis_base_ecclesial_communities_in_contemporary_perspective_23.pdf.

30. "The Spread of the Early Church," Christianity.com, accessed November 7, 2019, https://www.christianity.com/church/church-history/timeline/1-300/the-spread-of-the-early-church-11629561.html.

31. James Allaire and Rosemary Broughton, "An Introduction to the Life and Spirituality of Dorothy Day," Catholic Worker Movement, accessed November 7, 2019, https://www.catholicworker.org/dorothyday/life-and-spirituality.html.

32. "Aguinaldos Navideños," *El Boricua*, accessed November 7, 2019, http://elboricua.com/aguilnados.html; "Parranda," Wikipedia, accessed November 7, 2019, https://en.wikipedia.org/wiki/Parranda.

5. World Struggles, Parish Struggles

1. Status Animarum, Annual Statistical Parish Reports submitted to the Roman Catholic Archdiocese of New York, 1945–1975, Reports from Saint Athanasius R.C. Church, Bronx, New

York, obtained at the Archives of the Archdiocese of New York, at St. Joseph Seminary, Yonkers, New York, March 27, 2015.

2. "Father John Byrne," *Catholic New York*, December 20, 1984, 13.

3. Status Animarum, Annual Statistical Parish Reports submitted to the Roman Catholic Archdiocese of New York, 1945–1975, Reports from Saint Athanasius R.C. Church, Bronx, New York, obtained at the Archives of the Archdiocese of New York, at St. Joseph Seminary, Yonkers, New York, March 27, 2015.

4. Charles G. Bennett, "City's Economic Picture Mixed," *New York Times*, June 8, 1968, 33, col. 1.

5. Will Lissner, "U.S. Study Finds City's Poorest Are Puerto Ricans in the Slums," *New York Times*, November 17, 1969, 32, col. 1.

6. Richard E. Mooney, "Parley on Jobs for Puerto Ricans Cites 'Frustration and Despair,'" *New York Times*, May 22, 1968, 94, col. 2.

7. Peter Kihss, "Woes of Puerto Ricans in New York Found Increasing," *New York Times*, July 25, 1968, 25.

8. "Table A-7, Selected Housing Characteristics by Location in a Census Tract with a Poverty Rate of 20 Percent or More: 1970, New York, N.Y., Bronx County," United States Census, Department of Commerce, 1970.

9. "Table H-1, Occupancy, Utilization and Financial Characteristics of Housing Units: 1970," Census Tracts, New York City (part in Bronx County), United States Census, Department of Commerce, 1970.

10. "Table H-1, Occupancy, Utilization and Financial Characteristics of Housing Units: 1970," Census Tracts, New York City (part in Bronx County), United States Census, Department of Commerce, 1970.

11. "Table H-2, Structural, Equipment and Financial Characteristics of Housing Units: 1970," Census Tracts, New York City (part in Bronx County), United States Census, Department of Commerce, 1970.

12. Mooney, "Parley on Jobs," 94.

13. "Table P-7, General and Social Characteristics of Persons of Puerto Rican Birth or Parentage: 1970, Census Tracts with 400 More Persons of Puerto Rican Birth or Parentage, New York City (part in Bronx County), United States Census, Department of Commerce, 1970.

14. "St. Athanasius Church," Wikipedia, accessed November 11, 2019, https://en.wikipedia .org/wiki/St._Athanasius_Church_(Bronx).

15. "Sister Margaret Dowling, S.C.," *Catholic New York*, May 24, 2007, accessed November 11, 2019, http://www.cny.org/stories/sister-margaret-dowling-sc,4981; Robert L. Stern, *Bienvenidos, But . . . The Archdiocese of New York and Ministry to Hispanics, 1952–1982* (New York: Roman Catholic Archdiocese of New York, 1982).

16. "In Memoriam: Sister Ann Marie Lafferty, S.C.," Sisters of Charity, July 22, 2019, accessed November 11, 2019, https://www.scny.org/in-memoriam-sister-ann-marie-lafferty-sc/; Ann Marie Lafferty, in interview with author, November 11, 2016.

17. "Narcotics Addicts on Increase in City," *New York Times*, April 18, 1950, 22.

18. Clayton Knowles, "City Youth Addicts Estimated at 7,500," *New York Times*, November 25, 1953, 14.

19. John Wicklein, "Parish Is Seeking Care for Addicts," *New York Times*, February 23, 1959, 25; "Church Plea Made for Narcotics Bill," *New York Times*, March 28, 1960, 31, col. 1.

20. Peter Kihss, "100,000 Addicts Reported in City," *New York Times*, December 14, 1967, 52, col. 1.

21. Kihss, "100,000 Addicts," 52.

22. Kihss, "100,000 Addicts," 52.

23. Michael T. Kaufman, "Youths in Morrisania Section of Bronx Plagued by Narcotics," *New York Times*, October 31, 1969, 38, col. 2.

24. Kaufman, "Youths in Morrisania," 38, col. 2.

25. David K. Shipler, "Bronx Glue Angels Fly High," *New York Times*, August 3, 1968, 27, col. 1.

26. Thomas F. Brady, "Care Center Chief Sees 100,000 Child Addicts Here by Summer," *New York Times*, January 25, 1970, 37, col. 1; "Sharp Rise Is Found in Narcotics Users in the City Schools," *New York Times*, June 15, 1962, 29.

27. Grace Lichtenstein, "Addict Care Need Called Limitless," *New York Times*, November 29, 1970, 75.

28. Richard Severo, "Children's Narcotics Center Established in the Bronx," *New York Times*, October 7, 1969, 49.

29. Annual Report of the New York City Police Department, Howard R. Leary, Commissioner, Years 1960–1969, obtained via archives at Special Collections Room, Lloyd Sealy Library, John Jay College, City University of New York, June 25, 2015; "Major Crimes Up 20% in Nation," *New York Times*, June 16, 1967, 45, col. 7.

30. David Burnham, "Six Precincts in Slum Areas Produce Third of City's Violent Crimes," *New York Times*, January 29, 1968, 1, col. 2

31. Burnham, "Six Precincts," 1.

32. Burnham, "Six Precincts," 1.

33. Edward P. Eismann, "Unitas: Therapy for Youth in a Street Society," in *Handbook of Community-Based Clinical Practice*, ed. Anita Lightburn and Phebe Sessions (New York: Oxford University Press, 2005; "The Community Mental Health Act of 1963," Young Minds Advocacy, accessed November 11, 2019, https://www.ymadvocacy.org/the-community-mental-health-act-of -1963/; Mark Munetz and William Zumbar, "Community Mental Health Services: Historical Overview," Encyclopedia.com, accessed November 11, 2019, https://www.encyclopedia.com/ medicine/psychology/psychology-and-psychiatry/community-mental-health.

34. Eismann, "Unitas"; Edward P. Eismann, "Unitas: Building Healing Communities for Children: A Developmental and Training Manual," *Monograph No.8,* Hispanic Research Center, Fordham University, New York, 1982.

35. Mark L. Ruffalo, D.Psa., LCSW, "A Brief History of Electroconvulsive Therapy," *Psychology Today*, November 3, 2018, accessed November 11, 2019, https://www.psychology today.com/us/blog/freud-fluoxetine/201811/brief-history-electroconvulsive-therapy.

6. Organizing Priests

1. Eleanor Blau, "Archdiocese Here to Start an Advertising Drive to Recruit Priests," *New York Times,* November 20, 1973, 81; John Deedy, "Defections from Authority and the Institution Itself," *New York Times*, December 16, 1973, 244.

2. "Cody Accepts Proposals from Chicago Priests' Association," *National Catholic Reporter*, November 11, 1966, 7.

3. "Msgr. Schultheiss," *Catholic New York*, November 13, 1986, 33.

4. "Table P-2, Social Characteristics of the Population: 1970," Census Tracts, New York City (part in Bronx County), U.S. Census, Department of Commerce; "Table P-7, General and Social Characteristics of Persons of Puerto Rican Birth or Parentage: 1970," Census Tracts, New York City (part in Bronx County), U.S. Census, Department of Commerce.

5. "Cross Bronx Expressway," Wikipedia, accessed April 30, 2015, "http://en.wikipedia.org/w/index.php?title=Cross_Bronx_Expressway&printable=yes"printable=yes.

6. "Table P-2, Social Characteristics of the Population: 1970," Census Tracts, New York City (part in Bronx County), U.S. Census, Department of Commerce; "Table P-7, General and Social Characteristics of Persons of Puerto Rican Birth or Parentage: 1970," Census Tracts, New York City (part in Bronx County), U.S. Census, Department of Commerce.

7. "Dedication Held for Co-op City," Bronx Press Review, November 25, 1968; "Co-op City, Bronx," Wikipedia, accessed March 18, 2013, "http://en.wikipedia.org/w/index.php?title=Co-op_City_Bronx&printable=yes"printable=yes.

8. "Table P-4, Income Characteristics of the Population: 1970," Census Tracts, New York City (part in Bronx County), U.S. Census, Department of Commerce.

"Table H-5, Characteristics of Housing Units with Household Head of Puerto Rican Birth or Parentage: 1970," Census Tracts with 400 or More Persons of Puerto Rican Birth or Parentage, New York City (part in Bronx County), U.S. Census, Department of Commerce.

9. Status Animarum, Report of the Parish to the Roman Catholic Archdiocese of New York, submitted by 24 parishes of the South Bronx, Period: 1945–1975, The Archives of the Roman Catholic Archdiocese of New York, reviewed at the library of St. Joseph Seminary, Yonkers, New York.

10. "Spellman Death Marks End of an Era," National Catholic Reporter, December 19, 1967, 1; Alden Whitman, "Francis J. Spellman: New York Archbishop and Dean of American Cardinals," New York Times, December 3, 1967, 82; Thomas J. Shelley, "Francis Cardinal Spellman," in Encyclopedia of American Catholic History, ed. Michael Glazier and Thomas J. Shelley (Collegeville, MN: The Liturgical Press, 1997), 1347–1350.

11. "President Leads Tributes," New York Times, December 3, 1967, 81; Whitman, "Francis J. Spellman," 82; Shelley, "Francis Cardinal Spellman," 1347–1350.

12. Whitman, 82; Shelley, 1347–1350.

13. Whitman, 82.

14. Harold Faber, "Students Continue Work in Cemetery," New York Times, March 6, 1949, 49; Whitman, 82; Shelley, 1347–1350.

15. Whitman, 82; Shelley, 1347–1350.

16. Whitman, 82; Edward B. Fiske, "Religion after Spellman," New York Times.

17. Msgr. John Tracy Ellis, "Clergy Role in Picking Bishops Asked," National Catholic Reporter, March 15, 1967, 12; "Green Bay Priests Ask Voice in Naming Bishops," National Catholic Reporter, January 3, 1968, 12; "Priests Asked to Name Choices for Vacant See," National Catholic Reporter, January 24, 1968, 3.

18. Edward B. Fiske, "Priests Ask More Voice," New York Times, January 21, 1968, E16.

19. "Laymen Organize Nationally," National Catholic Reporter, July 5, 1967, 1.

20. Bernard Lyons, "Chicago Priests Seek to Define New Roles," National Catholic Reporter, December 6, 1967, 1.

21. "Text of Petition by Priests in the City," New York Times, January 21, 1968, 30.

22. John Leo, "What Selection Means: New Archbishop Seen as a Conservative with View Basically Like Spellman's," New York Times, March 9, 1968, 15; Marjorie Hyer, "47-Year-Old Auxiliary to Succeed Spellman," National Catholic Reporter, March 13, 1968, 1.

23. "Text of Priests' Memorandum Asking Cooke for Sweeping Changes," *New York Times*, March 14, 1968, 34, col. 3; Edward B. Fiske, "New Goals Asked for Archdiocese," *New York Times*, March 20, 1968, 44; "NY Priests Give Cooke Priority List," *National Catholic Reporter*, March 20, 1968, 1.

24. "Scientific Approach Sought in NY Decision-Making," *National Catholic Reporter*, March 27, 1968, 3.

25. Arthur Jones, "Fresh, Vital Happenings in Parishes Feed Murnion's Hopes for the Church," *National Catholic Reporter*, December 20, 1996.

26. Jerry DeMuth, "Clergy Vote to Form National Organization," *National Catholic Reporter*, February 21, 1968, 1.

27. "Lucey Rips Mckenzie—'Heresy' and 'Nonsense,'" *National Catholic Reporter*, November 29, 1967, 1.

28. Anthony Bannon, "In Buffalo, Priest Refuses to Leave Negro Parishioners," *National Catholic Reporter*, April 3, 1968, 5.

29. "Protest Follows Fast Transfer of Ohio Priest," *National Catholic Reporter*, March 27, 1968, 2.

30. "O'Boyle Suspends Fr. O'Donoghue, Faces Showdown with 54 Others There," September 11, 1968, 3.

31. "Decline of 89 Ends Years of Increases in U.S. Priests," *National Catholic Reporter*, May 1, 1968, 1; "7137 Priests Asked to Quit in 6 Years; Departures Soar in 69, Vatican Figures Show," *National Catholic Reporter*, July 9, 1969, 3; "70-Year Catholic Growth Rate Reversed," *National Catholic Reporter*, May 22, 1970, 1.

32. "Seminarians Show Considerable Drop," *National Catholic Reporter*, November 20, 1968, 7.

33. John Cogley, "Church Establishment in Ferment," *New York Times*, December 30, 1969, 22; John Deedy, "Defections from Authority and the Institution Itself," *New York Times*, December 16, 1973, 244.

34. Blau, "Drive to Recruit Priests," 81.

7. Social Action, Political Power

1. "Bronx Residents Protest Neglect; 300 Set Fires to Point Out Lack of Heat, Hot Water," *New York Times*, December 16, 1969, 51.

2. Michael B. Teitz and Stephen R. Rosenthal, "Housing Code Enforcement in New York City," *The New York City Rand Institute*, April 1971.
David K. Shipler, "Thousands Go Without Heat," *New York Times*, December 13, 1968, 62, col. 1.

3. Teitz and Rosenthal, "Housing Code."

4. Teitz and Rosenthal, "Housing Code."

5. Richard Severo, "In Hunts Point, This Year Is Like Any Other: Bad," *New York Times*. January 14, 1970, 49.

6. Teitz and Rosenthal, "Housing Code."

7. Charles G. Bennett, "Council Inquiry on Housing Asked," *New York Times*, July 3, 1968, 31; Charles G. Bennett, "Demolition Areas Are Picked Here; Massive Set to Begin to Destroy Deteriorating and Old Buildings; Mayor Lists 12 Sites," *New York Times*, March 26, 1967, 294.

8. David K. Shipler, "Thousands in City Go Without Heat," *New York Times*, December 13,

1968, 62, col. 1; Joseph P. Fried, "Owners Show Abandoned Tenements," *New York Times*, April 20, 1968, 19; Bennett, "Council Inquiry," 31.

9. "Furnace Fumes Kill Bronx Man," *New York Times*, January 17, 1970, 64; Peter Kihss, "More Landlords Face City Action," *New York Times*, September 30, 1970, 19.

10. Frank Handelman, in interview with author, February 15, 2015; Bronx Clergy Coalition—Mailing List of Members, Courtesy of Frank Handelman, former staff organizer; Bronx Clergy Coalition Newsletter—"The Bronx Clergy Coalition: Working Toward Better Housing, Health and Welfare Services for the Bronx," various editions, Courtesy of Frank Handelman, former staff organizer; Memoranda by staff to Bronx Clergy Coalition members, Early 1970s, Courtesy of Frank Handelman, former staff organizer.

11. "Catholics Plan $50 Million Drive to Combat Poverty in the Nation," *New York Times*, October 2, 1970, 8; "Catholic Campaign for Human Development," United States Conference of Catholic Bishops, accessed November 12, 2019, http://www.usccb.org/about/catholic-campaign-for-human-development/.

12. "Litany of Prayer" follows at the end of this section.

13. Ricdhard Severo, "In Hunts Point, This Year Is Like Any Other Year: Bad," *New York Times*, January 14, 1970, 49; "Priest Is Ejected After Scolding City Council About Bronx Slum," *New York Times*, February 18, 1970, 44; Charlayne Hunter, "Priest To Press Hunts Point Case," *New York Times*, February 19, 1970, 60; "Councilmen to Tour Hunts Point Homes," *New York Times*, March 3, 1970, 30; Jill Jonnes, "The Puerto Rican and the Priest," in *South Bronx Rising: The Rise, Fall, and Resurrection of an American City* (New York: Fordham University Press, 2002), 164–174.

14. Clayton Knowles, "Creation of a New Puerto Rican District Stirs Controversy," *New York Times*, January 22, 1970, 24.

15. Knowles, "District Stirs Controversy," 24; "Voting Rights Act of 1965," History.com, accessed November 13, 2019, https://www.history.com/topics/black-history/voting-rights-act; "The Voting Rights Act of 1965," Public Mapping Project, accessed November 13, 2019, http://www.publicmapping.org/what-is-redistricting/redistricting-criteria-the-voting-rights-act.

16. Knowles, 24.

17. "Badillo Announces He Is in Primary for Representative," *New York Times*, April 10, 1970, 49; Thomas Poster, "Badillo Flips His Hat in the Congress Race," *New York Daily News*, April 10, 1970.

18. "Community Aide in Congress Race; Vélez, Democrat, Is Seeking New Race in the Bronx," *New York Times*, March 17, 1970, 28.

19. Alfonso Narvaez, "Badillo Expected To Be in Close House Race," *New York Times*, June 20, 1970, 16.

20. Jesse H. Walker, "Coleman Bids for Congress," *Amsterdam News*, May 16, 1970, 1.

21. John Randazzo, "Priest Runs for Congress, First in the State," *New York Daily News*, April 15, 1970; "Runs for Congress," *National Catholic Reporter*, May 1, 1970, 24; Joe O'Sullivan, "Priest Runs Because 'Politicians Have Betrayed People,'" *National Catholic Reporter*, June 16, 1970, 8–9.

22. John Darnton, "Gigante vs. Vélez in Ring of Slum Politics," *New York Times*, November 13, 1973, 37; Jonnes, "Puerto Rican and the Priest," 164–174.

23. "Vincent Gigante," Wikipedia, accessed November 12, 2019, https://en.wikipedia.org/wiki/Vincent_Gigante.

24. "Badillo Is Apparent Winner," *New York Daily News*, June 24, 1970; "Breakdown of Voting in Primary Contests in City, Suburban and Upstate Districts," *New York Times*, June 25, 1970, 50.

25. Thomas A. Johnson, "A Man of Many Roles : Adam Clayton Powell, Former Harlem Representative, Dies," *New York Times*, April 5, 1972, 1.

26. "Priests in Politics," *National Catholic Reporter*, August 21, 1970, 10–11; John Duffy, "When the Priest Leaves the Pulpit for the Stump," *New York Times*, August 23, 1970, E9.

27. Duffy, "When the Priest Leaves," E9.

28. Edward Ranzal, "A Priest to Run for City Council," *New York Times*, February 13, 1973, 41; Martin Tolchin, "South Bronx: A Jungle Stalked by Fear, Seized by Rage," *New York Times*, January 15, 1973, 1.

29. Murray Schumach, "Catholic Priest in Bronx Also a Clubhouse Boss," *New York Times*, August 19, 1972, 25.

30. Edward B. Fiske, "A Visit to Archbishop Cooke's Domain," *New York Times*, October 13, 1968, SM50.

31. "Gigante Is Victor in Council Race," *New York Times*, June 14, 1973, 21; Emanuel Perlmutter, "Results of the Primary Election voting in the Contest Held Here on Tuesday," *New York Times*, June 16, 1973, 52; Beth Fallon, "Gigante Promises at Altar to Shield People of Disrict," *New York Daily News*, January 7, 1974.

32. "City Health Service Protested in Bronx," *New York Times*, March 5, 1969, 9; C. Gerald Fraser, "Doctors Criticize Lincoln Hospital," *New York Times*, July 25, 1969, 45.

33. Juan Gonzalez, "Vélez Larger than Life, For Good and For Ill," *New York Daily News*, December 3, 2008, accessed November 12, 2019, https://www.nydailynews.com/new-york/bronx/velez-larger-life-good-ill-article-1.353767; Douglas Martin, "Ramon S. Vélez, 75, 'El Jefe' of the Bronx," *New York Times*, December 4, 2008, B13.

34. Msgr. Michael Wrenn, "Remembering Msgr. Kelly," *Catholic Culture*, accessed November 12, 2019, https://www.catholicculture.org/news/features/index.cfm?recnum=33159.

° ° ° °

LITANY OF SOUTH BRONX CLERGY ON HOUSING –
City Council Hearing – March 1970

O God the Father of all men
HAVE MERCY UPON US
O God the son, who suffered at the hand of governors and chief priests
HAVE MERCY UPON US
O God the Holy Ghost who enlightens every man that comes into the world
HAVE MERCY UPON US
Hear our prayer, O Lord, as we cry out for the human in which Thy people dwell
In your compassion help those forced to live amid inhuman conditions, especially
in the South Bronx
LORD HEAR OUR PRAYER
From the pool of water in the kitchen, from the collapse of bathroom ceilings;
From water running down the bedroom walls.
GOOD LORD, DELIVER US
From bits of paint and plaster in the babies' beds
GOOD LORD, DELIVER US
From garbage in the hall and in the stairs, from garbage in the streets and in the
cellar, from garbage on the sidewalk and the cars, from garbage in the courtyard and
the alley and in every other place
GOOD LORD, DELIVER US

From Rats, Roaches and All Vermin
GOOD LORD, DELIVER US

From the sicknesses of little children from rat bites and lead poisoning; from colds, bronchitis and pneumonia; from malnutrition and from starvation
GOOD LORD, DELIVER US

From the abysmal hopelessness of families; from the rage of fathers; from the despair of mothers; from drunkenness and addiction and from apathy
GOOD LORD, DELIVER US

From a bureaucracy that cannot see and seeing cannot act
GOOD LORD, DELIVER US

From hearings that cannot comprehend
GOOD LORD, DELIVER US

From all excuses, postponements and delays; from redundant investigations, inquiries, studies and reports; from referral and reconsideration; and from all subcommittees
GOOD LORD, DELIVER US

From all emergency telephone numbers and emergency repairs that bring frustration faster
GOOD LORD, DELIVER US

From promises that are made but never kept; from housing meetings that are dreamed up but never held
GOOD LORD, DELIVER US

From the excuse that the City Council has no power, but only the Mayor; that the Mayor has no power, but only the State Legislature; that the State Legislature has no power, but only the Governor; that the Governor has no power, but only the Congress; that the Congress has no power, but only the President; and from all buck passing
GOOD LORD, DELIVER US

From attempts to belittle human dignity by labelling those who cry out for justice as anarchists, communists, trouble makers and corrupters of youth
GOOD LORD, DELIVER US

From the desperation of disruption and destruction
GOOD LORD, DELIVER US

O God of Abraham, Isaac and Jacob, protect this generation of Thy People.
LORD HEAR OUR PRAYER

O God of Moses, deliver the oppressed from bondage.
LORD HEAR OUR PRAYER

O God the Prophet, confront the conscience and stir up the will of all in power and authority.
LORD HEAR OUR PRAYER

Hear our prayer for the relief of human need.
LORD HEAR OUR PRAYER

Remember the soul of the child living in East 138th Street who died because of no heat in the building.
LORD HAVE MERCY

Christ have mercy.
LORD HAVE MERCY

O Lord, hear our prayer.
AND LET OUR CRY COME UNTO THEE
AMEN.

8. South Bronx—Commitment and Abandonment

1. Dennis Smith, *Report from Engine Co. 82* (New York: McCall Books, 1972).

2. Smith, *Engine Co. 82*, 11.

3. Deborah Wallace and Rodrick Wallace, "Benign Neglect and Planned Shrinkage," in *A Plague on Your Houses: How New York Was Burned Down and National Public Health Crumbled* (New York: Random House, 2001), 27.

4. Wallace and Wallace, "Benign Neglect," 27–29; Emanuel Perlmutter, "City Is Warned of Fire Plague; More Men Needed to Avert Danger, Union Head Says," *New York Times*, July 19, 1967, 45; David Bird, "Union Fights Fire Department Cuts," *New York Times*, 33, col. 1.

5. Wallace and Wallace, 27–38; Robert D. McFadden, "Computer Helps Fire Department," *New York Times*, February 21, 1971, 26, col.1;

6. Linda Greenhouse, "His Honor, the Mayor," *New York Times*, November 7, 1973, 58.

7. Chris Maisano, "The Fall of Working-Class New York," *Jacobin Magazine*, accessed November 15, 2019, https://www.jacobinmag.com/2017/07/new-york-fiscal-crisis-debt-municipal-politics-elections-socialists; "Text of Beame Statement Calling for Financial Restraint and Service Cutbacks," *New York Times*, August 1, 1975, 17.

8. "Economy," Gerald R. Ford Presidential Library, accessed November 15, 2019, https://www.fordlibrarymuseum.gov/library/document/factbook/economy.htm; "Gerald Ford, President of the United States," *Britannica*, accessed November 15, 2019, https://www.britannica.com/biography/Gerald-Ford.

9. Frank Van Riper, "Ford to City: Drop Dead; Vows He'll Veto Any Bail-Out; Abe, Carey Rip Stand," *New York Daily News*, October 30, 1975, cover page, 3.

10. Francis X. Clines, "Negotiations On," *New York Times*, September 10, 1975, 93.

11. Selwyn Raab, "Uniformed Services Studied for Savings; $185-Million-a-Year Trim in the Budgets of 3 Units Is Aim of Modernization Plan," *New York Times*, October 14, 1975; Edward B. Fiske, "Realistic Steps Urged in School Retrenchment," *New York Times*, October 18, 1975, 1, col. 6; Peter Kihss, "Productivity Pressed to Cut Welfare Costs," *New York Times*, October 21, 1975, 1, col. 7; David Bird, "City Hospitals' Role a Fiscal Crisis Issue," *New York Times*, October 22, 1975, 1, col. 7; Joseph P. Fried, "Strategy Sought to Cure City's Rising Housing Ills," *New York Times*, October 22, 1975, 1, col. 8; "Hospital Corp Votes to Shut Down Fordham Hospital," *New York Times*, October 31, 1975; Leslie Maitland, "50 City Hospital Clinics Will Close," *New York Times*, November 6, 1975; Michael Sterne, "City Fiscal Crisis Feeds on Itself," *New York Times*, December 27, 1975, 55; Edward C. Burks, "New York Transit System Is Facing Further Cutbacks," *New York Times*, December 7, 1976, 1; Pranay Gupte, "Garbage Collections Cut Down by Struggling Sanitation Agency," *New York Times*, February 4, 1977; "School Year Begins with Signs of Cutbacks," *New York Times*, September 14, 1976.

12. Paul L. Montgomery, "Third Ave. El Reaches the End of Its Long, Noisy, Blighted, Nostalgic Line," *New York Times*, April 29, 1973, 24; Ralph Blumenthal, "Now That El's Gone, Bronx Hub Sees a Brighter Future," *New York Times*, August 27, 1977, 36; "IRT Third Avenue Line," Wikipedia, accessed October 5, 2015, http://en.wikipedia.org/w/index.php?title=IRT_Third_Avenue_Line&printable=yes.

13. Montgomery, "Third Ave. El," 24; "IRT Third Avenue Line," Wikipedia accessed

October 5, 2015,http://en.wikipedia.org/w/index.php?title=IRT_Third_Avenue_Line&printable =yes.

14. David Vidal, ". . . While Hostos College Resists Its Elimination," *New York Times*, March 6 1976, 49, col. 5; "Statement by Gerald Meyer, Chapter Chairperson, Professional Staff Congress, Hostos, concerning the campaign of Hostos United/Hostos Unido to obtain the 500 Grand Concourse building for the immediate use of Hostos Community College at a press conference held at Hostos on March 30, 1976," CUNY Digital History Archive, City University of New York, accessed November 15, 2019, https://cdha.cuny.edu/files/original/afdde9b1394 dc7b70f35e3b75345ea4c.pdf.

15. "Struggle for Hostos Community College Celebrated," *Workers World* accessed November 15, 2019, https://www.workers.org/2016/03/24626/; "Save Hostos!," CUNY Digital History Archive, City University of New York, accessed November 15, 2019, https://cdha.cuny .edu/collections/show/172.

16. Attachment, South Bronx Catholic Association, Proposal to the Catholic Campaign for Human Development, United States Conference of Catholic Bishops, 1978.

17. Susan Baldwin, "City Council Delays 'In Rem' Role for HPD," *City Limits Community Housing News* 3, no. 3 (March 1978); Association for Neighborhood Housing and Development, (New York).

18. "Bronx Realty Protest Snuffed Out," *New York Times*, September 14, 1973, 43, col. 5.

19. Joseph Muriana, in interview with author, former Executive Director, Northwest Bronx Community and Clergy Coalition, Co-author of Bronx mortgages study, Fordham University campus, Bronx, New York, March 29, 2016.

20. Deborah Wallace and Rodrick Wallace, "A Plague on Houses—Contagious Fires," in *A Plague on Your Houses: How New York Was Burned Down and National Public Health Crumbled* (New York: Random House, 2001).

21. Joseph B. Treaster, "Police Will Press Drive on Arson in South Bronx," *New York Times*, May 22, 1975, 43, col. 7; James P. Brown, "South Bronx Is Burning," *New York Times*, December 24, 1974, 19, col. 1; Joseph B. Treaster, "Suspicious Fires Up in Slums Here; Buildings Looted," *New York Times*, September 2, 1974, 31; Alan S. Oser, "Bronx Fires Final Stage of Long Process," *New York Times*, June 20, 1975, 55, col. 1; Joseph P. Fried, "Serious Fires in New York City Have Jumped 40% in Last 3 Years," *New York Times*, June 20, 1977, 57.

22. Michael Goodwin, "The Profits of Arson Can Be Staggering," *New York Times*, March 11, 1979, E6.

23. Joseph P. Fried, "Housing Abandonment Spreads in Bronx and Parts of Brooklyn," *New York Times*, April 12, 1976, NJ1.

24. Clifford L. Karchmer, "Arson," *New York Times*, August 7, 1978, 17, col. 2; Fred C. Shapiro, "Raking the Ashes of the Epidemic of Flame," *New York Times*, July 13, 1975, sec. VI, 14.

25. Gelvin Stevenson, "Upsurge in Arson Calls for Insurance Reform," Opinion, *New York Times*, September 11, 1977, sec. VIII, 1, col. 4; Goodwin, "Profits of Arson," E6.

26. Joseph P. Fried, "There Are Many Motives, but Chief among Them Is Profit," *New York Times*, August 14, 1977, sec. IV, 4, col. 5; James F. Clarity, "Arson for Profit Reported on Rise, with Cost of $2 Billion Last Year," *New York Times*, May 22, 1977, 1; Karchmer, "Arson," *New York Times*, August 7, 1978, 17, col. 2.

27. Charles G. Bennett, "Demolition Areas Are Picked Here; Massive Drive Set to Begin to Destroy Deteriorating and Old Buildings," *New York Times*, March 26, 1967, 294.

28. "Mayor Submits Demolition Bill," *New York Times*, October 5, 1975, 50, col. 4.

29. Treaster, "Arson in South Bronx," 43, col. 7; Joseph B. Treaster, "35 Seized in South Bronx Arson but No Clear Pattern Is Found," *New York Times*, June 5, 1975, 41, col. 7; Joseph B. Treaster, "Arrests Continue in Drive Against Bronx Arson," *New York Times*, June 11, 1975, 47, col. 4; Joseph B. Treaster, "8 Landlords and Associates Are Indicted in Bronx Fires," *New York Times*, June 12, 1975, 77.

30. Joseph B. Treaster, "Arson Inquiry Pressed," *New York Times*, June 4, 1975, 41, col. 1; Joseph B. Treaster, "Officials Ask F.B.I. for Aid on Fires in South Bronx," *New York Times*, June 6, 1975, 37, col. 4.

31. Treaster, "Arson in South Bronx," 43, col. 7.

32. Fred C. Shapiro, "Raking the Ashes of the Epidemic of Flame," *New York Times*, July 13, 1975, sec. VI, 14.

33. Joseph P. Fried, "U.S. Inquiry Is Begun on Arson in Bronx," *New York Times*, June 20, 1977, 57.

34. Joseph B. Treaster, "Congressmen Urge City to Act in South Bronx Fire Epidemic," *New York Times*, May 20, 1975, L50.

35. Bill Kenkelen, "Streetwise Church: South Bronx," *National Catholic Reporter*, March 17, 1978, 7; "Three Additional Vicars Appointed for the Bronx," *The Catholic News*, October 7, 1976; November 4, 1976, Letter to South Bronx Clergy, inviting them to November 20th Vicar Installation Ceremony.

36. Kenkelen, "Streetwise Church," 7; Invitation Letter from Reverend Neil A. Connolly, Vicar of the South Bronx, to Terence Cardinal Cooke, Archbishop of New York, to attend June 4, 1977, South Bronx Catholic Vicariate "Day of Joy" at Cardinal Hayes High School, Bronx, May 12, 1977.

37. John T. Metzger, "Planned Abandonment: The Neighborhood Life-Cycle Theory and National Urban Policy," *Housing Policy Debate*, Vol. 11, Issue 1 (2000), Fannie Mae Foundation, Washington, D.C.); Deborah Wallace and Rodrick Wallace, "Setting the Scene," in *A Plague on Your Houses; How New York Was Burned Down and National Public Health Crumbled* (New York: Random House, 2001), 18.

38. Wallace and Wallace, "Benign Neglect," 24–25.

39. Roger Starr, "Making New York Smaller," *New York Times*, November 11, 1976, sec. VI, 32 and sec. IV, 7, col. 2; Glenn Fowler, "Starr's 'Shrinkage' Plan for City Slums Is Denounced," *New York Times*, February 11, 1976, 49, col. 5; Wallace and Wallace, 25–26.

40. Peter Kihss, "'Benign Neglect' on Race Is Proposed by Moynihan," *New York Times*, March 1, 1970, 1; Wallace and Wallace, 21–23; Vernon J. Williams Jr., "Benign Neglect," Encyclopedia, accessed November 15, 2019, https://www.encyclopedia.com/history/united -states-and-canada/us-history/benign-neglect; "Municipal Disinvestment," Wikipedia, accessed November 15, 2019, https://en.wikipedia.org/wiki/Municipal_disinvestment#Benign_neglect.

41. Wallace and Wallace, 26.

42. Wallace and Wallace, 26–27.

43. Bennett, "Demolition Areas," 294.

44. "What Must Be Done to Rebuild the South Bronx," South Bronx Catholic Association, 1977; "National Policy to Rebuild the South Bronx to Observe the Following Criteria," South Bronx Catholic Association, 1977.

45. Lee Dembart, "Carter Takes 'Sobering' Trip to South Bronx," *New York Times*. October 6, 1977, 66; Roger Wilkins, "After Carter's South Bronx Visit, His Urban-Aid Effort Is Being Watched," *New York Times*, 17.

46. Bernard Cohen, "South Bronx Snubbed on Redevelopment Plan," *City Limits*

Community Housing News, Association for Neighborhood Housing and Development, New York, March 1978, 4–5.

47. Maurice Carroll, "Badillo in Command of Project in Bronx," *New York Times*, April 5, 1978, 3, col. 6.

48. Joseph P. Fried, "Logue, Who Led U.D.C., Is Asked to Head Bronx Plan," *New York Times*, June 17, 1978, 25, col. 4; Joseph P. Fried, "Issue and Debate: Is South Bronx Revival Plan Simply Folly?" *New York Times*, June 19, 1978, NJ16.

49. Reverend Neil A. Connolly, "Sermon on the Streets," *New York Daily News*, October 1978.

50. David Medina, "South Bronx Group Acts to Push Carter Program," *New York Daily News*, October 27, 1978; "Not for Release before 10:00 a.m. Friday October 27, 1978," Press Advisory, Religious Council for the Renewal of the South Bronx, October 23, 1978.

51. "Bronx: Community Districts Facts-at-a-Glance 1987," New York City Department of City Planning.

52. "Table PL-P1 CD: Total Population, New York City Community Districts, 1970, 1980, 1990, 2000 and 2010," Population Division, New York City Department of City Planning, July 2011, New York.

53. "Table PL-P1 CD: Total Population, New York City Community Districts, 1970, 1980, 1990, 2000, and 2010," Population Division, New York City Department of City Planning, July 2011, New York.

9. New Ministers

1. Apostolicam Actuositatem, Decree on the Apostolate of the Laity, Solemnly Promulgated by His Holiness, Pope Paul VI, on November 18, 1965, Vatican Council II, Rome.

2. "Frequently Requested Church Statistics," Center for Applied Research in the Apostolate, Georgetown University, Washington, D.C., https://cara.georgetown.edu/frequently-requested-church-statistics/; "Catholics Gain; Nuns, Sems Decline," *National Catholic Reporter*, May 14, 1971, 1.

3. "Frequently Requested Church Statistics," Center for Applied Research in the Apostolate, Georgetown University, Washington, D.C., https://cara.georgetown.edu/frequently-requested-church-statistics/.

4. Art Winter, "More Nuns Seek Pastoral Duties," *National Catholic Reporter*, March 12, 1971, 1.

5. Winter, "More Nuns," 1; Art Winter, "More Nuns Train for Pastoral Roles," *National Catholic Reporter*, September 17, 1971, 7; "Nuns Run Chicago Parish," *National Catholic Reporter*, October 8, 1971; Sue Ciribani, "Permanent Diaconate Grows," *National Catholic Reporter*, June 11, 1971, 2; "Understanding the Ministry and Experience: Parish Life Coordinators in the United States," Special Report of the Center for Applied Research in the Apostolate, Georgetown University, Washington, D.C., Summer 2005; "Team Ministry (Canon Law)," *New Catholic Encyclopedia*, Second Edition (Washington, D.C.: Catholic University of America and the Gale Group, 2002), 782–783. .

6. Monsignor Robert Stern, in interview with author, New York, New York, November 11, 2015 and April 22, 2016.

7. Stern, interview.

8. Stern, interview; South Bronx Pastoral Center Board Reports, 1979–1985.

9. Stern, interview; South Bronx Pastoral Center Board Reports, 1979–1985; "South Bronx

Pastoral Center," Robert Stern website, accessed August 5, 2020, https://rlstern.net/the-south
-bronx-pastoral-center/.

10. Called and Gifted: The American Catholic Laity, Reflections of the American Bishops
Commemorating the Fifteenth Anniversary of the Issuance of the Decree on the Apostolate
of the Laity, United States Conference of Catholic Bishops, Washington, D.C., November
1980.

11. "Lay Ecclesial Ministers in the United States; Research Review," Center for Applied
Research in the Apostolate, Georgetown University, Washington, D.C. February 2015; "Lay
Ecclesial Ministry FAQs," United States Conference of Catholic Bishops, Washington, D.C.,
accessed December 18, 2015, http://www.usccb.org/about/laity-marriage-family-life-and-youth
/lay-ecclesial-ministry-faqs.cfm.

12. "Membership," Federation of Pastoral Institutes: Latinos United, Prophetic Voice!,
accessed January 6, 2016, http://www.fipusa.org/english/who.html.

13. P. David Finks, "CCUM: Noah's Ark for Social Ministers," *National Catholic Reporter*,
March 3, 1978, 1; John J. Egan, Peggy Roach, and Philip J. Murnion, "Catholic Committee on
Urban Ministry: Ministry to the Ministers," *Review of Religious Research* 20, no. 3 (Summer
1979): 279–290.

14. Tim Dunsworth, "Msgr. Jack Egan: Activist, Reformer, a City's Conscience," *National
Catholic Reporter*, June 1, 2001; Richard T. Conklin, "Jack Egan: Expert 'Connector,'" *National
Catholic Reporter*, April 28, 1972, 20.

15. Dunsworth, "Msgr. Jack Egan"; Lawrence J. Engel, "The Influence of Saul Alinsky on
the Campaign for Human Development," *Theological Studies* 59 (1998): 636–661.

16. Dunsworth, "Msgr. Jack Egan."

17. Richard T. Conklin, "Urban Ministry—Power to the Poor," *National Catholic Reporter*,
November 20, 1970, 3; "Which Way Urban Ministry? Risk-Taking Versus Organizing for Power,"
National Catholic Reporter, March 19, 1971, 1; Richard T. Conklin, "Activists Skip 'Churchy'
Issues; Urban Ministry Meeting Tackles Prisons, Schools," *National Catholic Reporter*,
October 20, 1972, 5; "CCUM Told a People's Agenda Must Include Coalition for Power,"
National Catholic Reporter, November 7, 1975, 2.

18. Institute for Social Ministry (Notre Dame) announcement, Summer 1978, *National
Catholic Reporter*, February 17, 1978, 7, Summer Listings section.

19. "Honoring Father Browne," West Side Spirit, June 25, 2019, www.westsidespirit.com;
"Henry Joseph Browne Papers" of Archival Collections, Columbia University Libraries, accessed
November 19, 2019, www.columbia.edu/cu/lweb/archival/collections/ldpd_4078408.

20. Diane Struzzi, "Rev. Lawrence J. Gorman," *Chicago Tribune*, February 24, 1999.

21. "Marjorie Tuite," Wikipedia, accessed November 19, 2019; "Marjorie Tuite," Women and
Leadership Archives of Loyola University Chicago, accessed November 19, 2019, http://libblogs
.luc.edu/wla/tag/marjoire-tuite; "Sister Marjorie Tuite; Advocate for Women," *New York Times*,
July 2, 1986, A20.

22. "Harry Fagan," Encyclopedia of Cleveland History/Case Western Reserve University,
accessed November 19, 2019, https://case.edu/ech/articles/f/fagan-harry; Jean McCann,
"Originator 'Sick of Committees'—Program Spurs Middle Class to Social Action," *National
Catholic Reporter*, January 26, 1973, 35; Mary Papa, "Minneapolis Middle-Class Federation-
'Do-Gooders' Adopt Alinsky Tactics," *National Catholic Reporter*, February 11, 1972, 19.

23. Industrial Areas Foundation, accessed November 19, 2019, http://www.industrial
areasfoundation.org; James Goodman and Brian Sharp, "Riots Spawned Community Efforts,"
Rochester Democrat and Chronicle, July 20, 2014, accessed November 19, 2019, www.democrat

andchronicle.com; "History," Communities Organized for Public Service (COPS), accessed November 19, 2019, www.copsmetro.com.

24. "Mission and History," Midwest Academy accessed November 19, 2019, www.midwest academy.com.

25. "Meet People's Action," People's Action, accessed November 19, 2019, www.peoples action.org.

26. "What Is Faith-Based Organizing?," Faith in Action (formerly PICO National Network), accessed November 19, 2019, www.faithinaction.org.

10. People for Change

1. George Vecsey, "Catholic Unit Plays Role in Self-Help Drives," *New York Times*, December 4, 1979, A23.

2. Harry Fagan, *Empowerment: Skills for Parish Social Action* (Mahwah, NJ: Paulist Press, 1979).

3. Laurel Rowe, "Police Call; South Bronx 'People' Cite Need," *Catholic New York*, May 30, 1982, 21; Sue McCarthy, "Agenda: Jobs; South Bronx People Eye Industry," *Catholic New York*, May 26, 1983, 22; "Bronx Housing Conference Set," *Amsterdam News*, May 12, 1984, 32; "Unity Conference in South Bronx," *Catholic New York*, May 16, 1985, 27; Ray Sanchez, "Who Are These People? South Bronx Parishioners Are Those Who Won't Give Up," *Catholic New York*, May 1, 1986, 21.

4. Dean Brackley, S.J., *People Power; Together We Can Change Things*, illus. Larry Nolte (Joe Gonzalez, 1st edition illustrator.) (Mahwah, NJ: Paulist Press, 1989); "People for Change Publish Comic Book," *Catholic New York*, June 28, 1984, 24, col. 1; "Un Libro Comico; Un Folleto Para Ayudar a La Gente Pobre," *Catholic New York*, July 5, 1984, 18; "Change Is Possible; Slide Show Documents South Bronx Success Stories," Laurel Rowe, *Catholic New York*, January 10, 1982, 19.

5. "Holy Week, 1985," *Catholic New York*, March 21, 1985, 33.

11. Another World, a Larger Mission

1. Consejo Episcopal Latinoamericano (CELAM), Latin American Bishops' Council, http://www.celam.org/; Bruce Calder, "Conference of Latin American Bishops,"Encyclopedia .com, accessed November 16, 2019, https://www.encyclopedia.com/humanities/encyclopedias -almanacs-transcripts-and-maps/conference-latin-american-bishops-celam.

2. "A New Church: From Medellin to Puebla," chap. 2, retrieved from Resources page of the website of Dominican Province of St. Albert the Great, Chicago, Illinois, accessed November 16, 2019, http://opcentral.org/resources/wp-content/uploads/sites/11/2014/09/crisis02 .pdf.

3. "'Justice'—Latin American Bishops, Medellin, Colombia, September 6, 1968," Spring Hill College Theology Department Library, accessed November 16, 2019, http://www.shc.edu /theolibrary/resources/medjust.htm.

4. "'Peace'—Latin American Bishops, Medellin, Colombia, September 6, 1968," Spring Hill College Theology Department Library, accessed November 16, 2019, http://www.shc.edu /theolibrary/resources/medpeace.htm.

5. "'Poverty'—Latin American Bishops, Medellin, Colombia, September 6, 1968," Spring

Hill College Theology Department Library, accessed November 16, 2019, http://www.shc.edu /theolibrary/resources/medpov.htm.

6. "Priest's Political Group Gets Communist Backing," *Catholic News*, 1966; Jorge Orlando Melo, "Camilo Torres, Primer Sacerdote Guerillero," *Colombia Es Un Tema*, accessed November 16, 2019, http://www.jorgeorlandomelo.com/camilo_torres.htm.

7. "Priest's Political Group Gets Communist Backing," *Catholic News*, 1966; Melo, "Camilo Torres."

8. Penny Lernoux, "Multinational Skullduggery in Central America: Nicaragua, Honduras, and Panama," in *Cry of the People* (New York: Doubleday Books, 1980), 95–107; Tim Merrill, ed., "The Sandinista Revolution," in *Nicaragua: A Country Study* (Washington: GPO for the Library of Congress, 1993), http://countrystudies.us/nicaragua/; June Carolyn Erlick, "In Nicaragua: Hopes, Not Bricks, Dreams, Not Dollars, as Country Builds," *National Catholic Reporter*, September 7, 1979, 7.

9. Lernoux, "Multinational Skullduggery," 90; "Ernesto Cardenal," Wikipedia, accessed November 17, 2019, https://en.wikipedia.org/wiki/Ernesto_Cardenal.

10. Lernoux, 102; Patricia Lefevre, "Fr. Miguel D'Escoto Put His Priestly Life at the Service of the Poor," *National Catholic Reporter*, June 13, 2017, accessed November 17, 2019, https:// www.ncronline.org/news/people/fr-miguel-descoto-put-his-priestly-life-service-poor.

11. Lernoux, 85–89.

12. Lernoux, 91–94.

13. Lernoux, 90; June Carolyn Erlick, "Cardinal: Violence Is Lesser Evil," *National Catholic Reporter*, November 17, 1978, cover.

14. Michael Hill, "Larry Pezzullo, Former CRS Executive Director, Passes Away," Catholic Relief Services, July 28, 2017, accessed November 17, 2019, https://www.crs.org/media-center /larry-pezzullo-former-crs-executive-director-passes-away; "Lawrence Pezzullo," Wikipedia, accessed November 17, 2019, https://en.wikipedia.org/wiki/Lawrence_Pezzullo.

15. "La Procesión de Minguito"/"Fiestas Patronales de Managua," Vianica.com—Explore Nicaragua en Linea, accessed November 17, 2019, https://www.vianica.com/sp/go/specials /27-fiestas-patronales-managua-santo-domingo.html.

16. "Catalogo de la Biblioteca Alvaro Arguello Hurtado, S.J.," Instituto de Historia de Nicaragua y Centroamerica, Universidad CentroAmericana (UCA) (Nicaragua), accessed November 17, 2019. http://ihnca.edu.ni/.

17. Penny Lernoux, "Torture—The Rise of Fascism: The Agony of the Church," chap. 1 in "Part One: Return to the Catacombs," in *Cry of the People*, (New York: Doubleday Books, 1980), 9.

18. Penny Lernoux, "Repression: The Recognition of Human Rights," in *Cry of the People* (New York: Doubleday Books, 1980), 33.

19. Penny Lernoux, "U.S. Capitalism and the Multinationals," in *Cry of the People* (New York: Doubleday Books, 1980), 255; Mark Winiarski, "Dom Hélder Tells NCR He Was under Ban, Blasts U.S. as Torture Exporters," *National Catholic Reporter*, March 31, 1978; Agostino Bono, "Military Government Alarming Bishops—Church Losing Battle in Brazil," *National Catholic Reporter*, February 16, 1973, 19; Gary MacEoin, "Dom Hélder: 130-Pounder with Staying Power," *National Catholic Reporter*, November 20, 1970, 9-A.

20. Gustavo Gutiérrez, *A Theology of Liberation* (New York: Orbis Books, 1988; originally published as *Teología de la Liberación*, [1971]); Leonardo Boff and Cleodovis Boff, "A Concise History of Liberation Theology," Resources Page of Spring Hill College Theology Department

Library, http://www.landreform.org/boff2.htm; Agostino Bono, "Gustavo Gutiérrez (interview)," *National Catholic Reporter*, February 15, 1974, 16.

21. Gustavo Gutiérrez, "Liberation and Development," in *A Theology of Liberation* (New York: Orbis Books, 1988; originally published as *Teología de la Liberación* [1971]), 22–25.

22. Gustavo Gutiérrez, "The Church in the Process of Liberation in Latin America," in *A Theology of Liberation* (New York: Orbis Books, 1988; originally published as *Teología de la Liberación* [1971]), 57; Paulo Freire, *Pedagogy of the Oppressed* (New York: Bloomsbury Press, 1970 in English, 1998, 30th Anniversary Edition).

23. Freire, *Pedagogy*; "Paulo Freire's Pedagogy of the Oppressed: Book Summary," *Educationist*, accessed November 16, 2019, http://www.theeducationist.info/paulo-freires -pedagogy-oppressed-book-summary/.

24. Gutiérrez, "Church in the Process," 68–71.

25. P. Verryman and J. P. Hogan, "Liberation Theology, Latin America," in *New Catholic Encyclopedia*, Second Edition (Washington, D.C.: Catholic University of America and the Gale Group, 2002), 546–550; Leonardo Boff and Cleodovis Boff, "Concise History"; Verryman and Hogan, "Liberation Theology, Latin America," 546–550.

26. "World Cup of Theologians: Chile—Sergio Torres," *Global Theology*, accessed November 17, 2019, http://globaltheology.org/tag/chile/; "Theology in the Americas Records, 1951–1988 (bulk in 1970s)," Archive Grid, accessed November 17, 2019, https://researchworks .oclc.org/archivegrid/collection/data/227180232.

27. "Theology in the Americas Records, 1951–1988 (bulk in 1970s)," Archive Grid, accessed November 17, 2019, https://researchworks.oclc.org/archivegrid/collection/data/227180232; Sergio Torres and John Eagleson, eds., *Theology in the Americas* (Maryknoll, NY: Orbis Books, 1976).

28. Penny Lernoux, "The Church's Role," in *Cry of the People* (New York: Doubleday Books, 1980), 390.

29. Penny Lernoux, "The Doctrine of National Security—Terror—the United States Teaches Latin America How," in *Cry of the People* (New York: Doubleday Books, 1980), 293–300 and 399–408; "Chilean Cardinal Reports Threats against His Life," *National Catholic Reporter*, April 1974; Charles Rooney, "Chilean Church, Unions Targets of Military Attack," *National Catholic Reporter*, December 15, 1978, 20.

30. Penny Lernoux, "The Church Divided," in *Cry of the People* (New York: Doubleday Books, 1980), 423;

Penny Lernoux, "Colombian Church Discovers That It, Too, Must Join Fights Against Oppression," *National Catholic Reporter*, December 8, 1978, 4.

31. Penny Lernoux, "Villains Afoot," in *Cry of the People* (New York: Doubleday Books, 1980), 283; "Yankee Go Home," series of nine articles from February to April 1979 focusing on Latin American and U.S. influence on economic, political, and military conditions in Latin America.

32. Lernoux, "Doctrine of National Security," 163.

33. "Timeline: Guatemala's Brutal Civil War," *PBS Newshour*, March 7, 2011, accessed November 17, 2019, https://www.pbs.org/newshour/health/latin_america-jan-june11-timeline _03-07; "Guatemala: Civil War Years," *Britanica*, accessed November 17, 2019, https://www .britannica.com/place/Guatemala/Civil-war-years.

34. "Mario Casariego y Acevedo," Wikipedia, November 17, 2019, https://en.wikipedia .org/wiki/Mario_Casariego_y_Acevedo; "Guatemalan Archbishop Safe after Right-Wing Kidnapping," *National Catholic Reporter*, March 27, 1968, 1.

35. "El Salvador," *Britanica*, accessed November 17, 2019, https://www.britannica.com/place /El-Salvador.

36. "El Salvador Civil War," *Britanica*, accessed November 17, 2019, https://www.britannica.com/place/El-Salvador/Civil-war; "El Salvador," Center for Justice and Accountability, San Francisco, California, accessed November 17, 2019, https://cja.org/where-we-work/el-salvador/.

37. "Who Was Romero," The Archbishop Romero Trust (United Kingdom), accessed November 17, 2019, http://www.romerotrust.org.uk/who-was-romero; "Romero Century 1977–1980," The Archbishop Romero Trust (United Kingdom), accessed November 17, 2019, http://www.romerotrust.org.uk/romero-century-1977-1980.

38. "Romero Century 1977–1980," The Archbishop Romero Trust (United Kingdom), accessed November 17, 2019, http://www.romerotrust.org.uk/romero-century-1977-1980.

39. "Romero Century 1977–1980," The Archbishop Romero Trust (United Kingdom), November 17, 2019, http://www.romerotrust.org.uk/romero-century-1977-1980.

40. "Romero Century 1977–1980," The Archbishop Romero Trust (United Kingdom), accessed November 17, 2019, http://www.romerotrust.org.uk/romero-century-1977-1980; Julian Filochowski, "Romero: Person and His Charisma with Pontiffs," Lecture given at Notre Dame University, Archbishop Romero Trust (United Kingdom), accessed November 17, 2019, http://www.romerotrust.org.uk/sites/default/files/Romero%20and%20the%20Pontiffs.pdf.

41. "Romero Century 1977–1980," The Archbishop Romero Trust (United Kingdom), accessed November 17, 2019, http://www.romerotrust.org.uk/romero-century-1977-1980.

42. "Archbishop Slain in El Salvador; Was Foe of Junta," *Newsday*, March 25, 1980, 1; "Who Was Romero," The Archbishop Romero Trust (United Kingdom), accessed November 17, 2019, http://www.romerotrust.org.uk/who-was-romero; "Romero Century 1977–1980," on The Archbishop Romero Trust (United Kingdom), accessed November 17, 2019, http://www.romerotrust.org.uk/romero-century-1977-1980.

43. Edmund Newton, "4 Americans Raped, Slain," *Newsday*, December 5, 1980, 7; Maura Clarke, "Amid Terror in El Salvador, Faith Abides," *Newsday*, December 26, 1980; Penny Lernoux, "The War Against the Latin Church," *Newsday*, December 21, 1980.

44. "Testimony of Rev. J. Bryan Hehir for the United States Catholic Conference," before the Senate Foreign Relations Committee, on Policy Toward El Salvador, March 11, 1982.

45. "History of CISPES," Committee in Solidarity for the People of El Salvador, accessed October 26, 2015, http://cispes.org/section/history-cispes.

46. "History of CISPES," Committee in Solidarity for the People of El Salvador, accessed October 26, 2015, http://cispes.org/section/history-cispes.

47. Rev. Neil A. Connolly, "Jesus Wasn't Trendy," *Catholic New York*, August 11, 1983, 13.

12. New Leadership

1. "John O'Connor (Cardinal)," Wikipedia, accessed February 17, 2016, https://en.wikipedia.org/wiki/John_O%27Connor_(cardinal); "New York's Sixth Cardinal: John Cardinal O'Connor," *Catholic New York*, May 23, 1985, cover.

2. Thomas J. Shelley, "Terence Cardinal Cooke (1921–1983)," in *Encyclopedia of American Catholic History*, ed. Michael Glazier and Thomas J. Shelley (Collegeville, MN: Liturgical Press, 1997), 378–380; "Terence Cooke," Wikipedia, accessed February 16, 2016. https://en.wikipedia.org/wiki/Terence_Cooke.

3. Rachel Black and Aleta Sprague, "The Rise and Reign of the Welfare Queen," *New America Weekly*, September 22, 2016, accessed November 15, 2019, https://www.newamerica.org/weekly/edition-135/rise-and-reign-welfare-queen/

4. "John O'Connor (Cardinal)," Wikipedia, accessed February 17, 2016, https://en.wikipedia.org/wiki/John_O%27Connor_(cardinal).

5. "Pope John Paul II," Wikipedia, accessed February 17, 2016, https://en.wikipedia.org/wiki/Pope_John_Paul_II.

6. "Pope John Paul II," Wikipedia, accessed February 17, 2016, https://en.wikipedia.org/wiki/Pope_John_Paul_II.

7. "Pope Tells People of Bronx Not to Despair," *New York Times*, October 3, 1979.

8. "Pope John Paul II," Wikipedia, accessed February 17, 2016, https://en.wikipedia.org/wiki/Pope_John_Paul_II.

9. Chris Kraul and Henry Chu, "Latin American Catholics' Problem with Pope John Paul II," *Seattle Times*, April 11, 2005; Marjorie Hyer, "Conservatives Seen in Control at Puebla; 'Theology of Liberation' in Retreat at Latin American Bishops' Meeting," *Washington Post*, January 28, 1979, accessed November 17, 2019, https://www.washingtonpost.com/archive/politics/1979/01/28/conservatives-seen-in-control-at-pueblatheology-of-liberation-in-retreat-at-latin-american-bishops-meeting/ffad74b0-677c-4ed5-951a-7b675d93860f/.

10. "Joseph Ratzinger as Prefect of the Congregation for the Doctrine of the Faith," Wikipedia, accessed November 15, 2019, https://en.wikipedia.org/wiki/Joseph_Ratzinger_as_Prefect_of_the_Congregation_for_the_Doctrine_of_the_Faith.

11. "Testimony on U.S.–Central American Relations," Testimony of the Most Reverend John J. O'Connor, Archbishop of New York/For the U.S. Catholic Conference Before the Subcommittee on International Operations of the Committee on Appropriations, U.S. House of Representatives, April 18, 1985, http://www.usccb.org/issues-and-action/human-life-and-dignity/global-issues/latin-america-caribbean/central-america/testimony-on-us-central-american-relations.cfm.

12. Lawrence E. Lucas, *Black Priest, White Church: Catholics and Racism* (Trenton, NJ: Africa World Press, 1989).

13. "New Clergy Assignments," *Catholic New York*, June 22, 1985.

14. Leo Mahon, *Fire under My Feet: A Memoir of God's Power in Panama,"* (New York: Orbis Books, 2007); "San Miguelito," Archives and Records, Archdiocese of Chicago, accessed November 15, 2019, https://archives.archchicago.org/photo-exhibit/san-miguelito.

INDEX

Page numbers in italics indicate a photograph. Locations of parishes, neighbourhoods, streets, and establishments are in the South Bronx unless otherwise noted. The abbreviation NC refers to Cornelius A. (Neil) Connolly.

Angel Garcia was a community organizer and Executive Director of South Bronx People for Change, a Church-based direct action and membership organization cofounded by Fr. Connolly. Born in Puerto Rico, and a graduate of Regis High School, Princeton University, and Pace University, Garcia is a long-term resident of the South Bronx and has been active on social justice issues and worker cooperatives.

EMPIRE STATE EDITIONS

SELECT TITLES FROM EMPIRE STATE EDITIONS

Allen Jones with Mark Naison, *The Rat That Got Away: A Bronx Memoir*

Salvatore Basile, *Fifth Avenue Famous: The Extraordinary Story of Music at St. Patrick's Cathedral*. Foreword by Most Reverend Timothy M. Dolan, Archbishop of New York

Edward Rohs and Judith Estrine, *Raised by the Church: Growing up in New York City's Catholic Orphanages*

Janet Grossbach Mayer, *As Bad as They Say? Three Decades of Teaching in the Bronx*

William Seraile, *Angels of Mercy: White Women and the History of New York's Colored Orphan Asylum*

Andrew J. Sparberg, *From a Nickel to a Token: The Journey from Board of Transportation to MTA*

Anthony D. Andreassi, C.O., *Teach Me to Be Generous: The First Century of Regis High School in New York City*. Foreword by Timothy Michael Cardinal Dolan, Archbishop of New York

Daniel Campo, *The Accidental Playground: Brooklyn Waterfront Narratives of the Undesigned and Unplanned*

Gerard R. Wolfe, *The Synagogues of New York's Lower East Side: A Retrospective and Contemporary View, Second Edition*. Photographs by Jo Renée Fine and Norman Borden, Foreword by Joseph Berger

Howard Eugene Johnson with Wendy Johnson, *A Dancer in the Revolution: Stretch Johnson, Harlem Communist at the Cotton Club*. Foreword by Mark D. Naison

Joseph B. Raskin, *The Routes Not Taken: A Trip Through New York City's Unbuilt Subway System*

Phillip Deery, *Red Apple: Communism and McCarthyism in Cold War New York*

North Brother Island: The Last Unknown Place in New York City. Photographs by Christopher Payne, A History by Randall Mason, Essay by Robert Sullivan

Stephen Miller, *Walking New York: Reflections of American Writers from Walt Whitman to Teju Cole*

Tom Glynn, *Reading Publics: New York City's Public Libraries, 1754–1911*

Greg Donaldson, *The Ville: Cops and Kids in Urban America, Updated Edition*. With a new epilogue by the author, Foreword by Mark D. Naison

David Borkowski, *A Shot Story: From Juvie to Ph.D.*

Craig Saper, *The Amazing Adventures of Bob Brown: A Real-Life Zelig Who Wrote His Way Through the 20th Century*

R. Scott Hanson, *City of Gods: Religious Freedom, Immigration, and Pluralism in Flushing, Queens*. Foreword by Martin E. Marty

Dorothy Day and the Catholic Worker: The Miracle of Our Continuance. Edited, with an Introduction and Additional Text by Kate Hennessy, Photographs by Vivian Cherry, Text by Dorothy Day

Pamela Lewis, *Teaching While Black: A New Voice on Race and Education in New York City*

Mark Naison and Bob Gumbs, *Before the Fires: An Oral History of African American Life in the Bronx from the 1930s to the 1960s*

Robert Weldon Whalen, *Murder, Inc., and the Moral Life: Gangsters and Gangbusters in La Guardia's New York*

Joanne Witty and Henrik Krogius, *Brooklyn Bridge Park: A Dying Waterfront Transformed*

Sharon Egretta Sutton, *When Ivory Towers Were Black: A Story about Race in America's Cities and Universities*

Pamela Hanlon, *A Wordly Affair: New York, the United Nations, and the Story Behind Their Unlikely Bond*

Britt Haas, *Fighting Authoritarianism: American Youth Activism in the 1930s*

David J. Goodwin, *Left Bank of the Hudson: Jersey City and the Artists of 111 1st Street*. Foreword by DW Gibson

Nandini Bagchee, *Counter Institution: Activist Estates of the Lower East Side*

Carol Lamberg, *Neighborhood Success Stories: Creating and Sustaining Affordable Housing in New York*

Susan Celia Greenfield (ed.), *Sacred Shelter: Thirteen Journeys of Homelessness and Healing*

Elizabeth Macaulay Lewis and Matthew M. McGowan (eds.), *Classical New York: Discovering Greece and Rome in Gotham*

Susan Opotow and Zachary Baron Shemtob (eds.), *New York after 9/11*

Andrew Feffer, *Bad Faith: Teachers, Liberalism, and the Origins of McCarthyism*

Colin Davey with Thomas A. Lesser, *The American Museum of Natural History and How It Got That Way*. Foreword by Kermit Roosevelt III

For a complete list, visit www.fordhampress.com/empire-state-editions.